Michael Leapman, an award-winning author and journalist, is a former foreign correspondent and editor of *The Times* Diary. A Londoner by birth and inclination, he has lived in the capital nearly all his life and written and edited several books about the city, its buildings, its people and its history. The most recent is *The World for a Shilling*, the extraordinary story of the Great Exhibition of 1851.

Inigo

The Life of Inigo Jones,
Architect of the English Renaissance

MICHAEL LEAPMAN

review

First published in 2003
by REVIEW

First published in paperback in 2004
by REVIEW
An imprint of Headline Book Publishing

10 9 8 7 6 5 4 3 2 1

Michael Leapman would be happy to hear from readers with
their comments on the book at the following e-mail address:
mhleapman@msn.com

ISBN 0 7553 1003 9

Typeset in Goudy by Palimpsest Book Production Limited,
Polmont, Stirlingshire
Printed and bound in Great Britain by
Clays Ltd, St Ives plc

Headline's policy is to use papers that are natural, renewable
and recyclable products and made from wood grown in sustainable forests.
The logging and manufacturing processes are expected to conform
to the environmental regulations of the country of origin.

Headline Book Publishing
A division of Hodder Headline
338 Euston Road
London NW1 3BH

www.reviewbooks.co.uk
www.hodderheadline.com

For Jacob James, the newest Leapman

CONTENTS

LIST OF ILLUSTRATIONS

NOTES ON STYLE, DATES
AND MONEY

I have used Inigo's first name instead of his surname throughout. This is inconsistent with my treatment of other people in the book, but I am not the first to have done it. In any case, after living closely with him for two years, I feel we ought to be on first-name terms.

Until 1752, the new year in England began on 25 March instead of 1 January. Thus a date written in the seventeenth century as 28 February 1611 would be, in today's terms, 28 February 1612. It is now conventional to convert such dates into the modern January–December calendar and that is what I have done: otherwise we would have had to learn that Charles I was beheaded in January 1648 instead of 1649.

When quoting from seventeenth-century documents I have revised the spelling, syntax and punctuation to make their meaning clear to modern readers.

As far as money is concerned, I have made no attempt to give modern equivalents for sums I quote. It is meaningless to try, given the sharply varying values placed over the years on such central commodities as labour and property. Adding two zeros to the seventeenth-century figure gives a very rough idea of current value, but in some cases seriously understates it.

It may be necessary to tell younger readers that a pound was divided into twenty shillings and a shilling into twelve pence. A guinea was one pound and one shilling. A mark – occasionally used as a unit of English currency in the seventeenth century – was worth two-thirds of a pound.

On pages 357–62, following the final chapter, is a list of surviving buildings and monuments designed by Inigo, including one or two where the attribution is probable rather than definite. I have added some practical details for intending visitors.

TIMELINE

As discussed on page XI, all dates have been converted to the modern January–December calendar. Where the names of masques and other entertainments appear without qualification, it signals the year of their first performance.

1573	Inigo Jones born in Smithfield, London, on 15 July.
1589	James VI of Scotland marries Anne, fifteen-year-old princess of Denmark.
Early 1590s	William Shakespeare begins to make a reputation as a dramatist and actor.
Late 1590s	Inigo's first journey to Italy.
1603	Inigo in Denmark, in retinue of Earl of Rutland. Queen Elizabeth dies. James VI of Scotland becomes James I of England.
1604	Begins collaboration with Ben Jonson on their first court entertainment, *The Masque of Blackness*, performed January 1605.

1605	Designs theatrical performances at Oxford for royal visit. Failure of Gunpowder Plot to blow up King and Parliament.
1606	*Hymenaei*. Edmund Bolton, inscribing a gift book, urges Inigo to spread the knowledge of Italian art and architecture to England.
1607	*Lord Hay's Masque*.
1608	*The Masque of Beauty*.
1608	On Lord Salisbury's initiative, Inigo acts as guardian of Tobie Matthew, a Catholic recusant newly released from prison. Salisbury asks him to submit a drawing for his New Exchange, and to design an entertainment at Hatfield. Also designs A *Hue and Cry after Cupid* for the wedding of Viscount Haddington.
1609	*The Masque of Queens*. Visits Paris and the south of France.
1610	Designs Barriers and other tournaments for Henry, Prince of Wales, as well as *Tethys' Festival*.
1611	*Oberon, the Fairy Prince* and *Love Freed from Ignorance and Folly*. Appointed Surveyor to Prince Henry. Attends Thomas Coryate's Philosophical Feast.
1612	Admitted as member of Middle Temple. Prince Henry dies.
1613	*The Lord's Masque* and *The Memorable Masque* celebrate Princess Elizabeth's marriage to Frederick V, Elector Palatine. Inigo joins official party accompanying newly-weds to Heidelberg, where he and Thomas Howard, Earl of Arundel, set out for eighteen-month trip to and around Italy.
1614	Visits Rome and Naples, as well as the magnificent

cities of northern Italy. Meets leading artists and architects including Vincenzo Scamozzi, pupil and disciple of Palladio.

1615 Returns to London and is appointed Surveyor General to James I. Designs *The Golden Age Restored*.

1616 Works on buildings for the King at Newmarket and makes a start on the Queen's House at Greenwich for Anne of Denmark. Shakespeare dies.

1617 *The Vision of Delight*. Undertakes many minor architectural projects for the court.

1618 *Pleasure Reconciled to Virtue*. Work on Queen's House suspended because of Anne of Denmark's illness. Inigo appointed to commission to enforce building regulations in London.

1619 Anne dies and Inigo designs her hearse. Begins work on new Banqueting House for Whitehall. Made a trustee of Edward Alleyn's new college at Dulwich.

1620 Surveys Stonehenge for the King. Sir Anthony Van Dyck visits England. Pilgrim Fathers set sail for America.

1621 Designs gateway for Lionel Cranfield at Beaufort House, Chelsea, now at Chiswick House.

1622 *The Masque of Augurs*. Banqueting House completed.

1623 *Time Vindicated to Himself and to his Honours*. Charles, Prince of Wales, and the Duke of Buckingham travel to Madrid seeking to arrange marriage between Charles and the Infanta, but return empty-handed. Meanwhile Inigo begins work on a Catholic chapel for the Infanta at St James's Palace.

1624 *Neptune's Triumph for the Return of Albion* written but not performed because of diplomatic complications.

1625   *The Fortunate Isles and their Union.* James I dies and is
succeeded by Charles I. Inigo designs James's catafalque.
Charles marries Henrietta Maria, daughter of the King
of France. Inigo appointed to a fifty-man commission to
enforce building regulations.

1626   *Artenice.*

1627   Charles I buys Duke of Mantua's art collection.

1628   Designs improvements to Somerset House and its garden. John Webb becomes his apprentice. Parliament
presents Petition of Right to curb King's freedom of
action. Charles begins eleven years of rule without
Parliament. Buckingham assassinated.

1629   Designs Cockpit Theatre in Whitehall.

1630   Made Justice of the Peace for Middlesex. Begins work
on chapel at Somerset House.

1631   *Love's Triumph Through Callipolis* and *Chloridia* provoke
terminal row with Ben Jonson. Work begins on Covent
Garden development. Start of dispute with parishioners
of St Gregory's Church.

1632   *Albion's Triumph* and *Tempe Restored.* Appointed to
catalogue the royal coin collection. Anthony Van Dyck
arrives as court painter.

1633   *The Shepherd's Paradise.* Work begins on restoration
of St Paul's Cathedral. Charles exempts Inigo from
knighthood and some taxes because he is 'tired ...
broken and ... frail of body'. Ben Jonson made to
eliminate character of Vitruvius Hoop from *The Tale
of a Tub* after objections from Inigo.

1634   *The Faithful Shepherdess, The Triumph of Peace, Coelum
Britannicum* and *Love's Mistress.* Advises on new south

front at Wilton House. Designs monument to his friend, the poet George Chapman.

1635   *The Temple of Love* and *Florimène*. Rubens' ceiling paintings installed in Banqueting House.

1636   Entertainments for King and Queen at Oxford – *The Floating Island* and *The Royal Slave*. Screen for Winchester Cathedral.

1637   Wooden masquing house, 'the Queen's dancing barn', built in Whitehall. Scots rebel against imposition of Protestant prayer book. Ben Jonson dies.

1638   *Britannia Triumphans* and *Luminalia*.

1640   *Salmacida Spolia*, the last masque. Charles forced to recall Parliament. Rubens dies.

1641   Fits up Westminster Hall for trial of Earl of Strafford, who is beheaded. Summoned to House of Lords to answer complaints by St Gregory's parishioners.

1642   Civil War begins. King forced to leave London: Inigo lends him £500. He and Nicholas Stone bury their valuables on Lambeth Marsh.

1645   Captured at Basing House.

1646   Appears before Committee for Compounding and fined £1000. King forced to leave his temporary capital at Oxford, and is captured by Scottish army.

1647   Inigo assists in design of cube room and double cube room at Wilton House, following fire. Scots hand Charles over to Parliamentarians, and he is confined on Isle of Wight. Nicholas Stone dies.

1648   Second Civil War breaks out.

1649   Charles I executed outside Banqueting House.

1651   At Battle of Worcester, Cromwell defeats Charles II, who escapes to France.

1652   Inigo Jones dies at Somerset House, a few days before his seventy-ninth birthday, and is buried at St Benet's Church in the City.

INTRODUCTION

NO ENGLISH ARCHITECT exerted a more profound influence than Inigo Jones on those who came after him. That is why his claim to greatness does not rest solely on the few buildings that survive from his restricted output. While meticulous and of supreme quality, they do not trumpet the genius of their creator as incontrovertibly as the more accessible works of successors such as Wren, Hawksmoor, Gibbs and Soane.

Yet without Inigo's pioneering vision, his fierce passion for the classical architecture of ancient Rome and his decisive break from medieval and Elizabethan traditions, the work of those successors would have looked very different. When the Palladian style was revived in England in the eighteenth century, he was rightly revered as its inspiration. From that revival grew the stately Georgian buildings that even today determine the character of so many British towns, cities and country estates.

It was Inigo, then, who set the stage on which later generations of British architects could display their creativity. But buildings are not simply works of art: they tell us a great deal about the times and circumstances in which they were conceived. The Banqueting House in Whitehall was envisaged as part of a splendid new royal palace that Charles I and James I could never build because they could not persuade Members of Parliament to vote them sufficient funds. Then, as now, it stood out as a jewel amidst humdrum neighbours. St Paul's Church in Covent Garden is aggressively plain because seventeenth-century Protestants and Puritans were deeply suspicious of the gaudy display of the Catholic Church that the nation had abandoned a hundred years earlier. Designing the lovely Queen's Chapel in St James's, initially meant for a Catholic princess, Inigo had to be careful that the splendour of the interior was not reflected in its external appearance, for fear that it would inflame passers-by.

Architecture was only one of his great talents. Most of his drawings that have survived are not of buildings but of settings and costumes for the increasingly elaborate masques that were an integral part of court life in the reigns of James I and Charles I. He introduced to England a number of devices for changing and moving scenery that are still used in theatres to this day. Not only did he design and mount the masques but he set the themes for many of them, aimed specifically at reinforcing the Stuarts' ultimately doomed belief in the Divine Right of Kings. The conviction with which he converted that philosophy into lavish stage spectacle bolstered Charles's intransigence in his dealings with Parliament, leading to the Civil War and the King's execution. The court was too absorbed in its own plots and intrigues to care about the deep resentment that displays of royal extravagance – Inigo's masques among them – were provoking among the sober, puritanical middle class of yeomen and tradespeople.

It is impossible to judge with certainty the true depth of Inigo's royalist sympathies. Did he share the Stuart belief in Divine Right or was he a mere placeman earning his living by obeying orders? The evidence is conflicting. The poet and dramatist Ben Jonson, with whom he was at loggerheads for much of his career despite their many collaborations, repeatedly lampooned him as a servile, pretentious and talentless courtier who would do anything to please his patrons.

Yet that does not quite square with his record in the court bureaucracy. As Surveyor General to both James and Charles he was in effect their personal planning officer. The records that have survived suggest that he filled the role with arrogance and insensitivity, believing that, as a designated servant of the Crown, he was entitled to exercise its absolute authority on his own account. Retribution came when he was captured and humiliated by Parliamentary troops in the siege of Basing House in 1645, and made to forfeit part of his wealth. Four years later the King was executed outside the Banqueting House, and in 1652 Inigo himself died at the age of seventy-eight.

Most books about him concentrate on a particular aspect of his achievements. In 1966 John Summerson wrote a superb monograph, focusing on the architecture, which was republished in a revised edition in 2000. In 1973, Stephen Orgel and Roy Strong compiled the monumental *Inigo Jones: The Theatre of the Stuart Court*, whose two richly illustrated volumes give a comprehensive account of his work on the court masques. The last full-length, rounded biography was written by another architectural historian, J. Alfred Gotch, in 1928, since when many new discoveries have been made that serve to alter our perception of the man and some aspects of his life and achievements. In bringing these together and placing them in the context of the stormy politics of his time, and in breathing life into the friends, enemies and acquaintances within his social circle, I have attempted to achieve the most complete portrait yet of a man whose influence, despite the adversities imposed by his times, survives to the present day.

A reviewer of the hardback edition of this book found it hard to comprehend how the man who designed such chaste, elegant buildings should also have been responsible for the masque designs – many of which, by the tastes of today, seem vulgar and excessive. As Roy Strong wrote in *Britannia Triumphans*: 'Jones has suffered from the compartmentalisation of modern scholarship. Historians of painting discuss the [Banqueting House] ceiling, historians of architecture the Banqueting House . . ., historians of literature the court masques. But all three are offsprings of the same mind and imagination.'

Chapter One

TERROR AT BASING HOUSE

H E HAD KNOWN FOR DAYS that it would come to this. As a foggy dawn broke over old Basing House, almost the last Royalist redoubt in Hampshire, England's greatest living architect and designer was shivering in his bedroom. An old and sick man, he could have slept only fitfully. The previous day's persistent barrage of rifle fire, along with the more menacing thud of cannon, had subsided as darkness fell; but the enemy were still at the gates.

Now, on Tuesday 14 October 1645, the firing had begun again at first light. Soon came a new sound to mingle with the terrifying crash of masonry as the ordnance hit its target – the sound of voices raised in panic, of bare and slippered feet scampering along the corridors. Before long he heard the clatter of heavy boots and the harsher, jubilant tones of men he could not identify. As he had feared, the long siege was over. Inigo Jones, who had been holed up at Basing House for months, recognised that now, at the age of seventy-two, he must face the ordeal of capture and the possibility – even the likelihood – that his life's journey would shortly come to an undignified end.

There had been plenty of previous alarms since he and other court servants had taken refuge with John Paulet, the gallant fifth Marquis of Winchester, in his house near Basingstoke that had come to be known as 'Loyalty House'. (The words 'Aimez Loyauté' were engraved on many of the windows.)[1] Inigo was among a small community of fellow artists seeking protection from the rampaging Parliamentarians. His companions included at least three who moved in the same privileged court circle as he did: William Faithorne, a young printmaker and portrait painter; the actor William Robinson; and Sir Robert Peake, a dealer in prints and paintings, newly knighted by the King. (The long-held belief that Wenceslaus Hollar, the Bohemian engraver and map-maker, was one of the besieged group has been challenged by his most recent biographer.)[2]

Although he was born in comparative poverty, Inigo's later life had been sheltered and prosperous. This was no more than he felt his due after the years of study, travel and toil that had turned him into the country's leading authority on the visual arts, in particular the European classical tradition. The son of a London clothworker, he had educated himself by travelling across Europe with wealthy patrons, studying the work of the great architects and artists and acquiring one of the finest architectural libraries in the country. His chief patron had been Thomas Howard, the Earl of Arundel, who had built up England's richest collection of paintings, sculptures and antiquities at Arundel House, his London home.

Inigo had accompanied Howard to Italy and advised him what works to buy and display. He had, too, been a member of the glittering, ephemeral court of Prince Henry, the eldest son of James I, whose good taste and intellect had convinced many that his succession to the throne would herald a golden age; but he died before his father. Had he lived, he would surely not have plunged the country into this disastrous Civil War, as his stubborn brother Charles had done.

Inigo had been a confidant and adviser on matters of taste and style to both James and Charles, the first two Stuart kings, as well as to their queens, Anne of Denmark and Henrietta Maria. Even though they never had the money to construct the splendid palaces that they coveted, it was to Inigo that the royal family turned to design the few stately buildings they were able to afford. At the same time, he had socialised, debated and caroused with some of the brightest intellects of the age, including the playwright Ben Jonson, the poets John Donne and George Chapman, and the actor and philanthropist Edward Alleyn. He had associated on equal terms with artists of the highest international repute, such as Sir Peter Paul Rubens and Sir Anthony Van Dyck.

He had designed the elaborate and costly staging of the masques that Jonson wrote in flattery of the royal family, until the relationship of the two proud, incompatible men ended in recrimination. He had enjoyed a formal position at court as Surveyor General, organising the Kings' construction works and trying to regulate the rapid spread of buildings across the capital. If landowners wanted to improve their houses or build new ones, he was the man who recommended whether they should be allowed to do so. He was a Justice of the Peace and had briefly been a Member of Parliament, though making little impression on fellow legislators.

All that was in the past. The stage on which he had cut so grand a figure had been pulled from under him and his fellow courtiers. In the end, the extravagance with which the monarchs, while pleading poverty, indulged their tastes for luxury and lavish spectacle, and their insistence on their divine right to rule as autocrats without recourse to Parliament, had provoked the vicious Civil War. The court had been forced to leave London, a Parliamentary stronghold, and to establish itself on a reduced scale at Oxford, one of the dwindling number of cities still loyal to the Crown. The King's supporters – and Inigo was certainly to be counted among them – had dispersed.

He had originally been invited to Basing House to give some professional advice on fortifying it. 'He was gotten thither for help to the house,' in the words of a hostile pamphleteer.[3] In his library – or possibly in his luggage, for he seldom travelled without books – were at least three Italian manuals on building military defences. In two of them he had made detailed annotations in the margins, showing that he had given meticulous thought to the principles involved, with a view to putting them into effect. In Gabriello Busco's *L'Architettura Militare*, he had highlighted a section about building fortifications on hill sites, such as Basing.[4] The outlines of the defences he designed –

ramparts projecting like the points of a star – can still be seen on the ground today, outside the ruined house. Yet they could not ward off the inevitable.

Since the summer, Parliament's disciplined New Model Army, called the Roundheads because of their short-cropped hair, had made deep inroads into the former Royalist heartland in the west of England. In July they had taken Bridgwater in Somerset and in September Prince Rupert, the King's dashing German nephew, surrendered the vital stronghold of Bristol. Basingstoke was now in Parliamentary hands and it would surely not be long before the King lost control of Oxford, only fifty miles north.

Many times the Roundheads had sought to prise the Marquis of Winchester and his beleaguered guests and followers from their refuge and to block its supplies of food and ammunition. Basing House, from the top of steeply rising ground, commanded fine views in all directions, so it was hard to take by storm. The previous year, 1644, it had been besieged from May to November; but the Parliamentary troops, although they greatly outnumbered the defending garrison, had been repulsed. Supplies had got through, relieving the periodic shortages of such staples as flour, beer and spirits.

Inside the house, though, nerves had become tenser as the winter dragged on, and there were increasingly serious disputes between the Protestants and Catholics who formed the garrison. The religious differences that had in part provoked the Civil War proved so potent that they could not be suppressed even when the very survival of the house and its occupants was so clearly at stake. The Marquis, a Catholic, petitioned the King to have the Protestant garrison commander, Colonel Marmaduke Rawdon, relieved of his post. Rawdon left in May 1645, taking his crack troops with him. They were replaced by less experienced men, some in their early teens.[5]

The Parliamentary assault, commanded by the veteran Colonel John Dalbier, began again later that summer, which was unusually hot and dry. In October Dalbier was reinforced by Lieutenant-General Oliver Cromwell, the most renowned and gifted of the Roundhead commanders. Having scored a decisive victory in June at Naseby in

Northamptonshire, Cromwell marched his men south to take Devizes and Winchester, then came to mastermind the final assault on Basing House. He brought with him some 7000 men and five large cannon. The Marquis badly needed reinforcements, but Royalist troops were fully stretched on other fronts. Without help the garrison, amounting to scarcely more than 300 soldiers, had no realistic chance of holding out, although they continued to display confidence. Less than a week before the final assault, some men had left the house at night and rustled nearly four dozen cattle from a nearby farm, to assure an ample supply of meat.

Basing House before the siege

There were two houses at Basing. The old one was in a circular compound at the very top of the hill, on the site of a stone and flint castle built by the Marquis's ancestors in the twelfth century. Alongside it, to the north-east, was a modern house, more comfortable to live in but harder to defend. This new house, though, had been made uninhabitable by a heavy bombardment three weeks earlier that had brought a high turret crashing down. A later volley killed one of the Countess of Winchester's maids, narrowly missing the Countess herself.[6] But the garrison in the old house, where Inigo and the other guests were staying, continued to resist. Its defenders threw grenades in the direction of the Parliamentary forces and burned a bridge that linked the two houses.

To no avail. Inigo had watched over the last few days as Cromwell's troops, horses and guns had gathered in the valley beneath the bronze-leaved trees on the hillside beyond. Now he could hear men advancing along the corridor. His room was stormed by a group of soldiers, some of whom would have recognised the frail old man with the snow-white beard as a symbol of all they despised about the effete, extravagant House of Stuart. Shouting in triumph, they seized and stripped him.[7] Clothing, especially of the quality expected from a member of the court, was a valuable commodity, a legitimate spoil of war. Having removed it, his captors wrapped Inigo in a blanket and carried him downstairs.

There any man of sensibility – and he was certainly one – would have been sickened to see the bodies of around seventy-five of the Marquis's men, killed inside the walls breached by Cromwell's massive cannon. Robinson the actor had been slain by an officer who accused him of taking part in an anti-Roundhead satire. As one of the Parliamentary news sheets put it: 'He was in Drury Lane a comedian but now he acted his own tragedy.'[8] The women of the house had been spared except for one of the three daughters of Matthew Griffith, an outspoken Royalist clergyman who preached at St Dunstan-in-the-West in the City of London. She had been killed when trying to persuade the soldiers – successfully, it transpired – to spare her father.

Hundreds of Parliamentary troops were obeying their commander's orders by smashing or looting the exquisite furniture, tearing down curtains and chandeliers, defacing family portraits and pocketing anything that looked to be of value. They bore away in triumph the large quantities of food that the inmates had hoarded. A contemporary news sheet reported:

> The rooms and chambers in both houses were completely furnished, which afforded the soldiers gallant pillage, provision of victuals for some years rather than months – four hundred quarters of wheat, three hundred flitches of bacon, two hundred barrels of beef, forty thousand pound weight of cheese, beer, divers cellars full and that very good. A bed in one room furnished at cost £1300, a great store of popish books with copes and such utensils, silver plate valued at above £5000, some cabinets and jewels and other treasure.[9]

One soldier walked off with sixty pieces of gold, another with three bags of silver. Some of the food and the household goods were sold to local people at bargain prices. Adding to the chaotic scene was a fire that had been started by one of the besiegers' fireballs and was spreading quickly. By the end of the day the house would be completely destroyed and the populace invited to remove the stones to use for their own purposes.[10]

Inigo despised chaos. His architecture had been based on discipline, order and mathematical calculation, on determining a set of principles and abiding by them. In the notebook that he kept during his visit to Italy in 1614 he had spelt out his philosophy that a well-designed building had to be 'solid, proportional according to the rules'. Now there were no rules. The authority of his King had been usurped by men with no claim to legitimacy except in the spurious concept of the people's will. Yet he had no choice but to submit to their commands.

With the Marquis, Peake, Faithorne, Griffith, four Catholic priests (also stripped of their clothing) and several other prominent captives, he was taken to the Bell Inn at Basingstoke, just opposite the Fleur de Lys, where Cromwell is reputed to have lodged. The Bell had a lock-up vault suitable for short-term prisoners. Three days later they were put in a wagon headed for London, to learn their fate from the Parliamentary leaders. The Marquis was sent to the Tower of London where, after complaining of lack of comfort, he was allowed to bring in a servant.[11] Several other of the captives were imprisoned or, in Faithorne's case, exiled; but Inigo was soon given his freedom, at the cost of the confiscation of his assets – later restored on payment of a fine of more than £1000.[12]

The fall of Basing House effectively marked the end of the efforts of the loyal English aristocracy, the Cavaliers, to protect King Charles I's throne and, ultimately, his life. The first stage of the Civil War was almost over. The monarchy, that seemingly impregnable institution in whose service Inigo had spent most of his adult life, was on the point of being dissolved, and would not be restored until after his death. In the heat and terror of the moment, it is unlikely that he was minded to contemplate how far he had himself contributed to the disaster. The stately buildings he designed were monuments to power and majesty. His costumes and stage effects for the highly political masques – the most popular entertainment at the Stuart court – had, by their ostentation and extravagance, burnished the image of an institution devoted to pleasure, excess and arrogant self-aggrandizement. It was all anathema to the strict Puritans whose frugal philosophy now held sway in the rebel army.

The Parliamentary press was jubilant when it was confirmed that Inigo had been captured. Anybody at court who had not declared unreservedly for the revolutionary cause was assumed to be an incorrigible Royalist. One pamphlet described him sarcastically as 'the great builder, the King's surveyor and contriver of scenes for the Queen's dancing barn'.[13] The pamphleteer added this curt footnote, referring to the ruination of Basing House as Jones was taken away: 'He was an excellent architector to build, but no engineer to pull down.'

That was not, strictly speaking, his epitaph. He lived for another seven years in semi-retirement, still occasionally providing drawings for his protegé John Webb, including one for the new south front and the remarkable double cube room at Wilton House, seat of the Earls of Pembroke. He died on 21 June 1652, shortly before his seventy-ninth birthday, at Somerset House in London – in happier days the home of his first royal patron, Anne of Denmark, wife of King James I.

In truth, he had lived too long. As far back as 1633 the King had issued a warrant exempting him from taxes and other obligations to the state because he was 'now old, broken and by his labours frail of body'.[14] On the end-papers of his treasured copy of the architectural treatise by the Italian Andreas Palladio he had written numerous recipes for medicines to treat the ailments that increasingly plagued him. And once, in a reflective mood, he had made this note in the margin of his equally cherished book by Marcus Vitruvius, the architect of ancient Rome whose work inspired Palladio and other creators of the classical revival of the sixteenth, seventeenth and eighteenth centuries: 'Time ruins all things.'[15]

We can only imagine his feelings as he learned – or may have even seen in person – how his sovereign Charles I had been beheaded outside the finest building that he, Inigo, had ever created: the Banqueting House in Whitehall. It was a work devoted to the glorification and gratification of royalty; an objective that cannot have escaped those who chose it for their act of regicide, and certainly would not have escaped its architect. The Banqueting House would come to be regarded as his enduring masterpiece, the pinnacle of a body of work severely restricted by his role as architect to a chronically impoverished court.

Inigo Jones in middle age: a self-portrait

By the time Inigo died, the Puritans and Republicans would be firmly in control of the levers of power and, so it seemed, likely to hold on to them. He had exploited his genius to climb to a position of prominence in a cultural context that had been superseded. At some point during his journey he had made a wrong political choice; but he had still survived much longer than the average man and woman in an age where recurrent plagues and deadly political intrigues had sent hundreds of thousands of his contemporaries to premature graves. Eventually history would grant him the renown that his creativity deserved: but, shivering in his blanket on an autumnal Hampshire hillside, how was he to know that?

Chapter Two

FOUNDATIONS

INIGO JONES WAS BORN in a small house in one of the narrow streets around Smithfield, on the north-west edge of the City of London, on 15 July 1573. He was baptised four days later in the church of St Bartholomew-the-Less, whose fifteenth-century tower still stands alongside St Bartholomew's Hospital. The parish served by the church then, as now, was restricted to the hospital itself and the buildings within its precinct; so it appears certain that this is where Inigo's family had their home. Not everyone who lived there had any direct connection with the hospital, which then accommodated the needy as well as the sick.

Smithfield was not a salubrious district. Still the 'smooth field' after which it had been named, it was the noisy, pungent site of London's main cattle market, the precursor of today's wholesale meat market. It was also a traditional venue for duels and public executions. Twenty years before Inigo's birth, in the reign of Mary Tudor, more than 200 Protestant martyrs were burned at the stake there in the continuing religious turmoil that would scarcely abate during his lifetime. Fastidious Londoners sought to steer clear of Smithfield's smells and dangers, though they might make an exception for the three days every August when normal life was suspended and the area given over to the popular though disorderly Bartholomew Fair, founded as a cloth fair in the twelfth century.

London in the sixteenth century

Inigo's father was also named Inigo. Tradition has it that he came to London from north Wales, and he is described in official documents as a clothworker. The architect John Webb, Inigo's pupil and close associate in later years – as well as the husband of his cousin – published some tantalisingly cursory biographical notes about his mentor after his death, in which he suggested that his father may have been a rich wool merchant. There is no wholly convincing explanation for the unusual Christian name that he passed on to his son: it appears to be a corruption of Ignatius, but Webb hints that there may have been a Spanish connection. Inigo senior's marriage record is missing, so his wife's name is uncertain, though since children were often called after their parents it was possibly Millicent, the name given to their first child, born in 1570 and dead less than a year later. Three other children failed to survive infancy but three daughters – Joan, Judith and Mary – reached adulthood and were, like Inigo, beneficiaries of their father's will.

In about 1585 the Jones family left Smithfield and moved to the parish of St Benet, between St Paul's Cathedral and the Thames.[1] There was then a substantial community of Welsh people in this district, possibly servants and attendants at nearby Castle Baynard, descended from those who came to London with the conquering Henry Tudor one hundred years earlier. As Henry VII he rebuilt the castle and used it as one of his principal palaces, conveniently close to the King's Wardrobe, where the monarch's robes, bedding and clothing were kept. It is no more than a coincidence that the church of St Benet, rebuilt by Wren after the Great Fire of 1666, is today the London headquarters of the Church of Wales, holding services in Welsh.

In 1589, Inigo senior was taken to court for a debt of £80 owed to a baker, which has been seen as evidence that the family was not prosperous: the cloth trade in London had been in decline since the middle of the century. Yet when he died a widower in 1597 he left a will that hints at a measure of respectability and some means. The document was correctly drawn up by a scribe, and among his listed possessions was a quantity of books – amenities not normally then found in poor households. He asked to be buried next to his wife beneath the chancel of St Benet's, which would have cost more than a grave in the churchyard. Maybe the dispute with the baker arose not through insolvency but stubbornness: if so, it was a quality he passed on to his son.

The young Inigo must have received at least a rudimentary education. His nineteenth-century biographer Alan Cunningham speculated that he may have been prevented from going to a university because his family was Catholic.[2] He began his working life as an apprentice joiner, a humble trade for which the poet and playwright Ben Jonson was to mock him in later years. The eighteenth-century antiquary George Vertue quotes Sir Christopher Wren as saying that Inigo was apprenticed to a joiner in St Paul's Churchyard. If so, he soon abandoned the saw and chisel for the visual arts. Vertue says he was an accomplished painter of landscapes and he is described as a 'picture maker' in the household accounts of the Earl of Rutland, recording a payment of £10 made to him in 1603.

By then he had almost certainly returned from his first trip to Europe, on which he embarked a year or two after his father's death. As Webb, putting words into his mouth, wrote: 'Being naturally inclined in my younger years to study the arts of design, I passed into foreign parts to converse with the great masters thereof in Italy.'

By 1605, in an account of his summons to Oxford to design an entertainment for the visit of James I to the city, he was already being described as 'Mr Jones, a great traveller'.

It is certain that his itinerary on that early trip included Italy and Denmark, but there is no evidence to show how he went, or with whom. The concept of the Grand Tour was in its infancy – indeed the precise term had not yet entered the language – but Italy's reputation as the fountainhead of European culture was well established. The traveller James Howell would write in 1642: 'Italy hath been always accounted the nurse[ry] of policy, learning, music, architecture and limning [drawing and painting].'

But most travellers were the scions of wealthy and noble families. It is unlikely that a young man of presumably limited means would possess either the funds or the inclination to travel on his own, although if he already had court connections he might have taken advantage of Queen Elizabeth's policy of encouraging and sometimes subsidising promising young men to see the world.[3]

The link with the Rutland family has encouraged speculation that he went abroad in the retinue of Lord Roos, the Earl's brother, who is known to have been on the Continent at around that time. It has been suggested that he was an 'Elizabethan homosexual' who went to Italy as part of a 'dandified and intellectual circle' including the Earl of Essex, the Earl of Southampton and the Earl of Rutland.[4] According to Vertue, though, his patron was William Herbert, who became Earl of Pembroke on the death of his father in 1601. Vertue cites no source for the assertion, however, and is not always reliable.

*   *   *

Travelling abroad was no simple matter in the early seventeenth century. There were both physical and diplomatic obstacles to be overcome. Not many voyagers could afford a well-upholstered coach; but even if they could, or were on horseback or their own feet, the journey was to some degree uncomfortable and dangerous. Because of this, travellers who were confident of their capacity for survival, and who enjoyed a gamble, could take out a kind of reverse travel insurance, by which they would be compensated not for falling victim to misfortune but for avoiding it. They would put up a sum of money before they went and receive between two and ten times the amount if they returned safely, depending on the length and danger of the trip. Fynes Moryson, an early travel writer, said this was never a respectable transaction, but one resorted to only by 'bankrupts, stage players and men of base condition'.[5] Shakespeare referred to it in *The Tempest* (act III, scene 3), where he used the phrase 'putter-out of five for one' to describe a traveller going to a dangerous destination, with odds of five to one given against his safe return.

Diplomatically, on a continent riven by competing and fervently held religious beliefs, travellers were regarded with suspicion by their own governments as well as those of the countries they were visiting. To be allowed to leave England they had to secure a passport signed by the Privy Council, which set out how long they could be abroad, how much money they could take with them, and how many servants. The Council would be reluctant to grant permission if it thought the applicant was likely to be contaminated by Catholicism while out of the country. For the converse reason, some Catholic states were wary of welcoming the subjects of a Protestant kingdom. In large cities, travellers had their documents perused and their motives questioned before they were allowed to proceed.

Because of these difficulties, it became common for English travellers in Europe to pretend to be something else. In 1607 Sir Charles Cornwallis, the King's ambassador in Madrid, reported to the Earl of Salisbury:

There come hither divers Englishmen under other shapes, some passing for French, others for Italians and some for Flemings ... [they] counterfeit their names as their nations, which makes it very difficult to understand what in truth they are.[6]

Travel literature was popular, as it is now, and the difficulties of journeying overseas were described in a number of contemporary books and pamphlets. Robert Dallington, in *A Method for Travel*, published in 1605 (the year of the Gunpowder Plot), warned readers to stop their ears against religious propaganda, 'lest they be open to the smooth incantations of an insinuating seducer, or the subtle arguments of a sophisticated adversary'. In particular,

I must precisely forbid him the fellowship or company of one sort of people in general: these are the Jesuits, underminers and inveiglers of green wits, seducers of men in matters of faith and subverters of men in matters of state, making of both a bad Christian and a worse subject.

Monks and friars, on the other hand, were described as jovial and companionable, not pressing their faith on strangers.

Inigo's own religious loyalties cannot be pinned down with certainty. *The Dictionary of National Biography* says with confidence that both he and his father were Catholics, a view shared by his twentieth-century biographer.[7] Certainly he was friendly with many Catholics in his early years: Edmund Bolton and Tobie Matthew were two, both converts to the faith as young men and both stubborn in their refusal to abandon it. He also had a long friendship with the Earl of Arundel, Thomas Howard, a member of one of the country's leading Catholic families – though he eventually became a Protestant for political convenience.

Despite those connections, Catholic emissaries to the court of Charles I in the 1630s did not regard Inigo as a co-religionist. Gregorio Panzani, the Pope's man in London, described him in a despatch home as 'Puritanissimo fiero', although that need not be taken too literally. Panzani clearly disliked Inigo's proud manner and may have been using the word as a generalised term of abuse, in the same sense as a contemporary writer, Barnaby Rich, who described somebody as 'a puritan, a precise fool, not fit to hold a gentleman company'.[8]

At about the same time a French envoy blamed Inigo for the delay in completing the Catholic chapel being built for Queen Henrietta Maria at Somerset House in London, accusing him of hampering the work deliberately because he did not approve of the Queen's religion. The probability is that Inigo, like many others anxious to maintain a position at court, chose to espouse whatever religious views were acceptable at the time. There is nothing in his surviving writings to indicate that he was burdened with dogmatic beliefs. At least once he was entrusted with a diplomatic mission abroad, so he must have been thought reliably resistant to Catholic propaganda. His rejection of traditional Gothic architecture, so strongly associated with the rituals of organised religion, may have reflected his departure from the old faith.

Dallington's advice on how a traveller should look after himself physically in foreign lands was a little sketchy. He warned: 'Beware of their wines, which agreeth not with some natures and are hurtful to all in hotter countries, except sparingly taken or well qualified with water.' As for exercise, riding and fencing were recommended but tennis could be over-strenuous and dancing, he believed, made some men look ridiculous. Most travellers would need between £80 and £150 for the journey and 'they say he should have two bags, the one of crowns, the other of patience'.

About the actual mechanics of travel, Dallington was silent. Only noblemen with their retinues travelled in carriages: less exalted folk went on horseback or in ox-carts or public coaches. They could buy a horse on their arrival on the Continent and sell it when they left, or rely on post horses that they changed at inns on the route – an expensive option, because they were often made to pay for taking the horse back to its base. The roads were bad, especially in adverse weather, and bridges few and sometimes unsafe.[9]

All this meant that progress could be painfully slow. Travellers would thus be forced to stay at many inns on their route, and these varied enormously in quality. The French were recognised as the best innkeepers. In Italy clean sheets were a rarity and in Germany it was often necessary to share a room or even a bed with other travellers.

German landlords also had a reputation for being strict about meal times.[10] To top it all, there was constant danger from wild animals and footpads, especially in northern Italy. A French tourist of the time recorded that Venetians always turned corners in the middle of the road, for fear of what may lurk in the shadows if they kept too close to the walls.[11]

Inigo's itinerary on that first visit almost certainly included Venice. Webb wrote that he had 'many years resided' in the city and circumstantial evidence suggests that he was there in 1601 when he bought his precious copy of Palladio's *I Quattro Libri dell' Architettura*, in whose broad page margins he would for most of his life make notes of his thoughts on architecture and other matters. A note on a flyleaf reads 'Venice 1601' and a price of two ducats. If that is indeed where and when Inigo acquired the book, it is the earliest intimation that he was planning to pursue a career in architecture. It also suggests that by then he had been long enough in the country to speak Italian at a level where the book could be of use to him.

In the two decades since his death, Andrea Palladio had become one of the most renowned of the Italian architects, partly because of this formidable book, first published in 1570. Thirty years before that, Sebastiano Serlio had begun to publish a scholarly six-part work which soon became a standard textbook of Renaissance architecture. In England, a few Elizabethan builders had started to experiment tentatively with his designs.[12] Palladio, though, was more productive than Serlio and his book, in addition to giving detailed practical descriptions of many of his buildings, acknowledged a greater debt to the classical architects of ancient Rome – in particular Marcus Vitruvius, whose own work, *I Dieci Libri de Architectura*, is one of the few contemporary records of Roman styles and techniques to have survived.

Venice in 1600 was as irresistible a magnet for lovers of art and architecture as it is today. Its interlocking canals were lined with gorgeous Renaissance palazzos and churches, many containing the works of the city's greatest painters – Bellini, Giorgione, Titian, Veronese and Tintoretto. Antonio da Ponte's Rialto Bridge had been completed nine years earlier. This, and the extraordinary set of medieval buildings around St Mark's, would certainly have given the young Inigo an inkling of the possibilities of confident and imaginative architecture, even if they had no direct influence on his developing style. For that, he looked to the clean lines and balanced proportions of the three churches that Palladio designed there, all with the colonnaded 'temple front' that Inigo would copy many years later at St Paul's Church in Covent Garden.

Webb's assertion that on his trip Inigo met some of the 'great masters' of design could refer to Vincenzo Scamozzi, a leading disciple of Palladio, who had returned to Venice from Paris in 1600. It is certain they met during Inigo's better-documented second visit to Italy in 1614, but it is possible that they first became acquainted on this earlier occasion. Certainly the young and largely untutored Englishman would have needed someone to guide and advise him on the buildings he ought to see and the books he should buy to further his architectural knowledge.

Given his demonstrated interest in Palladio, he would surely not have missed the chance of travelling some twenty miles west of Venice to visit Padua, the architect's birthplace as well as the home of one of Europe's leading universities: a paradise for someone with his intellectual curiosity. (William Harvey, the physician who later discovered the secret of blood circulation, was studying medicine there at the time.) A little further on is Vicenza, the town where Scamozzi was born and which contained, as it still does today, a concentration of Palladio's exquisite villas and palazzos, which Inigo would revisit and explore in greater detail during his later trip. Further west still are the Roman remains at Verona, including a theatre that influenced Palladio's Teatro Olimpico at Vicenza.

There is a tradition, supported by the seventeenth-century diarist John Evelyn, that Inigo's first itinerary included an extended stay in the port of Livorno; and that its arcaded central piazza, with a church occupying one side of it, was his model for Covent Garden many years later. Some say he had a hand in designing the church on Livorno's piazza, but since that was completed in 1595, by the architect Alessandro

Pieroni, it would mean that he had made a separate journey to Italy before his father's death. James Lees-Milne speculated that on his first visit to Italy he may have been apprenticed to Pieroni, who lived until 1607.[13]

While in the Livorno area, Inigo would have admired the celebrated Romanesque buildings of Pisa, just a few miles north: Bonanno Pisano's tower was already leaning significantly. He would, too, have absorbed the art treasures and theatrical innovations to be seen in Florence, a little further away to the east. It is unlikely, though, that he ventured any further south, and specifically not to Rome, because of the political and religious complications that would have resulted from visiting the global headquarters of the Catholic Church.

Exactly when Inigo left Italy, and where he went, have been disputed, though it is fairly certain that he was in Denmark in 1603. The death that year of Queen Elizabeth marked the end of the Tudor period. Her crown passed to her nearest relative, James VI of Scotland, the son of her cousin Mary Queen of Scots, who had been executed by Elizabeth for plotting against her. James had been King of Scotland since his mother's abdication, when he was only a year old: but his accession to the English throne, as James I, was controversial. There was a powerful faction – including the explorer Sir Walter Raleigh – opposed to the idea of a Scottish king, especially the son of a former pretender to the throne. A plot to depose him in favour of Arabella Stuart, second in line of succession, was foiled not long after the new King arrived in London.

Inigo may have travelled directly to Copenhagen from Venice, without returning to England first. Webb says that the Danish King, Christian IV, 'sent for him out of Italy' but for what exact purpose is unknown. The King, then a young man of twenty-six (although he had already been fifteen years on the throne) was an enthusiastic promoter of learning and an ambitious builder, founding at least seven towns and cities in Scandinavia, including Oslo, the Norwegian capital, originally called Kristiana. It would have been in character for him to seek to engage an untried architect, only a few years older than himself, if he had heard good things about him on the court grapevine or through his sister, Anne of Denmark, who had married James VI in 1589.

Another piece in the jigsaw of likely connections is the Earl of Rutland, who went to Denmark in 1603 on behalf of the new King, to present Christian with the Order of the Garter.[14] Inigo seems to have been included in the Earl's party, because his name appears as 'Mr Johns' on a list of guests at an official function on 10 July.[15] The Earl's £10 payment to Inigo was recorded a few days after Rutland returned to England, which suggests that Inigo, too, was back by then and that the sum may have been for services rendered during the visit. One possibility is that Inigo was already in Denmark when Rutland arrived and was able to give him practical help and advice before returning with him to England, although his being described in the accounts as a picture maker suggests that the payment might have been for something in that line of work.

It would be intriguing to know whether Inigo had already decided, before he set out on his travels, to study and ultimately to practise architecture, or whether it was the purchase of the Palladio book that sparked the idea. The first known reference to him as an architect comes in an inscription in a book given to him by his friend Edward Bolton on 30 December 1606. Bolton was an historian, a poet and a devout Catholic who all his life resisted pressure to join the Church of England, a determination that limited his opportunites of advancement at court. The book he gave Inigo was a collection of poems by Gianfrancesco Bordino in praise of Pope Sixtus V, who in a reign of only five years had commissioned many fine new buildings. In it Bolton wrote in Latin:

> 30 December 1606. As an earnest and a token of friendship which is to endure forever with Inigo Jones, I, Edmund Bolton, give this little book. To his own Inigo Jones, through whom his hope is that sculpture, modelling, architecture, painting, theatre work, and all that is praiseworthy in the elegant arts of the ancients, may some day insinuate themselves across the Alps into our England. MERCURY, SON OF JOVE.[16]

The friendship appears not to have endured forever. Like so many, it failed to survive the two men's markedly contrasting fortunes. After several spells in debtors' prisons, Bolton died in poverty in the early 1630s, when Inigo was at his most prosperous and would clearly have been in a position to help had he been so inclined. Yet he would spend much of his career trying to live up to Bolton's hopes. The classical buildings of Palladio, Serlio and their followers had left an enduring, liberating impression on him, alien as they were to anything that had as yet been attempted in England.

If he was to develop an English classicism he would have to start virtually from scratch, for there was precious little in the Elizabethan tradition that he could build on. This is what singles him out from those who came after him. Men such as Christopher Wren, James Gibbs, Nicholas Hawksmoor, John Soane, Robert Adam and John Nash – inspired architects all – created beautiful buildings, but they would not have been possible without Inigo's bold break with the past. It was he who, as Bolton had urged, would change the course of English architecture, even though it would be some years yet before he had the chance to begin.

Chapter Three

INIGO'S LONDON

IN 1598, WHEN INIGO WAS TWENTY-FIVE and about to embark on his European adventure, John Stow, a meticulous historian and antiquarian, published the first edition of his *Survey of London*. It provides a detailed description of the City and suburbs where Inigo grew up, the narrow streets and alleys he walked time and time again, and the crowded jumble of buildings that had been allowed to accumulate higgledy-piggledy, according to no overall scheme of things.

You could scarcely walk anywhere in London without being in sight of at least one of its scores of medieval churches: Stow counted 114 in the twenty-six wards. They were in the main forbidding structures, their grey stone spires and towers blackened by soot, many in a state of disrepair since the break with the Church of Rome in 1534. Filling the spaces between them were half-timbered houses, shops, cook-houses, galleried inns, brewhouses and tenements, characterised by oriel windows and upper floors overhanging the highway. Scruffy warehouses and quays were scattered along both banks of the crowded river. Many streets, in particular those leading up from the quays, were lined with market stalls, grouped according to the commodity they were selling. Their names survive today: Milk Street, Bread Street, Poultry . . .

The City had been getting more and more congested because the population was expanding fast. From 50,000 in the 1550s it had risen to nearly 200,000 at the turn of the century. The many acres of land that had been seized from the Church following Henry VIII's Dissolution of the Monasteries in 1537 had been used to build either town houses for the gentry or cheap tenements for the poor.[1] In July 1580 Queen Elizabeth issued a proclamation deploring 'such great multitudes of people brought to inhabit small rooms, whereof a great part are seen very poor . . . heaped up together, and in a sort smothered with many families of children and servants in one house or small tenement'.

So she barred any new houses or tenements within the City and a three-mile radius of any of its gates 'where no former house hath been known to have been in the memory of such as are now living'. Even if the edict had been rigorously enforced – and the evidence is that it was widely flouted – speculators could get round it simply by building larger structures on existing foundations and cramming in as many people as they could.[2]

It all made for an ugly, unsanitary environment: in the previous ten years there had been four severe outbreaks of bubonic plague, killing many thousands.[3] The architectural historian Andrew Saint has given a vivid description of the Elizabethan city's fabric:

> Owners of ampler properties along the main streets squeezed minuscule tenements in 'courts' on to every available piece of back land, at growing risk to safety and health. London Bridge, the busiest and most valuable thoroughfare of all, was jam-packed with buildings and shops. Most houses were still individual, piecemeal affairs, timber-built, of three stories at most, long and narrow and with their gable ends turned to the street. Retailing, manufacturing and warehousing were for the most part carried on in or behind such houses. Precision crafts like fine metal-work, document-copying, and the new trade of print-setting tended to migrate to the top floors where light was good, whereas noxious or noisy jobs like tanning, slaughtering or stabling took place in yards. As yet few houses had special shopfronts, and storage was confined to cellars, ground floors and garrets.[4]

Inigo's last parental home was a modest one, close to the parish church of St Benet's, where he, his mother and his father would be buried. The church itself was on Paul's Wharf, south of St Paul's Cathedral, at its junction with Thames Street. The old Gothic cathedral, begun in the twelfth century, dominated the City and provided plenty to engross a young man interested in monumental architecture. At 650 feet long it was larger than its successor, the present cathedral, built by Christopher Wren after the Great Fire of 1666. Both the nave and the chancel were twelve bays long and between them, above the crossing, was a squat tower, bereft of its spire since being struck by lightning in 1561. The east end featured a large window of seven lancets surmounted by a rose. A detached bell tower stood close to the south-east corner, and there was a splendid fourteenth-century chapter-house, in the Perpendicular style, to the south-west. Since the Reformation, though, the cathedral had deteriorated markedly, due to the lack of funds for its maintenance. The nave had become a place for meeting, shopping and doing business, or simply escaping from the weather.[5]

Other substantial buildings in the neighbourhood were the headquarters of the craft guilds and city livery companies – just how substantial depended on the company's wealth. Some still occupy the same sites, including the Painter-Stainers' Hall on Little Trinity Lane, which Inigo would frequent. There was also a convenient local theatre – the Blackfriars Playhouse, housed in the former Black Friars' monastery, dissolved in 1538. One of London's earliest theatres, it opened in 1556 in what had been the monks' refectory, but closed temporarily in 1584. It reopened in 1597 as a private theatre, so avoiding strict control by the authorities. This second theatre was larger, housed this time in the former assembly hall, with spacious galleries, on-stage seating and sophisticated lighting, which might have given Inigo ideas for his own special effects when he came to design masques. Until 1608 it was leased to the Children of the Chapel Royal, a boys' company whose repertoire included plays by Shakespeare, Jonson and Marlowe. Then it was taken over by the King's Men, London's leading adult company, led by the actor Richard Burbage.[6]

There were more places nearby where Inigo could indulge his

interest in the stage. He just had to walk across the sturdy 400-year-old London Bridge to reach the Rose in Southwark, controlled by the famous impresario Philip Henslowe. In the last years of the century it was joined on the south bank by two more venues for the burgeoning companies of players – the Swan and finally the Globe, where many of William Shakespeare's plays were first performed. The three theatres were in a district controlled by the Bishop of Winchester, whose palace dominated the south bank: 'a very fair house, well repaired, and hath a large wharf and landing place,' according to Stow. Everything in the Bishop's domain was outside the strict jurisdiction of the City of London, so the area attracted public entertainments of various levels of raffishness. As well as theatres, there were bear-baiting pits, taverns and stews (brothels), along with the notorious Clink prison, for locking up people who exceeded the limits even of the Bishop's tolerance of disorderly behaviour.

Back on the north bank, between London Bridge and the Tower, was the Custom House, controlling trade in the busy port. Built in 1559, it was topped by characteristic Tudor turrets.[7] Now walking west past busy wharves, Inigo would come to the Fleet Bridge, across the stinking Fleet River, where much of London's sewage flowed into the Thames and thence to the sea. On the west side of the mouth of the Fleet, Bridewell Palace was an imposing brick building set around three courtyards, constructed for Henry VIII in 1520. In 1553 the young Edward VI had ceded it to the City authorities as a workhouse, prison and orphanage.

Until the fifteenth century the priority in designing houses for the gentry had been security rather than elegance: in tempestuous times, an Englishman's home truly had to be his castle. The nation's grand mansions, like its places of worship, had for 500 years been constructed in varying versions of the Gothic style. But where the builders of churches and soaring cathedrals had been encouraged to create awe-inspiring monuments to their faith, domestic architecture was, for the most part, largely functional.

Scant regard was paid to sophistication or symmetry. Engravings of important late medieval mansions show them clinging to

the pattern of the fortified house, a series of barely related structures grouped around a central courtyard, entered through a manned
guard-house and fringed by high walls to keep out hoi polloi. In
the country, many were still surrounded by moats. Smaller houses
were even more functional, with sparse decoration. The traditional
white walled and black beamed Tudor cottage reflects its structural
elements rather than any conscious attempt at architectural distinction.
Only in more pretentious buildings, such as Little Moreton Hall
in Cheshire, was this style embellished to make an architectural
statement.

Arundel House in the Strand

The Dissolution of the Monasteries had freed land not only in the
towns but in the countryside. The large churches, and the monks' usually
spartan accommodation blocks alongside them, stood on prominent sites
admirably suited for stylish living; but the buildings themselves scarcely
fitted the lifestyle of the aspirational aristocrats, seeking to establish
a reputation for opulence and discernment, into whose hands they
had fallen. Many were therefore pulled down, and the stone used
to construct purpose-built mansions – the so-called 'prodigy houses'
whose flamboyance reflected the confidence and wealth of the new
ruling class. Henry VIII himself took over some of the monastery lands
and buildings, and by the time of his death he possessed forty-two
palaces.[8] The fashion for sumptuous houses took hold under Queen

Elizabeth, but all the same Francis Bacon was guilty of exaggeration when he wrote towards the end of the reign: 'As Augustus said that he had received the city of brick and left it of marble, so may Elizabeth say she received a realm of cottages and hath made it a realm of palaces.'[9]

Architects, in today's sense, scarcely existed. The first recorded use of the word in English was in the middle of the sixteenth century. Buildings were designed primarily by the carpenters, bricklayers or stonemasons who constructed them. Robert Smythson, the best-known Elizabethan architect, was a master mason by trade.[10] These craftsmen's most important qualifications were the technical and mathematical skills required to erect a building that would not fall down or let in the rain, plus sufficient ability as draughtsmen to put a working plan on paper. On matters of aesthetics they would defer to the landowners who commissioned them – or often their surveyors, who had overall responsibility for managing all matters on an estate relating to the use of land, including the buildings on it.[11]

In the nature of things, the ideas put forward by the owners and surveyors would chiefly have been inspired by features of houses owned by friends and neighbours that they had seen and admired. Sir Roger Pratt, a seventeenth-century follower of Inigo, commented that, when it came to planning new houses, men 'are apt to think nothing well but what is comfortable to that old-fashioned house which they themselves dwell in, or some of their friends'.[12] Such conservatism left little scope for cutting-edge architecture.

Not that the landowners and builders were totally insulated from what was happening elsewhere in the world. Italian and French books and engravings began to circulate in England in the second half of the sixteenth century, and more and more pioneer travellers went to view the innovative buildings being created on the Continent. The fashion for brick and terracotta as building materials started to make heavy, visible timber frames redundant.[13] All the same, most of the great brick buildings of that period – such as St James's and Hampton Court palaces, Horeham Hall in Essex and Knole in Kent

– remained essentially Gothic in form. Contemporary drawings and paintings of the vanished Tudor palaces at Richmond, Greenwich, Nonsuch and Oatlands make them seem outlandish to modern eyes. They reveal a surfeit of turrets, spires, pinnacles, finials and ebullient decorative features that resemble a Disney film set depicting a mythical enchanted kingdom.

Slowly the influence of the Renaissance began to seep across the Channel from Europe, first into the design and decoration of monuments and tombs and by the 1550s into full-scale buildings. In 1563, John Shute's book, *The First and Chief Grounds of Architecture*, introduced to Britain the five classical orders of decoration of the heads of stone columns and pilasters, drawing on the work of the Venetian architect Sebastiano Serlio, published earlier in the century.[14] Soon such columns began to appear in the fabric of the new great houses of England, along with other European devices including sculptures, porticos, entablatures and pediments. But they were introduced more or less at random, plucked from the vocabulary of classical design without any understanding of its grammar. The Palladian concepts of proportion and harmony had still to be understood. It was not yet accepted that, to be truly imposing, a house ought to be symmetrical, with balancing features on either side of a central entrance. Although Robert Smythson employed classical details on mansions such as Longleat, Wollaton Hall, Burghley House, Burton Agnes and Hardwick Hall, the buildings remained quintessentially English in form: you would not have seen their like in Venice or Paris.

By 1603, the end of Queen Elizabeth's reign, the golden age of the English country house had begun. The nineteenth-century architectural historian Alan Cunningham described Elizabethan great houses as 'the illegitimate offspring of the Grecian and Gothic', adding that they were 'inferior in elegance to the one and in magnificence to the other'. He explained: 'No rule, indeed, was followed, no plan formally obeyed.' Because there were no architects as such, there was no overarching theory of architecture to give unity to a body of work. Summerson has written:

There is no 'Elizabethan Style'. Elizabethan architecture consists of the Tudor-Gothic tradition, ever more and more diluted ... Although foreign fashions in ornament, and sometimes in plan, were excitedly adopted, they were adopted for the intrinsic pleasure they gave rather than from any sense of achievements greater than their own.[15]

A prominent example was Thomas Gresham's Royal Exchange, built in 1567 at the very heart of the City of London, on the same site as the present exchange. Four streets and more than eighty houses were demolished to make room for this pioneering building based on the Bourse at Antwerp, where Gresham had earlier resided as an official English trade representative. The Exchange was essentially a venue for negotiating deals, a commodity exchange combined with a retail shopping centre. Because nothing similar had been built in London before, Gresham imported craftsmen from the European mainland and the result was, for its time, a startlingly un-English building. Arcades, adorned with Doric columns, surrounded the courtyard where the main business of the Exchange was transacted. The shops were on the floor above, behind niches containing statues of royalty.[16] Inigo would have recognised the style from his Italian journey, and would have admired it.

Stow recorded several great houses in the vicinity of St Benet's Church. Castle Baynard, Henry VII's former palace, was the largest. Anthonis Van Den Wyngaerde, in his panorama of London drawn around 1558, showed it as a substantial pile with crenellations over the main river entrance and a number of Gothic round towers topped by pointed spires. Huntingdon House, dating from the fourteenth century, was the London home of the Earls of Huntingdon and the closest mansion to Paul's Wharf. Berkeley's Inn, near the adjacent Puddle Wharf, was described by Stow as 'an ancient building of stone and timber' built by the Berkeley family but now 'all in ruin and letten out in several tenements, yet the arms of Lord Berkeley remain in the stone work of an arched gate'.

Derby House was given to the College of Arms in 1555: the present college was built in 1688 on the same site, on what is now Queen Victoria Street. Just west of it was the College of Advocates and Doctors of Law, known popularly as Doctors' Commons, a law court where cases concerning the Church and the Admiralty were heard. Stow again noted approvingly that it was 'built of stone' rather than the prevailing timber. To the north-west, Ely House had been the home of the Bishops of Ely since the late thirteenth century, its imposing gatehouse fronting onto Holborn.

But for some years now, the bishops and the aristocracy had been moving away from the City itself, into the open spaces to its west. That is where Inigo would have had to walk to see the best examples of 'modern' architecture. From Fleet Bridge he would head west along Fleet Street, whose rows of booksellers and printers were broken up on the south side by the front courtyard of the medieval Salisbury House – today Salisbury Square – the residence of the Bishops of Salisbury until the Dissolution. (Its name was changed to Dorset House in 1603 when the then owner, Thomas Sackville, was created Earl of Dorset.) Still walking west, Inigo would pass close by the Inner and Middle Temple, then as now an enclave of lawyers, with the old round church and the hall where Shakespeare's *Twelfth Night* was first played in 1601.

Crossing the border of the City into the Strand, he entered a different environment, in terms of both the landscape and the prevailing culture. There had never been any love lost between the workaday City, which justifiably regarded itself as the source of the nation's wealth, and Westminster, the realm of court government and Church, with its attendant grandeur and excess. The truth was that each needed the other: the nation could not thrive without business, nor equally without competent governance. But the rivalry between factions grew ever more bitter under the first Stuart kings, and was among the causes of the terrible conflict that would divide the nation a half-century later.

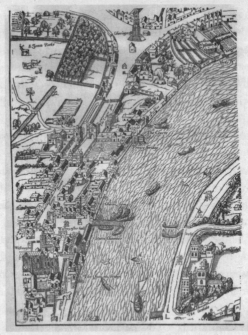

Whitehall and the Strand: a section of Ralph Agas's map of about 1630

Physically, where Fleet Street joined the Strand, the narrow alleys and tenements gave way to a broad road lined with the gateways to the town houses of the gentry, and between them shops catering to the busy traffic between the City and Westminster. Behind the street frontage were the extensive gardens of these 'Strand palaces'. On the south side of the street they stretched down to the Thames, each with its imposing watergate to allow river access. On the other side, immediately behind the houses, were orchards and fields – notably Covent Garden, the off-site garden of the Westminster convent. The church of St Martin-in-the-Fields still to a large extent lived up to its name, looking out across the open green space of what is now Trafalgar Square.[17] Within Inigo's lifetime the developers would move in and the fields disappear under streets and alleys of solid houses for the middle classes, interspersed with jerry-built tenements for the poor.

The most easterly of the mansions on the river side was Leicester House, the former home of Robert Dudley, Earl of Leicester. West of it was the former residence of the Bishops of Bath, now Arundel House, with which Inigo would become intimately associated through his friendship with Thomas Howard, Earl of Arundel. A compound rather than a single structure, it maintained the medieval pattern of being built around a courtyard entered through a gatehouse. So did its neighbour Somerset House, completed in 1550 (and demolished 200 years later), the first true Renaissance building in London. Its central gatehouse, arched and colonnaded, was adorned with one of the earliest examples of strapwork, a device imported from Antwerp, where decorated bands of ornament embellish the internal and external architecture.[18] After James I's accession it would become the official residence of Anne of Denmark and then of Henrietta Maria, and Inigo carried out extensive work on redesigning the interior, parts of the exterior and the garden.

Next to it was the rambling, thirteenth-century Savoy Palace, with crenellated outer walls. The oldest of the Strand palaces, the Savoy received its name through being owned, for a few years after it was built, by the Count of Savoy, a relative of Henry III's wife, Eleanor of Provence. It had been used since the mid-sixteenth century as a hospital and refuge for indigents.

Almost opposite, on the north side of the street, Exeter House was home to members of the powerful Cecil family. Adjoining it was Bedford House, built in 1586, with prominent gables on the street front and a tower to the west. Its garden – rather larger than those on the other side of the Strand because it was unconstrained by the river bank – stretched as far north as Covent Garden, where Inigo was to exercise his genius both in architecture and town planning. Further west, St Martin's Lane, running into the Strand from the north, was lined on both sides with recently built cottages: the playwright Ben Jonson lived in one for much of his early life.

Back on the south side, Robert Cecil acquired the property next to the old Savoy Palace and built Cecil House which, confusingly, became known as Salisbury House when he was made Earl of Salisbury in 1605. Next to it was Durham House, home of the Bishops of Durham, part of which would be acquired by Cecil to build the New Exchange and give Inigo his first known architectural commission. Then came York House, home of the powerful Bacon family, where Francis Bacon was born in 1561. It gained its name from having briefly been the residence of the Archbishop of York when the historic York Place, just around the bend of the river to the south, had been commandeered by Henry VIII and transformed into Whitehall Palace, the main London residence of the Tudor monarchs.

Cardinal Wolsey had been the last Archbishop to live at York Place, but was forced to give it up in 1529 when he fell from royal favour. Inigo would come to know Whitehall Palace well, living and working on its perimeter for the most productive period of his life. Its buildings were a mish-mash of the styles of the previous 200 years. The newest and most lavish had been put up by Wolsey, an ambitious builder who introduced to London an idiosyncratic style of external decoration, alternating squares of white stone and flint, producing a chequerboard effect familiar to us today from the East Anglian wool churches. The best-known example was the so-called Holbein Gate (despite the name the painter Hans Holbein played no part in its design), straddling King Street, the public thoroughfare on the line of present-day Whitehall. Another sixteenth-century palace gateway to the south was constructed from brick and stone.

The shabby appearance of Whitehall Palace at the end of the sixteenth century belied its regal status. It had been poorly maintained for years. The timber-framed Banqueting House, built in 1581, was coming to the end of its useful life: James I would have it replaced in the early years of his reign, and when that new building burned to the ground in 1619 it would give Inigo the chance to design his enduring masterpiece.

York House was divided from the palace by Northumberland House, the most modern Strand palace of all, begun at the very end of Queen Elizabeth's reign. It was among the last of the great Tudor buildings, with characteristic turrets at the corners and a portal by Gerard Christmas, where an oriel window was flanked by extravagantly decorated pilasters. It was demolished in 1874 so that Northumberland Avenue could be constructed to link the newly built Victoria Embankment with Charing Cross and Trafalgar Square.

Were Inigo to have ventured into the countryside just west of the metropolis he would have marvelled at Cope Castle, later called Holland House, built in 1606 on a site within today's Holland Park. This fine early Jacobean building occupied three sides of a formal entrance courtyard lined with an arcade decorated with strapwork. Its most distinctive features were a series of stepped Dutch gables on the roofs and pinnacles on either side of the central block. North, in the village of Highgate, was Lauderdale House, dating from the sixteenth century, one of the last great houses with timber-framed construction.

South of London was Wimbledon House, one of the residences of the powerful Cecil family, built in red brick with attractive white stone quoins, occupying three sides of a courtyard on top of a hill, with terraces built into the slope. East of Greenwich Charlton House, also in brick, is another typical mansion of the period and parts of it have been speculatively attributed to Inigo. It was built for Adam Newton, tutor to Prince Henry, James I's eldest son, and Inigo would certainly have visited it after 1610, when he joined the Prince's court as his surveyor.

The largest and most pretentious of the later prodigy houses was Audley End in Essex, on the site of a former abbey. The first Earl of Suffolk, James I's Treasurer, began building in 1605 but it was not completed until 1614. The elaborate entrance gate, contained within four turrets, led into the first of two courtyards. The entrance block to the main house, directly opposite, was attached at right angles to two ranges that filled the other two sides of this first court. Beyond that, a second courtyard was totally enclosed by the main portion of the house, topped with many turrets – the part that remains standing today. The King, visiting the house, famously remarked that it was big enough for a Treasurer but too big for a King. This turned out to be an ominous piece of irony, for in 1618 Suffolk was accused of embezzlement, stripped of his office and sent to the Tower of London. Only the central range of the house has survived.

This, then, was the fashionable architecture that prevailed in

Inigo

England as Inigo was learning his craft, a confusing jumble of traditions and overseas influences only half digested. Imagine, then, the shock to his senses when he first set eyes on the buildings of Italy – cool, disciplined and elegant, conforming to mathematical rules and philosophical principles. They were, quite simply, a revelation.

Chapter Four

PALLADIO THE PEERLESS

A NDREA PALLADIO WAS BORN Andrea dalla Gondola in
Padua in 1508. By the time he was sixteen he had moved to
Vicenza and joined the guild of bricklayers and stonemasons. He was
a mason for at least twelve years and as such, after he had served his
apprenticeship, he would increasingly have taken a hand in the design
of the monuments and decorative work that he carved: his first tentative
steps towards architecture proper. Then in 1536 came the opportunity
that would change his life. He was engaged to work at a villa at
Cricoli, near Vicenza, owned and designed by Giangiorgio Trissino –
a wealthy patrician, poet and philosopher, a devotee of architecture
and an enthusiastic mathematician.

Thirty years older than dalla Gondola, Trissino was impressed with
the young man's imagination and his grasp of architectural principles.
He urged him to study mathematics and Latin, the latter so that he
could read the works of Vitruvius, the inspiration for the design
of the Cricoli villa. It was Trissino who named the young man
Palladio – a reference to Pallas Athene, the Greek goddess of wisdom, as well as to a character in an epic that Trissino was writing
about the expulsion of the Goths from Italy. The work, published

in 1547, was packed with architectural descriptions and references to Vitruvius.[1]

Trissino was a man of great influence in Vicenza. At his villa he entertained those of the local gentry interested in patronising the fine arts, and introduced Palladio to them. It was a good time to be an architect. Many of the grand houses in the area had been damaged or destroyed in the War of the League of Cambrai in the second decade of the century, when the Venetian Republic came under assault from an alliance of neighbouring states supported by France and Spain; but now prosperity was beginning to return.

There were historical reasons why Vicenza's aristocrats were keen for their new houses to be the envy of other parts of the region. Once an independent city state, Vicenza had been part of the Venetian empire for more than a hundred years and was regarded by outsiders as a poor relation of the magnificent city and port to its east. To restore Vicenza's self-esteem, those grandees who could afford to rebuild their mansions wanted them to rival the very best that Venice could boast.

To establish a distinctive and influential body of work, an architect needs to operate in a climate of expansion and confidence. Palladio lived in just such times, and he rose to their creative challenge. Inigo would have no such luck but, only two decades after his death, Christopher Wren was able to establish his reputation – and claim his deserved place in history – because of the urgent demand for new churches in London following the Great Fire of 1666. Later, a breed of rising industrialists and entrepreneurs provided employment for the architects of scores of opulent Georgian country houses across Britain. Then the steep population increase of the Victorian era created a demand for middle-class housing, churches and factories.

Vicenza in the mid-sixteenth century offered similar opportunities. Throughout the early 1540s, Palladio increasingly became involved in the design of villas and palazzos for members of his patron Trissino's exalted circle. The earliest building that can be attributed to him with certainty is the Villa Godi at Lonedo, completed in 1540 and notable for its careful symmetry, with some features clearly derived from Trissino's villa at Cricoli. Shortly afterwards the young man was working on his first mansion in Vicenza, the Palazzo Civena. A palazzo was a nobleman's main city residence, a grand affair usually built around a central courtyard. Villas, not designed for year-round residence, were smaller, often omitting the courtyard. The villas that Palladio built were principally located in the lush, fertile countryside of Veneto; some on the banks of the Brenta, the charming canal linking Venice with Padua.

Palladio had yet to visit Rome. He was basing his early designs on the works of Vitruvius and Serlio, the first of whose textbooks was published in the 1530s, and on the treatise of the fifteenth-century architect Leone Battista Alberti, who set out the principles of what we now call the Renaissance style. In the 1420s Filippo Brunelleschi had pioneered the move away from Gothic and Romanesque, idioms that had held sway in Europe for many centuries, and sought to reintroduce classical Roman principles and motifs, including strict adherence to the orders for the capitals at the tops of columns. The first four orders – Tuscan, Doric, Ionic and Corinthian – had been listed by Vitruvius and the fifth, Composite, was identified by Serlio. The Corinthian and Composite orders feature acanthus leaves, introduced into Greek architecture and sculpture in the fifth century BC.

Brunelleschi and his followers agreed with Vitruvius that 'all the secrets of art consist in proportionality'[2] and that their work must be based firmly on rules and discipline. The classical movement, which Palladio would bring to its sublime peak, was strongly rooted in the scientific principles of mathematics and harmony. The core belief, expressed by Leonardo da Vinci among others, was that proportion and harmony in architecture were related to the same qualities in music. Both were seen as deriving ultimately from the proportions of the human body, and there was a universal harmony that held good for all the arts – a philosophy not too distant from today's fashionable cult of *feng shui* in interior design. Da Vinci and his followers, including Palladio, thought that the proportions of rooms should be calculated on a scale derived from harmonic chords. As the twentieth-century architectural historian Rudolf Wittkower explained it:

> As man is the image of God and the proportions of his body are produced by divine will, so the proportions in architecture have to embrace and express the cosmic order ... In the eyes of the men of the Renaissance, musical harmonies were the audible tests of a universal harmony which had a binding force for all the arts.[3]

That would become central to Inigo's credo, too.

Not until 1545, when Palladio was already in his late thirties, did Trissino arrange his protégé's first visit to Rome, where the two men could examine together not only the work of the leading Renaissance practitioners of the last hundred years but also – and in Palladio's case most significantly – what remained of the ancient classical buildings and statues. For an aspiring architect, indeed for anyone with a passion for the visual arts, Rome was the centre of the sixteenth-century universe. Many of the best artists from Florence, Venice and other Italian regions, as well as from northern Europe, had found their way there. Men such as Vasari, Tibaldi, Mabuse and Michelangelo himself were producing work of supreme quality.

By the middle of the century the simplicity of the early Renaissance movement was being embellished by a style known as Mannerism, involving the introduction of decorative detail alien to the purity of the original classical inspiration. Giulio Romano's palazzos and villas in Rome and his work on the ducal palaces in Mantua are prime examples, as is Michelangelo's Biblioteca Laurenziana in Florence. Mannerist elements appeared in some of Palladio's later buildings, but overall he was opposed to extraneous decoration – a view that Inigo would come to share wholeheartedly.

When Palladio and Trissino arrived in Rome, Michelangelo, who had painted the ceiling of the Sistine Chapel more than thirty years earlier, was still active at seventy, and would live for another nineteen years. He was about to embark on his most monumental architectural undertaking, the exterior of St Peter's Basilica begun by Bramante, a close follower of Leonardo da Vinci. (After Bramante's death in 1514 the work was carried on by Antonio da Sangallo, who died in 1546, and it was still not complete when Michelangelo himself died in 1564.) Palladio could admire Bramante's pioneering work here and at the churches of Santa Maria della Pace and San Pietro. Equally, he would have been inspired by the churches and palazzos of Raphael who, by the time of his death in 1520, had won a high reputation as an architect as well as a painter.

Palladio and Trissino stayed in Rome until 1547 and on his return Palladio published two guide books to the classical remains. In the dedication to his *I Quattro Libri dell' Architettura*, published in 1570, he acknowledged the vital contribution that this and later visits made to his understanding of architecture, especially the chance he had to view the ancient ruins at first hand. Although he had studied many drawings of them, when he visited them he found them 'worthy of much greater attention than I had at first thought'.[4]

On his return to Vicenza he entered and won a competition to redesign the medieval Palazzo della Ragione, the central market hall, or Basilica. His ingenious solution was to put a new skin around the original buildings in the shape of a two-tier arcade – Doric columns on the ground floor and Ionic above – surmounted by statues and a roof shaped like the upturned hull of a ship. Anxious to allow as much light as possible to penetrate into what would otherwise have been a gloomy interior, he placed oculi (small round openings) above so-called Serlian arches – wide archways flanked by two narrower flat-headed openings, separated by pillars. Described by Serlio in his 1537 book, this device was so often used subsequently by Palladio and his contemporaries, especially for windows, that it is sometimes called a Palladian or Venetian window.

By now his fame was spreading further among the wealthy landowners of Vicenza, Padua and Venice, and he was showered with commissions to design new palazzos and villas for them. He was able to hire a staff of bricklayers and masons and, according to his first biographer Paolo Gualdo, was generous with his time in teaching them the essentials of the craft.[5] An early commission was for the Palazzo Chiericati in Vicenza, imposing if rather heavy compared with some of his later work. The grand entrance frontage, rigidly symmetrical, is divided by two tiers of columns into eleven bays, with a broad flight of steps leading to the entrance in the centre and statues fringing the roof. A loggia overlooks the interior courtyard. Today the palazzo houses the municipal art museum.

Construction of grand houses in the sixteenth century was slow, and the supply of money for materials and labour not always constant. The work would be halted if the noblemen for whom the houses were being built found that their ambition had outstripped their resources. This explains why several of Palladio's projects remained only half finished. Among them was the Palazzo Thiene in Vicenza, begun by Giulio Romano but taken over by Palladio in 1546, shortly before Giulio's death. It was a tremendously important commission because Marcantonio Thiene was reputedly Vicenza's richest man and the palazzo, as originally conceived, would have reflected that.

Built on four sides of a courtyard, it would have taken up an entire city block; but what was actually built covers only about an eighth of this area. Like the Palazzo Chiericati it has eleven bays, but with a porticoed temple front covering the middle three, investing the design with added grandeur. Palladio was the first architect to design villas and palazzos with temple fronts, bringing to domestic architecture what had previously been thought of exclusively in the context of places of worship and other public buildings. At the Palazzo Thiene he also employed another favourite device that Inigo later adopted – rustication, or rough-hewn stone that contrasted with more conventional smooth dressed surfaces.

Trissino died a few years after the pair returned to Vicenza, but in 1554 Palladio went back to Rome for two years, making a further close study of the classical ruins and writing a short guidebook to them, *Le Antichita di Roma*. He also collaborated with the scholar Daniele Barbaro in redrawing the plates for a new translation of Vitruvius's architectural treatise. Barbaro was another who exerted a strong influence on Palladio, in effect succeeding Trissino as his chief patron. Barbaro was a firm advocate of the logical, structured approach that would be a feature of the Palladian style. In his commentary on Vitruvius, he wrote:

> It is not enough to order the measurements singly one after the other, but it is necessary that those measurements be related to each other, that is to say that there must be some proportion between them ... One cannot sufficiently praise the effect of proportion, on which is based the glory of architecture, the beauty of the work and the miracle of the profession.[6]

Barbaro persuaded the religious authorities in Venice to commission three churches from Palladio: San Giorgio Maggiore, Il Redentore and the façade of San Francisco della Vigna, all characterised by temple fronts made up of two pediments, a central one overshadowed by a larger one covering the whole width of the building. Later, Barbaro himself commissioned Palladio: to build a villa at Maser, near Treviso, for himself and his brother Marcantonio, a Venetian ambassador. The long, low structure, with a rusticated temple front-age in the centre, is laid out in the pattern of an opulent ancient Roman villa, fit for a man of ambassadorial rank, and is decorated with a superb set of frescoes by Veronese. Rudolf Wittkower has called it 'one of the most perfect Renaissance creations in northern Italy'.[7]

As Palladio's reputation grew, so did the demand for his services. Among his outstanding buildings of the 1560s was the Palazzo Barbaran-Porto in Vicenza, almost adjacent to the Palazzo Thiene and used today as the headquarters of the International Centre for the Study of Palladio. Some of his later work featured gigantic pilasters running the full height of a building, instead of the more common double row of shorter columns. This so-called 'giant order', usually regarded as a Mannerist element, was introduced by Michelangelo in his plan for the Roman Capitol in the middle of the century. Palladio employed the device most dramatically at the uncompleted Loggia del Capitaniato, facing the Basilica across Vicenza's main square, which he began in 1571 as a residence for the Venetian Governor. He used the giant order again on two other buildings in the city, the Palazzo Porto Breganze (also unfinished) and the Palazzo Valmarana.

His villas, built as they were for rest and recreation rather than as a nobleman's chief residence, showed an appropriately lighter touch than his palazzos, as well as sensitivity to the site. The best of them blended with and enhanced the landscape, in particular Villa Capra, commonly called La Rotonda, the remarkable and often-imitated building of four equal façades, placed dramatically on a hill just outside Vicenza. Palladio himself wrote that it had 'the aspect of a grand theatre'.

Villa La Rotunda, Palladio's masterpiece near Vicenza

On the banks of the Brenta he built Villa Foscari, called La Malcontenta, reputedly because of the unhappy expression of a woman depicted in one of its frescoes. He evolved what was in effect a stock pattern for villas, varied only to take account of the surrounding countryside and the clients' wishes in respect of ornament. Based as far as possible on Roman models, the layout was simplicity itself, with symmetry and order the essential qualities. The main rooms were placed evenly on two sides of the cube-shaped entrance hall. Domestic services, such as kitchens and laundry rooms, were on the lower ground floor, beneath the *piano nobile*, which was reached by a flight of steps up to the main entrance. As he wrote in *I Quattro Libri*: 'It is to be observed that those [rooms] on the right correspond with those on the left, so that the building may be the same in one part as in the other.'[8]

Palladio's last design was among his most remarkable. Straddling as it did the territory between architecture and the theatre, it was to exert a powerful influence on Inigo, much of whose own professional life was played out in these two spheres. In 1558 the Accademia Olimpica in Vicenza, an exclusive club devoted to fostering the arts, sciences and classical studies, had asked him to design a temporary stage set for a pageant celebrating Hercules, who, as the mythical founder of the Olympic Games, had a special place in the academy's iconography. It was the academy's first theatrical venture since it had been established in 1555, with Palladio as one of the twenty-one founder members. There were at the time very few permanent theatre buildings in Europe: plays and other performances were generally mounted on temporary stages, erected outdoors or in large halls, for special occasions such as carnival time in Venice.

Encouraged by the success of the pageant and its staging, the academicians commissioned Palladio in 1561 to build a full-blown but temporary wooden theatre inside the great hall of the Basilica, whose exterior was still being rebuilt to his designs of 1546. They stipulated, perhaps at the architect's own suggestion, that the theatre should be 'similar to that of the ancient Romans'. Two plays were initially produced in it, one a tragedy by Palladio's late patron, Trissino. The layout of this wooden theatre was in part based on the designs of Vitruvius that Palladio had drawn for Barbaro's book. As in Roman theatres, the audience was seated in a semi-circle facing the stage, beneath a balcony adorned with statues. Behind the acting area was a *frons scenae* with three arched entrances, again decorated with statues.

Not for another nineteen years, in 1580, did the Academy decide to erect a permanent theatre and they naturally looked to Palladio – now over seventy – to design it. Each leading academician was asked to give money to help pay for the building, and in return he would be honoured by having his statue, in Roman dress, erected on a pedestal as part of the theatre's permanent decor.

Palladio placed the statues on the *frons scenae*, mostly on the upper tier, above the entrances to the back of the stage – a large formal arch in the centre and a smaller opening on either side. To further compliment the donors, statues of the Virtues mingled with their own images. Palladio would never see the finished theatre – one of his lasting masterworks – because he died that August, when work on it had scarcely begun. His follower Vincenzo Scamozzi constructed a remarkable perspective stage backdrop in high relief, on a steeply raked base, representing streetscapes in Thebes and used for the theatre's opening production of Sophocles's *Oedipus Tyrannus* in 1585.

Even though a great many of Palladio's buildings survive, his enduring reputation owes as much to *I Quattro Libri* as to his portfolio of built work. Over the years the book became a bible, as well as a pattern reference, for Inigo and his many other followers. It was based principally on his own designs, not all of which were actually constructed, and it may have been intended as much as a catalogue for potential customers as a statement of his professional philosophy.

His meticulously drawn plans, with measurements included, were well coordinated with the text. In the first book he covered orders, ornaments and nuts-and-bolts matters such as materials and staircases. The second was devoted to his designs for villas and palazzos – sometimes, with the benefit of hindsight, he introduced improvements to what had actually been built. This book also contained plans of houses from ancient Rome. In the third, he gave the same treatment to public buildings such as basilicas, churches and bridges, and examined the principles of town planning. The fourth book depicted and discussed ancient Roman temples.

Palladio's illustration of a loggia

The title page allowed no doubt as to the high regard in which Palladio held his calling: it was illustrated with the allegorical figures of Geometry and Architecture pointing upwards to a crowned figure of Virtue. In the first chapter of the first book he declared his unequivocal allegiance to the Renaissance principle of harmony, and to Vitruvius's stress on symmetry, by defining beauty in terms of mathematics:

> Beauty will result from the beautiful form and from the correspondence of the whole to the parts, of the parts between each other, and of these again to the whole; so that the structures may appear an entire and complete body, wherein each component agrees with the other and all components are necessary for the accomplishmant of the building.

He recommended seven basic shapes for rooms: circular, square, and five standard rectangles – a square and a third (3:4), a square and a half (2:3), a square and two-thirds (3:5), two squares (1:2) and one where the long side of the rectangle constituted the diagonal of a square made on the short side. Height should be a mean between length and breadth, although he conceded that, in exceptional cases, the architect had to be free to make his own judgment on the height of the room, the dimensions of windows and other details. There were strict rules about nearly every aspect of a building. For instance, the distance between columns and pilasters, and the measurements of their bases, had to relate to their width, the proportions varying between the five orders.

Inigo made careful notes and translations of many of these details in the margins of the copy of *I Quattro Libri* that he is believed to have bought in Venice in 1601. As early as page 7 of the first book he recorded the author's advice that timber for building must be cut in winter and fall 'and in the decrease of the moon'. Three pages later he warned against building on soft or crumbly ground. Further on, Inigo noted Palladio's observations on doors and windows:

> The entrances are varied according to the greatness of the houses, as I observed at Vicenza where there are the best that I ever saw . . . To make the principal door observe the greatness of the building, quality of the person and what things are to pass through it . . . If windows be little the room will be dark, if too big uninhabitable for cold and heat . . . The windows above must be the sixth part lower than them below and if there be any higher they must so diminish . . . Windows all of a bigness though the rooms vary . . . In the corners no windows for strength.[9]

Many of Palladio's nostrums were strictly practical: for instance, he recommended that barns should face south, away from the prevailing wind, so that the hay would not get spoiled in rain. Inigo's response, as shown in his annotations, was equally pragmatic. At the start of Book Two, Palladio discussed the craft of designing buildings for specific functions, yet with an eye to the available budget:

> Grand gentlemen, the greatest of the Republic, will require houses

with loggias and spacious and ornate rooms so that they can entertain those who await the master . . . For lesser gentlemen, lesser buildings are seemly, costing less and with fewer adornments. For lawyers and advocates, one should build in such a way that their houses have pleasant, decorated places to walk in so that clients may remain there without tedium. The houses of merchants should have places where merchandise can be stored in such a way that the landlord need not fear burglars.

Inigo's curt précis of this advice was: 'Advocates must have fair places for their clients to walk in. Merchants must have places to put their merchandise in.' And this was his interpretation of Palladio's rules about arranging rooms in houses for maximum comfort:

The chambers for summer must be large and laid towards the north and those for winter little and towards the south and west. The chambers for the spring and fall placed towards the east and that they look on gardens. Studies and libraries likewise.[10]

Further on, he translated Palladio's version of the modern estate agent's dictum: location, location, location.

[It is] a beautiful and commodious thing to build upon a river a country house for transportation; besides one may easily water gardens and other grounds. Still waters engender ill airs. High and lightsome places where the air is moved continually by the winds and by falling of the ground, the moist and ill vapours are purged, the people are well coloured and not troubled with gnats nor such vermin. Water that hath an ill taste or is tinted [is] not good.[11]

Here he was betraying his concerns about health, especially his own, which he confirmed by copying out several recipes for medicines on the book's fly-leaves.[12] In Book Three, Inigo noted Palladio's observations on piazzas: 'Piazzas necessary for divers purposes. Piazzas giveth ornament. In sea towns, near the port. In land, in the middle . . . Triumphal arches give great grace to piazzas.'[13]

In 1615, Scamozzi published his own two-volume treatise, *L'Idea*

Della Architettura Universale. According to a date written on the title page, Inigo acquired his copy on 25 March 1617, and was again interested in the practicalities of the craft. Towards the end of volume two he made some notes on bricklaying: 'The columns of brick must be left to dry and be defended from the rain until the mortar has taken good hold, then put on the capital.' Both Palladio and Scamozzi usually had their columns built in brick and covered with terracotta to give the impression that they were of solid stone.

Like Palladio, Scamozzi was concerned with architectural discipline, with forgoing excessive ornament for its own sake. Inigo shared their view, and in reading his Italian books he constantly highlighted sentences that confirmed it. At the beginning of Scamozzi's second volume he noted: 'Some think all ornament unnecessary . . . God adorned the world.' Inigo clearly agreed, and translated Palladio's thoughts on it thus:

> Although variety and things new may please every one, yet they ought not to be done contrary to the precepts of art, and contrary to that which reason dictates; whence one sees that although the ancients did vary, yet they never departed from some universal and necessary rules of art.[14]

That was the most important principle that the Italian architect was eager to pass on to succeeding generations, and one that he applied consistently to his own peerless work.

In the eighteenth century the cause would be taken up by a generation of British Palladians including Colen Campbell, author of *Vitruvius Britannicus*, who would write of 'the great Palladio, who has exceeded all that were gone before and surpassed his contemporaries'. But, as Campbell also recognised, it was Inigo who introduced, to a nation not quite ready to embrace it, the principle that there could be no beauty in architecture without order and above all reason. Inigo drew the lesson not only from Vitruvius, Palladio, Alberti and other architectural practitioners and theorists but, reaching back into the history of thought, from the ancient philosophers. A voracious reader, he owned copies of many of their books and conducted, through his marginal notes, what were in effect tutorials with himself. He believed that an architect had to take pains to develop a broad range of expertise in various fields that would enable him to address the spiritual aspect of his designs as well as the practical.

Plutarch's *Moralia* was a prime source for his thoughts on music and the central doctrine of harmony, 'a heavenly thing', as he noted in the margin of page 229. Three pages later he observed: 'Music must be adorned with other senses, philosophy especially . . . No sort of harmony hath in it any absolute propriety.'

He also saw parallels with the disciplines of architecture and design. Translating Plutarch, he wrote that there were two aspects of a harmonious creation: the effect and 'the things that make the composition'. Perfection was achieved by 'mingling the parts and composing them', so they could be appreciated both sensually and intellectually. 'Discord and disproportion are all one.' He went into further precise detail about how the tune, the voice and the words commingled for a song's final effect, and why the ancients put musical instruments in the hands of the Gods.[15]

Yet he understood, too, that art could never be an entirely mechanical process, produced according to a rigid formula. Indeed he believed that Vitruvius, in most respects one of his heroes, paid rather too much heed to the mathematical aspects of architecture, at the expense of the creative side. On page 25 of his copy of Vitruvius's *I Dieci Libri de Architectura* he wrote, 'Methinks that Vitruvius might as well prefer the grammarian to the philosopher as the mathematician to the architect.'

The margins of this and other of his books are filled with maxims about the nature of art and the proper conduct of life, as well as admonitions to himself. On page 84 of Vasari's *Lives*, where the author discussed the qualities needed by architects, Inigo noted: 'One must begin betimes to learn the good principles; seeking to understand the parts and the manner that he means to follow.' Earlier in the same book he highlighted: 'What design is, to imitate the best of nature . . . Good manner comes by copying the fairest things.' He stressed, too, the observation that 'painting is imitation' along with the social point: 'Where there are poor there are thieves.'[16] And on page 95 of his copy of Xenophon's *L'Opere Morali*, he noted: 'Those are loved of God who are good in any good profession.'

His bitter disputes with Ben Jonson, and with other rivals at court, led no doubt to his underlining passages in Aristotle's *Ethics* about contentious and difficult men, about flatterers and men who were 'glad of another's hurt'. Other maxims that he translated in the margin were 'Repose and sport are necessary in this life' and 'Art is a habit to do a thing with right reason' – where he underscored the last word. But before he could acquire that habit, and put all those compelling theories about art and life into practice, he would have to secure a position in society from which he could exert an influence on English cultural life. And at the start of the new reign and the new century, that could only mean a place at court.

Chapter Five

THE ODD COUPLE

ANNE OF DENMARK, James I's queen, was almost certainly instrumental in introducing Inigo to the English court, but exactly how it happened is a matter for conjecture. Since he had already been in the employ of her brother Christian IV, the Danish King, it is possible that Christian simply recommended Inigo to her. Yet the young artist was also connected with the Earl of Rutland, a figure of some influence at Whitehall Palace, who might have effected the original introduction to Anne. Either way, in 1604 Inigo was engaged to work on the stage and costume designs for the Queen's first masque, to be performed on Twelfth Night, 6 January 1605, less than two years after she had come to London from Scotland. She insisted on taking part in it herself, although she was six months pregnant.[1]

Anne had married James in 1589, when she was only fifteen and he had been King of Scotland for twenty-two of his twenty-three years. At the Scottish court she quickly developed an appetite for life's pleasures, and a reputation to go with it. After a few years of marriage, rumours of her infidelity began to circulate – scarcely surprising given the King's unappetising appearance and apparent bisexuality. One of her alleged lovers, the Earl of Gowrie, was murdered in 1600 on

James's orders, although he probably had other motives besides his wife's honour.[2]

Anne had a taste for strong drink that she might have picked up from her husband, although it could equally have been hereditary for her brother Christian was also known for it. Ben Jonson, for one, believed it was in her genes, and paid enthusiastic tribute to her capacity in an entertainment he composed for the royal couple when they visited Sir William Cornwallis in Highgate in May 1604:

> Here mistress; all out. Since a god is your skinker;
> By my hand, I believe you were born a good drinker.
> They are things of no spirit, their blood is asleep
> That, when it is offered them, do not drink deep.[3]

(A skinker is a man who serves drinks – a tapster or barman in modern parlance.)

The hard-drinking Queen's principal passions, though, were dancing, music and spectacle. For the last fourteen years she had lived first in Edinburgh and then in Stirling, where her opportunities to indulge these enthusiasms – and indeed for any kind of social life – had been limited. Imagine her excitement at the prospect of London which, although not yet a truly cosmopolitan city, was at least developing a taste for lavish entertainment. Almost as soon as she arrived in the English capital she began to seek ways of making her own contribution to the merriment of the court.

It is unclear why she should have thought Inigo qualified to design a masque. He had probably seen similar entertainments on his travels, and he may have worked on one during his stay in Denmark. Quite apart from his creative flair, the talent for precise and practical draughtsmanship that is evident in his many surviving drawings would have endeared him to the carpenters, scene painters and dressmakers charged with following his designs.

Before starting work, though, he would have to meet his collaborator. Although the seventeenth-century masques were chiefly memorable for music, dancing and lavish display, they needed, too, a suitable plot and dialogue. To supply those vital elements, Queen Anne engaged Ben Jonson, already established as one of London's most popular playwrights and poets. He and Inigo, both in their early thirties, had probably never met before that first historic script conference with the Queen in 1604 when, according to Jonson's account, she set out her requirements for the theme of the entertainment. Her demands were specific and of an eyebrow-raising nature that would have fazed a less resourceful author and designer. To put it baldly, she wanted a plot that would allow her and the ladies of court to black up and play negresses. The two men went away and devised *The Masque of Blackness*.

Writing to order could not have come easily to Ben Jonson. His temper, as quick and fiery as his wit, had already got him into serious and near fatal trouble. He was a chancer, who had killed two men and spent four short terms in prison. The most intriguing contemporary account of his early life came from his own lips, in conversations with William Drummond, Laird of Hawthornden, with whom he stayed in the winter of 1618/19 after walking from London to Scotland. Drummond methodically wrote down details of their conversations and, in the end, gave his own assessment of the playwright:

> He is a great lover and praiser of himself, a contemner and scorner of others, given rather to lose a friend than a jest, jealous of every word and action of those about him (especially after drink, which is one of the elements in which he liveth), a dissembler of ill parts which reign in him, a bragger of some good that he wanteth, thinking nothing well but what either he himself or some of his friends and countrymen hath said or done. He is passionately kind and angry, careless either to gain or keep.

Gerard Langbaine, a seventeenth-century critic, put it more succinctly in his 1691 *Account of the English Dramatic Poets*: 'He was a man of very free temper and withal blunt, and somewhat haughty to those that were either rivals in fame or enemies to his writings.'

His unbounded confidence in his own abilities was all the more irritating for being so clearly justified. Combined with a vicious tongue, a stubborn contempt for authority and regulation and a disregard for the consequences of his actions, it made him the most difficult of men to work with; as the more feline, calculating Inigo would quite soon discover.

Jonson was born in 1572, a year before his future collaborator. He never knew his father, a minister of the Church who had been imprisoned in the reign of Queen Mary and died a month before Jonson's birth. He told Drummond that he believed his grandfather had come from Scotland, via Carlisle, to serve Henry VIII in some capacity. After his father's death, Jonson's mother soon married again, to a bricklayer, and the family lived in Hartshorn Lane, a narrow alley close to the Thames, where Charing Cross station now stands.

He first went to the school attached to the church of St Martin-in-the-Fields, just across the Strand, and then was admitted to the prestigious Westminster School, next to the Abbey, where his daily route from home took him through the precincts of Whitehall Palace. At Westminster he came under the tutelage of the historian William Camden, who taught him Latin and acquainted him with the classics. Jonson acknowledged his debt to his schoolmaster in an epigram:

> Camden, most reverend head, to whom I owe
> All that I am in arts, all that I know,
> (How nothing's that?) To whom my country owes
> The great renown, and name wherewith she goes . . .
> Many of thine, this better could than I
> But for their powers, accept my piety.

The fourth line is a reference to Camden having revived the Latin name Britannia for the British Isles.

The 'reverend head' encouraged Jonson to go on to St John's College, Cambridge, but if he did (the college records for the relevant years are missing) he stayed only a few weeks, possibly because his family could not afford the fees. He briefly took up his stepfather's trade of bricklaying but was soon conscripted into the army to serve in Flanders, where English soldiers were supporting the Protestants of northern Europe against the imperial aims of Catholic Spain. He saw some front-line action and in later life boasted of having killed an enemy soldier in single-handed combat.

Returning to London, he married Anne Lewis at the church of St Magnus the Martyr, by London Bridge, in November 1594. Their first two children died young: a daughter Mary in infancy and a son Benjamin in an outbreak of bubonic plague in 1603, aged seven. Like several other spirited Elizabethans with no obviously marketable qualifications, Jonson drifted into acting with a provincial touring company. The growing popularity of dramatic entertainments had spawned a number of groups who spent much of their year criss-crossing the country, performing in the houses of aristocratic patrons or in the courtyards of inns and other semi-public places in towns and villages.

The plays and pageants at first had mainly biblical themes, but the repertoire soon widened to include tragedies, usually based on British or classical history, and comedies satirising aspects of contemporary life. The London-based companies recruited promising actors and writers from the touring groups, and Jonson was hired by Pembroke's Men, partly funded by the Earl of Pembroke. They performed at a theatre called the Swan in Southwark, close to the better-known Rose.

Permanent commercial theatres were a recent innovation. To work out of a fixed base, as opposed to performing in a different town every two or three days, put an immense strain on the repertoire. Whereas travelling companies could present the same play day after day, the resident ones were forced to change their programmes frequently to satisfy a core audience too small to support a run of more than a few performances. So fresh scripts were sought wherever they could be found, and the more literate actors in the company were encouraged to turn their hands to writing them. That was how some of the greatest plays in the English language came to be created, by such actor/authors as Shakespeare, Jonson and Heywood.

Jonson made his explosive but ill-starred debut as a playwright in 1597, collaborating with Thomas Nashe on a piece called *The Isle of Dogs*, in which he also acted. The text has not survived but it was judged seditious by Queen Elizabeth's Privy Council – an easy body to offend – possibly because it referred to current shortages of essential supplies.

Both Nashe and Jonson were imprisoned for two months, along with two of the actors, and for a while all the playhouses in London were closed. The Swan did not reopen, and on his release Jonson became associated with Philip Henslowe's company, the Admiral's Men, playing at the Rose. But his first big success, *Every Man In His Humour*, was performed in 1598 by the rival Lord Chamberlain's Men at the Curtain Theatre in Shoreditch, with William Shakespeare, already a popular playwright, playing a leading role.

Only days after the new play opened its author was in prison again, this time for killing a man in a duel at Hoxton Fields, close to the Curtain Theatre. The victim was Gabriel Spencer, an actor in Henslowe's company and one of those imprisoned with Jonson after *The Isle of Dogs*. Jonson claimed that he had himself been injured in the arm in the encounter, and boasted to Drummond that he had gained victory despite his sword being ten inches shorter than his opponent's.

The jury found him guilty of murder, a capital offence; but he was saved from the gallows by his education. First offenders were entitled to claim 'benefit of clergy' if they were sufficiently versed in Latin to read the first verse of Psalm 51 (*Miserere mei, Deus* . . .) before the court. Jonson did so and was released, although not before the base of his thumb was branded with a T (for Tyburn) to prevent him claiming such immunity again. He had spent only two weeks in Newgate prison awaiting trial, but in that short time he was converted to Catholicism by a priest, probably a fellow-prisoner.

On leaving Newgate he did not immediately return to the theatre: unsurprisingly, Henslowe was in no mood to welcome back, as though nothing had happened, a man who had killed one of his best actors. Instead, Jonson briefly returned to his former employment and was admitted to the Bricklayers' Company. But he was unable to earn a living at the trade and in January 1599 he was arrested for debt and sent to Marshalsea, the debtors' prison in Southwark. The debt was paid for him, perhaps by a theatre acquaintance, and by August of that year he was back writing for a forgiving Henslowe. There were, after all, not many authors who combined his sharp wit, sense of dramatic construction and gift for poetry; and the theatregoers' appetite for new work showed no sign of abating. As well as writing for Henslowe he produced a sequel to his first hit for the Lord Chamberlain's Company, this one called *Every Man Out of His Humour*, one of the first productions at the newly built Globe Theatre. Like many sequels, it was less successful than the original.

The following year he wrote his first play to incorporate elements of the masque. *Cynthia's Revels*, created for the boys' company at the Blackfriars Theatre, included music, songs and Greek mythology. The plot involved an impoverished playwright, Criticus, who wrote a masque and was invited to fill a position at court.[4] This could have been meant as a thinly veiled job application, but was in any case a remarkable piece of prescience, for he would shortly be appointed the main royal masque writer. In the prologue to *Cynthia's Revels* he set out the philosophy of drama for which he became noted and which formed the basis of his later differences with Inigo: 'Words above action, matter above words.' Put more plainly, the plot is what counts.

Jonson never managed to ingratiate himself with the court of Queen Elizabeth but came to the notice of her successor and his wife very early in the new reign. In June 1603, after King James had already arrived in London, Anne of Denmark made her separate progress south from Scotland. One of her stopping places was Althorp, the Northamptonshire home of Sir John Spencer, and Jonson was invited to devise an entertainment for her there. Although it was a comparatively short piece, involving dancing and verses in praise of the new Queen, it clearly made an impression on her.

Before long, though, he was again in trouble with the authorities over something he had written. That year his Roman tragedy *Sejanus* had been produced at the Globe by the King's Men, the new name for the Lord Chamberlain's Men. Leading roles were played by Richard Burbage and William Shakespeare, whose last recorded stage appearance this was. Although it had a mixed reception, the King and Queen invited the company to perform it at Hampton Court during the Christmas period.[5] Yet despite the royal endorsement, the Privy Council thought they detected traces of 'popery and treason' in the play, which had boldly – or foolhardily – depicted a conspiracy against a monarch and an assassination at court. They called Jonson before them to explain himself, but took the matter no further.

More evidence of his quarrelsome nature, if it were needed, came in a feud he conducted at about this time with two rival playwrights, John Marston and Thomas Dekker. He satirised them in his plays and they did the same to him in theirs. But Queen Anne, whose wilful determination matched that of Jonson, was not deterred by his controversial reputation from inviting him to collaborate with Inigo on her first court masque. After considering her desire for a scenario that involved black ladies, the pair devised a plot in which dark nymphs from Africa became pale-skinned when exposed to the enlightenment personified by King James and by Britannia, the spirit of his newly unified realm.

A Daughter of Niger from *The Masque of Blackness*, 1605

Although the allegory is unacceptable by today's political and social conventions, its core message set the tone for the series of masques written and performed for the court of James I and his son Charles. All of them were dedicated to honouring the virtuous monarch, to asserting his divine right to rule and to deriding his enemies, who would invariably end up either totally routed or converted to the royal cause, as the kingdom entered a golden age of peace and contentment. The two queens, Anne of Denmark and then Henrietta Maria, were invariably represented as paragons of spotless, unassailable virtue.

Under King James, many of the masques reinforced the concept of union between his two kingdoms, England and Scotland. In Charles's time they took on a more blatant nationalist character, as can be gauged from the titles: *Albion's Triumph*, *Coelum Britannicum* (the British heaven), *Britannia Triumphans*. In *Salmacida Spolia*, the last of the court masques, performed in 1640, one of the characters was called the Good Genius of Great Britain. In modern corporate jargon, the masques would be called mission statements. Their purpose was to reinforce both national unity and the legitimacy of the Stuarts, citing their benevolent intentions and their moral aptness to lead the nation, as well as their hereditary entitlement to the throne.

Inigo's scenery and costumes were integral to these loyalist objectives. Representatives of right and wrong, of good order and chaos, were distinguished by their trappings. Courtiers wearing magnificent, ethereal creations of silk and taffeta were borne on clouds to and from their heavenly palaces. The forces of evil wore ragged clothing and grotesque masks and often inhabited dark caves. In staging, the sight lines were so arranged as to converge on the King's throne in the centre of the auditorium, giving him the perfect view. Inigo achieved this through the use of perspective. He was one of the first English artists to understand the technique, which he probably picked up in Italy.

The message of the masques was clear and passionate: its weakness was that it was so narrowly disseminated. Only friends of the court could attend the performances, and it was not from them that any challenge to the monarchy would be coming, or at least not yet. Those excluded from the celebrations would receive second- or third-hand reports of their opulence and excess, which sounded to many rather too much like the ritual of the Catholic Church that they feared and hated.

There was, inevitably, a great deal of hypocrisy in this idealisation of the monarchy. James was certainly no paragon; not physically nor in terms of his behaviour. The most vivid description of him that survives – a partisan one, to be sure – is from Sir Anthony Weldon, a former aide to the King who later supported the Parliamentary side in the Civil War. In his *The Court and Character of James I*, published in the Commonwealth period, he wrote that the King was of a timorous nature, in that he wore quilted doublets to guard against attack by stiletto. (If he did wear these seventeenth-century equivalents of modern bullet-proof vests it was surely a reasonable precaution, given the controversies and plots that surrounded his accession.)

This is how Weldon described James's appearance:

His eyes large, ever rolling after any stranger that came in his presence . . .; his beard was very thin; his tongue too large for his mouth, which ever made him speak full in the mouth, and made him drink very uncomely, as if eating his drink, which came out into the cup on each side of his mouth.

Not only did he slobber but he never washed his hands, just 'rubbed his finger ends slightly with the wet end of a napkin', and would not change his clothes 'until worn out to very rags'. He had suffered since a child from a weakness in his legs, which meant that he often needed support from others when he walked and, as Weldon tells us: 'His walk was ever circular, his fingers ever in that walk fiddling about his cod-piece.'

He 'drank very often', usually wine and Scottish ale, but it seldom went to his head.[6] He was also foul-mouthed. When advised that his people would like to see more of him, he is said to have exclaimed: 'God's wounds! I will pull down my breeches and they shall also see my arse!'[7]

His indiscriminate taste for liquor was noted by a man in a good position to know about it – Sir Theodore Mayerne, the court physician. He wrote that in his drinking the King:

errs as to quality, quantity, frequency, time and order. He promiscuously drinks beer, ale, Spanish wine, sweet French wine, white wine, Muscatel and sometimes Alicante white. He does not care whether the wine be strong or not, so it is sweet.[8]

As for the court over which he presided, an equally partisan description came from Lucy Hutchinson, the widow of a colonel in Cromwell's army, in her *Memoirs of the Life of Colonel Hutchinson*:

The court of this king was a nursery of lust and intemperance; he had brought in with him a company of hunger-starved poor Scots, who coming into this plentiful kingdom surfeited with riots and debaucheries, and got all the riches of the land only to cast away. The honour, wealth and glory of the kingdom were soon prodigally wasted by this thriftless heir, the nobility of the land utterly debased by setting honours to public sale, and conferring them on persons that had neither blood nor merit fit to wear ... The generality of the gentry in the land soon learned the court fashion, and every great house in the country became a sty of uncleanness. To keep the people in their deplorable security until vengeance overtook them, they were entertained with masques, stage plays and all sorts of ruder sports. Then began murder, incest, adultery, drunkenness, swearing and all sorts of ribaldry to be not concealed but countenanced.[9]

The King's appreciation of the company of comely young men also became the subject of whispered comment. One contemporary writer stated baldly that he was 'more addicted to love males than females'.[10] In his favour it can be said that he was genuinely a man of peace, seeking to settle disputes by diplomacy rather than military action or threats, and that his reign coincided with a period of comparative prosperity. Yet even allowing that some accounts of gross excesses at court will have been exaggerated to score political points, it would still have presented a challenge to Inigo as much as to Jonson to depict the King and his courtiers as the fount of beauty, virtue and grace.

The cynical explanation of why they agreed to do it is that they simply closed their eyes to reality and wrote whatever their paymasters required. They were the pipers and those who paid them called the tune.

The more charitable view is that they saw their work as educative and improving, believing that by presenting the audience with a vision of an ideal world to which they could aspire they were not merely bolstering the monarchy but at the same time offering instruction in morality. Certainly there is no real hint of scepticism or lack of commitment in Jonson's texts, nor in Inigo's designs.

From a modern standpoint, the masque is a bewildering form of entertainment. It arose out of an elaborate ritual for receiving guests that had been developed in great houses in Tudor times. Known as 'disguisings', the proceedings began when the guests, wearing masks and fancy dress, paraded before their hosts bearing gifts, accompanied by torch carriers. There followed a pageant, often representing military or maritime adventures and played on a transportable, extravagantly decorated stage on wheels.[11] (The word 'pageant' was originally used to denote this mobile stage, as well as the entertainments once presented on it.)

Guests and hosts would pay lavish mutual compliments in the form of poetry, full of allusions to the classics and Greek mythology. Then, still in their masks and costumes, they would join each other for dancing that would grow less formal – and in some company decidedly unrestrained – as the evening wore on. Spectacle was everything. A version of the ceremony was developed in parts of Italy, where again masked courtiers, after performing their tributes, plucked dancing partners from the audience.[12]

Combining these rituals with longer dramatic pieces, and using a fixed stage, was also an idea that originated at Continental courts. It led to the development of changing scenery, of which Inigo was a pioneer in England. Previously, where entertainments had been thought to need a variety of different scenes, they had been laid out in separate parts of the auditorium, forcing the audience to switch their attention from one to the other as the action demanded. That may have been practical when the plays were performed in halls, but not in purpose-built theatres with fixed seating. That was why Elizabethan and Jacobean dramas in public playhouses were usually staged with scarcely any scenery. By introducing devices to change the settings on a single platform Inigo provided a constant focus, supported by his introduction of the proscenium arch, also from Italy, which served to frame the stage and hide some of the machinery necessary to achieve his effects.[13]

Proscenium and garden scene fom *The Shepherd's Paradise*, 1633

Jonson is credited with the first use of the word 'masque' to describe these court entertainments, deriving it from the masks worn by the characters;[14] and he developed a rigid formula for them. They began with songs and verses in praise of the person or persons being honoured, packed with the classical allusions to which the playwright had been directed by his mentor, Camden. Jonson owned a copy of Cesare Ripa's *Iconologia*, the standard source book on Renaissance symbolism and mythology published at the end of the sixteenth century, and he frequently drew from it.[15]

The antimasque – a raucous dialogue between actors representing chaos and disorder, the villains of the piece – was introduced by Jonson in 1608, apparently at the suggestion of Queen Anne. It was acted before the masque itself as a sort of foil, to heighten the lyrical and uplifting effect of what was to follow and to give dramatic shape to the entertainment. It also allowed Jonson to exercise the wit and the talent for feisty and irreverent badinage that he later displayed in plays such as *Bartholomew Fair* and *The Devil Is an Ass*. The antimasque was the one part of the evening where the words were usually allowed to take precedence over the visual effects, even though Inigo's costumes for the low-life characters grew ever more imaginative and bizarre.

Along with the preliminary songs and verses, the antimasque was performed by professional actors borrowed from London theatre companies. The principal elements of the masque, the dances and symbolic tableaux, fell to the noblemen and ladies of the court; but to speak lines in public was regarded as beneath their dignity and beyond their competence. Stephen Orgel has observed:

> Masquers are not actors; a lady or gentleman participating in a masque remains a lady or gentleman, and is not relieved from observing all the niceties of behaviour at court. Queen Anne and her ladies danced in the masque because dancing is the perquisite of every lady and gentleman. It was, however, unthinkable for the Queen to become an actress and play a part.[16]

The formal dance, accompanied by music but no words, was the heart of the masque. As Prospero admonished when he produced his masque in Shakespeare's *The Tempest*: 'No tongue. All eyes. Be silent.'

To be among the dozen or so courtiers invited to dance in a royal masque was a signal honour and one that it would be impolitic to decline, particularly if a member of the royal family was taking part. For the dukes, duchesses, earls, countesses, and some senior knights and their ladies, it was evidence of status and favour. There were few starring roles, except when the Queen (and in Charles's reign the King) or the royal children were among the dancers. For the rest, each masquer was equal. It was a team effort in which the participants had to display mutual respect and solidarity, even though in real life they may be scheming against each other in one of the many court intrigues. They were expected to know the steps of the dances and, to ensure that they did, they would be trained by dancing masters for several weeks before the performance.

The music for the dances, tableaux and songs was a mixture of traditional tunes and those written especially for the occasion by court musicians, among them Nicholas Lanier, who would become Master of the King's Music. The musicians rehearsed the masquers by taking them through the steps of the different dances – some newly arrived from Europe, such as the galliard, lavolta and coranto.[17] The orchestras were large. In February 1619 Giovanni Battista Gabaleoni, the London representative of Savoy, reported seeing a court masque accompanied by forty violins and a wind section.[18]

When the main dance was over, the masquers quit the stage and joined the audience in revels, to which the vow of silence no longer applied. Nor, it seemed, did many other conventional restraints, according to the evidence of Sir Edward Peyton, an anti-monarchist Member of Parliament: 'The masques and plays at Whitehall were used only for incentives of lust: therefore the courtiers invited the citizens' wives to these shows, on purpose to defile them in such sort.'[19]

Between 1605 and 1640, a new masque would be produced most years, often on Twelfth Night and invariably in January or February. Male and female members of the court would take part at a time when women were still barred from appearing on the professional stage. Anne had passed on her enthusiasm to her sons Henry and Charles, who also liked to show off their dancing skills. King James never joined them, no doubt because of his feeble legs.

Samuel Daniel, in his introduction to the 1610 masque, *Tethys' Festival*, indicated how important a part of court life they had already become, just seven years into James's reign:

> Shows and spectacles of this nature are usually registered among the memorable acts of the time, being complements of state, both to show magnificence and to celebrate the feasts to our greatest respects.

Invitations to the masque, for those on the fringe of the court circle, were greatly coveted, and in his antimasques Jonson made at least two references to the difficulty of getting past the doorkeepers. In *Love Restored*, the 1612 production, he had the sprite Robin Goodfellow go through more than forty disguises in an attempt to inveigle himself in, but to no avail. And in *Chloridia* in 1631, Jonson's last court masque, the Postilion declared: 'Had hell-gates been kept with half that strictness as the entry here has been tonight, Pluto would have had but a cold court.'

Nor could those who were turned away plan to see the show later in the run, for normally the author's and designer's creative effort, and the great expense, were directed towards only one or two performances.

The best eyewitness account of the experience of attending a masque came from Orazio Busino, chaplain to the Venetian Embassy in London, who was invited to *Pleasure Reconciled to Virtue* on Twelfth Night in 1618. It was one of the last to be held in the Banqueting House built for King James in 1609, before it burned down in January 1619, allowing Inigo to design its replacement.

> In a large hall arranged like a theatre, with well-secured boxes all around, the stage is placed at one end, and facing it at the other end His Majesty's chair under a large canopy, and near him stools for the foreign ambassadors.

By Busino's account, the diplomatic guests arrived at 4 p.m. They were made to wait a while in an ante-room of the palace before the master of ceremonies fetched them and led them to the box customarily reserved for the Venetian representatives. That was when things began to go wrong:

> Unfortunately, we were so crowded and uncomfortable that had it not been for our curiosity we would have given up or expired. Moreover we had the additional curse of a Spaniard who came into our box by courtesy of the master of ceremonies, asking for two fingers of room, though we had no space to run around in and, by God, he placed himself more comfortably than all of us.

It would be two hours before the King eventually arrived. To while away the time Busino admired the architecture of the building, then turned his attention to his fellow guests:

> Though they claim to admit only those favoured with invitations, nevertheless every box was full, especially with most noble and richly dressed ladies, six hundred and more in number, according to the

general opinion; their clothes of such various styles and colours as to be indescribable; the most delicate plumes on their hats, and in their hands as fans; and on their foreheads strings of jewels, and on their necks and bosoms and in their girdles, and on their garments in such quantity that they appeared so many queens.

While confessing that his vision was poor, the chaplain was still able to give excited descriptions of what the women were wearing:

The plump and buxom show their bosoms very openly, and the lean go muffled up to the throat, all of them with men's shoes, or at least with very low slippers. Face masks are as important to them as bread at table, but for these public spectacles they put them aside willingly.

Jonson, too, testified to the gaudy attire of the women in the audience, again in *Love Restored*, where he had Robin Goodfellow speak of their 'superfluous excesses' in 'flaunting wires and tires [fine fabrics], laced gowns, embroidered petticoats and other taken-up braveries'. Small wonder that Inigo felt obliged to exercise his imagination to the utmost to ensure that his masquers were clothed more fancifully than his audience.

For *Pleasure Reconciled to Virtue*, the King arrived in the hall at about 6 p.m., accompanied by his senior courtiers and the Spanish and Venetian ambassadors, while some fifteen or twenty cornets played a fanfare. The King went to his throne, the ambassadors sat on stools and the other dignitaries went to the benches that had been reserved for them. The seating of the ambassadors always presented tricky problems of protocol, with the constant danger of offending those who considered that their status demanded a position closer to the King than they had been allotted, or who did not want to be in the same room as an ambassador of a hostile state. Boycotts were fairly frequent, and sometimes the King avoided the problem by selectively withholding invitations – or on one occasion by cancelling the performance altogether.

Busino described the masque in great detail.[20] When it ended the King went to the hall, where a buffet supper had been prepared for the performers.

He [the King] glanced round the table and departed, and at once like so many harpies the company fell on their prey . . . The meal was served in bowls or plates of glass; the first assault threw the table to the ground, and the crash of glass platters reminded me exactly of the windows breaking in a great midsummer storm. The story ended at two hours after midnight, and half disgusted and exhausted we returned home.[21]

The envoy may have misunderstood the significance of that apparent accident. The overthrow of the supper table at the end of a masque was one of the most peculiar traditions associated with the entertainment – a signal, perhaps, that for the rest of the evening the customary restraints on polite behaviour were in abeyance. Eyewitness accounts suggest that it was a regular ritual occurrence – 'the strange custom of the country', as one described it.[22] By tradition, it was said to have been introduced by James Hay, Earl of Carlisle, a Scottish courtier who came to London with James I in 1603, and a man noted for his ostentatious extravagance. When the original cold spread had been scattered, it was replaced by hot food from the kitchen – the so-called 'double dinner'.

Such excess will have displeased the higher-minded members of the court circle, such as Sir Francis Bacon. In an essay on masques and triumphs, he wrote: 'These things are but toys . . . but yet, since princes will have such things, it is better they should be graced with elegancy than daubed with cost.'[23]

Chapter Six

THE LOOKS, THE LAUGHTER AND THE SPORTS

B Y THE WINTER OF 1604/5 Queen Anne had been established in London for over a year and had been able to arrange a programme of seasonal entertainment richer than anything attempted in Queen Elizabeth's reign. On 20 January 1605, Ottaviano Lotti, the Florentine agent in London, sent a despatch home about it:

> At this time, more than at other seasons, all the people turn their minds to festivities and pleasures, but their majesties' courtiers in particular show themselves all the more ardent in this because of their capacity to spend money, and because it is proper for them to entertain one another . . . This year, therefore, new scenes and most lovely theatres have been built. Not an evening has passed without the performance of some lovely play in the royal household in the presence of their majesties, and then in a different fashion two most superb masques have been staged.[1]

One of the masques was for the Earl of Pembroke, the other for the Queen. Lotti was in no doubt which he preferred. He wrote that *The Masque of Blackness*, the Queen's masque, the first fruit of the partnership of Inigo and Ben Jonson, was performed 'with much more magnificence and rarer invention than the other'.

It was one of the coldest Twelfth Nights anyone could remember. On 6 January 1605, the Thames, which normally lapped around the eastern wall of Whitehall Palace, was frozen solid.[2] Those who considered themselves lucky to have been invited to *The Masque of Blackness* might have had second thoughts as, shivering, they skirted puddles of ice to reach the draughty Elizabethan Banqueting House, built of wood twenty-four years earlier. Yet as soon as the King made his formal entry and climbed onto his throne, and the proceedings got under way, the audience would have recognised that the effort they had made to prise themselves from their warm firesides had been well worth it. They were confronted with a vision of greater splendour and ingenuity than had ever been seen in England.

The stage, forty feet square and raised four feet off the ground, had been made for the occasion and fitted with wheels, so that it could be moved away and reused when the masque was over.[3] In the published text, Inigo's scenery and effects were described in detail. The curtain in front of the stage depicted a landscape of small woods and clearings, where hunters went about their sport. When it was allowed to drop to the ground, 'an artificial sea was seen to shoot forth, as if it flowed to the land, raised with waves which seemed to move, and in some places the billow to break, as imitating that orderly disorder which is common in nature'.

The churning sea, often accompanied by thunderstorms, was to become a recurring symbol in Inigo's masque designs; a metaphor, as the text suggested, for a disorderly realm. When virtue and order triumphed, as they always did, the sea would become calm and the landscape would change from threatening rocks and dark forests to sunlit hills, starlit skies and city streets furnished with sublime classical buildings. As Orgel and Strong point out, in his long career as a masque designer, Inigo would produce 'innumerable permutations of the same visual argument'.[4]

In front of the roaring sea sat six tritons, with blue hair, the lower part of their bodies covered, mermaid-like, to represent fishes' tails. Then the white god Oceanus and the black god Niger entered, mounted on a pair of giant sea-horses. After them came the daughters of Niger, twelve blacked-up aristocrats dressed in azure and silver, their hair formed into cones and crowned with feathers and pearls. They were accompanied by twelve white nymphs of Oceania bearing torches, their hands and faces blue, their hair a brighter blue, wearing green jackets with gold puff sleeves.[5]

> The masquers were placed in a great concave shell, like mother of pearl, curiously made to move on these waters, and rise with the billow; the top thereof was stuck with a chevron of lights which . . . struck a glorious beam on them as they were seated one above another, so that they were all seen.

More spectacle was to come. Six large sea monsters swam alongside the shell, each bearing two men holding more torches, made from the shells of molluscs. The backcloth represented a large sea painted in perspective.

For the most part Inigo's effects were produced by hand-operated machinery below the stage: the billowing sea, for instance, was created by raising and lowering painted cloths.[6] Clouds were painted on the Banqueting House roof.[7] The description of the scene in the text of the earlier masques was probably written by Jonson, although later Inigo would write it himself. Whoever wrote it for *The Masque of Blackness* was careful to give full credit to the designer for his ingenuity: 'So much for the bodily part,' he wrote, as he ended his detailed account of the staging, 'which was of Master Inigo Jones his design and act.'

With the scene set, the plot was acted out. Niger told Oceanus that his daughters had become dissatisfied with being black and had been advised by an oracle to seek out a place whose name ended in 'tania' and was lit by a greater light than the sun. The moon then appeared, in human form, dressed in silver and white on a silver throne amongst the clouds high above the auditorium. Having characters enter from the sky, often borne on clouds, was a favourite device throughout Inigo's career, and the effect was heightened by impressive lighting effects. The moon's head-dress was described as being:

crowned with a luminary or sphere of light which, striking on the clouds and heightened with silver, reflected as natural clouds do by the splendour of the moon. The heaven about her was vaulted with blue silk, and set with stars of silver which had in them their several lights burning.

The moon told Niger to look no further for the promised land. A country named Britannia was:

ruled by a sun . . .
whose beams shine day and night, and are of force
to blanche an Ethiop and revive a corpse . . .
This sun is temperate and refines
All things on which his radiance shines.

After this brazen flattery of King James, the masquers left their shell and began to dance on the stage in pairs, each carrying a fan decorated with a suitable symbol: the Queen's was a golden tree laden with fruit, celebrating her pregnancy. With the dance ended, a tenor voice representing the sea sang the short song 'Come Away', written for the occasion by Alfonso Ferrabosco, a prominent lute player and musical instructor to Henry, Prince of Wales. It is one of the few songs from the masques to have survived.[8] When it was over the masquers descended from the stage and danced with men of their choice. Eventually they climbed back into their shell, which moved off stage at a stately pace.

Although this was a more spectacular display than most of the audience had ever witnessed, there were still sceptics who refused to be impressed. Sir Dudley Carleton, a much-travelled diplomat, described the evening in a caustic letter to a friend:

There was a great engine at the lower end of the room, which had motion, and in it were the images of sea-horses, with other terrible fishes, which were ridden by Moors: the indecorum was that there was all fish and no water. At the far end there was a great shell, in the form of a scallop, wherein were four seats. On the lowest sat the Queen with my Lady Bedford; on the rest were placed the Ladies Suffolk, Derby, Rich, Effingham, Ann Herbert, Susan Herbert, Elizabeth Howard, Walsingham and Bevil. Their apparel was rich, but too light and courtesan-like for such great ones.

In another letter he went further in his criticism:

Their black faces, and hands which were painted and bare up to the elbows, were a very loathsome sight, and I am sorry that strangers should see our court so strangely disguised.

The evening ended on an unseemly note that, as we have seen, may have set a precedent:

In the coming out a banquet which was prepared for the King was overturned, table and all, before it was scarce touched. It were infinite to tell you what losses there were of chains, jewels, purses and such like loose ware, and one woman amongst the rest lost her honesty, for which she was carried to the porter's lodge, being surprised at her business.[9]

That was the less than dignified reality behind the glittering façade of the court masque. For Inigo, producing his exquisite and scholarly designs for an evening that would end on such a dissolute note must have made him feel like a classical pianist performing in a brothel. Certainly it was some distance from the rose-coloured vision conveyed by Jonson in *The Fortunate Isles and their Union* in 1625:

> Spring all the graces of the age
> And all the loves of time;
> With all the pleasures of the stage
> And relishes of rhyme:
> Add all the softnesses of courts,
> The looks, the laughter and the sports;
> And mingle all their sweets and salts,
> That none may say the triumph halts.

A queen from *The Masque of Queens*, 1609

The masquers' costumes, reflecting not just the softnesses but the extravagances of the court, were among the chief pleasures of the royal stage. Fine and costly clothing was a key element in court life. Some 450 of Inigo's designs for costumes have survived, more than for any other aspect of his work. Like his scenery and stage machines, they were derived mainly from Italian sources, from entertainments that he saw on his visits there and from books he brought back with him. To accuse him on that account of plagiarism, as some have, is to ignore the fact that most art of the period, not least the plays of Shakespeare, was founded on earlier work by others.

Whatever their origin, Inigo's designs testify to his talent for catching the surreal mood of the text and satisfying his audience's appetite for the exotic. The masquers themselves, extravagantly bejewelled ladies and gentlemen of the court, wore stylish robes and head-dresses: these were Jonson's 'sweets'. The 'salts' were the actors in the antimasques who portrayed absurd and grotesque figures – pygmies, acrobats, satyrs, pugilists, animals – and were clothed accordingly.

It was about fantasy, about creating an impossibly ideal world where softness, beauty and virtue triumphed over the basest human instincts. To create such a world the authors and designers of masques had to discard realism and aspire to its very opposite. This was much easier for Inigo to accomplish visually than for the author to do in terms of plot and dialogue. Yet almost alone among the masque writers Jonson managed to create works of meaning and beauty, compelling enough to assert themselves against the overpowering visual context in which the words were spoken and sung. But even he, in the end, could not wrest control of the piece from the man who conceived how it would look. Appearance was paramount.

Inigo would not have guessed, when he sat down to create the costumes for that first masque, that he would soon be caught in a treadmill, that as the years progressed he would have to produce ever more outlandish spectacles to amaze courtiers who had by now come to expect every new work to provide the ultimate feast for the senses. Thomas Campion, who wrote *The Lord's Masque* in 1613, described one of the more fanciful scenes Inigo devised for it: 'Sixteen pages, like fiery spirits, all their attires being alike composed of flames, with fiery wings and bases, bearing in either hand a torch of virgin wax, come forth below dancing a lively measure.'

Inigo's drawing of one of the sprites confirms the accuracy of the description. Indeed, his drawings of the costumes and the stage settings are works of art in their own right. According to Webb, Sir Anthony Van Dyck, portraitist to King Charles's court, praised Inigo's draughtsmanship as 'not to be equalled by whatsoever great masters in his time for boldness, softness, sweetness and sureness of touch'.

Essentially, though, the drawings were conceived as working documents, often accompanied by detailed instructions to those charged with interpreting them. On a design for a character in the antimasque of the *The Temple of Love* in 1635, he specified a man in a robe of russet girt low with a great belly . . . long moustachioes, the sleeves short . . . in the naked fat sleeves buskins to show a great swollen leg, on his head a cap coming forth before like a peak and from it great leaves hanging down with great ears, a great head and bald and a little cap *alla Venetiane* . . . like a Sir John Falstaff.[10]

On another, for the 1632 masque *Albion's Triumph*, he wrote:

For the tailor. That in putting in the person of Innocence, which is the uppermost of the five, the robe do hide all the feet and fall over a little so as none of the throne which is gilt be seen, but only the cloud which falls away.[11]

The drawings confirm that this was not an era of prudery. Several costumes for women masquers – for instance in *Tethys' Festival* in 1610 – left their breasts uncovered, as the Venetian ambassador noted with some disapproval when he attended *Pleasure Reconciled to Virtue* in January 1618.

Many of the costumes were highlighted with silver and gold that relied for their effect on carefully designed lighting. The record of Inigo's lighting requirements for *Albion's Triumph* stipulates four dozen torches, sixteen dozen 'lights according to those of the branches of good wax', three dozen ordinary torches and two hundred 'sises', a particular kind of candle used at court and in churches.[12]

Lighting had been an integral part of the masque since Elizabethan times, when the procession of masquers would be accompanied by trains of torch-bearers. With only naked flames at his disposal, Inigo achieved effects comparable with those of modern stage lighting designers with their banks of computer-controlled spotlights. He could conjure a pale light for the waning moon, suffused with clouds, and suddenly switch to a brilliant torch-lit spectacle where the light would catch the glint of the precious metals and jewels in the sets and costumes. Lights in glass cases would be lowered from the ceiling and made to move above the stage, sometimes to deflect spectators' attention from the scene-shifting below.

Inigo's machinery for changing scenes was innovatory in England

and, like his costumes, based in part on Italian models, some going back to Roman times. Vitruvius discussed stage machinery in Book Ten of his architectural works, from where Inigo gleaned the idea of *periaktoi*, large vertical prisms mounted on rods with parts of a different scene on each side to allow three scenes in a single spectacle – a primitive version of the mechanism used today on advertising hoardings that display three posters consecutively. On page 256 of his copy of the *Dieci Libri* he noted in the margin: 'I think that the scene changed according to the occasions given in the acts by taking of the cloths painted from the triangle machine as I have often used in masques and comedies.'

Another, simpler device that he often employed was the backcloth with a different scene painted on either side, fitted on to a revolve operated from below stage.[13]

In the 1611 masque, *Oberon, the Fairy Prince*, he introduced two techniques that are still in use to some extent today. Sidewings are pieces of painted scenery that jut out from the side of the stage, placed on an inwards sloping line that would, if continued, meet at the centre of the horizon, so as to assist the illusion of perspective. They also help to conceal backstage clutter and provided a refuge for actors waiting in the wings. Shutters are backcloths sliced in half vertically and placed on grooves at the rear of the stage, so that they slide in from both sides and meet in the middle. When drawn back they reveal a different backcloth. By this method the number of possible scene changes is limited only by the space available for the grooves.[14]

With experience he was able to create aerial effects more sophisti-cated than the dangling moon in *The Masque of Blackness*. He could make the masquers enter on clouds or in chariots that would fly across the top of the stage rather than being lowered from the ceiling. In *The Lord's Masque* he split the stage in half horizontally, with clouds drifting across the top half. By 1638, in *Luminalia*, he had devised a full-blown aerial ballet.[15] It all made a telling contrast with his architecture. Whereas he took great pains to make his buildings appear solid and dignified, with scant external decoration, for the masques he could throw off restraint and give full rein to his imagination and his flair for the exotic. They were the two distinct aspects of his creative genius, coming together only on those occasions when he incorporated classical buildings, sometimes his own, into his stage designs.

Masquers seated in a cloud in *Love Freed from Ignorance and Folly*, 1611

The effects and the lighting were a revelation for the audience at a time when public theatres operated either with rudimentary scenery or none at all.[16] Playwrights and commentators regularly expressed amazement at the fertility of Inigo's imagination and his technical ingenuity. In 1631, in James Shirley's play *Love's Cruelty*, Hippolit described the splendours of the court masques, showing how they inspired awe in those not privileged to attend them:

A scene to take your eye with wonder, now to see a forest move, and the pride of summer brought into a walking wood; in the instant, as if the sea had swallowed up the earth, to see waves capering about tall ships . . . In the height of this rapture, a tempest so artificial [expertly contrived] and sudden in the clouds, with a general darkness and thunder, so seeming made to threaten, that you would cry out with the mariners in the work, you cannot escape drowning . . .

Eubella responded: 'Fine painted blessings!'

The expense of the costumes, the scenery and the theatrical illusions that went with them seems not to have bothered a court constantly claiming poverty and seeking more money from Parliament. Surviving bills show that the cost varied greatly between masques. *The Masque of Queens* in 1609 came to more than £3000, whereas two years later *Love Freed from Ignorance and Folly* was mounted for a mere £719 1s 3d.[17] At the same time, the average annual rent for a decent London house was around £50.

Detailed accounts for *Love Freed* show that Inigo and Jonson were both paid £40 for their contribution – Jonson 'for his invention' and Inigo for 'his pains and invention', underlining that the final form of the masque was regarded as a joint responsibility. The fact that only Inigo is cited for his pains suggests that he may have taken a practical hand in constructing and installing the scenery and machines that he designed. The fee was apparently a standard one, because it crops up in connection with other masques in King James's reign. The man who taught the ladies of the court the steps of the dances was valued higher, at £50, with his assistant netting £20. The musicians received £2 each and twelve professional dancers £1.

The number of people employed in creating these fleeting entertainments is established by a note on the back of a design for one of Inigo's last masques, *Britannia Triumphans*, performed in 1638:

On the roof twenty men, quartering twenty men, on the windows twelve, on boarding the floor twelve, making ready the boards eight men, degrees [steps] and galleries twenty men, on the passages at the ends, ten men at one end, tilers eight. For the masques the master carpenter, for the stage shutters and clouds twelve and putting boards together for scenes of relieve [seven men named] with five more.[18]

While labour charges remained roughly constant, what chiefly determined the cost of a masque was the quality and quantity of the materials used. For *Tethys' Festival* – another 1610 masque, in which the nine-year-old Prince Charles took part – the silk merchant's bill for gold and silver braid alone came to £1984 8s 2d, nearly three times the entire cost of *Love Freed*.[19] The sets were less expensive. In *The Masque of Queens*, the most important piece of scenery was the House of Fame, for which several of Inigo's drawings survive. On the back of one of them is an account of expenses: £12 12s 10d for materials and £8 16s 6d for labour.[20]

A year after Charles I came to the throne in 1625 he decided to dispense with the annual masque, as an economy measure. It was probably his stagestruck French wife, Henrietta Maria, who persuaded him to restart them in 1631; but he capped the cost of each masque at £1400 and made the knights and ladies of the court pay for their own costumes, which could come to well over £100 each. To keep to this figure, old dresses and scenery were kept to be recycled in later masques, where formerly some of them had been given to the troupes of professional players who provided the actors for the antimasques. This library of masque costumes was a precursor of the extensive wardrobes that today's theatre companies maintain.[21]

Performances of the masques continued until the King and Queen were forced to leave the capital at the start of the Civil War. By that time they had become a staple ingredient of the mystique with which the couple sought to surround the beleaguered monarchy.

After *The Masque of Blackness* in 1605, word soon spread of the marvellous effects Inigo had created. In August of that year, King James, Queen Anne and their eldest son Henry were to make a visit to Oxford and would expect to be entertained royally. Inigo, described as a 'great traveller' in a waspish account of the visit by an academic from Cambridge, was invited by the university authorities to equal or surpass his January efforts in the Banqueting House. They wanted him to provide sensations, inspired by his travels, that would truly dazzle the royal party.

The university agreed to pay him £50 for the work – £10 more than he had received for the royal masque – but for that he would have to provide settings for four productions on successive nights.[22] He was not, however, responsible for designing or positioning the stage and seating in the great hall at Christ Church, where the entertainments were held. That was the job of Simon Basil, the King's Surveyor,[23] and it provoked the first of several controversies surrounding the visit.

Two days before the King was due to arrive, an advance party of four peers went to Oxford to examine the accommodation and other arrangements for the royal guests. They complained that the position of the King's throne in the auditorium meant that few in the audience would be able to see him properly. What was the point of a public appearance if it would be invisible to most of the public? The Chancellor and Vice-Chancellor initially resisted altering the position of the throne, arguing that this was where the King would get the best view, but in the end they moved it to a raised platform near the rear of the hall, where it proved hard for him to hear what was going on.[24]

Inigo produced two apparent innovations for the Oxford theatre-goers. One was the first recorded use of his 'triangle machines' to effect three changes of scene, the other a raked stage instead of a flat, horizontal one.[25] In spite of this, the sour Cambridge visitor declared that his 'rare devices . . . performed very little, to that which was expected'. Fortunately, the locals were more impressed. Isaac Wake, a fellow of Merton, wrote enthusiastically about the changing scenery:

> The cloths and houses of the scene were skilfully changed by means of a machine time and again according to all the necessary places and occasions, so that the whole form of the fabric of the stage suddenly appeared new, to everyone's amazement, not only from day to day for each production but even in the course of a single performance.

He marvelled, too, at the realistic moving clouds. Of the settings for the tragedy *Ajax Flagellifer*, played on the second night, he wrote:

> It is not easy to tell how wondrously all this nourished by turn our ears and eyes. The whole fabric of the scene and its artificial apparatus of hangings was renewed time and again, to everyone's amazement. By

which means you saw the living image of Troy, and the Sigean shore; then the woods and deserts and horrid caves, the lair of the Furies; these suddenly vanishing, you gazed surprised on the lovely form of the tents and the ships.

The King and Queen were harder to please. Each performance lasted more than three hours and James frequently showed his impatience, threatening to walk out of one of them and falling asleep at another. Anne, for her part, was offended by the appearance of semi-naked men during the masque on the first night. The King declined to attend the final play, a pastoral by Samuel Daniel, though as it turned out, the Queen and Prince Henry enjoyed it more than they did the first three.[26]

Jonson, meanwhile, was in trouble with the authorities again, this time because of a play called *Eastward Ho!* that he had written for the company of boy players at the Blackfriars Theatre in collaboration with George Chapman and John Marston, with whom he had by now made his peace. The play poked fun at the entourage of uncouth courtiers that the King had brought with him from Scotland, mimicking their broad accents and referring to 'thirty-pound knights' – the going rate for being so honoured. One of its principal themes was to contrast the idiocy and profligacy of the aristocracy, especially the new aristocracy, with the prudence and sharp common sense of businessmen in the City. The two rival power centres had been at loggerheads for centuries, and *Eastward Ho!* fanned the flames of their enmity.

One of the Scottish entourage complained about the play directly to the King, who had Jonson and Chapman imprisoned (Marston having made himself scarce). There was even talk of their having their ears and noses cut off, to punish them for such treasonable satire. From jail, Jonson wrote a sheaf of pained letters to some of his influential acquaintances and Chapman wrote to the King himself, who quickly relented and authorised their release. It was the last occasion on which Jonson would see the inside of a prison cell. He hosted a banquet to celebrate his release, with his old teacher Camden among the guests.

The most poignant moment came when his mother disclosed to the gathering that she had intended to smuggle poison to him if the mutilation threat had been taken further.[27]

The year 1605 was the most eventful of Jonson's career, provoking a full range of emotional responses, from the elation of the enthusiastic court reception for *Blackness* to the despair of his imprisonment and the threat of worse. There were more highs and lows to come. The year saw the instantly successful opening of one of his most enduring comedies, *Volpone*. And in the world beyond the theatre, it was when the King and his ministers escaped assassination in a plot that would have a permanent impact on English history and in which the accident-prone Jonson narrowly avoided becoming enmeshed.

In October 1605 he was invited to dinner by Robert Catesby, a wealthy Catholic, at his house in the Strand. The guests were all Catholics and at least two of them were privy to Catesby's plan to blow up the Houses of Parliament in less than a month's time, with the aim of killing the Protestant King and key members of his entourage and of bringing England back to Catholicism. It seems improbable, given the timing of the dinner, that the scheme was not discussed, unless the need for security prevented it.

When Guy Fawkes and his stack of explosives were found in a cellar adjacent to Westminster Hall on 5 November, Jonson was summoned by the Secretary of State Robert Cecil, Earl of Salisbury. Given his acquaintance with the conspirators, and the unfortunate similarities between their Gunpowder Plot and that depicted in his controversial 1603 play, *Sejanus*, he must have feared being treated as a suspect. But he denied any knowledge of the plan which, had it succeeded, would have deprived him and Inigo of their promising new source of regular income.

In any case, Cecil's purpose in summoning Jonson was not to accuse him of anything but to ask him to use his Catholic connections to determine the extent of the Catesby conspiracy. The playwright was unable to discover anything useful. The following January he was named as a recusant, meaning someone who refuses to attend services of the Church of England. There is no record that he was ever fined or otherwise punished for the offence, and he would abandon the Catholic faith four years later.[28]

Amongst all these diversions, Jonson still found time to work on his next collaboration with Inigo: not strictly a court masque but a double-headed entertainment to help celebrate an important society wedding. On Twelfth Night in 1606, just two months after the discovery of the plot to destroy the monarchy, Robert Devereux, the fourteen-year-old Earl of Essex, married Frances Howard, a year his junior, the daughter of the Earl of Suffolk. It was a blatantly political marriage, uniting two of the most powerful dynasties in the kingdom. It had been brokered by the King, partly as a means of gaining the support of the two formerly feuding families. Devereux's father had been executed in 1601 for attempting to provoke a popular uprising against Queen Elizabeth, and the boy was not permitted to assume his title until 1604, after the Queen's death. His bride's father, ennobled in 1603, had led the loyal troops who put down the Essex rebellion.

Inigo and Jonson were commissioned to create two events, a masque for the wedding night and a 'barriers' for the following day. A barriers was a traditional kind of formalised, scripted jousting, where champions of two opposing sides (in this case allegorised as Truth and Opinion) approached each other across a low fence or barrier and engaged in verbal as well as physical exchanges before burying their differences and uniting. Inigo was required to produce stunning scenery, costumes and effects for both occasions. The masque was called *Hymenaei* and Ferrabosco once again wrote the music.

The first scene set the theme, dominated by a Roman altar with the word 'union' inscribed on it in gold, signifying the union not only of the young man and woman but also of their great families, as well as celebrating the recent union of the English and Scottish Crowns. Behind the altar was a large globe, suspended from the roof by an invisible wire, showing a silver and blue map of the world on the side facing the audience. Flanking it were golden statues of Atlas and Hercules and above them a curtain with clouds painted on it, reaching to the ceiling. Masquers representing the newly-weds and

Hymen, the god of marriage, wore costumes that Inigo seems to have based on illustrations of Roman weddings. The couple were chiefly in white while Hymen wore a saffron-coloured robe, yellow socks and a crown of roses and marjoram on his head.

Then came the first dramatic effect. The globe turned and its bottom half was revealed as a hollow shell, where eight men sat, representing the four humours (melancholy, phlegm, blood and choler) and four affections (joy, hope, dread and sorrow). As the globe descended they drew their swords, surrounded the newly-weds and threatened to disrupt the union. But the figure of Reason, carrying a lamp and wearing a blue dress sparkling with stars and mathematical symbols, emerged from the top of the globe and deployed her powers of argument to pacify the disruptive elements. At that point the cloud-painted curtain was raised and revealed the figure of Juno, symbolising marriage, seated on a golden throne holding a sceptre, with a lion's skin at her feet and attended by two peacocks, the tableau surrounded by bright comets and meteors. Finally, eight female masquers descended from the heavens, dancing and linking hands to encircle the couple. Reason had triumphed.[29]

The barriers provided an equally striking if less elaborate spectacle. At the very start of the proceedings Inigo had contrived what Jonson called 'a mist made of delicate perfumes' to float across the audience, while beneath the stage musicians were playing noisy, cacophonous music, symbolising strife. There was little room for scenic grandeur since, after an earnest debate between Truth and Reason – identically clad in blue and white and wearing crowns of palm – thirty-two knights with pikes, swords and full battle paraphernalia marched on and engaged in energetic combat. At the end, as Jonson again described it, 'a striking light seemed to fill all the hall, and out of it an angel or messenger of glory appearing'. The angel reconciled Truth and Opinion, and peace returned.

The spirit of goodwill also appeared to have affected Jonson, who in his printed text of the masque, acknowledged that its 'design and act', as well as the costumes, were 'to the merit and reputation of Mr Inigo Jones, whom I take modest occasion in this fit place to remember, lest his own worth might accuse me of an ignorant neglect of silence'.

Was this just a passing thought or a piece of pointed ironic point-scoring? Had there already been behind-the-scenes sparring between the pair over who should get top billing? D.J. Gordon has observed that in the preface to *Hymenaei* Jonson drew a sharp distinction between, on the one hand, emotions relating to the soul and to human understanding, which were enduring, and those relating to the body, which were fleeting. As the creator of the heart and soul of the masques, he felt that he had a superior role to Inigo, whose physical devices and effects were transitory. As time went on and his reputation grew, Inigo would feel less and less able to accept Jonson's perception of their relative roles. The seeds of a famous quarrel were being sown.

Chapter Seven

FIRST STEPS IN ARCHITECTURE

O NE BIOGRAPHER BELIEVED that Inigo spent part of 1606 in Europe, back on his travels.[1] He cited as possible evidence Edmund Bolton's dedication in the book of Latin poetry that he gave him that December[2] which, by expressing the hope that the 'elegant arts of the ancients may some day insinuate themselves across the Alps into our England' could suggest that the two men were together in Italy when, or shortly before, the gift was presented. There is, however, no other evidence that Inigo left England between 1603 and 1609, and in 1606 he would have wanted to be in London for the visit of King Christian of Denmark, his recent patron.

James gave his brother-in-law a splendid welcome.[3] On 17 July the host King travelled in the state barge from Greenwich to Gravesend, where he was entertained on Christian's ship. Next day the flotilla sailed back to Greenwich, where Christian visited his sister Queen Anne, still confined to bed after the death the previous month of her day-old daughter, Sophia. He was accommodated in great style in Somerset House, called Denmark House to honour his visit. (Its name was not changed officially until 1617, when it became Anne's London residence. It reverted to Somerset House in the 1640s.)

Over the next fortnight the two kings indulged in their favourite pastimes, hunting and carousing, and the visit culminated in a triumphal procession through the City of London. Robert Cecil, Earl of Salisbury, who was now Lord Treasurer, entertained both kings at Theobalds House in Hertfordshire, where giant artificial oak leaves were strewn on the drive, bearing the message 'Welcome!'. Sir John Harington, a veteran courtier, described one evening's entertainment there as 'Mahomet's Paradise', adding: 'We had women, and indeed wine too, of such plenty as would have astonished each sober beholder.'

Many of the entertainers were drunk, and were to be seen 'sick and spewing in the lower hall'. A woman representing the Queen of Sheba spilled wine over Christian who then, attempting to dance, fell over and had to be carried to a couch.[4]

Another contemporary writer asserted that Christian was 'addicted to drunkenness, to which James had not the least objection'. The English king would surely not have been surprised by his guest's behaviour, given the immoderate habits of his sister; nor is he recorded as expressing any disapproval when Christian was accused of being 'indelicate of traits of manners to the ladies about the court', and specifically of behaving indecently towards the Countess of Nottingham, wife of the Lord High Admiral.[5]

Stories of such excesses at King James's court occur so frequently that they cannot all have been made up by his enemies. It would be a surprise if Inigo, a young man on the make, did not take some part in what seems to have been a pervasive court culture. A few years later he was one of a number of men, prominent in the arts, who formed a regular dining and drinking club in the City; but as he grew older his failing health would have ruled out too much intemperance, which anyway ceased to be acceptable at Whitehall once James had been succeeded by his ascetic son Charles in 1625. The remedies for a range of ailments that Inigo jotted down over the years in the back of his copy of Palladio contain several for diseases of the kidneys and for gout, that painful condition often ascribed to heavy drinking.[6]

* * *

The January 1607 court masque was written by Thomas Campion, poet and musician, to celebrate the wedding of Lord Hay (he of the double dinners) to Honora Denny, a high-born Englishwoman. The match was encouraged by the King in the name of Anglo-Scottish unity and the masque underscored that theme. Weldon stated that Inigo was the designer[7] but no drawings survive except the frontispiece to the published text, which does seem to have much of Inigo's ingenuity in it.[8] In the text it was noted that one scene included 'artificial bats and owls placed on wire . . . continually moving', and one particularly elaborate piece of staging seems to bear his stylistic signature. The masque was set mainly in a forest populated by Sylvans, who at one point started to sing,

> whereof that part of the stage whereon the first three trees stood began to yield, and the three foremost trees gently to sink, and this was effected by an engine placed under the stage. When the trees had sunk a yard, they cleft in three parts and the masquers appeared out of the tops of them, the trees were suddenly conveyed away, and the first three masquers were raised away by the engine.[9]

Just four months later, another masque by Jonson was performed at Theobalds House. It marked the handover of the house from Cecil to the King, who had grown so fond of it that he insisted on swapping it for the royal property at Hatfield. Robert Cecil and his father William, Lord Burghley, had been powers in the land since Queen Elizabeth's reign. The younger man, called the 'crookback earl' because of a deformity, had played a critical role in securing James's succession to the throne; but even so he felt obliged to agree to the exchange. The plot of Jonson's masque had the genius of the house mourning the loss of his former master, but rejoicing on hearing that the King and Queen were to take over. It is uncertain whether Inigo worked on the designs for this masque, which seem to have been rather basic by his standards:

> There was seen nothing but a traverse of white across the room; which, suddenly drawn, discovered a gloomy obscure place, hung all with black silks, and in it only one light, which the genius of the house held, sadly

attired; his cornucopia ready to fall out of his hand, his garland drooping on his head; his eyes fixed on the ground.[10]

The following year, Inigo and Jonson were working together again on two masques to be presented in the space of three months. *The Masque of Beauty*, the sequel to *Blackness*, was originally planned for 1606, but the Essex/Howard nuptials consumed the court's attention that winter, so it was postponed to Twelfth Night 1608. As *Beauty* opened, the black daughters of Niger – with four added to their number – had been granted their wish for white skins and fair complexions. They made their entrance on a colossal Throne of Beauty borne on an island floating in the sea. The throne, decorated with lights and garlands, was an architectural inspiration, divided by Ionic pillars into eight squares, each containing two of the sixteen masquers. Among Inigo's other decorative devices was an orchard of trees bearing golden fruit, two fountains and a maze made up of arbours and trees.[11]

The second of the 1608 masques celebrated the wedding of Viscount Haddington to Elizabeth Radcliffe, the daughter of the Earl of Sussex. The marriage, like that of Lord Hay, was welcomed enthusiastically by the King, for here was another of his Scottish knights marrying into a good English family. The young viscount, formerly Sir John Ramsay, was one of the King's closest henchmen, and had rescued him from an assassination attempt in Scotland in 1600. He was duly ennobled in 1606. Because of the importance the King attached to the match, Queen Anne took personal responsibility for ensuring the success of the masque that was to celebrate it. On 12 December 1607, the Florentine ambassador, Ottaviano Lotti, reported home on the excitement generated among court ladies by the preparations:

Her Majesty the Queen intends to be their director, in such fashion that there will be talk of very little else at this time, and the greatest occupation among the ladies will be with poets, musicians, dancers and great expenses.[12]

This was confirmed by a contemporary correspondent, Rowland White, who wrote to Lord Shrewsbury that the Haddington masque 'is now the only thing thought upon at court'.[13]

Jonson called the masque *A Hue and Cry After Cupid* and it contained the customary tributes to Hymen, the god of marriage, and to the joys of sacrificing virginity for the sake of married love. Inigo's stage design was chiefly memorable for the inclusion, perhaps for the first time, of something approaching a proscenium arch, the Italian device that he introduced to the English stage. This is how the setting was described in the published text:

> The scene to this masque was a high, steep red cliff, advancing itself into the clouds . . . before which, on the two sides, were erected two pilasters, charged with spoils and trophies of love . . . all wrought round and bold: and overhead two personages, triumph and victory, in flying postures, and twice as big as life, in place of the arch, and holding a garland of myrtle for the key. All of which, with the pillars, seemed to be of burnished gold, and embossed out of the metal.[14]

In a trick that would become in effect his trademark, Inigo had the cliff split in the middle to reveal the masquers and a revolving silver sphere picked out in gold, eighteen inches in diameter, all brilliantly lit.[15]

Whether or not he designed the Theobalds House masque, Inigo had certainly forged a relationship with Robert Cecil by this time – one that would at last allow him to take the first positive steps towards establishing himself in the profession to which Edmund Bolton had directed him and in which he would earn his lasting reputation. The first hard evidence linking Inigo with Cecil emerged in a significant episode at the beginning of 1608, just after the performance of *The Masque of Beauty*, when he was entrusted with the care of a convicted religious offender about to be deported. The man was Tobie Matthew, the Bishop of Durham's son. At thirty he was five years younger than Inigo, and he had been a youth of great promise, graduating from Christ Church, Oxford, when he was seventeen, and becoming a Member of Parliament at twenty-four. He received patronage from the statesman and writer Sir Francis Bacon but in 1605 went on an extended visit to Italy, where he was converted to Catholicism, justifying the reservations of the English authorities about letting impressionable young men travel freely on the Continent.

Matthew's conversion was effectively a bar to further political advancement; but he defied attempts by Bacon and the Archbishop of Canterbury to redirect him towards the Protestant faith. He refused to renounce his Catholicism or to take the oath of allegiance. In the summer of 1607, therefore, he was sent to the Fleet Prison for an indefinite period. After a few months he began a correspondence with Cecil, exploring ways in which he might be released. In a letter dated 4 February 1608, he noted that in previous correspondence Cecil had told him that 'if I would dispose myself to live out of the realm, your honour would favour me therein with your assistance'. Having considered the matter, 'I shall embrace the condition of living abroad, with the same resignation of mind that a merchant threatened with shipwreck hath, in the casting of his wares overboard.'[16]

On receiving the letter, Cecil moved quickly – but not, it would transpire, out of any overwhelming concern to end the young man's suffering. For although Matthew did not know it, his offer of voluntary exile came at a time when he was in a position to perform a signal favour for the Lord Treasurer. As Ben Jonson remarked pithily in one of his conversations with William Drummond: 'Salisbury never cared for any man longer nor he could make use of him.'[17]

For Cecil had a scheme. It was founded on the fact that the Royal Exchange, a centre for commerce of all kinds, had proved a tremendous success since Sir Thomas Gresham opened it in the heart of the City in 1570. Cecil believed that there was scope for a rival exchange on the Strand, where it would catch the considerable passing trade of merchants, lawyers and wealthy gentlemen travelling between the City, the Inns of Court and Whitehall. His own town residence, Salisbury House, was one of the 'Strand palaces' on the south of the thoroughfare, stretching down to the river. Next to it was the rambling Durham House, belonging to Matthew's father, the Bishop of Durham, with parts of it leased to various tenants.

Cecil thought that the Bishop's gatehouse, stables and outhouses, fronting onto the Strand, would be an ideal site for a westerly version of the Royal Exchange, and he sought to persuade the Bishop to get rid of his tenants. One had been the soldier and explorer Sir Walter Raleigh, a favourite of the late Queen but an enemy of Cecil, who had him evicted from the house shortly after James came to the throne.[18] (Raleigh was then charged with plotting against the new King and confined to the Tower of London for the next thirteen years.) Other parts of Durham House were leased to the diplomat Sir Dudley Carleton, the future ambassador to Venice; and to Tobie Matthew. By 1608, Matthew's lease was all that stood in the way of Cecil's scheme.

Matthew's letter from prison, therefore, came at a fortuitous time. Less than a week after receiving it, Cecil summoned the prisoner to appear before the Privy Council, where the devious Lord Treasurer put on an impressive show of sternness. He claimed he had not been a party to the decision to send the young man to prison: indeed he thought it so light a punishment for his offence that it might make him 'proud and perverse'. All this, though, was an elaborate deception. In fact Matthew was being offered an escape route. He was ordered to leave the country but given six weeks to put his affairs in order. During that period he was asked to nominate 'some friend of good account and well affected' who could act as his guarantor and in whose house he could stay. According to the court chronicler John Chamberlain, writing to Sir Dudley Carleton: 'He named Master Jones, who was accepted and is not a little proud of his prisoner.'[19]

It may have been that Inigo and Matthew were already friends; but it also seems likely that Cecil himself had proposed Inigo as guardian, for a reason made apparent by a letter from Matthew to Cecil on 24 February, only days after his release. In it, he refers to an offer made by Cecil 'by the means of Mr Jones' for 'the interest that I had in the gatehouse and stable row of Durham House'. Cecil was prepared to pay handsomely for this last piece in the property jigsaw that would allow him to go ahead with the New Exchange project. Inigo was authorised to offer £1200. Matthew described this as 'a very full value . . . a price rather to your Honour's disadvantage than otherwise'. He was thus happy to accept the 'undeserved favour' of a 'very provident and saving bargain'.[20]

The deal signed, Cecil quickly demolished the stables and the gatehouse, and work on his new building was soon under way. In April, Matthew went into exile in Spain and stayed on the Continent until 1617, when the King allowed him to return home, only to exile him again two years later when he still refused to take the oath of allegiance. Not until 1621 was he allowed to return permanently. In 1624 he was named, along with Inigo, as a founder member of a so-called 'Royal Academy' of men of learning that Edmund Bolton was going to set up; but the project was aborted when James I died the following year. In 1640, with Parliamentary opposition to Catholics growing, Matthew again left the country and settled in Ghent, where he died in 1655.

Cecil had every reason to be grateful to his successful go-between. As for Inigo, he had learned a valuable lesson in the arts of wheeler-dealing that make the political world go round: a lesson that he would put to good use when he sought to make his way at court. The incident provides an insight into the developing character of this ambitious man of thirty-five as he climbed the bottom steps of the ladder towards position and influence at the heart of government. Chamberlain's comment that Inigo was 'not a little proud of his prisoner' is the earliest of many references down the years that suggest he was a vain man, jealous of his status, keen for his worth to be recognised, wanting to be in charge.

It shows, too, that he was sufficiently well thought of, at least by Cecil, to be entrusted with the responsibility of keeping an eye on a man technically regarded as an enemy of the state, and at the same time helping conclude a potentially lucrative business deal. He would not have been accepted by the Privy Council as Matthew's guardian had there been any doubt about his own loyalty to the established Church and his ability to resist any attempt by his prisoner to convert him. Whatever Inigo's personal faith, he was too ambitious to allow it to interfere with his chances of advancement. To witness Matthew's travails at such close quarters would have reinforced that resolve.

Inigo's design for the New Exchange in the Strand

Inigo received two tangible rewards for his role in helping Cecil acquire the Durham House property. One was a commission for another stage design. He and Jonson were asked to devise an unspecified 'entertainment' at Salisbury House in May 1608, just weeks after the Matthew affair. On the back of a drawing of one of the costume designs is an account showing the expenditure of £12 12s 10d for materials, including £3 15s for paint, £4 12s for 'gold' and four shillings for the boat fare of the men who carried the materials to the house. There is an additional charge of £8 16s 6d for the labourers, named as Dolfin and his man, Daniel and his boy, the tall man, the little fellow and the black fellow. Jonson, Inigo and John Allen, the main actor in the piece, each received £20.[21]

His second reward was more significant: the chance to play a role in designing the New Exchange. A drawing now held at Worcester College, Oxford – believed to be the earliest of Inigo's purely architectural designs to survive – is certainly a scheme for the New Exchange. Its form clearly owes much to Palladio, but with the kind of Elizabethan flourishes that he would learn to suppress only after his second visit to

Italy. On the ground floor is an arcade of seventeen identical arches separated by pilasters and above them fifteen niches for statues. The three central arches are surmounted by a triangular pediment and above that is a tall tower on an elaborate base that Palladio would certainly have found too fussy. There are smaller towers at each end.

The New Exchange as built, to judge from the sometimes conflicting evidence of contemporary illustrations, did not conform precisely to Inigo's plan but seems to have been based on it, perhaps modified by Simon Basil, the King's Surveyor. The three towers were less ornate and the upper-floor niches replaced by windows.

Once Cecil had acquired the site, the building took shape remarkably quickly. The King and Queen, accompanied by their eldest son, Prince Henry, opened it on 10 April 1609 and again Inigo and Jonson provided the set-piece celebration, described as 'a royal entertainment in praise of trade'.[22] After one actor had spoken Jonson's lines lauding the New Exchange, a second, portraying an honest merchant, presented the King with rarities from India and China.[23] Despite Cecil's hopes the Exchange, given the grandiose name of 'Britain's Bourse', only really began to flourish after the Royal Exchange was destroyed in the Great Fire of 1666. Later it fell into decline as fashionable London shifted further west, and it was demolished in 1737.[24]

Cecil was a cunning, secretive man with few social graces. While he bestowed on Inigo and Jonson the favour and patronage due to men of their genius and accomplishment, they enjoyed no great intimacy with him. The relationship was still that of master and servants, a circumstance that irked the petulant Jonson, never a man to underestimate his own importance. One particular slight – or at least the playwright perceived it as such – rankled so persistently that he recalled it during his conversation with Drummond some ten years later. He complained that he and Inigo, invited to dinner by Cecil, had been placed at the end of the table furthest from the great man and had even, he maintained, been served inferior meat. When his host inquired whether anything was wrong, Jonson claimed to have told him: 'My Lord, you promised I should dine with you, but I do not.'[25]

Jonson was sensitive to such nuances: he had referred to the indignity of being seated 'below the salt' in his 1599 play *Cynthia's Revels* – one of the first known uses of the phrase in the language. There is no record that Cecil invited him to dinner again.

A second surviving drawing of Inigo's from about 1608 was for another project destined not to be completed as he designed it, or indeed at all. In that year the King, egged on by Cecil, ordered a survey of St Paul's Cathedral, London's principal place of worship since Norman times but, like many churches since the Reformation, falling seriously into disrepair. Inigo's design was for a new spire to replace the old one that had collapsed in a 1561 fire sparked by a lightning strike. The fire also destroyed the cathedral's roof and much of its fabric. Although these had been repaired shortly afterwards, a new spire proved too expensive.

The drawing shows a distinctly Palladian gallery set on top of the thirteenth-century tower, with short Italianate spires at each corner and a larger spire arising from an onion dome in the middle. It is again a hybrid of the Palladian and Elizabethan styles. The project was abandoned when an estimate put the cost of repairs and a new steeple at £22,537 2s 3d. By the time Inigo was able to work on renovations to the Cathedral, in 1633, his ideas had changed radically and the spire was not a part of the scheme.

There are other pieces of evidence to show that, towards the end of the century's first decade, architecture was beginning to consume more of Inigo's attention. A drawing almost certainly by him, in the collection of the Royal Institute of British Architects, has been identified as a design for a tombstone for Francis, the wife of Sir Rowland Cotton, who died in childbirth in 1606. The tomb, adapted to accommodate Sir Rowland himself some years later, survives at St Chad's Church at Norton-in-Hales in Shropshire. Although it differs in detail from the drawing, the similarities are so pronounced that there can be little doubt about the identification. The decoration includes several devices used by Inigo in his masque designs, another strong pointer to his having drawn it.[26] The commission may have come about because

Cotton operated on the fringe of the London literary scene to which Inigo was connected.

One other possible early foray into architecture resulted from James I's decision in 1606 to commission a replacement for the now dilapidated wooden Banqueting House built by Queen Elizabeth in 1581. Whether or not Inigo was directly involved in the design, he would certainly have taken a close interest, because it was the success of his and Jonson's masques, and the prospect of their becoming a regular feature of court life, that had prompted the King to demand a more impressive and permanent setting for them. He wanted a new hall built mainly of brick; consistent with his many proclamations urging developers in London to make more use of this enduring material and less of timber.[27]

Only a sketchy ground plan of the new royal entertainment venue exists and we have to rely on written accounts. These describe a large hall surrounded by a gallery supported on columns, with Doric capitals on the lower level and Ionic above. James was never very fond of it, claiming that the columns interfered with his view of the proceedings. Simon Thurley believes that it was designed by Robert Stickells[28] but Summerson wrote that Inigo was 'almost certainly the architect', citing the classical detail that was his hallmark.[29] This was the Banqueting House that burned down in 1619 to be replaced by Inigo's magnificent and enduring creation of 1622.

Inigo's combination of architectural talent with the design of scenery and costumes was not unique. Vitruvius specifically discussed stage machinery in his book of Roman architecture and a number of Renaissance architects dabbled in stage work.[30] While Inigo and Jonson were working on the entertainment for the opening of the New Exchange in April 1609, they were collaborating on a more ambitious project. *The Masque of Queens* was performed on 2 February that year and was possibly the first production in the 1606 Banqueting House. It was also the first time that Jonson had introduced a full-fledged antimasque into his script, explaining in the Introduction that he had:

now devised that twelve women in the habits of hags or witches, sustaining the persons of Ignorance, Suspicion, Credulity, etc., the opposites to good Fame, should fill that part, not as a masque, but a spectacle of strangeness.

The witches' scene was in some ways similar to that in Shakespeare's *Macbeth*, probably first performed a year or two earlier. Inigo devised as its setting a fiery hell, with roaring flames and smoke. The witches were described in the text as:

all differently attired, some with rats on their heads, some on their shoulders; others with ointment pots at their girdles; all with spindles, timbrels, rattles, or other venefical [malignant] instruments making a confused noise with strange gestures.

Jonson was anxious that the credit for this scene should properly be divided between him and his collaborator:

The device of their attire was Master Jones his, with the invention and architecture of the whole scene and machine. Only I prescribed them their properties of vipers, snakes, bones, herbs, roots and other ensigns of their magic, out of the authority of ancient and late writers.

The outstanding element in Inigo's design was the House of Fame, based on a description in Chaucer's poem of that name. It was a tall, hexagonal structure painted in gold to represent a highly decorative exterior with figures of classical heroes and poets and battle scenes. There was a large double door at floor level. Twelve masquers, young noblewomen dressed as queens of ancient civilisations and clad in appropriate costumes, were revealed sitting at the top of the house on a throne shaped like a pyramid. After a long declamation, the upper part of the house revolved and the figure of Fame herself appeared. The queens descended and passed through the doorway in three chariots drawn by eagles, griffins and lions, taking with them the witches, who had been overcome and trussed up. The masquers came forward again to perform their dances before returning to the House of Fame.

The bill presented by Andrew Kerwyn, the head carpenter, gives an account of the complex structure that Inigo asked him to build. The tasks he enumerated were:

> fitting and setting up of diverse running scaffolds, framing and setting up a great stage for a masque all the height of the Banqueting House with a floor in the middle of the same being made with sundry devices with great gates and turning doors below and a globe and sundry seats above for the Queen and ladies to sit on and to be turned round about.[31]

It was Inigo's most ambitious stage design so far, so widely admired that Jonson felt obliged to heap further praise on him in the published text. After a second explicit reference to his role, he wrote:

> All which I willingly acknowledge for him, since it is a virtue planted in good natures, that what respects they wish to obtain fruitfully from others, they will give ingenuously themselves.

But with Jonson – a master of irony, after all – you never knew quite where you were. However glowing his praise appeared, you could not help wondering whether there might be barbs barely concealed beneath the polished surface. What he might have been saying here was this: while he was more than ready to give his collaborator the credit due to him, was it not time that Inigo returned the compliment?

Not long after the opening of the New Exchange, Inigo was off on his European travels again, this time on a short visit to France arranged by Cecil. On 16 June 1609 the Lord Treasurer issued a warrant authorising a payment to Inigo of £13 6s 8d for carrying official letters to France.[32] On 3 July the English ambassador in Paris, Sir George Carew, wrote to Cecil confirming that Inigo had delivered the letters on 28 June.[33] A note in his copy of Vitruvius confirms that he was in Paris in 1609. While there he would have seen the Place Royale (now the Place des Vosges), completed just two years earlier as the first residential square in Paris. The thirty-six houses – nine on each of its four sides

– behind colonnaded arcades could well have influenced his own design for Covent Garden twenty-five years later.

The Pont du Gard, France

In his copy of Palladio is an annotation indicating that he also spent some time at the royal palace at Chambord, in the Loire Valley, and in his Vitruvius he noted that he had visited the Roman theatre in the southern city of Orange. Amongst the drawings in his collection was one of the Pont du Gard, the Roman aqueduct between Orange and Nimes, with a note attached confirming that he paid a visit there. The drawing is not by him, but a characteristically meticulous comment in his handwriting points out an inaccuracy: one of the large central arches, depicted as having three smaller arches above it, in fact has four.

To visit south-east France would have been a natural ambition for anyone seeking to emulate the architecture of the ancient Romans, for a surprising number of their structures had – and have still – survived there in a reasonable state of repair. The Pont du Gard itself is the most impressive, with its intact aqueduct running across the three tiers of arches. It was a tourist attraction even in Inigo's time. A guide for travellers in France and Italy in the late sixteenth century recommends it, along with the Maison Carrée and Temple of Diana at Nimes,[34] which Inigo also saw, according to notes he made in his edition of Palladio. He visited Arles, too, where many spectacular Roman reliefs were to be seen at the necropolis of Les Alicamps. There are important Roman arenas at Nimes, Arles and Orange; but in the seventeenth century he would have had an impeded view of their structure, since all three had been filled with houses and shops.

Until quite recently it was believed that Inigo passed through these towns on his way back from his later visit to Italy, but it is now generally accepted that he travelled south immediately after delivering his letters in Paris.[35] Edward Chaney argues persuasively that he went at the behest of Cecil, primarily to accompany his son William, Viscount Cranborne, who is recorded as visiting southern France, specifically Orange, in 1609.[36] The mail delivery to the ambassador was simply an added assignment to be carried out en route.

Inigo cannot have stayed long in France, for by the end of October he is recorded as taking another step towards establishing his credentials as an architect, once again working for Cecil. Having reluctantly agreed to cede Theobalds to the King, the Lord Treasurer undertook some major building at the former royal residence of Hatfield House, which he had been given in exchange. While keeping the central part of the old Tudor palace intact, he knocked down the wings and used the bricks to build a new house close to it. Inigo, fresh from his trip abroad, was invited there on 30 October 1609, when Cecil was finalising the plans for the centre block of the south front of the new house. He was provided with a horse from the stables alongside Salisbury House in the Strand, and rode the twenty-seven miles to Hatfield with one of Cecil's servants, returning two days later.

The following February the Earl paid Inigo £10 'for drawing of some architecture' at Hatfield. The arcading and dominant clock tower of the south front, in sharp contrast to the other side of the house, show clear Continental influence and it could be that Inigo had a hand in their design.[37] There is also, amongst the collection of his drawings at the Royal Institute of British Architects, an early sketch of what Giles Worsley has identified as a stable and covered riding house, with three large statues on top of its pediment.[38] The accepted date of this drawing, around 1610, means that it could well have been intended for Hatfield – Cranborne was a keen horseman – although there is no evidence that it was ever built.

After the French trip, the flavour of ancient Rome seeped not only into his architecture but also his stage work, especially in the motifs he used on buildings depicted in the backdrops. This was apparent in the setting he was asked to create for Prince Henry's Barriers, performed in January 1610. That key commission marked his introduction into the charmed circle of the Prince of Wales, a precocious young man widely lauded as the best hope for the future of England – and, it now seemed, for Inigo's chance of further preferment.

Chapter Eight

A PRINCE AMONG MEN

PRINCE HENRY, THE HEIR to both of James's thrones, was born in Scotland in 1594. Approaching manhood, he appeared to be everything his father was not: handsome, diligent, athletic, cultivated, well-dressed, orderly and self-effacing. He so abhorred foul language that he installed swear boxes in his houses and gave the proceeds to the poor. In only one respect was he more assertive than his father: where James's diplomacy was aimed at keeping the nation at peace, Henry was keen on the study of warfare, especially naval battles, and the practice of the martial arts. Though he was too young for his sexual preferences to be defined with any certainty, rumours of a liaison with the recently wed Frances Howard, Countess of Essex, suggested that he did not inherit his father's liking for comely young men.

From an early age he had, at the King's insistence, been removed from parental care and brought up in Stirling by a guardian, the Earl of Mar, and a tutor, Adam Newton. Between them they had taken such pains with his education that by the time the Prince arrived in London with his mother in 1603 he was a precocious boy, even something of a prodigy. By 1606, when he was twelve, the French ambassador sent this report of him back to Paris:

None of his pleasures savour the least of a child. He is a particular lover of horses and what belongs to them [but] he is not fond of hunting: when he goes to it, it is rather for the pleasure of galloping than that which the dogs give him. He plays willingly enough at tennis, and at another Scots diversion very like malle [golf]; but this always with persons older than himself, as if he despised those of his own age. He studies two hours a day, and spends the rest of his time tossing the pike, or leaping, or shooting with the bow, or throwing the bar, or vaulting, or some other exercise of that kind, and he is never idle.[1]

The daily hours of study were clearly productive. Henry had an inquisitive child's fascination with exploration and discovery, both in the geographical and scientific sense. He was intrigued by mechanical gadgets but also developed a love of the arts and literature. He could write French and had a growing knowledge of Latin and Greek. The Danish National Archives has a dozen letters written in Latin to his uncle, Christian IV, between when Henry was eight, and still living in Scotland, to a few weeks before he died in London in November 1612. Although they are not all in his own handwriting, and Adam Newton would have made sure there were no grammatical errors, they still indicate a boy of remarkable discipline and maturity.[2]

The image of Henry as a paragon of all the virtues is somewhat marred, though, by a look at his household accounts for the two years after he reached sixteen, when they were first kept separately from his parents'. In that time he lost an extraordinary £2681 gambling at dice, cards and real tennis, and spent even more on jewellery. His tennis balls alone cost him £312.[3] Yet courtiers seemed prepared to put this down to youthful extravagance – had not the great Henry V, after all, shared similar tastes as a young man? – and the consensus was that he would, when the time came, make a splendid monarch. Maybe he would even prove as popular as his father's predecessor, Queen Elizabeth, whose reign had already come to be characterised as a golden age. His Treasurer, Sir Charles Cornwallis, wrote after his death, 'Plenty and magnificence were the things that in his house he especially affected, but not without such a temper as might agree with the rules of frugality and moderation.'[4]

In 1609 James allowed his fifteen-year-old son to begin forming a court of his own, based at St James's Palace in Westminster and two palaces in Surrey: Richmond and Nonsuch, south-east of Kingston-upon-Thames. The following year he was formally declared Prince of Wales. Ambitious spirits soon latched on to this new fount of patronage and the Prince's court attracted some of the most glittering and talented men of the age, provoking the King to jealousy and petulance. 'Will he bury me alive?' he is said to have asked, conscious that his son's popularity could undermine his own place in his subjects' regard. Nor was he pleased when Henry openly opposed some of his policies, especially the desire to strengthen relations with Europe's Catholic monarchies. At some stage in his upbringing Henry had acquired a tough, uncompromising streak that contrasted with his father's broadly tolerant world view. Where James, although avowedly a Protestant, would admit Catholics to his circle, Henry made no such allowances. He stood for principle, not compromise. That was why he wanted the nation to be prepared to resume hostilities with Spain, the old enemy.

Aristocrats vied with each other for the youth's favour. For his close circle of advisers he chose, in the main, men who shared his passions for the arts and military exploits. In the first category came the young Thomas Howard, Earl of Arundel, who was to amass one of the country's finest collections of art and antiquities; his tutor Adam Newton, who had come to London with the Prince and remained a key figure in his retinue; and three pioneers of the emerging art of garden design – Sir Henry Fanshawe, Sir John Danvers and the Frenchman Solomon de Caux. Howard and de Caux, along with Isaac Oliver, the admired painter of portrait miniatures, advised the Prince on acquiring pictures from Europe, chiefly Italy. Internal alterations were made at St James's Palace to accommodate the pictures, as well as a library that had been given to the Prince by Lord Lumley, one of the earliest English collectors of books and paintings.[5]

Henry was the first member of the English royal family to buy art seriously. In this he was following the example of other ruling houses of Europe, whose collections would have been described to him by returning travellers, including Inigo. Several of the men that he chose to surround him had spent time in Europe. They could advise him how the other princely courts were conducted and report on the latest developments in architecture and the other arts. Among these was Sir Robert Dallington, a classical scholar (later Master of Charterhouse) who had been with the Earl of Rutland in Italy in the 1590s, in the party that may well have included the young Inigo.[6] As well as paintings, the Prince amassed a collection of rare coins that he asked Inigo, Howard, Fanshawe, and his Chamberlain Sir Thomas Chaloner, to value for him. On his death his brother Charles built on his pioneering work and greatly expanded the art and coin collections, but many of the most valuable items were sold and dispersed during the Commonwealth period.

Old soldiers and sea dogs in the Prince's circle included Charles Howard, Earl of Nottingham, and Sir John Holles: both had played leading roles in the defeat of the Spanish Armada. Henry displayed his growing independence from his father by forming a friendship with another nautical hero, Sir Walter Raleigh, a notorious opponent of the Stuart succession. The rules that the Prince laid down for his new royal household were equally designed to set it apart from his father's, which he regarded as extravagant and dissolute.[7] The Tuscan agent in London reported that he had decreed that all banquets should be conducted 'with decency and decorum, and without all rudeness, noise or disorder' – ruling out the orgiastic scenes into which the King's festivities so often descended.[8]

All this had to be taken into account by Jonson and Inigo when they fashioned the series of Barriers and masques that would mark Henry's installation as Prince of Wales in 1610. Not that they had much scope for challenging his wishes, because the young man, who had already over-ridden his father's objections to the militaristic nature of the proceedings, took a close interest in the preparations. In the

Barriers, performed on Twelfth Night at the Banqueting House, Henry played the role of Meliadus, Lord of the Isles, a Christian knight from the Arthurian legend who sent other knights on a quest to find the land where virtue reigned triumphant. They identified the newly unified Great Britain as the place, praising its ruler for his kingly virtues.

Inigo's setting for the first scene represented the Fallen House of Chivalry, a landscape of classical ruins, its crumbling arches mimicking those in the decaying Roman amphitheatres that he had seen in southern France the previous year. In Jonson's script the Lady of the Lake prophesied a revival of chivalry, identifying Meliadus as its agent. In the second scene, with the prophecy fulfilled, the ruined city had been restored to its ancient splendour. There followed a pageant of English monarchs, from Richard Coeur de Lion to Queen Elizabeth, and tributes to their military successes. There must have been music to accompany the dialogue: the recorded payments to musicians cover ten oboes, twenty-six lutes, two cornets, 'a company of violins' and twenty-one other instruments, as well as ten singers, coming to £152 in all. On top of that the devisers of the dances received £60, compared with a mere £20 paid to the actors.[9] After the pageant the ritualised jousting commenced, and continued until dawn.[10]

As with any complex dramatic production, getting all the elements in place at the right time had been one of Inigo's chief concerns, especially since he was working for a court from which it was notoriously difficult to prise ready money. Cash flow was a constant problem, evidenced by a note written by Sir Thomas Chaloner to Robert Cecil on 1 January. With only five days to go before the performance of the Barriers, the note gives a clear hint of incipient panic. Inigo had asked Chaloner for £150 to 'discharge the residue of that work which appertaineth to the show'. The note was endorsed by Sir Julius Caesar, Chancellor of the Exchequer, the most senior Treasury official below Cecil, who asked his staff to pay the money and draw up the necessary documentation for Cecil to sign, 'for this business must endure no delay'.[11]

In March, the year of celebrations continued with a tilt – an outdoor and more intricate version of Barriers – in the Whitehall tiltyard, the space now known as Horse Guards Parade. Its highlight was the appearance of an elephant bearing a palanquin, a rare sight at a time when overseas exploration was in its infancy. It fell to Inigo to design the beast's trappings and one of his drawings is in the Duke of Devonshire's collection, depicting the palanquin as an especially elaborate variation on a Roman sarcophagus.

Design for a palanquin for a pageant in 1610

The formal ceremony for Henry's inauguration as Prince of Wales took place on 30 May and the ceremonies lasted a week. Inigo was involved in designing the settings and costumes for at least two of them. One was an even more spectacular tilt than the earlier one, described in John Stow's *Annals* (continued by other hands after Stow's death in 1605):

> In the afternoon in the tiltyard there were diverse earls, barons and others being in rich and glorious armour and having costly caparisons, wondrously curiously embroidered with pearls, gold and silver. The like rich habiliments for horses were never seen before. They presented their several ingenious devices and trophies before the King and Prince and then ran at tilt, where there was a world of people to behold them . . . That night there were naval triumphs and pastimes upon the water, over against the Court, with ships of war and galleys fighting one against another and against a great castle builded upon the water.[12]

The naval triumphs were included in the programme to satisfy Henry's passion for stirring tales of nautical heroism. When darkness fell, fireworks were launched from the castle and the ships.

The theme of sea power was maintained in *Tethys' Festival*, staged next day, commissioned by Queen Anne, who played the title role of the sea goddess.[13] It was the first masque in which Henry's siblings, the fourteen-year-old Princess Elizabeth and nine-year-old Prince Charles, are known to have taken part. This time Inigo's collaborator was not Jonson but Samuel Daniel, an established court poet and playwright, as well as a groom of Queen Anne's privy chamber. He was more generous than Jonson in acknowledging Inigo's role, writing in the introduction to the published text:

> In these things wherein the only life consists in show, the art and invention of the architect gives the greatest grace, and is of most importance, ours the least part and of least note . . . and therefore I have interserted the description of the artificial part, which only speaks Master Inigo Jones.

As Daniel made clear, Inigo himself wrote much of the account of his scenes, describing them in meticulous detail. Spectators were confronted first with stars and clouds painted on a curtain, which was drawn back to reveal a castle and fortified town leading down to a harbour teeming with ships. This was meant to depict Milford Haven, where Henry VII had landed before winning the Battle of Bosworth Field and establishing the Tudor monarchy. The proscenium was formed of twelve-foot golden statues of Neptune and Nereus, the Old Man of the Sea, in front of pilasters bearing a frieze of nymphs and naked children in gold and silver.

Prince Charles was the first of the royals to appear, portraying Zephyrus, a benign wind, accompanied by eight children representing fountains. The King and the Prince of Wales, both in the audience, were presented with gifts from Tethys: a trident for James and a sword and scarf for Henry.

After another dance the music grew louder and three revolving circles of lights were lowered onto the stage. By the time they moved away the scene had changed to a golden grotto, with Tethys herself enthroned at the centre surrounded by a dozen nymphs representing rivers, all wearing sea-blue costumes and head-dresses made from shells. (The total cost of their costumes came to more than £1000.[14]) Princess Elizabeth, as the Thames, sat at her mother's feet. Above the throne, water flowed from a silver and gold fountain, while a larger fountain occupied centre stage.

Descending, the masquers paraded through the hall sinuously, like meandering rivers, before starting their dances and finally inviting members of the audience to join them. Then the masquers returned to the stage where the scene had changed once more, this time into a leafy grove. Inigo's settings and costumes were greatly admired but the court was less enamoured of Daniel's script. Indeed the author himself expressed dissatisfaction with his work on the masque. He found the conventions restrictive, and may not have been too disappointed never to be invited to write another.[15]

The prolific Ben Jonson was back on the team for the next production, *Oberon, the Fairy Prince*, performed on New Year's Day 1611 at the command of Prince Henry, who danced the title role. According to the Venetian ambassador, the Prince had wanted it to be staged on horseback, which would have presented problems for both author and designer. Fortunately for them, his father vetoed the idea.[16]

Scene from *Oberon the Fairy Prince*, 1611

Perhaps thankful for this reprieve, Inigo created his most sensational spectacle yet. This was the masque in which he introduced his sophisticated sidewings and shutters to effect his changes of scene.[17] When the spectators entered the Banqueting House they saw a large curtain in front of the stage, decorated with a map of England, Scotland, Wales and Ireland. As soon as the King and Queen arrived, accompanied by Princess Elizabeth and the ambassadors of Spain and Venice, the curtain was drawn and revealed a rock lit by a moon that moved slowly across the sky behind it. On the rock was an elderly sage, surrounded by fauns and satyrs. He was telling them about the imminent arrival of

Oberon, a great prince who would bring increased order and happiness to the nation.

They danced joyfully at the news. The rock cracked open to reveal a room in a palace dominated by a throne surrounded by shimmering coloured lights. 'A lovely thing to see,' wrote a diplomat, William Trumbull, who was in the audience. Then Prince Henry and thirteen knights appeared from the back of the stage, in a chariot drawn by two white bears.[18] The knights were dressed in gold and silver, with white and scarlet feathers on their heads – reminding Trumbull of splendidly costumed Roman emperors, except that they wore black masks. Inigo appears to have based the designs on prints by the Italian Renaissance artist Antonio Tempesta.[19]

A choir of boys, accompanied by ten men playing lutes, then sang the praises of the Prince and King James. After ten more boys, dressed as medieval pages in green and silver, had performed a dance, the masked noblemen displayed their own well-rehearsed steps, before the Prince plucked his mother from her seat in the audience to signal the start of the general dancing. At around midnight the King declared that he was tired and had the proceedings wound up:

> The masques being laid aside, the King and Queen with the ladies and gentlemen of the masque proceeded to the banqueting hall, going out after they had looked about and taken a turn around the table; and in a moment everything was thrown down with furious haste, according to the strange custom of the country. After this their Majesties withdrew and the ambassadors took leave.[20]

The costumes alone, as stated in Henry's accounts, cost £1412 6s 10d, including £16 for Inigo as their 'deviser'.[21] On top of that would have been the cost of the scenery, music and actors, and Jonson's fee for the words.

The two men had to create yet another masque the following month, this time for Queen Anne. No doubt because of the high expenditure on the Prince's entertainment, *Love Freed from Ignorance and Folly* was a low-budget production, coming in at a little above £700. Inigo's sets, with the masquers sitting in a cloud resting above the stage, were markedly similar in structure to those in *The Masque of Queens* two years earlier and he had probably recycled some elements as an economy measure. None of his advanced mechanics was in evidence; nor were any of the scenes painted in perspective.

Between the performances of the two masques at the start of 1611, Inigo's career was given a significant lift by Prince Henry, who appointed him his Surveyor of Works on 13 January, no doubt partly in recognition of his achievement with *Oberon* twelve days earlier. The young Prince had already shown, through other appointments, that he was intrigued by the artistic fashions emanating from Italy and France, and the well-travelled Inigo would prove a valuable addition to his team of salaried advisers. The formal work involved in the post would not be onerous: essentially it was to make sure that the Prince's two palaces remained in good repair, inside and out. Even that limited task was shared to some extent by the King's Surveyor, Simon Basil.

That the title of the post was surveyor, rather than architect, confirmed the still prevailing view that the design of buildings was primarily a technical rather than an artistic endeavour. Inigo's mechanical skills were what recommended him to Henry, who already had two men on his staff well qualified to advice him on the aesthetics of architecture. They were Solomon de Caux, better known to posterity as a garden designer, and Constantino de' Servi from Florence, who had experience in creating masques. Both were paid substantially more than Inigo's three shillings a day.[22] As in modern sport, overseas stars were invariably valued higher than home-grown talent.

Yet despite the limitations of Inigo's new role – and however slighted he may have felt by his comparative pittance of a fee – a position at court, especially at such a new and vibrant court as this, was to be coveted. Even if it would never make him truly rich it gave him a measure of financial security and, more important, an entrée into the society of men who might have more challenging and lucrative commissions at their disposal. He is recorded as having undertaken two specific tasks for the Prince during his first few months. One was the alterations to the library at St James's Palace, to provide a home for Lord Lumley's gift of books, and the other some work on shoring up three small islands in the grounds of the Prince's palace at Richmond. The latter appears merely to have been a structural task: the more prestigious assignment of designing fountains went to de' Servi.[23]

The specifics of Inigo's job may have lacked the glamour he would have liked, but it was not long before his social life began to reap the benefit of his appointment to Henry's court. In particular, he was admitted to the early seventeenth-century equivalent of London's café society. Around the city were a number of taverns where groups of people with like interests – commerce, literature, the arts – would gather regularly to gossip and carouse. The most famous was the Mermaid on Friday Street, near St Paul's Cathedral. There, Ben Jonson would preside over a table that reputedly included such celebrities as Sir Walter Raleigh and the playwrights William Shakespeare, John Fletcher and Francis Beaumont, who immortalised the proceedings in verse:

> . . . What things have we seen
> Done at the Mermaid! Heard words that have been
> So nimble and so full of subtle flame,
> As if that every one from whence they came
> Had meant to put his whole wit in a jest,
> And had resolv'd to live a fool the rest
> Of his dull life . . .

Inigo does not appear to have been a member of that sparky, largely literary circle but he was part of another congenial crowd, 'the right worshipful fraternity of Sireniacal Gentlemen', that met at the Mermaid on the first Friday of every month. It was clearly possible to join more than one such group for Jonson was again among its seventeen members. The so-called 'High Seneschal', or convenor, was Lawrence Whitaker, later to be Inigo's close colleague in the royal Office of Works.[24] Other members were courtiers, scholars, writers, publishers, booksellers and travellers. Among them were John Donne, the poet and future clergyman, and Sir Robert Cotton, an MP, antiquary and creator of the finest library of the age by the Thames at Old Palace Yard, where the House of Lords now stands.

The Cotton Library's records, now in the British Library,[25] show that Inigo was one of several of the Mermaid group included in the select list of aristocrats, scholars and statesmen allowed to borrow from the enormous collection of rare books and manuscripts. It is also possible that the architect was responsible for two memorials to Cotton's ancestors at his family church, All Saints' at Conington, near Peterborough. One is to the twelfth-century Prince Henry of Scotland and the other a joint commemoration of Thomas Cotton, who died in the early sixteenth century, and his wife Joan Paris. As David Howarth has pointed out,[26] they are designed in the same strict proportions of height to breadth as Inigo's monument to the wife of (the unrelated) Sir Rowland Cotton at Norton-in-Hales in Shropshire,[27] and bear other similarities: for instance, all three feature an altar flanked by Corinthian columns. The assumed date of the Conington pair, about 1615, would mean that Inigo designed them soon after his return from his second trip to Italy. The classical influence, the restraint and the lack of Elizabethan flourishes are unusual in England at that period.

The name of the Sireniacal fraternity arose from the association between the mythical sirens (half women, half birds) and the mermaids (half women, half fish) after whom the tavern was named. It was also probably meant to bring to mind the Cyrenaic philosophers, who put pleasure before all else.[28] Documentary proof of its existence came from its most charismatic member, the adventurer Thomas Coryate (pronounced corry-at). Born about 1577, the son of the rector of Odcombe in Somerset, Coryate left Oxford University without graduating and soon afterwards appeared alongside Inigo on Prince Henry's payroll, though in an unknown capacity. It is possible that he was a jester, or some other kind of entertainer, for there is a record of his being shut up in a trunk and released, amid great hilarity, at a court function.[29]

Coryate's fame rested chiefly on his travels. These began in May 1608 when he left Dover on his own with the intention of reaching Venice by whatever means presented itself: hiring horses, begging lifts in passing wagons, or talking himself on to a boat when the route took him along rivers. Between Amiens and Paris he was given a ride in a horse-drawn coach, an elite form of transport at the time. The outward journey via Lyons, Turin, Milan and Padua took him six weeks. In August he set out for home, determining that this time he would go most of the way on foot. He passed through Switzerland, Strasbourg, Heidelberg and Cologne and by October he was back in England, where he put his walking shoes on display at Odcombe Church to advertise his achievement.

His account of the enterprising journey was published in 1611 as *Coryate's Crudities*, with the subtitle: 'Hastily gobbled up in five months' travelling in France, Savoy, Italy . . .', going on to give a full list of the countries he visited. The volume ran to nearly 800 pages, and of these more than a hundred were filled with verses from fifty-nine of his acquaintances. They included Inigo and Jonson, who coordinated the publication and wrote the preface, where he portrayed Coryate as a man obsessed by travel:

> The mere subscription of a letter from Zurich sets him up like a top: Basel or Heidelberg makes him spin. And at seeing the words Frankfurt or Venice, though but on the title of a book, he is ready to break doublet, crack elbows and overflow the room with his murmur . . . He is always Tongue-Major of the company, and if ever perpetual motion be to be hoped for, it is from thence.

The contributed verses praised – or more often gently mocked – Coryate's achievement, in the joshing, sardonic tone you would expect from regular drinking companions. It is clear from them that Coryate's sense of fun was a principal feature of the weekly meetings. Inigo's doggerel was typical. It began with a pun on his friend's home town – 'Odd is the Combe from whence this Cock did come' – and went on to note that, in Venice, he 'slipped into the stews [brothels]', where he 'trod a tough hen of thirty years of age' – no unsubstantiated slur, for Coryate boasted about the lustful encounter in the book. Inigo's poem became fashionably xenophobic when it followed its subject into France. According to the custom of that country, he wrote, Coryate should have starched his beard, ruffled his hose and 'worn a foul shirt twelve weeks'. After describing what must have been a personal foible –

> '. . . when thou drink'st thou makes a crab-tree face,
> shakes head and wink'st'

– the poem ended with an exhortation to readers to buy the volume.

Coryate's book was a lively travelogue, packed with incident and with vivid, enthusiastic descriptions of European landscapes and people. There was a particularly detailed account of the Palladian buildings of Vicenza, which would exert so great an influence on Inigo's own work. Venice provided Coryate with 'the most glorious and heavenly show upon the water that ever any mortal eye beheld'. The book was notable, too, for introducing the Italian word 'umbrella' into the English language: Coryate was fascinated by the unfamiliar 'things that minister shadow unto them [Italian travellers] for shelter against the scorching heat of the sun'. In the English climate they would turn out to be more useful against rain.

He was intrigued by the fashionable women's shoes known as chopines, with cork soles up to eighteen inches deep. Originally introduced to keep dainty feet clear of the dirty streets, they had developed into brightly painted fashion items, so exaggerated that they would sometimes caused their wearers to topple over. (Shakespeare's Hamlet, greeting the strolling players, tells one of the boy actors: 'Your ladyship is nearer heaven than when I saw you last, by the altitude of a chopine.') Other unfamiliar aspects of Venice that Coryate noted were the mountebanks on the streets, and women being allowed to act on the professional stage, which would not occur in England for another fifty years.

The book's illustrations included a fine fold-out drawing of the Roman amphitheatre at Verona and another of the author standing on the legendary Great Tun of Heidelberg, a barrel built in 1591 with a capacity of 24,000 gallons. To mark its publication, he held what came to be known as the Odcombonian Banquet, or 'philosophical feast', not this time at the Mermaid but at the Mitre in Fleet Street, another tavern popular with the *literati* of the time. The fourteen guests included Inigo, Donne and Lionel Cranfield, a rising politician destined to become Lord Treasurer and Earl of Middlesex before falling from grace in a corruption scandal in 1624. As well as being one of Inigo's patrons and an important link with the ruling élite, Cranfield appears to have been a close friend: in 1613 he noted in his accounts that he had spent sixpence on buying tobacco for the architect.[30]

The feast was commemorated in a long poem in Latin, possibly written by the lawyer and poet John Hoskins, another guest. A translation by John Reynolds begins:

> Whoever is contented
> That a number be convented
> Enough but not too many;
> The Mitre is the place decreed,
> For witty jests and cleanly feed,
> The betterest of any.

The poem offered terse pen sketches of the guests, including Inigo, described as 'neither unlearned nor profane'. In Reynolds's version he was dubbed 'Inigo Ionic-pillar', a free translation of the more straightforward '*Ignatius architectus*' in the original.

The author went on to give a long description of the genial host of the group:

> When Coryate is fuddled well
> His tongue begins to talk pell-mell
> He shameth nought to speak . . .
> To pass the sea, to pass the shore,
> And Fleet-street it all Europe o'er,
> A thing periculous [i.e. perilous].
> And yet one pair of shoes, they say,
> And shirt did serve him all the way . . .

And the poem ended:

> Thus every man is busy still,
> Each one practising his skill,
> None hath enough of gain.
> But Coryate liveth by his wits,
> He loseth nothing that he gets,
> Nor plays the fool in vain.[31]

Although at thirty-four he was not much younger than some of his fellow celebrants, Coryate's footloose and irreverent spirit was what made him attractive to them. Most of the others around the table were, like Inigo, in the process of discarding their youthful excesses for the more sober pursuits of middle age, principally jostling for power and status at the Stuart court. Though few will have had any real desire to emulate Coryate, they could only envy his devil-may-care approach.

In 1612 he went off on his travels again, this time determined to explore further east than Venice. Just before he left, his fellow Sireniacal Gentlemen issued him with a joke 'passport' to smooth his path. He sailed to Constantinople, then walked for much of the way through Greece, Egypt, the Holy Land, Persia and India, from where, in 1615, he wrote a letter greeting the members of the fraternity by name. In it, he made mention of the passport, 'that elegant safe-conduct, which, a little before my departure for England, your Fraternity with a general suffrage gave me for the security of my future peregrination'.

The principal purpose of his letter was to introduce a potential new member to the group, the Reverend Peter Rogers, and to 'entreat your generosities to entertain him friendly for my sake to exhilarate him with the purest quintessence of the Spanish, French and Rhenish grape which the Mermaid yieldeth'. No doubt his friends did as he bade; but they were not to enjoy Coryate's stimulating company again. After many adventures he was still in India, planning soon to return to his congenial haunts, when he died in December 1617.

Inigo's membership of that so-called 'worshipful fraternity' could be a factor in the recurring legend that he played a role in the early history of English freemasonry. The secret society of 'speculative' freemasons, with its unusual rituals and philosophy, is assumed to have developed as a spinoff from the London Company of Freemasons, a conventional City guild established in the fifteenth century. (A freemason was a mason who worked in freestone, a superior type of stone free from blemishes.) Freemasonry in its modern form was established in 1717, with the formation of the original Grand Lodge of England, an amalgamation of several pre-existing lodges. Records from before that date are sparse, and some supposed lists of admissions almost certainly refer to the

London Company of Freemasons rather than to a separate secret organisation. Freemasons describe God as the Great Architect, and it is not surprising that they should seek to enrol actual architects into their ranks: Sir Christopher Wren is known to have been admitted in 1691.[32]

Inigo's alleged connection seems first to have been documented in 1738 by Dr James Anderson in the second edition of his *Constitutions of Freemasons*, the first official history of the society. Anderson was apparently relying on an account written by Nicholas Stone, the stonemason who often worked with Inigo and was one of his closest friends. Stone is said to have recorded that Inigo was Grand Master of the Freemasons from 1607 until 1618, and again from 1636 until his death in 1652. Unhappily, the relevant document is believed to have been destroyed in 1720, and no other direct evidence of Inigo's association with the freemasons exists.[33] The 'Inigo Jones Manuscript', a masonic record whose frontispiece is a drawing signed 'Inigo Jones, 1607', is thought to be a forgery.[34]

Inigo was not asked to design the 1612 Twelfth Night masque, Jonson's *Love Restored*, probably because his two productions the previous year, notably *Oberon*, had so drained the royal finances. The total bill for *Love Restored* came to a paltry £280,[35] and in the antimasque Jonson made reference to the shortage of funds and the consequent lack of music and spectacle.

There was, though, better news for Inigo in February, when he received the honour of being admitted as a member of the Middle Temple. This did not mean that he had become or intended to be a lawyer. At that time about a quarter of those admitted to the Inns of Court were 'special admissions', men who had distinguished themselves in any field or who happened to know somebody who had influence at the inn. There were several lawyers in the Sireniacal fraternity and some were attached to the Middle Temple. They included the poet John Hoskins and Richard Martin, a wit and an immoderate drinker who had been expelled from the Temple in 1591 for riotous behaviour, but later reinstated. One of the benefits of membership was the right to live in an apartment at the Temple; but if Inigo did take advantage of that perk it could only have been for a short time.[36]

Unhappily for him, both of Inigo's principal patrons died in 1612. Robert Cecil, whose health was never robust, passed on in May, but by then he had already lost much of his influence at court. In 1610 he had failed to persuade the King to cut down on his extravagance and to accept the so-called Great Contract, by which he would have been granted a fixed annual payment from the House of Commons instead of amassing revenue from the swathe of feudal dues on which his Exchequer relied. Acceptance of the Contract could well have prevented the Civil War and the dire fate that was to befall his son Charles, but James refused to countenance the limits on his freedom of action that were an intrinsic part of the proposal.

In 1611 Cecil forfeited his primacy among James's advisers to the fresh-faced twenty-two-year-old Robert Carr, a former royal page whom the King had made a viscount in 1611, later to become Earl of Somerset. By 1612 Cecil's own finances were in a parlous state, partly due to his expenditure on the new Hatfield House, so Inigo might not have received many more commissions from his early benefactor even had he lived. In any event, following Cecil's death, his future now depended on his new employer, Prince Henry.

For much of that year Henry involved himself in questions of matrimony, which in his circle did not denote affairs of the heart but of high diplomacy. He was exceptionally close to his sister Elizabeth, a year younger than him, who was betrothed to Frederick V, Elector of the Palatinate (in what is now Germany). Henry welcomed the marriage because it would seal the alliance between two of the most important Protestant states in Europe. As for his own future, there was talk at various times of engagements to the daughters of the Spanish king, of the Prince of Savoy and of the late Henry IV of France, who had been assassinated in 1612. Prince Henry made it known that he was not attracted to any of those options and would prefer to follow his sister's example by taking a German Protestant spouse. Meantime came rumours of his affair with the young Countess of Essex, whose marriage Inigo and Jonson had helped to commemorate six years earlier.

A few days after Frederick's arrival from Heidelberg in October, to prepare for his wedding to Elizabeth the following February, Henry began to feel feverish and unwell. From 25 October he was forced to stay in bed and relays of doctors were called to diagnose and treat his mysterious illness. They resorted to bleeding and the other remedies of the time, but to no avail. Henry died on the evening of 6 November and was buried in Westminster Abbey, with full state honours, two days later. Inevitably there were rumours that he had been poisoned by enemies of the kingdom, but later research has shown fairly conclusively that the cause of his death was typhoid fever.

The court and the nation were in shock. A vigorous youth, accomplished both in the manly arts and cultural pursuits, Henry had surely been destined to steer Great Britain and its monarchy back to the glories of their heroic past. Now, within days of taking to his sick bed, he had been snatched from the nation whose future he would have shaped. Hundreds of panegyrics to him were penned for public and private consumption, such as this from the Earl of Dorset, writing to the diplomat Sir Thomas Edmondes: 'Our rising sun is set ere scarce he had shone, and . . . all our glory lies buried.'[37]

Prince Henry's accounts show that Inigo was fully paid for his term as Surveyor, lasting less than two years, although he probably had to wait a while for his money. He received a payment of £88 2s 6d for the first nineteen months, to 1 October, with an extra £5 11s to cover the thirty-seven days until the Prince's death. He also received an extra £30 under the heading 'gifts and rewards'. Wages for people he employed and materials for works under his control came to a hefty £2828. More puzzling items in the accounts seem to be connected to the masques and other revels performed for the Prince. There were 16s for 'two Frenchmen that made silk', £8 for 'the Antidoteman', 12s for an Italian juggler and 15s for 'a Grecian stranger'.[38]

Suddenly the revels had ended. Inigo, along with about 500 others employed at Henry's court, had his own future to worry about as well as that of his country. The obvious move for many of them would have been to join the court of Henry's younger brother Charles, the new heir to the throne, but this avenue had been blocked by the King. His jealousy of the quality and prestige of the men in his eldest son's circle had not faded with Henry's death. In an attempt to avoid the situation arising again, he told Charles and the Lord Chamberlain not to employ any of Henry's former servants without his express permission.[39]

In any event, Charles was not blessed with anything like the prestige or potential of his elder brother. Even Henry – his sum of fraternal affection expended exclusively on his sister – poked fun at him: he told him he should be a bishop because the long gown would hide his legs, deformed by rickets. Now this feeble, derided youth would inherit the future that should rightfully have belonged to his brother. The puny Charles, to put it callously, had the last laugh. The nation's tragedy was that it would not share the joke.

Chapter Nine

PILGRIM'S PROGRESS

N O SOONER HAD THE COURT EMERGED from its period of mourning for the young prince than it switched to celebratory mode for the wedding of James's sixteen-year-old daughter, Princess Elizabeth, to Frederick V, Elector of the Palatinate. The elaborate ceremony was held at Whitehall Palace on St Valentine's Day, 14 February 1613, and James, sparing no expense, authorised a budget of nearly £100,000 for lavish public festivities. Following the precedent set at Prince Henry's investiture three years earlier, a pageant was staged on the Thames that included a flotilla of mock battleships, while hundreds of fireworks were ignited from four floating castles.[1]

Inigo designed the settings for two spectacular masques performed on successive evenings. On the first evening, *The Lord's Masque* was presented at the Banqueting House, written for the occasion by Thomas Campion, the author of the 1607 court masque. Inigo employed many of his characteristic devices. In the opening scene the stage was dominated by a rock, divided horizontally. The upper half quickly dissolved into a drifting cloud, in which the masquers sat surrounded by gold.[2] Soon the scene changed again and spectators were presented with a view of London and the River Thames. The whole effect was greatly admired, not least by Campion, who wrote in his introduction to the text:

> Master Inigo Jones . . . in all . . . the workmanship which belonged to the whole invention showed extraordinary industry and skill; which if it be not as lively expressed in writing as appeared in view, rob him not of his due, but lay the blame on my want of right apprehending his instructions for the adorning of his art.

It is hard to judge whether the author was being altogether sincere or indulging in some Jonsonesque irony, perhaps referring to a dispute with Inigo over the text. If taken at face value, Campion's display of modesty seems to confirm that, in his case if not in Jonson's, Inigo had already established himself as the senior partner, devising the theme and the setting for the masque before the author set to work on the script. His costumes, including sixteen pages dressed like fiery spirits,[3] matched the splendour of the settings.

Inigo was at the peak of his productive genius in this genre, so peculiar to its period. On the next night the Inns of Court staged their own celebration of the wedding and, as a new member of the Middle Temple, it would have been ungracious of him to refuse their request to design it. Moreover the author of *The Memorable Masque* was the poet George Chapman, who had been imprisoned with Ben Jonson for writing *Eastward Ho!* eight years earlier and was now one of Inigo's closest friends.

The show began with a parade from the house of the Master of the Rolls in Chancery Lane to Whitehall, where the masque was staged in the great hall. (It would have been impossible to get the Banqueting House rearranged after the previous night's revelry.)[4] The parade was headed by fifty gentlemen on horseback, 'richly attired and as gallantly mounted, with footmen particularly attending'. There followed a troupe of boys dressed as baboons, wearing 'Neapolitan suits and great ruffs', mounted on asses and small ponies; then musicians on two lavishly decorated floats preceding the masquers themselves, also on horseback, dressed as Red Indians from Virginia.

That theme may have been chosen at the behest of the mourned Prince Henry, who had been keen to revive interest in developing the American colony and who had played a key role in planning his sister's wedding celebrations. Chapman, like Inigo, had been close to the Prince and wrote one of the many poems lamenting his loss. He acknowledged that it was Henry who encouraged him to complete his famous translation of Homer, begun in the last years of the sixteenth century. Inigo may have designed the title page of the completed work when it was eventually published in 1611.[5]

As the parade arrived at the Whitehall tilt-yard, the King and the newly wed couple were there to greet it. Moving into the hall for the masque itself they were confronted by a gigantic golden rock reaching almost to the ceiling. Alongside it was a silver octagonal temple on a hill, topped with pilasters and a silver dome. In the first speech of the masque Chapman poked gentle fun at Inigo's frequent use of crags and cliffs in his settings: 'Rocks? Nothing but rocks in these masquing devices? Is invention so poor she must needs ever dwell amongst rocks?' Clearly both Chapman and Inigo were aware of some of the absurdities and clichés inherent in the conventions of the form; for the poet would scarcely have kept the line if it had not been approved by his friend.

As if in response to the taunt, the rock began to move towards the audience, then 'split in pieces with a great crack', at which point the antimasque was played out. Later the upper part of the rock was transformed into a cloud and, drifting away, revealed a gold mine where the twelve masquers sat, attended by torch-bearers. As the sun gradually set over the cliffs behind, the musicians and singers performed songs celebrating the virtues of love and marriage.

It was an expensive production: the cost to Lincoln's Inn, only one of the two sponsoring inns, was £1086 8s 11d.[6] Inigo's fee was £110. The account books of Lincoln's Inn show two separate payments, of £100 to him personally and a separate £10 to 'Mistress Jones for her brother Mr Inigo Jones'.[7] This suggests that he remained in contact at this time with at least one of his three sisters, and that they might have been living together. A bachelor in his position would have needed someone to take charge of his household.

The citation on the title page of the published version of *The Memorable Masque* shows again how Inigo was coming to regard his role in the proceedings as more vital than that of the author of the text. Probably composed by Chapman, it announced that the work had been 'invented and fashioned, with the ground and special structure of the whole work, by our kingdom's most artful and ingenious architect, Inigo Jones. Supplied, applied, digested and written by George Chapman.'

There is nothing to suggest that Chapman felt himself demeaned by being deprived of top billing in favour of his designer, and he was a model of restraint in denying himself any complimentary adjectives. The great Ben Jonson would have seen no need to be so self-effacing.

Inigo's work on both wedding masques had been much admired, according to the evidence of commentators and correspondents. This may have influenced James in his decision to invite the architect to join his own staff, despite his general reluctance to employ members of his late son's court. In April it was announced that Inigo was to have the 'reversion' of the post of Surveyor-General of the King's Works, then held by Simon Basil. This meant that in normal circumstances he would be first in line to inherit the position when Basil died, for such appointments were invariably for life.

This was an extraordinary piece of good fortune for Inigo, less than six months after his chances of pursuing a career at court appeared to have been snatched from him by Henry's death. Waiting for Basil to die before filling his shoes could have been a grisly and frustrating process, but Inigo knew that the Surveyor was in poor health. The chances were that he would not have to wait too long.

He was anyway on a lucky streak. Not long before the announcement of his impending appointment, he received an invitation that would help him fill in the waiting time, while allowing him to pursue his principal passion. After the royal wedding, the Elector Frederick had to take his bride to Heidelberg, the Palatinate's capital, and introduce her to his people. Tradition demanded that they make a royal progress across northern Europe, accompanied by representatives of the English Crown. King James invited Thomas Howard, Earl of Arundel, the art collector and former leading light of Prince Henry's court, to be a senior member of the mission. Howard accepted – and asked Inigo to go with him.

Though gawky, reserved, plainly dressed and a touch self-important,[8] Howard was described by one contemporary as looking 'more like a nobleman than any of us'.[9] He had taken part in several of Inigo's masques at court, and the two men's shared enthusiasm for the fine arts would form the basis of a close friendship for many years. They might have met first in 1609, when Inigo went to Hatfield House to advise Cecil on architecture and Howard was helping Cecil to select paintings to buy to fill the walls of his new mansion.[10]

He had endured a tragic childhood, though not uniquely so in that time of religious turmoil. Before he was born in 1585 his father Philip, the first Earl of Arundel, had been imprisoned in the Tower of London for refusing to renounce the practice of Catholicism. Remaining stubbornly committed to his faith, he died there ten years later, having never been allowed to see his son and heir. (Despite, or perhaps because of his father's fatal adherence to the Roman Church, Howard had no strong religious allegiance himself, and would formally become a Protestant in 1616.)

Queen Elizabeth, angered by Philip's obstinacy, stripped Thomas, his heir, of all his hereditary titles. James I, though, was anxious to heal the religious divisions amongst England's great families, and awarded Thomas Howard the earldoms of Arundel and Surrey in 1604. In 1606 he married Aletheia Talbot, the wealthy heiress of the seventh Earl of Shrewsbury. Although Howard was never one of James's closest advisers, the King agreed to be named godfather to their first child.

After Aletheia's father's death in 1616, the couple would use their joint fortune to indulge a passion for collecting. At Arundel House, their rambling mansion in the Strand, they accumulated England's greatest collection of art and antiquities. It included an unparalleled group of paintings and drawings by Hans Holbein, inherited in 1617 from Lady Lumley, a member of the Howard family and the widow of the man who had donated his library to Prince Henry. At its height, Howard's collection numbered some 800 paintings and several hundred statues. The Dutch painter Peter Paul Rubens called him 'one of the four evangelists and a supporter of our art'.[11] Hungry for knowledge and guidance on matters of taste, he took advice not only from Inigo but also from another regular at the Mermaid club, the book collector Sir Robert Cotton.

Like Prince Henry, Howard was fired by the enthusiasm of Inigo and other travellers for Italian culture and architecture, and in 1612 he obtained a licence from the King to visit Italy, ostensibly for his health, for many of his family had suffered from consumption. Journeys to the Catholic states of Europe were still not encouraged by the Protestant court, but with the Gunpowder Plot now seven years in the past and fears of a Catholic revival receding, restrictions were beginning to be eased. England was by now on reasonable terms with some of the Italian states. Venice, for instance, was regarded favourably for having refused to accept the supremacy of Pope Paul V over its secular affairs, and James I appointed an ambassador there a few months after his accession. (The man he chose was Sir Henry Wotton, who later wrote a book on architecture but is best known for having invented the classic definition of an ambassador as 'an honest man sent to lie abroad for the good of his country'.)

On his way south on this, his first visit to Europe, Howard met Rubens, who painted his portrait at Spa in Belgium. But after only a few weeks in Italy, news came of the death of his patron and friend Prince Henry. Cutting short his intended stay, he returned from Padua to London as fast as he could manage. Now, as a result of the royal wedding, he was being given a chance to resume his European travels. He grasped it delightedly, realising that once the bride and groom had been safely delivered he would be well placed to continue his interrupted tour of Italy.

This time he decided to take his wife Aletheia along and to invite Inigo to travel with them as an artistic adviser. The up-and-coming architect, with the experience gained during his own visit a dozen years earlier, could instruct him about the architecture and evaluate the works of art that he might be tempted to buy. The knowledge of the Italian language that Inigo had acquired during that earlier trip would also prove invaluable. Inigo accepted the invitation with alacrity, for he too had unfinished business with the Italian masters.

On Saturday 10 April 1613 the newlyweds and their accompanying dignitaries set out from Whitehall in a carriage procession that included the King and Queen and Prince Charles, the new heir to the throne. Lord and Lady Arundel travelled with thirty-six attendants, including Inigo.[12] Other aristocrats in the party were the Duke of Lennox, steward of the King's household; Viscount Lisle, later Earl of Leicester, who had experience as a soldier and diplomat in the Netherlands; and Lord Harington, who as Princess Elizabeth's guardian was credited with having saved her from kidnap by the gunpowder plotters in 1605. (Harington was destined to die on the return trip from Heidelberg.)

They all spent Saturday night at Greenwich Palace, before proceeding to Rochester and Chatham where, on the 14th, the King and Queen headed back to London after a ceremonial inspection of the fleet. Prince Charles stayed on, because he wanted to remain with his sister – to whom, like Henry, he was greatly attached – until she embarked. But after spending five days with her and her husband at Canterbury he was summoned back to Whitehall on 19 April, so as to be there in time to take part in the festivities for St George's Day four days later. The others moved on to Margate, where on 21 April the bride and groom boarded the newly built 'Prince Royal', named for Henry. Unfavourable winds delayed their departure until the 25th. When they finally got to sea, the ships carrying other members of the retinue arranged themselves in semi-circular formation for the three-day journey across the Channel to Flushing.

Progress through the Netherlands and northern Germany was slow, because of the elaborate welcoming ceremonies arranged for the party in the Protestant cities along the somewhat circuitous route: Rotterdam, the Hague, Leyden, Haarlem, Amsterdam, Utrecht, Arnhem and Dusseldorf, which laid on the biggest show of all. From Bonn they proceeded by boat along the Rhine, sailing slowly past the high, romantic ruins of Godesburg Castle, largely destroyed in 1583. On the opposite bank was the formidable and still intact castle of Drachenfels framed by the spectacular wooded landscape of the Siebengebirge (seven

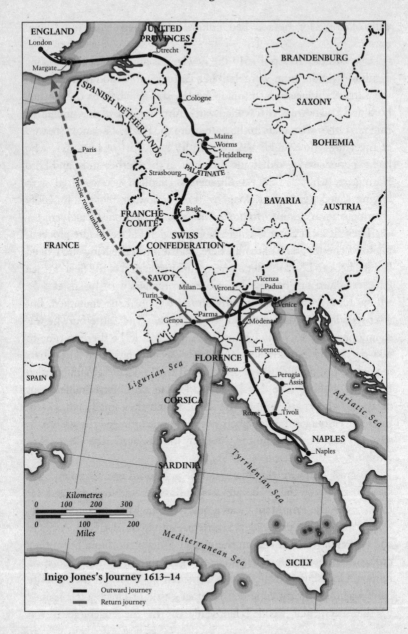

ENGLAND
London
Margate

UNITED PROVINCES
Utrecht

SPANISH NETHERLANDS

BRANDENBURG

SAXONY

BOHEMIA

Cologne

Paris

Precise route unknown

Mainz
Worms
Heidelberg

PALATINATE

Strasbourg

BAVARIA

AUSTRIA

FRANCHE-COMTÉ

Basle

FRANCE

SWISS CONFEDERATION

SAVOY

Vicenza
Padua

Milan   Verona

Turin

Venice

Genoa   Parma   Modena

Ligurian Sea

CORSICA

Florence

FLORENCE

Siena

Perugia
Assisi

SPAIN

Adriatic Sea

Rome   Tivoli

NAPLES
Naples

Tyrrhenian Sea

SARDINIA

Kilometres
0   100   200   300

0   100   200
Miles

Mediterranean Sea

SICILY

Inigo Jones's Journey 1613–14
    Outward journey
    Return journey

mountains). More castles and ancient settlements, grouped around medieval churches, loomed around nearly every bend, with neat rows of vines on the slopes between them. Once Elizabeth had taken her first step on Palatinate soil the pace became slower still, as the people turned out in force to greet their new princess at Mainz, Oppenheim and Worms, the town where less than a hundred years earlier Martin Luther had refused to renounce the Protestant theology that had so altered the politics of northern Europe, including Britain.

Inigo would not have had much opportunity to explore this or any other historic site as the party continued its triumphant progress. In any case, he is unlikely to have been much impressed by the predomin- antly Gothic buildings of the region, such as the Katharinenkirche in Oppenheim and the enormous Romanesque cathedral at Worms: they were part of an architectural tradition from which he was seeking to break free. On 7 June the royal party finally reached Heidelberg and was escorted into town through ceremonial arches by a thousand horsemen, to the thud of cannon in the background. The procession ended at the Elector's castle, on a hill overlooking the town and the River Neckar, where a new wing, today called the English wing, was being built for Elizabeth.

The wing was constructed in a severe neo-Palladian style, unlike anything else in the castle and rare anywhere in the Rhineland. There has been speculation that Inigo may have had a hand in its design. There is no hard evidence, and it is impossible to judge from what little remains of it today: chiefly the disfigured south wall, with two stories of plain rectangular windows and, above them, two large dormers. One suggestion[13] is that the Elector may have commissioned the work from the up-and-coming architect when he first went to London in October 1612 to meet his bride-to-be. It is also possible, given Inigo's experience of stage work, that he was involved – at least as an advisor – in the construction of a theatre in the castle in 1616, where Elizabeth thought to emulate her mother in presenting grand spectacles.

It is unlikely, though, that Inigo had a hand in the bizarre Elizabeth Gate, a lavishly decorated triumphal arch leading into the garden of the English Wing, improbably reputed to have been erected in a single night as a surprise gift from Frederick to his young wife. Its provenance is unclear but, by contrast, the history of the once magnificent formal garden to the east of the castle is well documented. It was designed in 1616 by Solomon de Caux, who with Inigo had been a member of Prince Henry's circle but had lost out in the scramble for places in King James's court. He had therefore accepted Frederick's offer to accompany him back to Heidelberg, where his garden was for a while hailed as the eighth wonder of the world. Only the remnants of a grotto and a splendid viewpoint over the river remind us of its splendours today.

The week-long celebrations of the royal couple's arrival in their capital included tilting, theatrical displays and hunting excursions. Inigo would almost certainly have found the time to see the Great Tun, within the castle precinct, that Coryate had described so graphically at the Mitre feast. He is likely, too, to have wanted to visit the University, the oldest in Germany. The British party stayed until 14 June, when most returned north to Cologne. But the Howards, with Inigo and a small group of servants, headed south-west, initially accompanied by the Duke of Lennox.

For some reason they were being mysterious about their intended destination and sought to give the impression that they were returning to London via Strasbourg and through France. Sir Dudley Carleton, who had recently replaced Sir Henry Wotton as the British representative in Venice, had been told of the Strasbourg plan, but he did not believe it. He reported, presciently, that in his view the travellers were heading his way: 'I hear my Lord had taken Inigo Jones into his train, who will be of best use to him (by reason of his language and experience) in these parts.'

Sure enough, when the party reached Strasbourg only Lennox returned to England. Howard's coterie moved on, as he had always planned, following the Rhine south as far as Basle, then crossing the Alps into Italy.

Aristocratic travellers in the early seventeenth century found that their noble status earned them precious few privileges on the open road. When it came to crossing the mountains everyone, regardless of rank, was at the mercy of the local suppliers of beasts of burden suitable for the task. Howard and Inigo had both endured the hardships of overland travel before. So too had Thomas Coke, a senior member of the Earl's entourage who had been with him on his earlier Italian visit. A letter written by Coke in November 1612 to the Earl of Shrewsbury, for whom he had been carrying letters to Italy, vividly described some of the hazards and delays of that first journey.

In France he had caught up with the train of a duke, whose twenty horses filled the narrow road 'so as I could neither get before him nor go with him'. Once he had managed to leave them behind, and then to cross the Alps, he was caught in a torrential rainstorm. It meant that he could not ford the river between Turin and Milan (probably the Ticino) but had to go across by boat. As the horse carrying his saddle-bag was being led on to the vessel,

> the horse fell in betwixt the bank and the boat and, not being able to rise the sloping bank, the boy holding up the horse's head by the bridle was fain to return to the boat to swim him back again to the other side, but the horse struggling broke his girth and away went the saddle and took with it my portmanteau with all my letters which were in it, for the which I am infinitely sorry, having by this misfortune disappointed both many noble persons in England and also my Lord here.

'My lord here' was Howard, staying in Padua at the time. Coke was determined to make clear to the Earl that he had done all he could to retrieve the saddle-bag:

> It rained all that night extremely yet I sent forth boats to see if it might stay at some bridge or stake and left money with the postman to send fishermen to fish for it when the waters might fall.[14]

The letters were not found. Again seeking to minimise any blame,

Coke went on to tell of similar mishaps to others crossing the river, including one Nicholas Fitzherbert, who was drowned 'two days after my misfortune'.

It says much for Inigo's and Howard's intrepid natures, and their determination to savour the works of the Renaissance masters, that they were both prepared to risk such perils for a second time. The most commonly used route to Italy in this period was the Brenner pass, the only Alpine crossing that could accommodate wheeled traffic. But this was too far east for the impatient Howard and his party. Since it was summer, they opted instead for the more difficult St Gothard pass, the shortest route to Milan, their first port of call. They would not have attempted the pass in winter when, according to one contemporary account, 'snow waters thundered like the sea and mules were buried in the snow'.[15] Even in summer there were dangers, from footpads and from wild animals such as wolves, lynxes and bears.

The road from Basle to the pass (6860 feet at its highest point) first follows the River Suhr beyond Lake Lucerne, then winds through the steep Leventina valley to Bellinzona, where the party's carriages and luggage carts had to be exchanged for mules and pack horses and, for the women, litters borne on men's shoulders. These were provided by cooperatives of villagers from both sides of the ridge, first formed in the thirteenth century. Some parts of the track – stretches are still visible alongside today's fine motor road – were narrow and quite vertiginous, and gaps had to be crossed using bridges of varying degrees of danger. At some spots walkways were suspended from the sides of rocks, and the many spectacular views and dramatic waterfalls that today delight tourists only served to increase the trepidation of nervous seventeenth-century travellers.

After a final climb between the peaks of Mount Tamaro and Mount Camoghe came the welcome sight of the hospice at the very top of the pass. The Swiss mountain hospices were run by monks and this one, rebuilt only in 1607 after its predecessor had been trashed by German soldiers, offered quite a decent standard of accommodation. And with the top of the pass finally reached, there was now leisure to appreciate the majestic views of the snow-clad peaks. Infanta Clara Eugenia, a Spanish noblewoman who made the crossing in 1599, wrote: 'I doubt whether there is a better view to be had in the world.'

The party spent the night there and began the descent – less wearying than the previous day's climb, but no less terrifying, even though the notorious old wooden Devil's Bridge, with no railings to protect travellers from mishap, had been replaced by a safer stone crossing twenty years earlier. After some five hours, as they approached the lakes of Lugano and Como, the gradients became less steep and they could see the Plain of Lombardy spread below. On the way down, the firs below the tree line on the high ground gave way to deciduous silver birches, willows and whitebeams. Soon, as the daylight started to fade, the fortified city of Milan came into view, with its prominent castle turret in silhouette. The travellers rode in through the north gate.

In his book *Touring in 1600*, E.S. Bates wrote:

Milan must no more be missed than Rome. It was the city of all Europe on which the question of peace and war permanently depended; being the key to the most debateable district. And as such, it may be imagined what the castle was then from what it is even in its present state . . . Then it was alive with the finest soldiers of the age, Spaniards; a small town, complete in itself, with rows of shops and five market-places. And the city itself was recognised as unsurpassed as a school both for the accomplishments that befitted a gentleman and for craftsmanship; for everything, in fact, that made life possible or pleasant.

On 16 July Howard wrote to Sir Dudley Carleton:

Upon Thursday last at night we arrived here at Milan safely, drawn on from Basle by the freshness of the weather, which was both beyond our expectation and the custom at this time of the year. Here we find it so hot as without danger we cannot (as they say) stir, till some rain fall. Some advise me to try the waters at St Cashan; and for physic at

Padua I know the year is too far spent, till the fall. Therefore what course I shall resolve on here I am altogether uncertain and must refer myself till the next post.[16]

His uncertainty was resolved sooner than he would have chosen. Milan was then ruled by fiercely Catholic Spain. Its Governor, Don John de Mendoca, Marquis of Hinojosa, declined to receive the Howards and their party. Angry at what he saw as a calculated act of hostility to him and to England, Howard left almost immediately, taking Inigo and the rest of the entourage with him.

At Parma, an independent dukedom ruled by the Farnese family, they received a more cordial welcome. It would have been surprising if, while in Parma, Inigo and the Earl did not take the opportunity of looking at some of the city's magnificent examples of Renaissance art, in particular Correggio's rich frescoes. His interpretation of the *Annunciation of the Virgin*, painted inside the cathedral dome, shows a complete mastery of perspective – the skill that Inigo would bring to perfection in his later masque designs.

Moving on to Padua, part of the Venetian state, the Howards established themselves in a villa two miles from the city. Sir Dudley Carleton went from Venice to pay his respects, promising to arrange a suitably lavish reception by the Doge when the time came for the Earl and his lady to move there. Carleton was not simply being polite. As the representative in a Catholic state of a Protestant ruler, an important part of his job was to keep tabs on British travellers, watching out in particular for any too overt display of Catholic sympathies that could lead to their conversion.

Inigo was in his element in Padua, at the heart of a countryside richly endowed with villas designed by his admired Palladio. He had almost certainly visited the city during his first Italian journey, as well as nearby Vicenza, a treasure trove of Palladian palazzos; but for a disciple of Palladio there was no limit to what could be learned from detailed and repeated study of his work. Inigo appears to have carried his copy of *I Quattro Libri dell' Architettura* with him on his travels, and thus could compare many of the architect's original plans with the buildings themselves. Moreover, Palladio's pupil Scamozzi, now over sixty, was living in Venice and appeared willing to pass on not only the insights handed down to him by the master but also a priceless collection of around 250 architectural drawings by both Palladio and Scamozzi himself – unsurpassable reference material for Inigo in his mission to establish an English Palladian style.[17]

He was an avid collector of drawings, not only of architecture but also of stage designs and costumes, which he also used in his work. Many of his own designs can be identified as having been inspired by Italian prints that he had bought. During his journey he also acquired prints and etchings for his own pleasure. One of his favourite artists was Francesco Parmigianino, the early sixteenth-century master, whose style of drawing he often mimicked. Part of Inigo's collection was acquired some years after his death by Thomas Herbert, the eighth Earl of Pembroke, who noted: 'Inigo Jones so fond of Parmigianino that he bought the prints of the imperfect plates, which are now here in this book.'[18]

Palladio's design for the Basilica at Vicenza

As Carleton had promised, when the group arrived in Venice the Doge welcomed them at a feast at the Arsenal. They returned early in September to Padua, where Aletheia remained for several weeks. Meanwhile Howard took Inigo and a few other members of his group – and possibly Scamozzi as well – to Vicenza where, according to a note that Inigo made in his copy of Palladio, they had arrived by 23 September. He would find it a wrench to leave.

Chapter Ten

IN THE STEPS OF THE MASTERS

F EW CITIES IN THE WORLD can boast such a coherent body
of work by a single architect as Vicenza, especially not by one born
nearly 500 years ago. For visitors in the twenty-first century, part of the
appeal of Palladio's masterworks lies in their age, in their sheer survival.
For Inigo it was the very opposite: all was new and stimulating. Here was
the work of a man who, drawing his inspiration from ancient Greece
and Rome, had refined and embellished the classical vision to create a
modern architectural idiom. The clean, stately lines, the sense of light,
space, balance and proportion, were a revelation to someone brought
up in the cramped, dark, higgledy-piggledy streets of London.

Before Palladio, Vicenza, like London, had been essentially a medieval town. It was appropriate that his first major commission there was
to put a new classical skin over the Gothic Basilica which, though never
finished according to his plans, quickly became the recognised symbol of
Vicenza. Another unfinished work that greatly impressed Inigo was the
heavily rusticated Palazzo Thiene. He recorded that, during his visit to
it, Scamozzi showed him the original plan and told him that it had
been drawn by the Roman architect and painter Giulio Romano, and
put into effect by Palladio after Romano's death in 1546.

Inigo admired the building enormously, and was delighted when one of the workmen on the site pointed to a pillar which he claimed had been carved by Palladio's own hand. Inigo made sketches of its entrance hall in the margin of his copy of the *Quattro Libri*, believing that entrances were the key to the success of a design: 'The entrances are varied according to the greatness of the houses, as I observed at Vicenza, where are the best I ever saw.'

He went on to praise the 'admirable discretion' of the Palazzo Thiene, explaining: 'Being slender the pillar answers the height of the place and the addition of bozzi [rough-cut rustication] answers to the strength and rustic of the rest.'[1] He was to incorporate rustication in many of his designs, including the Whitehall Banqueting House. He also noted Palladio's use of stucco over brick, one of his most common building techniques. Inigo's comment on La Rotunda, the well-known villa sited dramatically on a hill just outside the town, confirms that his priority in architecture was to give pragmatic factors at least as much weight as sublime beauty: he remarked merely that, despite its difficult site, it 'stands very solid and firm', adding: 'A great deal of money must have been spent in the building of this house and especially for the terraces.'

During this visit Inigo inspected and admired Palladio's last work, the Teatro Olimpico, which was to influence his own design for at least one theatre in London. He made notes on Palladio's interior and on the stage design, completed by Scamozzi after Palladio's death. It was an important model for his use of perspective in scenery, although his own backdrops were flat rather than three-dimensional as in the Vicenza theatre.

His great admiration for Palladio did not wholly extend to Scamozzi, in whose company he saw many of Vicenza's buildings including the Palazzo Trissino, which Scamozzi had designed but was not yet complete. Inigo wrote critically: 'There a great palace begun by Scamozzi but the order within agreeth not with that without, which is an Ionic portico. That within is Doric and lower.'

The two men obviously engaged in spirited discussions about architecture. Elsewhere, Inigo criticised Scamozzi as 'purblind' for not recognising that you have to enlarge decorative elements such as friezes and medallions if they are being placed high on a building, otherwise nobody will see them. And many years later, on his copy of Vitruvius's *I Dieci Libri*, he would observe waspishly: 'Most writers of architecture do leave over those parts which they understand not, as Scamozzi, Sir Henry Wotton.'

Wotton, the long-time ambassador in Venice, wrote one of the first English architectural textbooks, *The Elements of Architecture*, in 1624. It was greatly derivative from the books of Palladio, Scamozzi and their predecessors. It clearly did not impress Inigo, who was perhaps put out by it, because by then he may have had thoughts of writing such a book himself.

After Vicenza, the group split up temporarily. Howard rejoined his wife at Padua, then went off to Bologna and Florence, where his sightseeing plans were interrupted by heavy rain. The Countess rejoined him in Siena, where she had originally wanted to stay over the winter. The couple spent six weeks at the Monasteria della Grazie improving their command of Italian, while sending most of their retinue on to Pisa.[2] But by January they were in Rome, which Inigo may have reached independently, stopping off at Mantua. In his copy of Vasari's *Lives*, he records his visit to Mantua's splendid Palazzo Tè, where Giulio Romano's frescoes appear to have influenced some of his subsequent masque designs.[3] At the nearby Ducal Palace he would have had his first glimpse of the Duke's fabulous art collection, part of which he would help Charles I to buy some years later.

Although restrictions on travel were easing, in the normal course of events English tourists were still not permitted to go to Rome, headquarters of the Catholic Church. The royal licences to travel expressly forbade it, as Sir Dudley Carleton, always suspicious of Catholic propaganda, would have reminded Howard and his party. Robert Dallington, in *A Method for Travel*, described Rome as 'the seminary and nursery of British fugitives (and yet a place most worthy to be seen)'. One such fugitive was Inigo's old friend Tobie Matthew, who is recorded as having guided Howard round the city during his visit.[4] It would be surprising if Inigo had not also taken the opportunity of renewing his acquaintance with the man who had once been his official captive.

It was not only the English authorities who frowned on visits by Englishmen to Rome and made it hazardous to undertake them. The Inquisition was still a force to be feared and only six years earlier John Mole, Lord Roos's tutor, had been arrested there and died in prison. Howard was determined to ignore such precedents and warnings; but the danger that he courted in going ahead with the visit was brought home to him on his return, when he was rumoured to have been part of a Catholic plot against the Crown and was closely questioned by the Archbishop of Canterbury.[5] It was soon after this that Howard formally became a Protestant, perhaps as a defensive measure against any further accusations of the kind.

If Vicenza represented the flowering of Palladio's art, Rome was where it had its roots. Palladio came here in 1545 and it was during his two-year stay that he was inspired to adopt and develop the precepts of the architects and sculptors of the ancient world. It is unlikely that Inigo had travelled as far south during his first Italian tour; so when he arrived in Rome with Howard he would be seeing for the first time what had inspired Palladio nearly seventy years earlier, the city that the French author Michel de Montaigne had described at the end of the sixteenth century as 'not so much a ruin as a sepulchre of ruins'.[6] Howard and Inigo may have stayed with the Marchese Giustiniani, patron to some of the most important Roman artists and a particular admirer of Caravaggio, who had died three years earlier. (The Marchese's enthusiasm must have rubbed off on Howard, who later bought several Caravaggios for his Arundel House gallery.)[7]

Almost as soon as he arrived, Inigo began to record his impressions and observations in his copy of Palladio. On page 10 of Book Four he wrote, 'The 2 of January 1614, I being in Rome, compared these designs following with the ruins themselves.' For the next 123 pages he methodically went through the twenty-six ruined temples that Palladio had drawn. The Temple of Peace he judged 'the greatest and most magnificent of the city', although Palladio himself thought that the Temple of Jove was 'the greatest and most adorned of all that were in Rome'.

From Inigo's Roman sketch book

Inigo was not a man to accept received opinion, even on such subjects as the naming of temples. Where Palladio designated one of them 'Neptune's Temple', he observed, 'This is not likely for, Neptune being a robustious God, they made Doric temples and not Corinthian nor so adorned.'

He continued updating these notes all his life. Alongside the drawing of the Temple of Jove is a comment dated 13 June 1639, referring to a discussion he had in that year with a visiting Roman sculptor, who 'told me that the ruins of this temple is pulled all down to have the marble by the constable Barbarinos Collona by the Pope's permission. This was the noblest thing which was in Rome in my time. So as all the good of the Ancients will be utterly ruined ere long.'

After a few days in the city, finding the margins of *I Quattro Libri* too restricted to express the torrent of thoughts and impressions that his visit was inspiring, he decided to supplement them with a notebook, filling it with sketches and a few comments. On the fly-leaf he wrote, with a significant flourish, an unambiguous statement of his life's passion: 'Rome. I find no delight except in learning – Inigo Jones. 1614.' He was to repeat that memorandum to himself in his copy of Vitruvius's book on classical architecture.

Many of the entries in the notebook are dated, but their order does not appear consecutive. For instance, the entry for 19 January 1614 comes after entries for later in January. This must mean either that he did not start filling the notebook at the first page – which would be perverse – or that he was being inconsistent by mixing up his calendar years. The modern calendar year, running from January to December, had been adopted in most of Europe in the sixteenth century, whereas in England the year still officially began on 25 March, with our present calendar not adopted until 1752. If he used the calendar appropriate to the place where he was writing, an entry written just after he had returned to England for January 1614 (the month following December 1614), would have been a year later than an entry made in Rome for January 1614 (the month following December 1613). Another possibility is that he copied them into the book at a later date, from rough notes made while he was in Italy.

Whenever they were composed, his entries dated 19 and 20 January 1614 contain the most interesting – and most often quoted – of his observations about architecture. They suggest that his principal purpose was to turn his exploration of the eternal city into a treatise that would set out his architectural philosophy, possibly for eventual publication:

> 19 January 1614. As in design first one studies the parts of the body of man as eyes, noses, mouths, ears and so of the rest, to be practised in the parts before one commences to put them together to make a whole figure and clothe it, and consequently a whole story with all – so in architecture one must study the parts as loggias, entrances, halls, chambers, stairs, doors, windows and then adorn them with columns, cornices . . .

He went on to list a range of architectural ornaments including cherubs, shells, heads of beasts and much else. Next day he continued the theme:

> In all inventions of capricious ornaments one must first design the ground, or the thing plain, as it is for the use, and on that vary it and adorn it . . . according to the use and order it is of.

He suggested that many ornamental additions 'which proceed out of the abundance of designers and were brought in by Michelangelo and his followers' – what today we call Mannerism – are unsuitable for the exteriors of buildings, and ought to be confined to gardens, loggias or chimneypieces inside the house.

> For as outwardly every wise man carrieth a gravity in public places, where there is nothing else looked for, yet is inwardly easy and imagining what is free and sometimes licentiously flying out, as Nature herself does oftentimes extravagantly to delight: a man is sometimes moved to laughter, sometimes to contemplation, sometimes to horror. So in architecture the outward ornaments ought to be solid, proportionable according to the rules, masculine and unaffected; whereas, within the limits used by the ancients, to vary and compose the ornamental parts of the house itself and the movables within it is most commendable.

In other words, a sober external appearance need not mean an absence of gaiety and extravagance 'licentiously flying out' within. It has been suggested that in writing about the wise man carrying gravity in public places, but being more relaxed in private, he had in mind his friend and travelling companion, Thomas Howard.[8]

The entry on the first page of the book, after the flyleaf, is dated 21 January 1614. In it he examined the fine detail of the many paintings, sculptures and drawings that he was seeing on his journey. He was turning the visit into a self-taught course in the techniques of classical art, even including little homilies to himself about how to avoid the faults he perceived in his techniques of drawing and writing. He looked first at how artists handled drapery, relevant to his costume designs for masques:

> The folds come either from some high place or from a gathering or girdle. Folds must be bigger in the middle than at each end, like muscles . . . The falling folds that come from a gathering in must be narrow at the top and another broader and narrow at the bottom . . . The women's garments are open on the right side commonly.

He went on to examine the clothing of different categories of subject – consuls, soldiers, gods, emperors – and noted, with his customary eye for detail and proportion: 'The drapery of clothed figures must cover half the feet.'

He illustrated his conclusions with a few drawings, some depicting the clothing he was discussing and some the heads of statues. Further on, a whole page of bearded faces accompanied his comments on how to represent hair. He discussed the depiction of children in a similar fashion, and his notes on how to mix and use colours in painting ran to a page and a half. Limbs were the next subjects to fall under his spotlight: 'to consider each member, whether it be soft, fat or coarse, and when it sits on any hard thing as stone and the buttock must spread'. He gave as an example a painting by Titian of Mary Magdalene, in which a hand pressed her flesh.

There were pages of notes on Roman antiquities, almost certainly written while he was visiting the sites, and having something of the travelogue about them. 'The circuit of Rome now is sixteen miles. The gates, that are now eighteen in number, enclose the seven hills.'

Statistics engrossed him. As well as seven hills, there were seven aqueducts, eight bridges over the Tiber and twenty-nine principal roads, the Appian Way being the most celebrated, 'called Queen of the Ways' because the Roman triumphs passed along it, from the Vatican to the Capitol. He made no mention of the Catacombs along the Appian Way, which had only recently been discovered and were not yet open to the public. On Monday 24 February he wrote about ancient public baths, whose distinctive architecture was an important influence on Palladio, and about the principal Roman theatres ('that of Pompeii was built in stone in Campo del Fiori, that of Marcellus in the Palace of Sanoli'), each of which could accommodate as many as 80,000 spectators. When he saw them they were all in ruins, as was Vespasian's gigantic Colosseum.

In addition to the sketches in his notebook, he was producing more ambitious drawings as he travelled around. Two have been positively identified. One is a view of the Castle of St Angelo, dated 19 May 1614, and another a head of the painter Guercino da Cento, who may have been one of the 'great masters' that Webb records him as having met on his Italian visits (although Guercino was in fact eighteen years his junior).[9]

Portrait of Inigo drawn by Francesca Villamena in Italy, 1614

One artist whom Inigo indisputably met at this time was Francesco Villamena, a Roman engraver and illustrator, who drew the first known portrait of him, probably during his stay in Rome. He is represented as a stern man with penetrating eyes, a high forehead, unruly hair, heavy jowls and a neatly trimmed moustache and beard. It is rather less flattering than Sir Anthony Van Dyck's later, better-known portrait, but has many affinities with William Dobson's portrayal of Inigo as an old man.

Curiously, Villamena enclosed his image within an oval frame on what seems to be a funerary monument, bearing the Latin inscription: 'Inigo Jones: architector Magnae Britaniae [architect of Great Britain]', with the artist's name beneath. David Howarth explains this apparently lugubrious context by interpreting Villamena to be suggesting that Inigo had revived the spirit of classical architecture in Britain, until then thought dead.[10] The engraving is now at Chatsworth, with the Duke of Devonshire's collection of Inigo's drawings. The purpose for which it was made can only be guessed at; but it does indicate that Inigo, as Webb suggested, had been introduced into the circle of the best Italian artists and had already gained a reputation as an up-and-coming architect.

Thomas Howard, who had clearly been assiduous in promoting the talents of his protégé, was also busy on his own account. He obtained permission to excavate one of the many ancient sites in Rome and to send any statues he found back to London, where they formed the core of the museum he was creating at Arundel House. This is thought to have been the earliest British-led archaeological dig overseas. For good measure, Howard commissioned some new statues in the Roman style from Egidio Moretti, a promising young sculptor who had worked on the façade of St Peter's. Some of Moretti's statues, along with ancient marbles that Howard excavated in Rome, are now at the Ashmolean Museum in Oxford.

Apart from gaining inspiration from the ruins of a great city, Inigo may also have enjoyed an experience that bore on his other significant talent, stage design. In February 1614 the Perettis, one of the leading aristocratic families in Rome, put on a memorably sumptuous masque. The suggestion that Inigo was in the audience came twenty-one years later from the Papal legate in London, Gregorio Panzani. Describing in a letter Inigo's designs for *The Temple of Love*, he wrote that they appeared to have been inspired by what he saw at the Peretti event.[11]

The group stayed in Rome for about two months before heading further south to the busy port of Naples, with a population even then of nearly half a million. For most of the 130 miles they followed the old Appian Way, as Inigo described in Book Three of his Palladio:

This way was made by Apio [the Emperor Appius Claudius Caecus] to Capua [north of Naples]. The rest it is imagined that Caesar built, but last of all restored by Trajan. This way I observed in my voyage to Naples 1614 and yet remains much entire.

He recorded that even the blocks placed alongside the road, to enable horsemen to mount and dismount, were still there. And on the way he spotted and noted examples of several of the styles of architecture illustrated by Palladio.

Howard was engrossed in the more practical aspects of the journey. Keen to accompany Inigo to Naples, he had left his wife temporarily in Rome, and wrote to her on 14 March arranging for her to join them. He confessed that he had 'done nothing for a lodging' but added that the sights of the southern city could be seen in quite a short time. He warned her, too, that the journey would be uncomfortable: 'On your way hither you shall find vile hostelries, one mattress, one blanket, no bolster or anything else.'

As for the traveller's perennial difficulty of identifying an acceptable currency for expenses on the road, he told her to tell Coke, who had stayed with her, to 'put all his money in pistoles', that is, gold coins.[12] Undeterred by these dire warnings, Aletheia made the journey and joined them in good order.

It was certainly true that there was less to see in and around Naples than in Rome: the ruins of Pompei, buried under lava from Mount Vesuvius in AD 79, had yet to be excavated. Still, Inigo found plenty to interest and instruct him. He paid at least two visits to the former Temple of Castor and Pollux (by then the church of San Paolo Maggiore), whose decoration had been commended by Palladio as showing 'that which is done by reason and is gracious, though it vary from the usual way, is good and to be followed'. To this Inigo added a note: 'This I observed Sunday 23 March and indeed these capitals are excellent.'

One of his designs for a doorway at the Banqueting House, with a broken pediment, seems to have been based on the sixteenth-century doorway to this church.[13] That he was in learning mode was confirmed by a visit to the ruined Roman baths at Baia, on the peninsula just west of the city, where he observed:

There are many walls with more courses of brick and some great brick amongst, for the Romans varied these things according to their caprice, mingling one with another, so it showed well.

He was still in Naples on 1 May, when he bought a two-volume book about the city and wrote his name and the date in each volume.[14] By the end of that month the party had returned to Rome, for he mentions watching fireworks and a procession marking the ninth anniversary of the Pope's enthronement on 29 May,[15] and records that he visited the Roman Pantheon on 'the last of May 1614'. In early June the party set off east to Tivoli, where he saw the Temple of Vesta on the 13th, then north to Trevi, where he made a note about another temple on the 16th. They travelled north slowly, and by early July had reached Florence, where the Grand Duke laid on a lavish welcome for them.[16] On 30 July Inigo, possibly now separated from the main party, was back in Venice and records that on 1 August he again sought out Scamozzi. By mid-August he had been drawn back to Vicenza, Palladio's heartland, probably taking Scamozzi with him.

He caught up with the Howards again in Genoa, where he had time for more sightseeing, wandering through the narrow streets lined with stately Renaissance palaces, many decorated in the spectacular *trompe l'oeil* fashion that characterises this corner of Italy. It is possible that he and the Howards stayed in one of them, for in Andrea Doria's republic private property owners were obliged to entertain important visitors. As always, Inigo absorbed the fine detail of the design of the houses, noting in Book One of *I Quattro Libri*: 'I have observed that some loggias are made without the house and others within . . . most commonly in the midst [but] two in the corners are much used in Genoa.'

Other travellers took account of different aspects of the city. James Howell, in his *Instructions for Foreign Travel*, published in 1642, wrote: 'There are in Genoa mountains without wood, sea without fish, women without shame and men without conscience.'

It was there that Howard learned of the death of his great-uncle, Henry Howard, Earl of Northampton, who had beqeathed him his house in Greenwich.[17] He needed to return to London in some haste, but found himself delayed by being strapped for cash. The practical difficulties of travel in the early seventeenth century included that of transmitting money from country to country, especially in the large sums needed when you were purchasing works of art on the way. By September he lacked sufficient ready money to satisfy the rapacious landlords of the 'vile hostelries' on whose mercies he and his party would be thrust on the homeward journey. He therefore borrowed a quantity of gold and silver coins from Giustiniani, giving as surety two gold rings inlaid with diamonds. He repaid the debt almost immediately after his return to London, and the rings were duly returned to him.[18]

His departure was further delayed by illness; but the party eventually left Genoa late in October for Turin, where the arcaded Piazza Castello, designed by Ascanio Vitozzi in the late sixteenth century, may have been one of the inspirations for Inigo's design for Covent Garden, along with the Place Royale in Paris and the main square at Livorno that he had seen on earlier visits. From Turin the route took them to Paris, where, like any modern traveller returning from the Continent, Howard stocked up with cases of fine wine before they all returned to London for Christmas.[19]

Edward Chaney has described Inigo's 1613–14 journey as 'arguably the most significant Grand Tour ever undertaken'.[20] The sights that he absorbed during this, his second and last Italian journey, profoundly influenced his development as an architect and designer. He had not been out of England for as long as he was the first time, but his maturity and experience allowed him to absorb a greater understanding of the works of the Italian masters. He had, too, bought books and made contacts that would nourish his artistic development. Now forty years old, he was a little more than halfway through his long life. As he disembarked on the Kentish coast, he may not have known that his career as a traveller was over; but he would surely have been confident that his most productive professional years were still before him.

Chapter Eleven

ON THEIR MAJESTIES' SERVICE

W HEN INIGO RETURNED to London at the end of 1614 he found a court racked by scandal. Although he was not directly implicated in it, he had likely been acquainted with someone who was. Who could say whether that taint, however remote, might count against his chance of inheriting the job of the King's Surveyor when Simon Basil died? It was true that James had already granted him the reversion – but anything that the King could give he could just as easily take away.

At the centre of the sordid series of events was Thomas Howard's cousin, the former Frances Howard, Countess of Essex, whose wedding at the age of thirteen had been celebrated in 1606 with such dazzling pomp. The marriage may have been a political triumph, but it proved such a personal disaster that the bride claimed it had never been consummated. At twenty she had developed into a great beauty. Rumours of her liaison with the late Prince Henry might have been without substance, but what was certain was that she had become enamoured of Robert Carr, now the King's most influential adviser, who reciprocated her feelings. She was determined to escape from her marriage to Essex and to marry Carr instead.

The scandal revolved around the death of Sir Thomas Overbury,

Carr's former friend and mentor. Overbury had at first collaborated with Carr in his affair with Frances Howard, even to the extent of composing love letters and poems to help the young man woo her. But when marriage became a possibility he changed his view, out of self-interest. He feared that the bride would bring her own circle of advisers into Carr's household, and that his position would therefore be undermined. He threatened to discredit the two lovers with the King if they went through with the marriage plan.

When Frances Howard learned of Overbury's hostility to the match she was furious, and determined on a ruthless and extreme course of action. She would remove her dangerous enemy from the scene, if necessary by killing him. At first she sought to use a hired murderer, but other aristocrats, opposed to Overbury for their own political reasons, came up with a more subtle plot. They persuaded the King to offer him an ambassadorial post abroad. Overbury knew that to disobey such a royal command was regarded as a contempt of the Crown, punishable by imprisonment, but he was reluctant to forfeit his comfortable position at court and turned down the post. He relied – foolishly, as it turned out – on his old friend Carr to dissuade the King from inflicting any punishment on him; but he had fatally underestimated how far his opposition to the intended wedding had infuriated the two lovers, and Carr refused to intervene. As a result, in April 1613 Overbury was arrested for flouting the King's instruction, and imprisoned in the Tower of London.

Although her enemy was now scarcely in a position to exert a decisive influence on her future plans, Frances Howard had the bit between her teeth. She was still convinced that to kill Overbury was the only way to remove once and for all the threat to her scheme of marrying the man she loved. And to help her plot the murder she turned to one of London's most scandalous women, the widow Anne Turner. This is where the story brushes up against Inigo. For Mrs Turner was a fashion-setting dressmaker, and to produce the effects that breathed life into his costume designs Inigo needed to call on the services of the most accomplished tailors and seamstresses in London. Two twentieth-century books about the Overbury case state unequivocally that Mrs Turner worked for him in that capacity, although neither cites a contemporary source to support the assertion.[1]

The red-headed beauty was born in Suffolk in 1576. The widow of George Turner, a court physician, she was also the long-term mistress of another courtier, Sir Arthur Mainwaring, by whom she had three children. In the world of fashion, she was best known for making and introducing into England the French vogue for high yellow starched ruffs and matching sleeves. These achieved immense popularity in the early years of the century, although allusions to them in contemporary literature indicate that they were regarded as not wholly respectable, a badge of a louche and wanton lifestyle. In *Philosophers Satyrs*, published in 1616, Robert Anton wrote:

> Each fantastic corner of the land,
> Stinks with the infection of a yellow band.

And Ben Jonson made the same point in his play *The Devil Is an Ass*: 'Carmen are got into the yellow starch, and chimney sweepers.' The Dean of Westminster so disapproved that he forbade churchgoers to wear the ruffs.[2]

For a few years, only Mrs Turner seems to have had the recipe for the yellow dye (it involved saffron) so she built up a lucrative monopoly. It was not, though, her fashion sense that drew Frances Howard to seek her aid. By reputation Mrs Turner was also a procuress, an abortionist and a dabbler in the black arts of alchemy, necromancy and sorcery that had a substantial following in Elizabethan and Jacobean England. Queen Elizabeth placed confidence in the advice of the astrologer and sorcerer John Dee, who had died as recently as 1608. Among his principal living followers was Dr Simon Forman, based across the Thames in Lambeth. Anne Turner was his client, and when courtiers wanted to get in touch with him and his underworld of occult practices, it was to her that they would first turn. A seventeenth-century commentator described her as 'a gentlewoman that from her youth had been given over to a loose kind of life'.[3]

Frances Howard may have met the seamstress when she was having her costumes made for *The Masque of Queens* in 1609 and *Tethys' Festival* the following year. She confided in her in the early stages of her plan to leave the Earl of Essex and attach herself to Carr. Mrs Turner took the young Countess to Lambeth to see Dr Forman, who supplied her with two potions, one to dampen her husband's ardour and the other to excite the passion of her lover. Mrs Turner also bought some of the latter for herself, since she was seeking to secure marriage to the father of her children.

Inconveniently for the two women, Simon Forman died before their plan to kill Overbury could reach maturity. But through his network of sorcery Mrs Turner had come to know a pharmacist in the City prepared to sell poisons. They bought some and mixed it into pies, jellies and wine, then suborned guards at the Tower to give them to the prisoner. The poisons were slow acting but their cumulative effect proved deadly. Overbury was sick for several weeks before succumbing on 14 September 1613.

While the circumstances of his death aroused suspicion and gossip, the crime would remain undetected for nearly two years. Before her divorce could be permitted, though, the Countess still had to endure not just a long legal hearing but also a medical examination to prove her contention that she was still a virgin. She survived that, despite strong rumours that another, purer girl had been substituted, her face heavily covered throughout to conceal her blushes. The divorce was finalised and on 26 December 1613 Frances Howard married Carr, the newly created Earl of Somerset, in the chapel of Whitehall Palace. Like her first marriage ceremony, it was conducted in the presence of the King, who was so pleased with the match that he gave the bride jewellery said to be worth £10,000.[4] At last she had achieved her ambition. She was Lady Somerset, wife of the King's most powerful adviser.

The newly wed couple's happiness did not last long. Political machinations continued and by the middle of 1614 Somerset was beginning to lose favour at court, his place in the King's affections being taken by the younger and prettier George Villiers, later to become Duke of Buckingham. When Inigo returned from Italy, the rivalry between the two men was at its most intense. Somerset's enemies, as a weapon against him, began to revive the rumours about Overbury's death, with suggestions that the Earl's new wife, if not Somerset himself, was deeply involved. Statements were taken from people who worked at the Tower and in September 1615 the King asked Sir Edward Coke, the Lord Chief Justice, to look into the matter.

Coke quickly found out about the poisoned food and drink, and all the evidence pointed to Anne Turner as a principal plotter. She was quickly brought to trial and found guilty, upon which Coke characterised her as 'a whore, a bawd, a sorcerer, a witch, a papist, a felon and a murderer, the daughter of the devil Forman'.[5] The tale of deadly intrigue in the boudoirs of power engrossed London society. Queen Anne, in a letter home to Denmark, observed: 'In this court nothing is spoken of except poisoning and sorcery.'[6] Mrs Turner knew where to pin the blame. Interviewed by a priest after her conviction, she said she wished the King had better servants, there being nothing among them but 'malice, pride, whoredom, swearing and rejoicing in the fall of others'. She wondered that the earth did not open to swallow up so wicked a place.[7]

Soon it would swallow her. Despite confessing and repenting, she was hanged at Tyburn on 14 November, brazenly wearing one of her famous yellow ruffs – which remained in fashion for another decade despite her disgrace.[8] The enormous public interest ensured that a huge crowd turned out to see her die. The following May, Lord and Lady Somerset went on trial for their suspected involvement in the affair, which some believed was part of a wider Catholic plot directed at the King. Inigo, as one of his first duties as Surveyor-General, was charged with fitting out Westminster Hall with seating to accommodate the large number of spectators, hungry for scandal.[9]

Although found guilty, the Somersets were protected by their social position and by the former patronage of King James. He reprieved them from the death penalty but confined them to the Tower of London, where they were allowed to live in a style that befitted their station, if not their offence, until their release in 1621. By that time their marriage had turned sour and there was never any question of their returning to their previous prominence or influence at court.

*　　*　　*

While Inigo might have been embarrassed by any former connection with the notorious seamstress, on balance the scandal had a positive impact on his progress at court. The marriage of Carr and Frances Howard in 1613, having the blessing of the King, clearly had to be celebrated with a masque, even two. Jonson and Campion were commissioned to write them but Inigo, away on his Italian idyll, was not available to work on the designs. As it transpired, this was a tremendous piece of luck. While in Prince Henry's service, he had been somewhat overshadowed by the European architects and designers that the Prince had engaged at some expense, especially the Florentine Constantino de' Servi, who had been allotted the lion's share of the architectural work relating to Richmond Palace. With the Prince dead, de' Servi, like Inigo and many others, was looking round for alternative patronage.

In Inigo's absence the Italian was asked to design Campion's masque for the Somerset wedding. If successful, this would be his chance to gain favour with the King, even perhaps replacing Inigo as first choice for future masques. He prepared for the challenge meticulously, writing home to Florence for books containing designs for entertainments that had been performed there. But his efforts were to no avail. His settings, costumes and stage devices for the wedding masque were roundly criticised on all sides, especially by Campion, who complained that de' Servi had been too vain and secretive to consult the author before committing himself to the designs. The result was that the whole piece 'was of force drawn into far narrower compass than was from the beginning intended'. Moreover, the machinery did not work nearly as smoothly as Inigo's: the device for lowering the clouds proved cumbersome and noisy. The prolific correspondent John Chamberlain wrote: 'I hear little or no commendation of the masque made by the lords that night, only that it was rich and costly.'

The most comprehensive criticism came from Giovanni Battista Gabaleoni, the London agent of the Duke of Savoy, although it must be read in the context of a ferocious dispute that he had been conducting with the agent from Florence, de' Servi's home city, about who should be sitting closest to the King at the event. He reported back to his Duke:

He [de' Servi] has disgraced himself, if truth be told, and mis-spent much of these gentlemen's money . . . What they had thought would be a marvellous thing – the descent of a cloud with twelve lords, richly clothed and much adorned, who were to perform the masque – turned out to be that he had fixed a lowering device behind the cloud, just like one used in dropping a portcullis . . . When it came down one could see the ropes that supported it and hear the pulleys, or rather wheels, making the same noise as when they raise or lower the mast of a ship.

Inigo would never have countenanced that. And the envoy's report on the masque concluded:

Apart from having seen their majesties in good order and with great majesty, and also the great number of ladies, one could see nothing that came anywhere near meriting the inconvenience of the thousands of people who waited twelve hours without dinner.[10]

De' Servi's creative failure, and the poor critical response to his work, effectively assured the absent Inigo of an enthusiastic welcome on his eventual return. The loud grinding of the gears on the Italian's cloud-lowering mechanism showed that stage engineering was not as easy as Inigo made it look. So even if there had been damaging fallout from any association with the dangerous Mrs Turner, it counted for nothing against London society's new-found appreciation of his skills.

Nor did the case affect his relationship with his patron, Thomas Howard. The two men had become close during their travels in Italy, and for a time Howard was Inigo's most important link with the court. On 30 July 1615 he wrote to his Countess, at home in Arundel House, from Wiltshire, where he had been visiting the Earl of Pembroke at Wilton. The King was due to dine at Wilton the following week, and the Earl was anxious that Inigo should be among the guests, perhaps to discuss some work at the house. The letter discussed the arrangements for taking the architect to Wilton, and also mentioned a deal he was doing with one of Howard's agents to bring more antiquities and pictures from Italy.[11]

The Earl's appetite for such things had been greatly sharpened by their visit, and Inigo, as Cecil had discovered during the Matthew affair, was an enthusiastic and competent negotiator. A few months later he helped Howard evaluate twelve pictures that Carleton had acquired in Venice for Robert Carr before the errant Earl was sent to the Tower, where he was presumed not to be in a position to take delivery. They included six Tintorettos, three Veroneses and a Titian. Originally it was agreed that the works should be divided between Howard and the statesman Lord Danvers (later Earl of Danby), so Inigo carefully selected what he thought were the best half-dozen on Howard's behalf. In the end Danvers dropped out and Howard took them all, after Inigo had negotiated a price of £200.[12]

Howard was also making use of his new friend's architectural skills, if only in a small way. Internal alterations were under way at the house in Greenwich that the Earl had just inherited from his uncle, and which his new pictures would help furnish. Tragically, the work came to a sudden end the following January, when the house burned down, destroying all the paintings save for a single Tintoretto. Inigo would contribute, too, to the adaptation of Arundel House to accommodate Howard's growing collection of paintings, prints and sculptures, and to the design of two Palladian gateways in its garden that were drawn by John Smythson, son of the Elizabethan architect.[13] In Daniel Mytens's portrait of Howard, painted in 1618, the Earl is shown sitting outside a sculpture gallery that may well represent Inigo's design. It is decorated in a plain, somewhat severe classical style, so as not to detract from the impact of the statues ranged along the wall. At the far end it looks out across an iron railing to the Thames and the Surrey hills beyond.

It is probable that he designed other buildings for wealthy courtiers in this period, but documentary evidence is lacking and the buildings themselves have vanished. He is credited with a house in Holborn for Sir Fulke Greville, Chancellor of the Exchequer, and one in the Strand for Colonel Edward Cecil, later Viscount Wimbledon.[14] Yet although he was by now intimate with one of England's premier earls, and in growing demand both as an architect and for his royal stage designs, Inigo still lacked the security and status of office. That goal was finally achieved on 1 October 1615, two weeks after the death of Simon Basil, Surveyor of the King's Works. With de' Servi discredited, no rival candidate appeared on the scene to impede his promised inheritance of the position.

As Inigo stood on the brink of a promising future, it was appropriate that the masque for that winter, on which he and Jonson would have already started work by the autumn, was called *The Golden Age Restored*. None of Inigo's designs for it appears to have survived but Jonson's theme, the cleansing of a corrupt court, was certainly meant as a topical reference to the Overbury murder, with the spotless new favourite Villiers compared favourably to the tainted Carr, still awaiting trial when the masque was performed:[15]

> Now peace and love, faith, joys, all, all increase;
> And strife and hate and fear and pain all cease . . .
> Of all there seems a second birth,
> It is become a heaven on earth.

Inigo's return to the Whitehall stage was a triumph. The King liked the masque so much that he ordered a repeat performance a few nights later.

Inigo's salary in his new post was a mere 2s 6d a day,[16] sixpence less than he was paid by Prince Henry; but on top of that an array of perks went with the job. The royal accounts show that he received 8s a day for his 'entertainment', meaning the provision of servants; £80 a year for his 'avails' – perhaps business expenses – and 2s 8d a day for travel costs. He was, too, expected to look the part, at least on official occasions. A warrant from the King, dated 16 March 1616, instructed the Master of the Wardrobe to issue him with five yards of broad cloth for a gown, at 26s 8d a yard, to be decorated with a fur of budge (lamb's skin) at £4; four and a half yards of baize lining at 10s a yard; plus 20s to cover the work of tailoring and furring. According to the warrant, a new gown of the same design was to be delivered to the Surveyor on All Saints' Day (1 November) every year for the rest of his life.[17]

Along with Simon Basil's position he took over his house, although this did not strictly count as a perk because he had to pay rent of £46 a year for it to Basil's widow until Charles I relieved him of the obligation some years later. The house was in Scotland Yard, so named because the Kings of Scotland used to lodge there when they visited London, a purpose that became redundant when the two crowns were united. Scotland Yard, between Whitehall Palace and Charing Cross, had long been the site of the Surveyor's store yard. When Basil took over the position he obtained a lease for part of the property, pulled down some old buildings and built a modern house for himself, alongside his departmental office.[18]

Inigo must have been pleased that such a convenient residence went with the job. The local records for the poor rates show that he lived there for most of the rest of his life, even after he lost the Surveyor's position at the start of the Civil War. For the most part he is listed as the sole resident, except for one year, 1621, when Alice Revell is named alongside him. She was almost certainly the widow of Robert Revell, who lived next to Inigo in Scotland Yard until he died in 1620 and is described in the St Martin's burial register as a crown servant, presumably in the Surveyor's department. It is possible he was descended from John Revell, Surveyor-General between 1560 and 1563. His family connection would have ensured him a position in the department and that would explain why Inigo took in his widow following her bereavement. Their relationship, whatever it was, seems not to have lasted long, for her name does not appear on any further registers at his address.

Any euphoria that Inigo may have experienced, as he looked at the tangible benefits of his new post, will have evaporated as soon as he examined the books. From them, it was apparent that he had inherited a serious financial crisis. According to John Webb, his pupil and his first biographer, the office had contracted a debt of 'several thousands of pounds' under his predecessor, due to the King's extravagance in commissioning new buildings and improving existing royal residences. The Privy Council summoned the new Surveyor to discuss what could be done to resolve the crisis, 'the Exchequer being empty and the workmen clamorous'.

Inigo's response was to offer to forego his emoluments until the debt was cleared, adding that he had persuaded the other senior officials in the department to do the same.[19] Certainly the accounts show that expenditure was markedly lower during his term of office than in Basil's. From the time he inherited the job until shortly before the Civil War in 1640, the average annual cost of the King's works was £6717, as against £11,348 in the first twelve years of King James's reign.[20]

Inigo's first architectural assignment for the royal household was suitably modest, setting the tone for his cost-controlling regime. The task was to design a brewhouse and stable block at Newmarket.[21] Hunting was the King's favourite outdoor activity, and when he came to the throne in 1603 he found facilities for the pursuit sadly lacking. It was possible to hunt in the vicinity of the palaces near London – Eltham and Greenwich in Kent; Richmond, Oatlands and Nonsuch in Surrey – but the sport was better in the less populated countryside to the north-east. That was one reason why the King had pressed Cecil to swap Theobalds for Hatfield, and why he acquired land at Newmarket for a residence and stables. This first royal link with the Suffolk town would lead later in the century to James's grandson, Charles II, building England's finest racecourse there, and eventually to its becoming the headquarters of English horse racing. Inigo designed a number of buildings for King James at Newmarket[22] but not all were built and none remains standing.

While expenditure on royal works had been cut, it had not been frozen entirely. In 1616, when he had been in the job for just a year, Inigo was given the chance to design his first important building. Since the early fifteenth century, Greenwich, on the south bank of the Thames east of the City, had been the site of one of the most important royal palaces. Henry VIII and his daughter Queen Elizabeth were both born there and, as monarchs, spent as much time there as they could. It was at Greenwich that Sir Walter Raleigh famously spread his cloak across a puddle so that Elizabeth would not get her feet wet.

James made some use of the palace in the first years of his reign but in 1613 he turned it over, along with the surrounding park, to his wife Anne, as a peace offering after a torrid domestic dispute that began when the Queen accidentally killed the King's favourite hound while hunting.[23] The breakdown in relations was so complete that James compensated Anne not just with a palace but also with a diamond said to be worth £2000. Duly pacified, the Queen set out to develop her new property and was pleased that she could call on the skills of Inigo, who had done such great things in designing her masques.

The brief was not a straightforward one. About a hundred yards south of Greenwich Palace, going away from the river, was a much-used highway that divided the palace grounds from the park. The road was straddled by a Tudor gatehouse. Anne wanted this pulled down and replaced by a pleasure house for relaxing and receiving guests. It was to be a small house by comparison with a full-blown mansion or palace. Although there would be bedrooms, there were no extensive servants' quarters or kitchens because those were available in the main palace. The most formidable architectural challenge was that she wanted the building to follow the basic pattern of the gatehouse by occupying both sides of the road, linked by a bridge room that would allow her and her friends to cross from the palace to the park without getting their feet muddy or being forced to mingle with passers-by on the highway.

With a commission at last worthy of his talents, Inigo went to his bookshelves and leafed through his works on Italian architecture. From them, he conceived at least two designs for the new house, charging Anne £10 for one plan and £16 for the other. The one she chose was for a villa based on the letter H, with the central horizontal acting as the bridge over the highway, between two long ranges on either side. It was based on the villa at Poggio a Caiano, near Florence, designed in 1485 by Giulianio da Sangallo, that Inigo must surely have visited on his Italian journey.[24] That was also built essentially in two sections, linked by a large hall over a road.

The Tudor gatehouse was removed in the summer of 1617 and construction got under way. A year later, though, work was suspended, with only the ground floor completed, plus a basement on the north range. The two sides were still not linked by the bridge room. Part of the reason for the suspension was that Anne had fallen ill, but there seems little doubt that a more compelling motive was the rapidly escalating cost and the difficulty of finding ready money to pay the workers. By the time the building was temporarily abandoned, covered with thatch to keep out the elements, an estimated £4000 had been spent on it.

To have his first major royal project shelved while only half finished would have been a tremendous disappointment for someone so engrossed in his calling. Yet even in its incomplete state it was apparent that the Queen's House represented a concept of architecture that had not been seen in England before. In one of his letters to Carleton, Chamberlain termed it 'a curious device'. He was surely not referring just to the oddity of its being built in two sections but to the spare, geometric nature of Inigo's design, which would have looked incongruous set against the background of the traditional Tudor palace to its north. Inigo had adhered rigidly to one of the principles he had recorded in his Roman notebook a few years earlier: that the exterior of houses should exude a dignified quality, with little ornament, like a wise man putting on a mask of gravity in public places. His ground plan was equally disciplined, adhering to the Palladian principle of proportion, with balancing rooms grouped symmetrically around a cubic central entrance hall.

While working on the Queen's House Inigo had time for some smaller commissions, many of them also for the Queen. In the garden of Greenwich Palace itself he created an arbour and seats, made a new gateway from the palace into the park and a new window for the chapel.[25] He created a masque for her that was performed at Somerset House, her London residence – still called Denmark House, even though it was ten years since her brother Christian's visit. There, and at St James's Palace, Inigo designed some internal alterations, and he upgraded the Duke of Buckingham's lodgings in Whitehall. A ceremonial gateway to the vineyard at Oatlands, the royal house and hunting lodge between Walton and Weybridge in Surrey, was one of the improvements ordered by the Queen for a banquet she was giving for the Venetian ambassador.[26] It had two imaginative, slightly bulbous colonnades on each side of its arch, divided as though they had been pinched in at the waist.[27]

Gateways were a useful device for an architect experimenting with a new style with which his clients were largely unfamiliar. They performed much the same function as those miniature pieces of furniture once made by craftsmen to show off their repertoire of forms and designs. A gateway, usually inside or at the entrance to a garden, was purely decorative: nobody had to imagine living in it, or gazing at it for long if they found it too 'modern' to appreciate. Additionally, an architect basing his style on that of the ancient Romans could make pleasing connections with the triumphal arches that formed an important part of their cityscapes.

Inigo's best-known gateway was designed in the early years of his Surveyorship, but it was a private commission. The client was his friend Lionel Cranfield, a fellow guest at Coryate's Feast, whose climb up the perilous ladder of court favour had taken him so far to the positions of Master of the Wards and Chief Commissioner of the Navy. Cranfield had bought Beaufort House in Chelsea – once the riverside home of Sir Thomas More, Henry VIII's ill-fated Lord Chancellor – and asked Inigo to design a gateway to seal the approach to the house from the north.

It is a strictly classical design, a rusticated stone arch adorned with Doric columns supporting a triangular pediment, and it proved more enduring than Cranfield's political career. After rising to the position of Treasurer and being made Earl of Middlesex, Inigo's patron fell victim to the fickle nature of Jacobean public life and in 1624 was convicted by the House of Lords of taking bribes. He was imprisoned in the Tower for a while and fined a colossal £50,000, forcing him to sell the Chelsea house and ending his public career. The gate, by contrast, stayed where it was until Beaufort House was acquired a century later by Sir Hans Sloane, the royal physician and a founding father of the British Museum. In 1740 he gave the gateway to the Earl of Burlington, Inigo's most fervent eighteenth-century disciple, who had it re-erected in the garden of his Palladian villa in Chiswick, where it remains. A

Gateway designed by Inigo for Beaufort House, Chelsea

verse to celebrate the gift has been attributed to both William Kent and Alexander Pope:

> Ho! Gate, how came ye here?
> I came from Chelsea the last year.
> Inigo Jones there put me together;
> When I was dropping by wind and weather
> Sir Hans Sloane
> Let me alone
> But Burlington brought me hither.

A more substantial private commission during Inigo's early years as Surveyor-General was his first recorded design for a theatre. The drawings, now at Worcester College in Oxford, have been persuasively identified by John Orrell as being for the Cockpit Theatre (later known

. . . now at Chiswick House

as the Phoenix) in Drury Lane. Originally an actual cockpit, built of brick, it was acquired in 1616 by Christopher Beeston, an actor turned impresario, who had it converted into a theatre where his company, Queen Anne's Men, could perform in the winter. (In summer they played in the courtyard of the Red Bull in Clerkenwell.)

Beeston may have hired Inigo to design the conversion because his official position could help avoid any difficulties in getting approval from the planning authorities: the actor had already been in trouble over unauthorised extensions he had made to his house in Clerkenwell. The regulations forbade building on new foundations[28] but since this was an existing building, though much enlarged, it was allowed to go ahead.

Inigo's interest in theatre design is shown by the number of jottings he made on the subject in the margins of his Italian books on architecture. In Chapter Seven of Alberti's *L'Architettura* he carefully noted the differences between Greek and Roman theatres, regarding the height of the stage, the position of the doors and the shape of the auditorium. He took a keen interest in acoustics, in how 'to keep in and make the voice sound the more'. The Worcester College drawing shows the influence of Serlio and of Scamozzi, whose indoor theatre at Sabbioneta, between Parma and Mantua, would almost certainly have been on Inigo's Italian itinerary. The auditorium is round, with a semi-circular seating area that had been a feature of the former cockpit. The wooden interior was painted to resemble stone.[29] It was badly damaged in an apprentices' riot in 1617, less than a year after it opened.

One of the new Surveyor-General's most unusual assignments for the court was to design a silkworm house at Oatlands in 1616. Although silk originated in China and the Far East, the French and Italians had been producing it since the fifteenth century and James I made it a point of national pride to establish a British silk industry. So he issued an edict in 1607 to the effect that mulberry trees, on whose leaves silkworms feed, should be planted in every English county. The mulberry is a long-lived tree, and some of those planted as a result of his campaign are still with us after 400 years. Sadly, though, they are the wrong sort of mulberry. Only the red variety thrives in the English climate, while the worms prefer the white; so the King's plans for a lucrative new British industry were stillborn.

By 1616, though, the lesson had not yet been learned. The mulberry trees imported nine years earlier were now in full leaf, and James commanded that an outhouse should be built at Oatlands where the worms could form the cocoons from which the silk thread is extracted. Inigo must have looked at designs of such specialist buildings elsewhere and came up with a two-storey structure whose top floor was a single room lined with wooden shelving for the worms, while the ground floor was divided into four small rooms. But it was not purely functional: it had a decorated frieze, a crested tiled roof and one of the rooms boasted a carved mantelpiece.[30]

Early in 1617 the King and some 500 courtiers, including Howard, made the long journey north to visit Edinburgh, his Scottish capital. Inigo was given the job of furnishing a chapel for the royal party –

Inigo Jones (Hogarth)

Andrea Palladio

Thomas Howard, Earl of Arundel, and his wife Aletheia, in these separate paintings by Mytens, are depicted in the sculpture gallery designed by Inigo at Arundel House

Ben Jonson
(attributed to Abraham van Blyenberch)

Robert Cecil, Earl of Salisbury
(John de Critz the Elder)

The Pont du Gard in the eighteenth century

An aristocrat in masque costume (Marcus Gheeraerts the Younger)

Henry, the ill-fated Prince of Wales, enjoying field sports

James I in front of Inigo's
new Banqueting House
(Paul Van Somer)

The Rubens ceiling in the Banqueting House

The Banqueting House

Anne of Denmark outside Oatlands Palace

The Queen's House, Greenwich

Henrietta Maria (Van Dyck)

The Queen's Chapel, St James's

Somerset House in the eighteenth century (Canaletto)

Charles I (Mytens)

One of the two pavilions at
Stoke Park, Northamptonshire,
probably designed by Inigo

A scene from Luminalia (1638)

The double cube room at Wilton House

a tricky assignment because the strong Puritan streak among Scottish Protestants meant that he would have to avoid any too flagrant religious symbolism. He seems not to have travelled to Scotland himself but to have sent instructions with Nicholas Stone, a Devonshire man who had trained in Amsterdam between 1606 and 1613 and had returned to become London's best stonemason. He and Inigo would work closely together on several future occasions, and would become lifelong friends.[31] Stone was a designer as well as a master mason; the gateway outside the Oxford University Botanic Garden was once attributed to Inigo, but it is now accepted as the work of his friend.

The silkworm house and other such commissions were comparatively small beer for a man impatient to make his mark as the court's principal architect. Inigo's only other major royal assignment in his early years was, like the first stage of the Queen's House, destined to end in frustration. In 1617 he was asked to draw plans for a new Court of Star Chamber within the precinct of Whitehall Palace. In the Tudor and Stuart periods this court, named after its ceiling decoration, was an important instrument for exerting the authority of the monarch, especially when dealing with offences against the state. Made up of judges and privy councillors, sitting without a jury, there was always a strong political element to its decisions, usually enforced rapidly and without mercy.

Because the number of cases dealt with by the court had increased in the turbulent era that began in the last years of Elizabeth, King James wanted a larger and more impressive home for it; but from the beginning there were doubts whether he could afford such extravagance. Chamberlain wrote to Carleton that the King was keen to build it 'if there were money'. Inigo anyway went ahead with the design, which has come down to us in a version drawn by Webb after his master's death. It would have been the most characteristically Palladian of all his buildings. Above the rusticated ground floor was a portico, its pediment supported by four Corinthian columns. This was flanked by two bays on each side, while at either end of the frontage two tall, rectangular colonnades covered all three stories. It would have made a fitting companion for the Banqueting House that he was to design – and, finally, to see completed – a few years later. But in the end, frustratingly, all he was permitted to accomplish at the Star Chamber was a modest refurbishment.

Chapter Twelve

THE BANQUETING HOUSE:
HARMONY AMID DISORDER

EVEN IF HIS WORK as the King's Surveyor was turning out to be less fulfilling than he had hoped when he took on the role, Inigo's reputation and social standing continued to rise. In 1617 his old friend Edmund Bolton put a bold plan to the King for the establishment of a royal academy of the most eminent of his subjects, with particular emphasis on the arts and sciences. One of its functions would be to evaluate and in effect censor new publications. The optimistic Bolton proposed that Windsor Castle should be given over to the academy, turning the royal residence into a kind of British version of Olympus, the home of the omniscient Gods.

Members would be entitled to wear a distinctive ribbon and piece of jewellery and were to be divided into three categories. Two of these would be based largely on rank, including knights of the garter, the chancellors of Oxford and Cambridge Universities and sundry noblemen. The third group, called the 'essentials', would carry most prestige, embracing the best minds of their generation. Bolton's initial list included poets such as George Chapman and Ben Jonson; the diplomats Sir Kenelm Digby and Sir Henry Wotton; the judge Sir

Edward Coke; Inigo's former 'prisoner' Sir Tobie Matthew – and Inigo himself.[1]

The King was much taken with the idea – and so, more to the point, was his handsome favourite George Villiers, by now Duke of Buckingham. Thus encouraged, Bolton set about trying to put it into effect; but progress was slow and funding scarce, and it was not until 1624 that all the elements seemed finally to be in place. The King's death the following year put paid to the scheme, for his son Charles showed no interest. It would be another forty years, after the restoration of Charles II, before a body with comparable aims, though on a more modest scale, came into being as the Royal Society.

For Inigo to be included on Bolton's list of the great and the talented was an honour that he must have relished. To bring him down to earth, the Twelfth Night masque for 1618 earned him and Jonson poor reviews, almost for the first time since they had started their partnership twelve years earlier. The masque was *Pleasure Reconciled to Virtue*, in which the seventeen-year-old Prince Charles danced, and whose closing Saturnalia – and the discomfort of his seat – had so horrified Orazio Busino, the Venetian chaplain.[2]

Its subject was Hercules, confronted with the dilemma of whether to make pleasure or virtue the ruling passion of his life. In the end he decided that the two were not incompatible. While the pursuit of pleasure should not dominate, if enjoyed in moderation it still allowed plenty of time for the practice of virtue. This was essentially the philosophy that Inigo had expressed in his Roman notebook, when he wrote about wise men carrying gravity in public places, yet being 'inwardly easy' and moved both to laughter and contemplation. As Jonson wrote in the masque, it was possible:

> To walk with Pleasure, not to dwell.
> These, these are hours by Virtue spared
> Herself, she being her own reward.

Although he complained about conditions for the spectators, Busino's report on the masque itself was less critical than others'. He was impressed with Inigo's opening image of Mount Atlas, its peak in the form of a giant human head which 'rolled its eyes and moved itself with wonderful cunning'. Chamberlain described the action, demonstrating the evils of pleasure when taken to excess:

> In the first act a fat Bacchus, sitting on a cart pulled by four men, sang a song, then twelve men dressed in barrels appeared, followed by a dozen boys disguised as frogs, who did a grotesque dance with each other.

Bacchus's song was evidence of Jonson's versatility: at one moment writing lyrically of virtue being her own reward, at the next composing doggerel, if superior doggerel:

> Room, room, make room for the bouncing belly,
> First father of sauce and deviser of jelly.

Chamberlain resumed the tale:

> Mercury came on stage to make a speech praising the king. A guitar player, attended by a high priest wearing red robes, sang a number of Italian songs badly enough to upset Busino.[3]

Then Prince Charles entered, leading a dozen knights wearing black masks with feathers on their heads, prancing in the formation of a pyramid with the Prince at its apex.

After that the general dancing began; but it was altogether too desultory for the King, who had been sitting impatiently through the piece and was now unable to contain his anger. In describing what happened, Busino provided an insight into the qualities needed to be a royal favourite:

> Finally they danced the Spanish dance once more with their ladies and because they were tired began to lag; and the King, who is by nature choleric, grew impatient and shouted loudly: 'Why don't they dance? What did you make me come here for? Devil take all of you, dance!' At once the Marquis of Buckingham, his majesty's favourite

minion, sprang forward, and danced a number of high and very tiny capers with such grace and lightness that he made everyone admire and love him, and also managed to calm the rage of his angry lord.

The Venetian went on to describe how the young Prince of Wales made an elaborate show of bowing humbly to his father and kissing his hand, despite the exertions of the evening: 'Because of his youth, he does not have much breath; nevertheless he cut some capers with considerable grace.'

The King was not the only spectator dissatisfied with the night's entertainment. Edward Sherburn, another man-about-court who kept Carleton up to date with the London gossip, told him in a letter on 10 January:

It came far short of the expectation and Mr Inigo Jones hath lost in his reputation in regard some extraordinary device was looked for (it being the Prince his first masque) and a poorer was never seen.

Another observer, Nathaniel Brent, proctor of Oxford University, blamed Jonson rather than Inigo:

The masque on Twelfth Night is not commended of any. The poet is grown so dull that his device is not worth the relating, much less copying out. Divers [many] think fit he should return to his old trade of bricklaying.[4]

Despite this negative response and the King's impatience with the dancing, Inigo and Jonson now had to face the prospect of mounting the masque a second time, at the insistence of the Queen, who had been too ill to attend the first performance. It was decided to do it on Shrove Tuesday, only a few weeks away. Jonson sought to freshen it up by writing a completely new antimasque called *For the Honour of Wales*, involving some broad Welsh comedy. The same mountain was used in the opening scene, but instead of identifying it as Atlas, the Welsh rustics referred to it as a mountain in Wales.[5] This change may have been meant as a tribute to the Prince of Wales, although a mischief-maker could have seen some of Jonson's Welsh jokes as a jibe against Inigo's family origins. In any event, the hyper-critical Brent was still not satisfied, reporting that the second version contained 'some few additions of goats and Welsh speeches sufficient to make an Englishman laugh and a Welshman choleric'.[6]

Based purely on his position as Surveyor and masque designer, Inigo's relationship with the King would have been that of master and servant, lacking the intimate access to the monarch enjoyed by peers of the realm and gentlemen of the bedchamber. On the few occasions when he did enjoy such access it was through his continuing close friendship with Howard, as is shown in another tale passed on by Chamberlain. In the autumn of 1618, Howard and Inigo, who were staying at Theobalds, visited nearby Ware Park, where one of the most renowned Jacobean gardens had been created by Sir Henry Fanshawe. Sir Henry Wotton, the former ambassador in Venice, was extravagant in praise of the Ware bedding schemes in his book *The Elements of Architecture*.

Chamberlain was a frequent visitor to the house and he too had written glowing accounts of the horticultural paradise that Sir Henry was in the midst of developing when he died in 1616 at the age of forty-seven.[7] After his death the garden was still maintained by the family and 1618 saw an exceptionally good crop of fruit. Inigo and Howard sampled the grapes and peaches with delight, and must either have taken some back to Theobalds for the King to try, or at least given him a mouth-watering account of their succulence and flavour. The result was that the King asked to be provided with a supply of Ware fruit twice a week; although Chamberlain expressed doubt whether the Fanshawe family would ever receive (or indeed demand) payment.[8]

Inigo will have enjoyed his short breaks at country homes and gardens all the more because he was learning that many aspects of his position as Surveyor-General were centred on London and took him to the least salubrious parts of the capital. Designing new buildings was only part of it, and quite a small part at that. His toughest and most time-consuming task was to try to ensure that London's crude planning laws were adhered to, preventing the construction of anything that would cause inconvenience or hazard to others, or that tried to cram too many people into a restricted space, endangering the citizens' health.

Like Queen Elizabeth in her later years, both James I and Charles I regarded town planning as of great importance. The attractions of Stuart London – of which Inigo's masques and Jonson's plays were significant ingredients, along with the lure of fashionable shops – meant that the gentry, once content to spend most of their time in the country, swarmed to the City in ever growing numbers, swelling its population by some 4000 a year.[9] Not only did they bring with them scores of servants, putting further pressure on the amenities of the inner city, but their presence lured more and more artisans and traders, keen to serve this expanding market. It was a vicious circle. Supplies of food were stretched, so prices inevitably rose, provoking discontent among the poorer citizens.

In 1616, in a speech to the Star Chamber, the King, in forthright and colourful fashion, likened the uncontrolled growth of London to 'the spleen in the body, which, in measure as it overgrows, the body wastes'. It was essential, he insisted, that country gentlemen stayed in the country:

> Therefore as every fish lives in his own place, some in the fresh, some in the salt, some in the mud: so let everyone live in his own place, some at court, some in the city, some in the country.

He had no doubts about where to pin the principal blame for the rush to the capital, nor about its damaging effects on domestic harmony:

> One of the greatest causes of all gentlemen's desire, that have no calling or errand, to dwell in London, is apparently the pride of women: for if they be wives, then their husbands, and if they be maids, then their fathers must bring them up to London, because the new fashion is to be had nowhere but London: and here, if they be unmarried, they mar their marriages, and if they be married they lose their reputations and rob their husbands' purses.[10]

This was not a new complaint, nor one that was confined to London.

In the margin of page 251 of his copy of Alberti's *L'Architettura*, written in Rome in the fifteenth century, Inigo had made a note of this passage: 'The ancients desired not to enjoy both city and country houses. One who tends the city business must there live. The city is a magazine [repository] of stinks.'

Ben Jonson must have recognised that, among other attractions, it was his plays rather than the stinks that drew people to London. He compensated by doing his bit in supporting the King's campaign to persuade country-dwellers to stay at home. Before 1615 he wrote a poem, 'To Sir Robert Wroth', congratulating the knight, 'though so near the city and the court', on sticking to the pleasures of the country:

> . . . Nor com'st to view the better cloth of state;
> The richer hangings, or crown plate,
> Nor throng'st (when masquing is) to have a sight
> Of the short braverie of the night;
> To view the jewels, stuffs, the pains, the wit
> There wasted! Some not paid for yet.

Apart from the danger of social instability inherent in large-scale migration into London, it meant a growing demand for housing. Unless the quality of new buildings was strictly controlled, they would quickly turn into hovels, fertile breeding grounds for the epidemics of the bubonic plague that were recurring with ever greater frequency. A serious outbreak in 1603, the year that James came to the throne, had killed 30,000 people in London alone.[11]

By the end of Queen Elizabeth's reign the Privy Council had already begun to tighten up its enforcement of rules barring any building on new foundations, and some offending tenements were pulled down.[12] On 1 March 1605 the King issued a proclamation placing a moratorium on any new house building until the end of the following September. After that, all new houses should be made of brick or stone and have frontages of at least twenty feet, with stories at least ten feet high. Two years later a further proclamation forbade building any new houses around London except by special licence, while old houses were to be rebuilt under even more stringent regulations, ensuring that they 'cannot be inhabited but by persons of some ability'.[13]

Several prosecutions were brought, and a few offending houses demolished, but in the main it was only the relatively poor and powerless who were punished. Men of greater wealth and rank could simply pay a fee to the exchequer (and probably a bribe or two to individual officials) to gain exemption from the regulations. As Parliament became less and less willing to approve funds for James and later Charles, these fines became a useful source of royal revenue – and by the same token a less effective means of controlling urban sprawl.

On 16 July 1615, only months before appointing Inigo as his Surveyor, the King issued a further proclamation for 'an utter cessation of further new buildings' in London, except on old foundations and in brick, 'lest the surcharge and overflow of people do bring upon our said city infinite inconveniences'. He declared:

> Our City of London is become the greatest or next the greatest city of the Christian world . . . As it was said of the first emperor of Rome [Augustus] that he had found the city of Rome of brick and left it of marble, so we, whom God have honoured to be the first King of Great Britain, might be able to say in some proportion that we found our city and suburbs of London of sticks, and left them of brick, being a material far more durable, safe from fire and beautiful and magnificent.[14]

The quotation from Augustus harked back to what Sir Francis Bacon had written in the last years of Queen Elizabeth's reign, about her receiving a realm of cottages and turning it into a realm of palaces. In 1615, Bacon was James's Attorney-General, and it is likely that he had a hand in drafting the proclamation.

Noting that his previous edicts had not so far achieved the desired effect, the King went on to speculate that this was because he had 'carried so moderate a hand and so mixed our clemency with our justice, as the fruit of a reformation may not have too much of the sour grape'. But the time had now come to wield the big stick, to 'leave words and to act and execute our princely ordinance'. To implement this new determination to enforce the rules, he established a high-powered Commission for Buildings, including all thirty-three members of the Privy Council and twenty-two others, to examine and regulate construction in the capital. Inigo was not originally a member of the Commission, probably because it was created shortly before he became Surveyor General; but he had joined it at the latest by 1618. He certainly had a hand in drafting new proclamations in the following two years, imposing specific rules on new buildings: uniform frontages with walls of a minimum thickness; a bar on overhangs, bay windows and thatched roofs; no patching up of old, unsound structures.

In 1618 he was appointed, along with Thomas Howard, to a separate commission of seventy-five men, specifically charged with controlling building on and around Lincoln's Inn Fields. As the City spread west along the Strand and Holborn, this open space, together with nearby Covent Garden, was the obvious target for the next stage of urban sprawl. Originally at Lincoln's Inn there were three fields in separate ownership – Purse Field, Cup Field and Ficket's Field – covering a far more extensive area than the garden square that remains of them today. The first two had been owned by monasteries until the Dissolution.

In 1613 an application had been made to build on Purse Field, at the corner of Drury Lane and High Holborn. Local residents, including the Society of Lincoln's Inn, protested to the Privy Council, which refused permission for the development. The Council agreed with the protestors that the fields should be made into public walks, as:

> a means to frustrate the covetous and greedy endeavours of such persons as daily seek to fill up that small remainder of air in those parts with unnecessary and unprofitable buildings, which have been found the greatest means of breeding and harbouring scarcity and infection to the general inconvenience of the whole kingdom.[15]

The Council instructed Inigo and his fellow commissioners to draw up a plan for the fields to be 'framed and reduced both for sweetness, uniformity and comeliness into such walks, partitions or other plots and in such sort, manner and form both for public health and pleasure'.

This they duly did; but the remorseless pressure of the developers led to the gradual contraction of the scheme, as new buildings encroached on it from all sides over the next thirty years. By 1645, Lincoln's Inn Fields was notorious for Bacchanalian romps on Sundays, when hundreds of people would congregate, drinking freely, while black men 'and others of like rank' would 'make sport with our English women and maids'.[16]

So much for sweetness and comeliness. During his twenty-seven years as Surveyor General Inigo would become accustomed to such frustrations. As respect for authority dwindled in the years leading up to the Civil War, it became increasingly hard to enforce any of the Crown's rules and decisions. If offending houses were pulled down – and a row of twenty-three on Long Acre was demolished in 1618 – the developers swiftly rebuilt them. Others resorted to transparent ruses that showed their contempt for the system, like one George Peck, who built high brick walls round a field off Chancery Lane in 1624, claiming that its purpose was to confine his tame rabbits, while in fact it concealed his construction of some mean tenements.[17] In the end, Inigo's vain attempts to enforce unpopular measures not only made him look ridiculous but inevitably provoked the hostility of people with financial clout, some of whom would eventually be in a position to gain their revenge.

The Twelfth Night masque of 1619 provided an opportunity for Inigo to redeem his reputation after the disappointment of the previous year. He grasped it eagerly, to judge from this description by Giovanni Battista Gabaleoni, the Savoy agent in London:

> At the foot of the room opposite his Majesty a curtain which hid all the wall at that end was let drop, revealing a perspective with very lovely ornaments which stood in the air between the ceiling of the room and the solarium. In it were seated all the lords of the masque, in the most beautiful order. By means of a hidden device it descended very, very gently to the ground. Behind this perspective, in proportion to the lords' seat descended, and at their backs, there were seen in another perspective castles, towers, palaces, rooms and

pictures in foreshortening. In truth it seemed to me that I had never seen anything that gave more cause to wonder.[18]

Inigo wrote the words 'Palace of Perfection' on his drawing of the scene, which is the only clue to the theme of the masque, whose text and title have been lost. It deserves a place in history, though, as the last to have been performed in the 1609 Banqueting House, which burned to the ground on 12 January, just six days after the performance. There are conflicting accounts of exactly how the fire started, but most agree that the culprit was someone working to return the hall to normal after the masque. Once the fire had taken hold of the scenery, there was no chance of saving the mainly wooden structure. In the northerly wind, some neighbouring houses to the south were also destroyed and others had to be pulled down as a firebreak, to prevent the flames from spreading to the main royal quarters.

Inigo's house, although only a few hundred yards away, was north of the burning hall and therefore safe, though from his window he would have commanded a close-up view of the spectacular inferno, and was perhaps already anticipating the need to design a replacement hall. A crowd of spectators quickly gathered to watch the efforts of the firefighters, while others sought to see whether there was anything they could loot in the confusion.[19]

This was the first of two disasters that befell the King in the opening months of 1619 – disasters that the more superstitious of his subjects had predicted following the appearance of a comet in the skies above England during the previous November and December. The graver of the two was the death of Queen Anne on 2 March, at Hampton Court. Her health had been deteriorating since about 1612, and what was at first thought to be gout was eventually diagnosed as dropsy.[20] She had been confined to her bed for most of the winter and it had been clear for several weeks that the illness would be terminal. The King himself was also lying ill at Newmarket, and could not attend her deathbed. He recovered, but never remarried. Anne's funeral was delayed until May because, it was said, James had difficulty in raising the ready money to have her buried with full honours. Her death had robbed Inigo of his earliest royal patron and it must have been with some feeling that he designed her splendid hearse, drawn by six horses, which Chamberlain praised as 'the fairest and stateliest that I have ever seen'.[21]

Despite this tragedy, there was never any doubt that a new Banqueting House would be built, and quickly. Even if the King had been made to delay his wife's funeral for financial reasons, and had failed to find the funds to rebuild the Star Chamber, this was much higher on the scale of priorities. Since he and Anne had arrived in Whitehall the annual masque had become integral to the life of their court, and even though the Queen was now dead it was unthinkable that the tradition should not continue. A palace lacking a Banqueting House would be like a modern house without a bathroom, intolerable for those who lived there and derided by the neighbours to boot.

There was another, more political motive. For years, in defiance of public opinion, James had been manoeuvring to arrange a marriage between his surviving son and the King of Spain's daughter, the Infanta, to make allies of former enemies and help heal the divide between European Protestants and Catholics. By 1619 the negotiations looked promising, and if such a splendid marriage were to take place, it would be essential to provide a suitably grand venue for the celebrations.

For the same reason, this was the year James ordered a tapestry factory to be established at Mortlake, emulating his brother-in-law, the King of Denmark, as well as the King of France.[22] Tapestries were a potent status symbol in seventeenth-century courts, lining the walls of the great halls where state banquets were held and important visitors received. English-woven tapestries, decorating a splendid new Banqueting House, would be a source of national pride. In 1623 the seven Raphael cartoons depicting scenes from the Acts of the Apostles, now at the Victoria and Albert Museum, were bought from Genoa and used as templates for suitably splendid wall hangings for the new building.

James insisted that the work on the Banqueting House should be completed with the greatest possible speed and he appointed as its coordinator Lionel Cranfield, Inigo's client and former drinking companion. Alongside Cranfield was a five-man Commission including another friend and patron, Thomas Howard, by now the Earl Marshal. Here, at last, was Inigo's opportunity to put into practice some of the lessons he had been absorbing through his books and his travels for twenty years.

He appears to have had his copies of the precious architectural manuals constantly at his side as he was designing this, the most important building of his life. His Palladio contains notes made in March 1619 highlighting details that he would employ in the structure, such as double-cornered columns.[23] Within three months he had drawn detailed plans and worked out their cost, and on 19 April submitted them to the Privy Council. The building would be 110 feet long, 55 feet wide and 55 feet high – a perfect double cube, as prescribed by Vitruvius – and it would cost £9850.[24] Like most building estimates, that represented about half of what was eventually spent.[25]

With the exchequer so impoverished, where would the King find that kind of money? The economy was in the midst of what we would today call a recession, with trade stagnant. Parliament, if asked, would almost certainly regard expenditure on such an enterprise as frivolous. The writer John Aubrey, often inaccurate, says that the money was paid by the City of London as a fine 'for the prentices killing Dr Lamb in the streets for a conjuror'.[26] This was a reference to the astrologer John Lambe, attacked and fatally injured by a mob of apprentices for practising the black arts. But since this did not take place until 1628, three years after James I's death, the explanation cannot be true.

A more likely version comes from John Bagford, another late seventeenth-century antiquarian, whose manuscripts include an early biography of Inigo.[27] Discussing the Banqueting House, the author states: 'This fabric was at the charge of the states of Holland, according to an agreement upon the delivery of the Cautionary Towns into their hands as was stipulated.'

The Cautionary Towns were the Dutch ports of Flushing (Vlissingen) and Brill (Brielle). They had been occupied by the English since 1585 to help defend the Protestant Netherlands against the threat from Catholic Spain. In 1616, with the conflict in abeyance, they were returned to Dutch rule. If the Bagford account is correct, the Dutch compensated

England for its trouble, and the timely windfall went towards the King's pet project.

Early design for Banqueting House interior

Two of Inigo's preparatory drawings for the west side of Banqueting House, as seen from King Street (now Whitehall), are in the Duke of Devonshire's collection at Chatsworth. Both depict the basic design as built, with their clear references to the Palladian villas and palazzos that Inigo had studied so closely in Italy. Two horizontal rows of seven windows each, separated by two ranks of colonnades, stand above a semi-basement with smaller windows, rusticated in the second drawing. The three central sets of windows project forwards a foot or two from the others and are capped by a pediment, with statues at its three angles.

As Summerson has pointed out,[28] the central pediment was a familiar device used by Palladio and his contemporaries in their house designs, where it was placed above the steps leading up to the main entrance. The difference here – as in Inigo's design for the Star

Chamber, which included the same feature – is that the pediment would not have been over an entrance. The principal access to the new building was from the palace to its south, not from King Street. So the pediment and its statues, serving neither a practical nor a crucial symbolic purpose, were surplus to requirements and Inigo decided to forego them in his final Banqueting House design: perhaps reluctantly, for he was clearly fond of them.

The interior was essentially a single space. On all sides except the south a gallery separated the upper and lower rows of windows. Inigo pared down the subsidiary rooms to make this space as large as he could, given the limitation of the site. In this he was putting into practice a principle that he had translated in his copy of *I Quattro Libri*: 'Halls for feasts, triumphs, plays, masques and weddings . . . must be larger than the rest to receive many people.'[29] He turned to Palladio again when deciding on the size of the windows: 'If windows be little the room will be dark, if too big uninhabitable for cold and heat.'[30] In fact the lower windows were blocked for much of the time, to accommodate the tapestries that would adorn them.[31]

One of Inigo's priorities was to answer the King's tetchy criticism of the old building by ensuring that there were no columns to obstruct his view of the action. The free-standing pillars were replaced by pilasters set against the walls between the windows – Ionic on the lower range, Corinthian above – and continued along the shorter north and south walls. But although the Banqueting House was intimately connected with the court masques and other entertainments, they occurred no more than half a dozen times a year, so they could not dictate the architecture. When they were performed the hall had to be temporarily converted, a wooden stage erected at one end and raked rows of seats on scaffolds placed around the walls.

A more frequent use was for the reception of ambassadors and other dignitaries, so there had to be a prominent and suitably splendid location for the throne. From his abortive Star Chamber design he borrowed the Palladian device of a semi-circular niche, or apse, at the southern end, beneath a large round-headed window. This did not, in the end, find favour, possibly because the cloth canopy under which the King traditionally sat, as a symbol of his supreme power, was square, and looked odd placed within a semi-circular niche. The apse was removed only three years after the hall was finished.[32] In his enthusiasm to emulate Palladio's work, Inigo had ignored one of his basic principles of architecture: that a building must first and foremost be suitable for its intended purpose. As the American architect Louis Sullivan was to put it nearly 300 years later: 'Form follows function.' He ought, too, to have taken more account of an epigram that he translated from his copy of Vasari's *Lives*: 'An architect should think well before he begins his work.'[33]

The decorative details of the interior, as we see them today, have been altered since Inigo's time, and there is no complete set of plans that would allow us to reconstruct them. One clue lies in a drawing identified in Inigo's own hand as representing the 'elevation of the great door, Banqueting House, 1619'. It is framed by two Ionic columns linked by two garlands immediately above the door, all crowned by a broken pediment. It appears to be based in part on some doors by Scamozzi in the Doge's Palace in Venice.[34]

Inigo designed the ceiling with recessed compartments to accommodate paintings, but none had been commissioned by the time the building was completed and the whole surface was painted white, with twelve carved and gilded cherubs hanging from it. (They were removed in 1626.)[35] It seems likely that Sir Peter Paul Rubens was always the artist favoured by Inigo and King James to decorate the ceiling: a letter written by Rubens in 1621, saying that he was by instinct 'better fitted to execute works of the largest size rather than little curiosities', suggested that he had already been approached on the matter.[36] Prince Charles was enthusiastic about his work, and owned at least two of his paintings. But it would be another nine years – and five years after James's death – before Charles, as King, could afford to finalise the commission, by then conceived as an elaborate tribute to his father.

With the negotiations for the Spanish marriage apparently moving towards consummation, King James wanted his new Banqueting House to be ready by the end of 1620. This was unrealistic, if only because of the many hundreds of tons of stone that had to be brought from quarries all over the country: from Northamptonshire for the fascia, Oxfordshire for the basement, and the pillars from Portland in Dorset, where a new pier had to be built for shipping the stone to Whitehall.[37] Then the local contractor engaged to secure the Portland stone for the project had to be reprimanded for selling it instead to his private customers, at a higher price than the Crown was offering.[38] (This was a recurring problem: it surfaced again sixty years later, when Sir Christopher Wren was rebuilding St Paul's Cathedral.)

Even if the early stages of the work had been on schedule, by the time winter came it would certainly have been delayed by the weather, because the winter of 1620–1 was one of the coldest anyone could remember. The Thames again froze over, as it had when Inigo's first masque was performed in 1605. This time a frost fair was held on the ice, very close to the half-built Banqueting House. Stalls were set up there to serve food and drink and to sell souvenirs, while entertainers drew crowds to the whole length of the river between the City and Westminster. Looking towards Whitehall, they would have seen little evidence at that stage of the revolutionary new building being erected there.

The unfavourable temperatures, combined with the potent rival attractions of the Frost Fair only a few hundred yards away, meant that it was even harder than usual to secure reliable labour. On 16 August 1620, some months before the freeze set in, Inigo had written to Howard and the other Commissioners complaining that many of the masons had 'run away' while he was temporarily absent from London, and warning that others would do the same unless the ringleaders were punished.[39] The following day he wrote separately to Howard alone, making the same point and adding, 'Some are returned and for the rest if your Lordship do show some exemplary punishment causing them to be sent up as malefactors it will deter the rest from doing the like.'[40]

The worst offender was the master mason, William Cure. Although he had an official salaried position in the King's works department, and came from a long line of royal masons, he also ran a business as a monumental mason in Southwark, and seems to have preferred to work on his private commissions than at the Banqueting House.

Because of his persistent failure to report for duty, Inigo replaced him with Nicholas Stone, the mason whom he had briefed for the King's work in Scotland and who had already become a firm friend.[41] Two years later, after the Banqueting House was complete, Inigo and his deputy, Thomas Baldwin, reported to Cranfield that Cure had been absent for five months and even after his return had become 'careless and negligent'.[42]

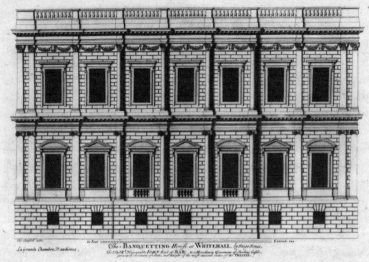

The Banqueting House

Despite these frustrations, the Banqueting House was close enough to completion by St George's Day, 23 April 1621, to stage its first official event, a ceremonial reception for the Knights of the Garter after their annual procession. Today we recognise it as Inigo's most important surviving work of architecture, a grandiloquent symbol of the Stuarts' concept of their divine right to rule; what Per Palme called 'the epitome of kingship'.[43] Yet in the two years in which its revolutionary shape and style had gradually been rising from the ashes of its predecessor, the public response had been muted and puzzled: nobody knew quite what to make of it.

There are surprisingly few references to the building in contemporary correspondence and journals, an exception being the irrepressible Chamberlain, who informed Carleton that it was 'too fair and nothing suitable to the rest of the house'[44] – the house being Whitehall Palace. In that he was surely right: the pristine, classical Banqueting House will have looked incongruous amid the jumble of miscellaneous Tudor buildings that constituted the palace. Both Inigo and the King must have seen it as the first element of the new Palladian palace that they were ambitious to build once the royal finances were sufficiently restored for such a large investment in grandeur and prestige.

In attempting to imagine today what it looked like in its original context, it is important to recall that Inigo's Banqueting House was not then the predominantly snow-white building that it became later. He was sparing with his use of white Portland stone on the exterior, probably so as to prevent it standing out too prominently from its surroundings. He used a warm beige Oxfordshire stone for the basement and a pinker Northamptonshire stone for the upper levels, while only the parapet, the pilasters and other decorative features were in Portland. Not until it was resurfaced by William Chambers in 1774 did Portland stone come to predominate.

What baffled contemporary Londoners was not so much the colour of the stones as the whole appearance of the building. The remorselessly regular 'harmonic' proportions did not conform to any concept of beauty as understood in Jacobean England. Palladio's dictum that 'beauty will result . . . from the correspondence of the whole to the parts'[45] had yet to become established in the English architectural lexicon. The idea of the perfect cube and double cube, the strict mathematical relation of the height of columns to their width, the Composite order solemnly and correctly superimposed on the Ionic, the proportionate spacing of the windows – all these were alien to a culture that took its greatest delight in gaudy spectacle; and where the science of mathematics was itself in its infancy.

Ben Jonson, characteristically, was concerned less about the look of the new building than the use to which it would be put. In his convivial and sarcastic mode he wrote *The Dedication of the King's New Cellar to Bacchus*, in praise of the vaulted basement where, alongside store rooms and other service areas, 'The King's Privy Cellar' was opened in 1624. This was a wine cellar and drinking room for James I, containing a grotto for which Isaac de Caux, the garden designer, charged £20, with an additional £10 for shell work added later.[46] Jonson hailed it with some suitably high-spirited lines:

> Since, Bacchus, thou art father
> Of wines, to thee the rather
> We dedicate this cellar,
> Where now thou art made dweller;
> And seal thee thy commission:
> But 'tis with a condition,
> That thou remain here taster
> Of all to the great Master.
> And look unto their faces,
> Their qualities and races,
> That both, their odour take him,
> And relish merry make him.

The merriment would not last much longer. But the Banqueting House, happily for succeeding generations, would survive the political perils to come.

Chapter Thirteen

THE WEAKNESS OF PRINCES

KING JAMES HAD COME TO REGARD his Surveyor-General as a man of many and varied abilities, a view that Inigo would not have been inclined to challenge. In 1620, on one of his regular progresses through the west country, the King, as had become his habit, stayed with Lord Pembroke at Wilton House. On his way he stopped at Stonehenge on Salisbury Plain, some ten miles north of the house, and asked about the origins of the giant stone circle that stood, unfenced and untended, in the long grass. Told that the landmark's history was obscure, he had a message sent to the knowledgeable Inigo, asking him to look into the question and report back.

Busy though he was, Inigo fulfilled at least the first part of the assignment. According to his nineteenth-century biographer, he pitched his tent close to the circle and cleared the ground around the stones. Using the experience he had gained in Italy at analysing the remains of ancient structures, he dug around the bases of the stones and carefully measured those that had fallen to the ground, even working out how much they weighed. Then he drew them to scale.[1] He does not, however, seem to have provided the King with his answer, and indeed nothing was heard of his conclusions until after his own death.

Only then, in 1655, did his protégé John Webb publish a little book entitled *The Most Notable Antiquity of Great Britain, Vulgarly Called Stonehenge . . . Restored*, had put together from the notes Inigo made about his investigation.

There was no science of archaeology at the time (the word came into use in its present-day sense only in the nineteenth century), even though Thomas Howard had organised a pioneering dig in Rome. The prevailing theory about Stonehenge, among the antiquaries who dabbled in such matters, was that it had been erected by Druids as part of their religious observances. Inigo – if we assume that Webb had correctly interpreted his notes – discounted that view, coming instead to the surprising conclusion that Stonehenge had in fact been built by the Romans in the early years of the first millennium as a temple to Coelus, or Uranus – in mythology the father of the Gods, the embodiment of Heaven.

Inigo's drawing of Stonehenge in 1620

The theory seems to have been based on his view that the Britons, Saxons and Danes did not have the mathematical knowledge or precision necessary to design such a structure, nor the machinery to move the stones. It provides fascinating evidence of how passionately he regarded the Romans as the fount of order and symmetry, the core values that drove his architecture. His illustration of Stonehenge, as it would have looked when built, shows a pristine circle in a very basic form of the Tuscan order. He described it as 'a plain, grave and humble manner of building, very solid and strong'. As drawn, the temple was made simply from blocks of stone, completely undecorated, broadening out at the base, arranged in a circle and supporting a ring of linking horizontal stones on the top. Inside the circle were six pairs of identical free-standing stones, similarly linked at the top.

To support his argument, Inigo drew on the work of William Camden, Ben Jonson's teacher, whose book *Britannia*, citing the historian Tacitus, asserted that the Roman governor Agricola built large monuments in Britain as a means of civilising the natives, to bring them the fruits of superior Roman culture and to keep them employed and out of trouble. As for the identification of Coelus as the God to whom the temple was dedicated, this was based on the fact that it was circular and in the open air. According to Vitruvius, these were characteristics of temples to celestial gods, the circle representing the heavenly sphere.[2]

The eighteenth-century scholar Horace Walpole commented perceptively: 'It is remarkable that whoever has treated of that monument [Stonehenge] has bestowed it on whatever class of antiquity he was peculiarly fond of.' And almost as soon as it was published, Inigo's theory was challenged. Indeed, so fierce was the reaction that Webb felt obliged to produce *A Vindication of Stonehenge Restored* ten years later, and today we know for certain that Inigo was wrong. Yet although his notes, as published, leave little room for doubt about his conclusion, it is arguable whether he was wholly committed to it. If he was, he would surely have gone into print during his lifetime, or at the very least passed his opinion to the King, at whose behest the inquiry was carried out.

So preposterous does the theory seem to us today that at least two admirers of Inigo have expressed doubt as to the authenticity of Webb's interpretation of it. Timothy Mowl and Brian Earnshaw have advanced the view that Webb, 'a natural confidence trickster with a fair talent for drawing', published the book simply to reinforce his credentials as Inigo's heir and successor, and may in effect have made the whole thing up.[3] On balance it seems an improbable scenario – and since Webb is the only source of information on much of Inigo's life and work, to discount him as a credible witness would cast doubt on his other biographical details, allowing scope for endless imaginative speculation.

If Inigo the naive archaeologist is a surprising piece of casting, what are we to make of Inigo the politician? His career as a Member of Parliament was largely accidental and, probably to his relief, rather short. James I's relationship with Parliament had deteriorated throughout his reign, due both to the increasing reluctance of its members to vote him funds to pay for his extravagant lifestyle, and to their opposition to his policy of rapprochement with Catholic Spain, exemplified in Prince Charles's proposed marriage.

Members of Parliament refused to go along with Cecil's Great Contract[4] unless they could also influence how the money was spent. This infuriated the King, whose core belief in his divine right to rule as he wished was only strengthened by the growing insistence of his subjects that they, too, had rights when it came to the allocation of their money to his purposes. He put his view most trenchantly in a speech to judges in 1616:

> That which concerns the mystery of the King's power is not lawful to be disputed, for that is to wade into the weakness of princes and to take away the mystical reverence that belongs unto them that sit in the throne of God.

The weakness of princes was a factor that would come fatally into play after his death. Meantime, after his rebuff over the Great Contract, he dissolved Parliament and in the ensuing ten years summoned it only once, and that briefly. In the absence of a Parliamentary subsidy, his main sources of revenue had become the sale of knighthoods and of monopolies on the supply of staple commodities such as salt, starch and wine.

By 1620, needing money badly for the marriage preparations, he had no alternative but to summon another Parliament. Since the wedding scheme was first mooted, though, it had become complicated by political developments abroad. In 1618 Spain had embroiled itself in a war against the Protestant states of Europe, later to be known as the Thirty Years War. By 1620 this had resulted in James's son-in-law Frederick being ousted by Spain both as Elector of the Palatinate and King of Bohemia, a throne he had unwisely accepted when it was offered him a few months earlier. Because he had occupied the throne of Bohemia for less than a year, Frederick became known as the Winter King, and his wife Elizabeth as the Winter Queen.

Being a firm Protestant, Frederick was popular in England, as shown by the widespread rejoicing that his marriage to James's daughter had provoked eight years earlier. The thought of an alliance with his enemy was anathema to many citizens and was denounced by Protestant clerics in churches across the kingdom, particularly in London. The defeat of the Armada in 1588 was, after all, still well within living memory, and the Spanish ambassador, Don Carlos Coloma, was routinely abused when he dared venture on to the streets of the capital. James argued that, by going through with Charles's marriage to the Infanta, he could exert leverage on Spain for the return of Frederick's throne; but this reasoning cut no ice with Parliament. When it met in January 1621 its members gave full vent to their strong opposition to any overtures towards Spain, and to the marriage especially.

Many seats in the House of Commons were effectively in the gift of senior peers who controlled the areas around their principal country estates. As Earl of Arundel, Thomas Howard had several seats at his disposal in that part of West Sussex dominated by his hereditary castle. (Lionel Cranfield, for instance, had been a member for Arundel itself.) Two of the Howard seats were in the borough of Shoreham-by-Sea, and for the 1621 Parliament the men chosen to fill them were Sir John Morley and Sir John Leedes. But in February Leedes was expelled from the House because he had inadvertently (as he claimed) omitted to take the oath of allegiance before assuming his seat.[5]

Keen to fill the unexpected vacancy with a man on whose loyalty to the Crown he could rely, Howard asked Inigo to step in. The two had remained close since their Italian journey. In a draft will drawn up in 1617 Howard asked that 'my most approved good friend Inigo Jones' should design tombstones at Arundel both for him and his father, still buried in the Tower. As a reward he bequeathed to Inigo 'a cup of gold of one hundred marks [£66] which I desire he will keep for my sake and continue to my wife and my children as he hath been unto me'.[6]

Inigo must have been flattered by the offer of a Parliamentary seat and, even if he harboured doubts about his suitability for the role, he was disinclined to offend his friend and patron. He therefore agreed to accept the post. It was convenient enough – the House of Commons was, after all, only a few steps from his Scotland Yard home – but he soon found that Parliamentary life was not for him. The mood of the House was overwhelmingly hostile to the court of which he was now a part. Following a summer recess, members expressed their views strongly in November in the so-called Apologetic Petition, urging the King to abandon the Spanish marriage plan. It provoked a furious response from James:

> You usurp upon our prerogative royal, and meddle with things far above your reach, and then in conclusion you protest the contrary; as if a robber would take a man's purse and then protest he meant not to rob him. For first, you presume to give us your advice concerning the match of our dearest son with some Protestant . . . and dissuade us from his match with Spain, urging us to a present war with that King: and yet, in the conclusion, forsooth, ye protest ye intend not to press upon our most undoubted royal prerogative; as if the petitioning of us in matters that yourselves confess ye ought not to meddle with were not a meddling with them.

When the Commons responded in kind, protesting at his attempts to bend them to his will, James dissolved Parliament in January 1622 and struck the protest from the Commons journal.[7] Three of the most recalcitrant members were arrested: John Pym, John Selden and Sir Edward Coke, who had been dismissed as Lord Chief Justice and had become one of the King's fiercest critics.

There is no record of Inigo's taking part in any of these impassioned debates during his year as a Member. He would certainly not have been counted among the King's opponents; but nor would he have wanted to raise his head above the parapet and speak out to defend an unpopular cause. He was not, after all, a natural public figure and had no real desire to act as one. In the conduct of his life, as in his work for the stage, he operated most effectively behind the scenes. What influence he enjoyed was gained by knowing the right people and being able to please and flatter them. Unlike his more volatile partner, Ben Jonson, he had never seen any point in making enemies gratuitously.

Parliament reassembled in February 1624, but Inigo was not among its members. Watching history being made was all very well, but a year in that supercharged atmosphere was more than enough. He was replaced by Anthony Stapley, who turned out to be a less reliable supporter of the royal cause: he was one of the Parliamentary leaders who signed Charles I's death warrant.

It was not as if Inigo lacked other things to do. His duties as the King's Surveyor were pressing on him, as a letter to Howard in August 1620 had made clear. As part of the negotiations for Prince Charles's projected marriage, a high-level ambassador from Spain was coming to visit the King and was to be accommodated at Hampton Court. The ambassador sent his steward to check the rooms a day or two in advance, and it was Inigo's job to go with him.

It was a prickly encounter. The steward, in Inigo's words 'utterly disliked' the rooms, especially what he perceived as a lack of sufficiently comfortable furniture, and demanded that alternative arrangements be made. It fell to Lord Nottingham, who had been James's ambassador to Spain since 1605, to pacify his opposite number, and the rooms were accepted as suitable, although the ambassador was eventually moved to more central lodgings at Ely House in Holborn.[8] The proud Inigo felt insulted and wounded by the contretemps, telling Howard that it was all the ambassador's fault for not sending someone over earlier 'to see how he was provided for and give notice what would please him'.[9]

Design for Prince's Lodgings in Newmarket

The development of the estate at Newmarket continued, with a hunting lodge built for Prince Charles in about 1619. No trace of it remains on the ground. Two drawings in the Royal Institute of British Architects collection are thought to represent alternative versions of the design, but it is impossible to say which of them was the final building. Both are strictly symmetrical, with a centre block of three window spans flanked by identical two-window blocks. In the version shown here, the central loggia above the entrance is divided by four Corinthian columns supporting a pediment with statues – the device that he eventually omitted from the Banqueting House design. Two more statues stand guard by the shallow steps leading up the the rusticated front doorway. It is a charming composition that appears to be influenced by Palladio's design for palazzo in Verona, as illustrated in *I Quattro Libri*. The other design was of similar proportions but had a steeper roof with dormer windows, the statues at the front were in niches and there were no columns.[10]

The more mundane work had to go on, too: repairs to the gatehouse prison at St Albans, maintenance at the Tower of London and other chores. In 1620 he had to adjudicate a complaint by glaziers at the poor quality of the glass from the country's sole manufacturer, Sir Robert Mansell, the powerful Vice-Admiral of England, who had bought the monopoly from the King in 1615. The glaziers alleged that the glass was 'scarce, bad and brittle'. Inigo and his deputy, Thomas Baldwin, upheld the complaint, judging the glass to be 'mixed good and bad together, and is very thin in the middle'.[11]

Although these bureaucratic tasks had to be performed, Inigo still made the time to work on private commissions, and was especially keen to serve clients who came from the ranks of the powerful. A drawing by his hand, dating from around this period, has a notation identifying it as a design for an Italianate house in Blackfriars for Sir Peter Killigrew, an influential courtier, although there is no firm indication that it was ever built.[12] Nobody was more powerful in the last decade of King James's life than George Villiers, the Marquis (later Duke) of Buckingham. Just before beginning the Banqueting House Inigo had done some work on upgrading Buckingham's lodgings at Whitehall: the King wanted his favourite comfortably housed, as close as possible to the royal apartments.[13] Inigo's design for the coffered ceiling of the dining room is among his surviving drawings.

Now Buckingham had bought New Hall in Essex, otherwise known as Beaulieu, a rambling palace built one hundred years earlier for Henry VIII. Chamberlain, writing to Carleton in September 1622, saw the £20,000 purchase as a great bargain, and recorded that Inigo was doing some work to convert it to 'the modern fashion'. Not long afterwards, though, the bulk of the work at New Hall was assigned to Balthazar Gerbier, a Dutch painter and architect who had come to England in 1616 and become something of a rival to Inigo for the approval and custom of courtiers.

When Buckingham took over York House in the Strand in 1621, Gerbier was given the task of adapting it and it was he who probably built the watergate – once attributed to Inigo – that still stands in London's Embankment Gardens. No love was lost between the two architects and the Dutchman was convinced he was the more accomplished. He claimed that Charles I had declared that the great hall of York House was as fine as the Banqueting House, and that when Inigo saw it he was covered with jealousy and shame, fearing that he would lose his position to its inspired creator.[14]

This was not the only instance where the self-seeking Gerbier reported that Inigo was overwhelmed with admiration for his exquisite taste. In 1624 he acquired a batch of pictures for Buckingham, including Titian's *Portrait of a Secretary*. In a letter to Buckingham, Gerbier described how he had shown the masterpiece to Inigo, who 'almost went down on his knees' before it.[15] While he certainly relayed the story primarily to impress his patron with his own judgement, it fits in with other accounts of Inigo reacting with great excitement at the sight of a work of art,[16] displaying his enthusiasm and reverence for the European master painters.

Gerbier could never outgrow his resentment of his rival. In a book published after Inigo's death, he was critical of the Banqueting House, citing among other faults the size of the hall and the weight of the pillars and pilasters, which he feared could cause the building to collapse on the heads of passers-by.[17] Despite a devastating fire later in the century, and months of aerial bombardment 250 years later, the building has survived a lot longer than its arrogant critic.

The first masque performed in the new Banqueting House was Jonson's and Inigo's *The Masque of Augurs*, on Twelfth Night 1622, with Prince Charles again taking part. The hall was filled with row upon row of tiered seating, covering the whole area of the floor apart from the stage and the King's own hallowed space.[18] The political thrust of this masque was to glorify the proposed Spanish match, and two senior Spanish envoys were guests of honour.[19] This caused diplomatic difficulties, since the overweening and militantly Catholic Spaniards were highly unpopular with most of the countries that maintained embassies in London. James's solution was to invite only the Spaniards but when the Venetian representative, Giralomo Lando, got wind of this he reported back to Venice:

There was some idea not to invite me to the masque, which is one of the two annual ceremonies attended by the ambassadors. France was not asked because Spain had been. When I heard that they proposed to leave me out because Spain and I did not visit each other, I tactfully contrived to convey that your serenity [the Doge] ought not to be deprived of the customary honour on that account, and finally I gained my point, to which I attached importance. The ceremony was most sumptuous.[20]

In every way the masque should have been an auspicious occasion, but the mischievous Jonson did his best to put a damper on it by joking in his antimasque about the impoverished state of the court's finances, for which the cost of the Banqueting House was partly responsible: 'Neither the King's poet, nor his architect, had wherewithal left to entertain so much as a baboon of quality.'[21]

Augurs was notable, too, as the first – but by no means the last – of their joint efforts in which Jonson was bold enough to poke fun openly at his collaborator. Again in the antimasque, he invented a ludicrous character named Vangoose, almost certainly meant to be Inigo, described as 'a rare artist and projector of masques'.[22] As part of the plot, Vangoose created an antimasque of his own and, when challenged that it was unrealistic to the point of absurdity, replied: 'If it go from the nature of the thing it is the more art: for dear is art, and dear is nature.'

The allusion may seem obscure today, but the Jacobean audience would have had little trouble in identifying the reference to Inigo's fanciful, unnatural stage designs, especially since Jonson had taken similar liberties with the architect's reputation some years previously. In *Bartholomew Fair*, written in 1614, Lanthorn Leatherhead, a puppeteer and toy salesman, was portrayed as a manipulator of stage effects and lights: 'O the motions that I, Lanthorn Leatherhead, have given light to in my time.' Earlier in the play Lanthorn was teased for his self-importance and the company he kept at the Mermaid and the Mitre:

Put him a-top o' the table, where his place is, and he'll do you forty fine things. He has not been sent for, and caught out for nothing, at your great city suppers, to put down Coryate and Cokeley,[23] and be laughed at for his labour.

In Jonson's 1616 volume of *Epigrams*, the verse entitled 'On the Town's Honest Man' also appeared to be directed at Inigo. The anonymous subject, identified throughout the poem as the neutral 'it', was sycophantic:

> A subtle thing, that doth affections win
> By speaking well o' the company it's in.

'It' spoke ill of people behind their backs, then denied doing so, and shied away from challenges to a duel, however great the insult offered. The use of the words 'architect' and 'engineer' in the final lines seem to confirm the identity of the victim of the satire:

> . . . By defect
> From friendship, is its own fame's architect,
> An engineer, in slanders, of all fashions,
> That, seeming praises, are yet accusations.
> Describ'd, it's thus: Defin'd would you it have?
> Then, the town's honest man's her errant'st knave.

That this is a precise reflection of Jonson's opinion of Inigo was confirmed in his conversation with William Drummond of Hawthornden after his walk to Scotland in 1619.[24]

> He said to Prince Charles of Inigo Jones, that when he wanted words to express the greatest villain in the world, he would call him an Inigo. Jones having accused him for naming him behind his back a fool, he denied it; but, says he, 'I said he was an arrant knave, and I avouch it.'

The phrase 'arrant knave' seems proof enough that Inigo was the 'errant'st knave' of the epigram. Given the depth of Jonson's hostility towards him, it is surprising that the partnership survived for as long as nine years after *The Masque of Augurs*. Yet in 1622 the poet seemed anxious to avoid an open breach, and in the preface to the masque he was meticulous in apportioning the credit that Inigo had earned, even if treading a fine line between sincerity and sarcasm:

> For the expression of this, I must stand; the invention as divided betwixt Mr Jones and me. The scene, which your eye judges, was wholly his, and worthy his place of the King's Surveyor, and Architect, full of noble observation of antiquity and high presentment.

Despite their growing rivalry, Inigo and Jonson continued to collaborate on an ever-increasing number of masques and court entertainments throughout the first half of the decade. In January 1623 Chamberlain wrote that he could not recall there ever being so much dancing and feasting among the royal entourage, apparently oblivious of the growing political tension between Parliament and the Crown. The young Prince Charles's enthusiasm for disporting himself on stage had become infectious. He danced again in that year's masque, *Time Vindicated to Himself and to His Honours*, postponed from Twelfth Night to 19 January because the King was not well. Its chief purpose was to mark the return home of the French ambassador.

It included three changes of scenery. The first was a perspective view of Whitehall in which Inigo, never a slouch when it came to self-promotion, had placed his new Banqueting House in a prominent position. Yet at least one of the spectators thought the sets were below his usual level of excellence. The Venetian ambassador reported home:

> Last Sunday the masque took place, danced by the prince and ten other cavaliers. After various preliminaries and appearances of no great account, they descended in disguise from the sky in a cloud. It was a spectacle of some pomp and beauty but not attaining the royal standard of excellence.[25]

Prince Charles, a few weeks after dancing his delicate measures on the boards of the Banqueting House, left the country, along with Buckingham, on the most bizarre mission ever undertaken by an heir to the British throne. With the King's health declining, Buckingham could see that it was in his interest to ally himself closely with his presumed successor, and both men were impatient for a conclusion of the painfully slow progress of negotiations with Spain about the proposed marriage. Ignoring James's doubts, they decided to travel to Madrid in person. Their intention was to slice through the thick strands of diplomatic and ecclesiastical red tape that had been hindering the proposal, allowing Charles to sweep the Infanta off her feet and bring her back in triumph.

Knowing how much hostility there was to the match, they borrowed the plot from many a Shakespearean comedy by leaving England in false beards, pretending to be John and Tom Smith, servants to a member of the royal household. They were almost rumbled when Buckingham, whose fine clothes belied his pretended status, gave the Gravesend ferryman a bag of silver as a tip. The man assumed his two passengers were going to Dover to cross the Channel to fight a duel, illegal in England. He reported them to the local magistrate, who was just too late to apprehend them.[26]

Admirably swashbuckling though the scheme appeared in concept, it presented practical problems for the court, and for Inigo in particular. If the Infanta was indeed to return as Charles's bride, she would need somewhere to live and, just as important, somewhere to worship. The provision of a chapel for her had been an unshakeable Spanish demand throughout the negotiations. Since the Reformation there had been no Catholic chapels in the royal palaces. Inigo was instructed to design two, one in St James's Palace, where the Infanta was to live, and one in Somerset House, where some of her court would be accommodated. With her arrival expected in early summer, there was no time to lose.

Of the two, the St James's chapel was given the priority. A former pheasantry was pulled down to provide a site near the palace, and Inigo was asked to carry out the work 'with great state and costliness'.[27] Given the court's chronic poverty, that was a rare and welcome instruction. As Vitruvius had written, in a sentence that Inigo had underlined in his copy of *I Dieci Libri de Architectura*: 'Cost gives magnificence and authority to buildings.' Yet there was a caveat: for he would have known, without being told, that in this case the costliness and magnificence must not be reflected in the building's exterior. It had to be plain and understated, with none of the lavish ornament that so provoked Protestant hostility. Any extravagances must be reserved for the interior, which would be seen mostly by faithful Catholics.

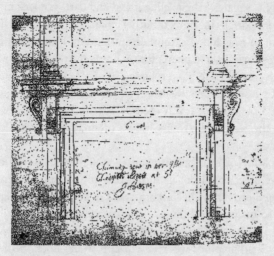

Chimneypiece for the Queen's Chapel

His design met that criterion perfectly: a modest, inoffensive front-age, with three bays and an unassertive central entrance, beneath a cornice conventionally decorated with lions' heads and capped by a triangular portico. With its tall, round-headed central window, flanked by two more with straight heads, it harked back to the three central bays of the Prince's Lodging at Newmarket that he had designed a few years earlier. Originally there were small wings on the north and south sides. Today only the latter remains, but aside from that the chapel, a double cube (fifty-six feet long, twenty-eight feet high and wide) standing inconspicuously between St James's Palace and Marlborough House, is in all essentials much as Inigo conceived it, the first English place of worship designed in the classical tradition rather than the Gothic. Christopher Wren drew on many of its details in the London churches that he rebuilt after the Great Fire of 1666.[28]

The elegant interior was showier than the exterior, but still restrained by comparison with Catholic churches on the Continent. The barrel ceiling, drawn from a design by Palladio, was compartmented into twenty-eight squares, their gilded egg-and-dart borders crafted by Matthew Goodrich in timber, rather than in plaster, as had been the custom in England. [29] Another outstanding feature was the large tripartite East window, in plain glass, echoing the theme of the frontage in that the central pane has a rounded head – a 'Venetian window', as illustrated by Serlio. This was the first known example in England of this pattern of window, much used by Wren. The royal pew, on the gallery at the west end, retains Inigo's original monumental fireplace in Reigate stone.

On 16 May 1623 the Spanish ambassador laid the foundation stone, but the architect could not give the work his exclusive attention, for the expected arrival of the Infanta and Prince Charles brought other additions to his workload. Even if the precise date was still uncertain, plans had to be made for a formal reception for the future King and Queen at Southampton, where their ship would dock. So in June a group of officials travelled to the port to see what needed to be done, in Chamberlain's words, 'for mending the highways and for shows and pageants'. Inigo – qualified in all three categories – was in the party, as were Thomas Howard and Edward Alleyn, the veteran actor, theatre owner and founder of Dulwich College.

The three were old acquaintances, going back to when they were all attached to Prince Henry's household. Inigo had an additional point of contact with Alleyn's world of the commercial stage through the work he had done on Beeston's Phoenix Theatre in Drury Lane. He and Howard had been in Dulwich for the opening ceremony of Alleyn's college in September 1619, and were signatories of the trust deed. The previous year Howard had given Alleyn a guided tour of the art treasures of Arundel House, and in 1622 Alleyn reciprocated by showing Howard work in progress on rebuilding his Fortune Theatre in Finsbury after it had burned down.

Chamberlain, clearly a sceptic about the royal marriage, doubted whether it was really necessary for such a high-powered delegation to journey all the way to Southampton to prepare for the Infanta's arrival. In his view,

> two or three herbingers[30] or suchlike officers might have performed all this as well as so many prime counsellors, but that we must show how diligent and obsequious we are in anything that concerns her [the Infanta].[31]

In the event all the diligence and obsequiousness proved in vain, for the mission of Charles and Buckingham to Madrid was a farcical failure.

They had removed their ludicrous disguises once they arrived in Paris, then ridden through France, where Charles fell off his horse at least four times. They crossed the Pyrenees and arrived in the Spanish capital at the beginning of March. It was scarcely surprising that the King, Philip IV, should regard their sudden arrival with grave suspicion. Since the marriage negotiations had started nearly a decade earlier, they had hinged on whether James would agree to allow English Catholics to worship freely and in public. As soon as the King indicated that he would make that concession, the Spaniards added new and impossible conditions, including Charles's conversion to his intended wife's faith. For James's part, in addition to the Spanish dowry, he wanted an assurance that his son-in-law Frederick would be restored as ruler of the Palatinate.

For both sides, those terms proved a step too far. Charles and Buckingham stayed in Madrid all summer – indeed at one point King James feared they were being held hostage. From the fleeting glimpses that he was allowed of the Infanta, the immature Charles had convinced himself that he was truly in love with her, but for most of his stay he was not allowed within arm's length of the object of his passion. After a hot, frustrating summer the two men left the city in September. Riding fast to the north coast, they were met by the British fleet in Santander and, surviving an accident when their ship capsized in rough seas, arrived home the following month without their hoped-for prize.[32]

No doubt they were disappointed by their failure, but the reaction of the London populace was quite the opposite. Defying rain, the citizens celebrated and lit bonfires, not only – or indeed chiefly – to mark the Prince's safe return, but to hail the final burial both of the marriage project and of King James's political dalliance with the Spaniards. The King liked to see himself as the English Solomon, using his wisdom to pacify warring factions, but he would end his reign in a renewed conflict with the old enemy. In 1624 Parliament finally voted him the money he had long sought, but its purpose was to allow him to wage a trade war against Spain and to defend the country against possible attack by Philip.

As for the lovesick Prince Charles, he rebounded quickly from his failed wooing. He and the King began to sound out Louis XIII, King of France, about a marriage between the Prince and the King's fourteen-year-old sister, Henrietta Maria. Ironically, the couple had first met when Charles was passing through Paris earlier that year, on his way to Madrid. This time the negotiations were swift and the marriage contract was signed before Christmas.

For Inigo, this speedy resolution of the heir's matrimonial future was unalloyed good news, because it meant that he scarcely had to interrupt work on the chapel at St James's. The French princess was also Catholic, and she too would need a chapel. Who knew, she might even need a pleasure house at Greenwich as well?

Chapter Fourteen

HONOUR THY FATHER

T HE PRINCE'S SAFE RETURN from his misguided mission, his survival of the accident at sea and the public celebration that followed, gave Inigo and Jonson a ready-made subject for the 1624 Twelfth Night masque, *Neptune's Triumph for the Return of Albion*.

> Now he is safe, and Fame's not heard in vain,
> But we behold our happy pledge again . . .
> And every songster had sung out his fit;
> That all the country and the city wit
> Of bells and bonfires and good cheer was spent,
> And Neptune's guard had drunk all that they meant.

The masque, published the following year, was never in fact performed, for two principal reasons. First, the King's health was continuing to decline and secondly there was another dispute about diplomatic precedence. The King wanted to invite the Spanish ambassador, in the hope of repairing the damage done to relations between the two countries by Prince Charles's escapade, but his French counterpart angrily refused to sit in the same room as the envoy from Madrid.

The King was already worried about the anti-Spanish tone of the piece. Forever the populist, Jonson had taken the side of the majority by expressing relief at the failure of the marriage plan and urging reprisals against Spain. Some excisions of overtly political references had already been ordered, but in the end, given the diplomatic complications, the King decided to abandon the whole masque.[1]

This was particularly frustrating for Inigo because the stage directions suggest that he had created yet another of his ambitious and innovative devices, where an island moved to the front of the stage to join up with the shore, then receded to reveal a palace. Luckily he was able to use the same sets the following year, for *The Fortunate Isles and their Union*, in which Jonson, equally loath to let his best work go to waste, recycled some of the more lyrical passages from *Neptune's Triumph*. Luckily for Inigo, these did not include the antimasque, where Jonson had once again seized the opportunity of satirising his collaborator. Much of it would have taken the form of a dialogue between a poet (Jonson) and a cook (Inigo). The cook, jealous of his privileges, declared: 'This is my room and region too, the Banqueting House! And in matter of feast and solemnity nothing is to be presented here but with my acquaintance and allowance to it.' And he described himself as:

> A master-cook! Why, he is the man of men
> For a professor! He designs, he draws,
> He paints, he carves, he builds, he fortifies,
> Makes citadels of curious fowls and fish;
> Some he dry-ditches, some moats round with broths,
> Mounts marrow-bones, cuts fifty-angled custards,
> Rears bulwark pies and, for his outer-works
> He raiseth ramparts of immortal crust . . .
> He is an architect, an engineer,
> A soldier, a physician, a philosopher,
> A general mathematician!

Jonson had by now eschewed any mystery and subtlety in his references to Inigo: nobody can have been in the slightest doubt about the cook's intended identity, especially not the cook himself. Yet though he ended the antimasque with a couplet that confirmed his belief in his own prime importance in the creation of the masques, Jonson appeared at the same time to be trying to cool the growing rivalry between the couple. He had the cook exhort him:

> And, brother poet, though the serious part
> Be yours, yet envy not the cook his art.

It would have been a shame to waste such wit. Two years later he recreated the cook in his play *The Staple of News*, where many of the lines mocking Inigo were reproduced verbatim. Despite his own admonition to himself, Jonson's envy and resentment of his pretentious collaborator were now so potent that they could not be contained; nor could his expression of them be thwarted.

It was fitting that *The Fortunate Isles*, lauding the benefits of a unified kingdom and a wise ruler, was the last masque that James I would see. It reflected perfectly the image that he had tried, in his rough-hewn way, to cultivate – even if history, in allotting him part of the blame for the catastrophe that was to befall his son, would be less generous to his reputation.

He died at Theobalds on Sunday 27 March 1625 and it fell to Inigo to design the catafalque for his body. The new King, Charles I, wanted his father commemorated in a suitably grand and solemn style. In 1621 Thomas Howard had been appointed Earl Marshal, whose duties then (as now) included the responsibility for organising such royal ceremonies as state funerals. He headed a commission that met for the first time two days after the King's death and ordered that the body should be taken in a torchlight procession to Somerset House the following Monday evening. There it lay in state beneath a canopy, with a life-sized effigy of James on the coffin, surrounded by eight candlesticks that Charles had bought on his Spanish trip. It stayed there for four weeks, with a view to a funeral at the end of April.[2] So long a period between death and burial would scarcely be acceptable today, but Inigo needed plenty

Catafalque for James I

of time to get the catafalque built. When he failed to meet the first deadline, the funeral was postponed until 7 May.

The catafalque, where the coffin was placed during the funeral service, was widely admired. Chamberlain called it 'the fairest and best fashioned that hath been seen'. Based on one designed by Domenico Fontana for the funeral of Pope Sixtus V in 1590, it took the form of a miniature temple crowned with an octagonal dome of exaggerated height, decorated with flags and shields and supported on Doric columns. It stood on a square plinth with statues of grieving women at each corner, representing religion, justice, war and peace.[3] At the base of the dome were seated figures sculpted by Hubert Le Sueur. Because it was a temporary structure it was made of perishable materials: the figures were of plaster of Paris draped in calico, rather than being carved in marble.[4] For the funeral, the King's Wardrobe issued court mourners with 30,000 yards of black cloth, to the value of £28,251.[5]

Charles did not let his father's death interfere with his marriage plans. On 11 May 1625, only four days after James's funeral, he was married to Henrietta Maria at a ceremony in Paris, where a French nobleman acted as proxy for him. When the fifteen-year-old Queen arrived in London in June, the couple sailed from Greenwich to Somerset House in formal procession; but that was the only public ceremony in London to celebrate the marriage. The new King's aversion to close contact with the multitudes meant that there was no repeat of the wedding ceremony itself: nor did he mark his accession with a parade, as James had done.

The Queen brought with her a number of French attendants, whose principal purpose was to ensure that the young woman was not persuaded into straying from the Catholic faith. Before long Charles, resenting the influence exerted by these attendants, threw them all out; but he recognised that he was obliged to provide Henrietta Maria with a place to worship, and Inigo was instructed to see that work on the Queen's Chapel at St James's was quickly resumed. Within a year, by Easter 1626, the chapel was sufficiently complete for the young Queen, accompanied by a clutch of ladies-in-waiting, to walk from Somerset House, along the Strand and Pall Mall, to St James's Palace, to inspect her private place of worship.[6] The plan to provide another one for her at Somerset House, where she was living, was delayed for a few years, but Inigo was required to convert part of the cellar at Greenwich Palace into a temporary chapel.[7] Henrietta Maria was fond of Greenwich, and it would not be long before she would ask Inigo to complete the pleasure house that he had begun for Anne of Denmark.

Charles was keen to stress the continuity of policy between his administration and his father's. On 2 May 1625, five weeks after assuming the Crown, he issued a proclamation on town planning that reaffirmed all the building rules and restrictions imposed in the two previous reigns. That they were still necessary was confirmed that year by the worst outbreak of the plague since 1603 – coincidentally the year James came to the throne.[8]

The new proclamation, with its meticulous attention to the detail of permitted construction standards, showed every sign of being drafted by Inigo. It ruled that all visible external surfaces, including jambs (window surrounds) must be in brick or stone, and that timber window frames were not to be fitted until the jambs were in place. Walls of two-storey buildings had to be the thickness of one and a half bricks, and if there was a third storey then the ground floor walls had to be two bricks thick. The walls must be 'direct and straight upwards' (i.e. no overhangs) and the windows taller than they were broad. The heads of shop windows should be arched, to carry the weight of the walls above. There were even rules about when bricks should be made – between Annunciation Day (25 March) and the end of August – and their price at the kilns: no more than eight shillings per thousand.[9]

Most of the regulations were dictated by sanitary considerations – what today we call health and safety – more than by aesthetics. Soon after Charles's accession Inigo had to bury any fastidious instincts and involve himself in a direct way in the problems of drainage and sewage caused by London's population explosion. They affected him personally, for Scotland Yard, where he had his house, was one of the main trouble spots. Waste from the increasingly populated areas around St Giles and St Martin's Lane tended to gather there and, worse, much of it travelled still further south, ending up close to the royal quarters in Whitehall Palace. At the beginning of 1626, Inigo, in his capacity as Surveyor of His Majesty's Works, and Thomas Baldwin, the Comptroller, wrote an official report on the problem. It painted a vivid, horrifying picture. Rain would carry soil from Long Acre into St Martin's Lane, which was 'now full of great muckhills, all which by default of the scavengers is at this time near three hundred loads, which upon every rain is brought down before the King's palace'. By no means a dainty dish to set before the King.

The scavengers were those whose unenviable task it was to remove muck and rubbish from the streets, but they could not keep up with the rate at which it was now being generated. There were more dunghills in the lanes linking St Martin's Lane with Covent Garden, which increased the nuisance, while some newly built stables in the area compounded the problem. The report recommended that the parish of St Martin's should be charged with taking away the offending heaps, recouping the cost from those who had produced the rubbish. The parish of St Giles should build new and bigger sewers, and everyone should carry away their soil in carts rather than piling it up in the streets.[10]

Whether or not those recommendations were put into effect, the capital remained a chronically unhygienic city. In 1630 Inigo was made a Justice of the Peace for Westminster and Middlesex. Among his first tasks in the role was to report to the Privy Council on the steps taken to prevent the spread of plague: shutting up houses, burying the dead by night and inspecting houses before they were allowed to reopen. The magistrates also had to take action against those who resisted their houses being closed, or went out into the streets without authority.[11]

The tasks that fell to a JP covered an even broader range than those of a Surveyor-General. One of Inigo's recorded acts was to command thirty-seven innkeepers and twelve poulterers not to allow any small acates – provisions such as butter and eggs – to be sold on their premises by people from the country, who were taking trade from local shopkeepers.[12] In 1631 he and another magistrate were ordered by the Privy Council to enforce an order on Scipio Squire, a property speculator, to pull down a two-storey house he had built in Long Acre in defiance of the royal proclamations.[13] And he soon found himself having to witness countless oaths of allegiance, as people whose loyalty to the Crown was suspect were pressed to affirm it in the increasingly dangerous political climate.

Inigo filled the roles of the methodical surveyor and conscientious magistrate – carefully measuring the thickness of walls, monitoring the price of bricks and grappling with sewage and health matters – with as much seeming enthusiasm as he did his creative endeavours.

This was fortunate, for demand for his other principal skill, stage design, was in a temporary decline. The reign had begun with a production of *Artenice*, a French pastoral drama by Honorat de Racan, performed in French by the Queen and the attendants who had accompanied her from Paris. (This was shortly before Charles sent them all packing.) It was an historic event, the first recorded occasion in which actresses had appeared on an English stage. The King, knowing how controversial it was likely to be, allowed only a very few intimates to attend the performance. Chamberlain noted: 'I have known a time when this would have seemed a strange sight to see a Queen act in a play but *tempora mutantur et nos* [times change and so do we].'

Proscenium for *Artenice*, 1626

In King James's time, women of the court had danced in the masques, but custom, decency and piety had until now barred them from speaking roles. The Puritans, an increasingly powerful religious and political force, detested the notion. In Elizabethan and Jacobean plays and entertainments, female characters were played by boys, and on the commercial stage this convention lasted until the Restoration.

In France, though, actresses had begun to appear at the beginning of the seventeenth century. Henrietta Maria, who enjoyed treading the boards, was determined not to be deterred from her pleasure through fear of provoking scandal in her new realm. Inigo did her proud, engineering seven changes of scenery in *Artenice* and some sensational effects of sound and light. The play opened with a moonlit village scene, partly based on an engraving by Serlio and including a classical temple. This was transformed into a wood and, following a dramatic storm, the moon reappeared, this time over mountains. For the masque that followed he designed a backdrop incorporating the Thames and Somerset House, the Queen's home.[14]

After that controversial start, there appears to have been a hiatus in the production of masques. Charles, though still a keen dancer, may have felt he had other priorities; and Henrietta Maria was as yet too young to fill the shoes of Anne of Denmark, whose entrepreneurial flair had been such an important factor in inspiring the early masques and shows of James's reign. The whole tone of the new court was chillier and more formal, less given to pleasure. The King's small, slight figure, his withdrawn bearing and his occasional stammer, stood in contrast to his father's coarse ebullience. Soon after Charles's accession the Venetian ambassador reported home: 'The King observes a rule of great decorum.'[15] The widow Lucy Hutchinson, the Parliamentary supporter who had been so disapproving of James's lifestyle, wrote:

> The face of the court was much changed in the change of the King, for King Charles was temperate, chaste and serious; so that the fools and bawds, mimics and catamites, of the former court, grew out of fashion.

No wonder, then, that the old King's erstwhile favourites were nervous, uncertain whether his son would continue to value their advice and presence. Under James, courtiers had become accustomed to virtually uncontrolled access to the royal bedchamber, where they would go to plead their own or their friends' causes, but the practice ceased abruptly under Charles. At only twenty-four, he was still short of confidence and jealous of his privacy.

In the event, Inigo, unlike some other royal servants, would have little difficulty in ingratiating himself and securing his admittance into the young sovereign's inner circle. By now a long-standing member of the court, he was there by virtue of his professional skills rather than because of aristocratic status or favouritism. Indeed he was closer to the new King than he had been to his father, given their mutual interest in the visual arts and their fruitful collaboration in several masques over the past fifteen years. Many an old trouper will testify that backstage comradeship, along with the shared terrors of public performance, can be a potent and enduring bond.

Among those who fared less well at court, at least in the early years of the reign, was Inigo's friend and patron Thomas Howard. Entrusted with the key role in preparing the state funeral, he had got off to a good start; but soon afterwards he fell seriously out of favour with the King, through no apparent fault of his own. The cause was the clandestine marriage between Lord Maltravers, Howard's eighteen-year-old son and heir, and Lady Elizabeth Stuart, the fifteen-year-old daughter of the Duke of Lennox, one of the Scottish noblemen who had come south with King James. Charles had been scheming to arrange Elizabeth's marriage to Lord Lorne, son of the Earl of Argyll, as a means of healing the bitter rift between the Stuart and Campbell clans – Campbell being the family name of the Argyll dynasty.

The King was convinced that Howard, despite his fervent denials, had engineered his son's impulsive marriage. Egged on by Buckingham, a long-time enemy of the Earl Marshal, the King banished Howard from his court and had him locked up in the Tower for some weeks before allowing him to move to his mother's house, where he was made to remain, virtually a prisoner.[16] For nearly two years his movements were restricted and it was only after Buckingham's untimely death – knifed by a disgruntled soldier in 1628 – that he won his way back to favour.

That December, the King signalled the end of Howard's disgrace by visiting Arundel House, accompanied by Henrietta Maria, to look at his increasingly renowned art collection.[17] Although the healing of the rift between his two most important patrons would have come as a great relief to Inigo, there is no evidence that he played any mediating role: his concern not to compromise his own status at court may have persuaded him to let events take their course. If by mischance Howard's fall from favour had proved permanent, to be seen to take his part would have cost Inigo everything he had so far achieved. Loyalty could be carried too far.

Charles was the first English sovereign to show a serious interest in the visual arts. He shared his brother Henry's taste for classical painting and sculpture, ancient coins and medals, and he inherited some of the works that the late Prince had begun to collect. Just before Charles became King, Rubens wrote to a friend describing him as the greatest lover of painting among all the princes in the world.[18] In this respect he was a much more inspiring patron than the philistine James, and both Howard and Inigo were eventually able to use his enthusiasms to their advantage in gaining his confidence. They were prominent in the group of intimates whose opinion the King would seek as he developed his collections.

According to the inventory made by Abraham Van der Doort in 1639, some items in the royal collection had either been selected by Inigo or sold or donated by him. They included an altar-piece and some important pictures. One was a portrait in wax of Henry VIII 'in a worm-eaten, rotten frame' and another a miniature drawing by Isaac Oliver depicting Prince Henry wielding a lance: Inigo may have acquired it while he was in the late Prince's service. Van der Doort also hinted at disputes among the King's advisers, including Inigo, about who should have access to some of the most valuable parts of the collection, especially the coins and medals. He suggested that some of the rarest items may have been removed and disposed of without authority.[19] Inigo had gained a reputation for expertise over a broad area and in 1631 he was one of three men appointed to value the King's collection of coins.[20]

Vying with Inigo as the most influential of the new King's cultural advisers was Nicholas Lanier, a court musician under James, who had written, played and sung much of the music for the royal masques. Charles, immediately on his accession, appointed Lanier Master of the King's Music and also took his advice on expanding his art collection. He played a prominent role in the acquisition in 1628 of the collection of the Duke of Mantua, the most important batch of paintings ever bought by an English monarch.

Lanier went to Italy on the King's behalf in 1625, first to Rome, where he bought more than thirty paintings for £20,000, then Venice, where he heard that Duke Ferdinando of Mantua was hard pressed financially and wanted to sell part of his family's renowned collection, including paintings by Titian, Rubens and Raphael. At first the deal, negotiated by a Venetian agent, did not run too smoothly: Ferdinando died, as his dissolute successor Duke Vincenzo did soon afterwards, and Charles, as was his habit, was slow to pay the agreed sum. But the delay worked in Charles's favour. The next Duke, Carlo di Nevers, agreed in addition to part with the biggest prize of his collection, Mantegna's series of nine *Triumphs of Caesar*, now hanging at Hampton Court. A price of £15,000 was agreed, but when the Mantua pictures were eventually despatched, some came into contact with mercury in the ship's hold and had to be restored after their arrival.[21]

In the end it was worth it, for when the paintings were hung in Charles's palaces they constituted one of the world's finest collections of Renaissance art, a fitting background for a prince of cultured tastes to act out his destiny as the divinely ordained ruler of his people. Yet there was a negative outcome to all this spending on high art. Charles, more aggressive than his father in foreign affairs, had decided to support the people of the Netherlands in their attempt to drive out the occupying Spaniards. He needed money to conduct both this campaign and a later one against France. Though neither war lasted long they proved a drain on the exchequer, especially Buckingham's bungled raid on Cadiz in the first year of the reign.

Parliament's reluctance to supply the necessary funds was stiffened when its members observed how much the King was spending on indulging his artistic whims. Combined with his arrogant and high-handed manner, and the suspicion that he had Catholic leanings – a dangerous inclination less than a century after Henry VIII's Reformation – this extravagance could only aggravate the tension between the Crown and Parliament that had been evident in James's time. The first crisis of the reign broke in 1627, only two years after Charles's accession. When Parliament denied him the money he sought for making war, he tried to exact forced loans from his knights, claiming that this was his inalienable right as King. Five knights refused to pay and he had them arrested. Seeking to appease Parliament after the men were released the following year, the King agreed that he would not in future resort to imprisonment for those who declined to pay forced loans.

This was not enough to cool the anger of Members, who presented him with a Petition of Right – an ancient method of calling monarchs to account – demanding an end to all arbitrary imprisonment, forced loans and the compulsory billeting of soldiers on citizens. Charles accepted the petition but was almost immediately accused of failure to observe it, by continuing to raise illegal taxes. In March 1629, his patience exhausted, he dissolved Parliament, though he could not prevent the passing of three resolutions condemning him. For the next eleven years, known as the period of personal rule, he would make do without the recalcitrant politicians who claimed to be representatives of the people.

His financial position was eased when the conflict with Spain came to an end, through a peace deal brokered by an unlikely envoy. Peter Paul Rubens, born in Germany and now living in Antwerp, was one of the most admired of the Flemish school of painters. He had never been to England but in 1625 attended the wedding celebrations in Paris for Charles and Henrietta Maria. There he met Buckingham, who became a friend and client, buying a substantial quantity of the artist's pictures. Because of his connections with the Spanish court, Rubens supported the Spanish occupation of the Netherlands and sought to persuade Buckingham, and later Charles himself, to end their opposition to it.

In August 1628 – coincidentally the month of Buckingham's assassination – Rubens went to Madrid to discuss possible peace terms with the Spanish King. In April 1629 he brought those terms to London, staying until he succeeded in gaining acceptance for a treaty the following year. During his visit he painted a portrait of Thomas Howard and inspected his collection of marbles, declaring in a letter to a friend that 'I have seen nothing in the world more rare, as regards antiquities'.[22]

During his stay Rubens accepted the commission to execute the ceiling paintings for Inigo's Banqueting House. He had first been approached in 1621, when the old King was still alive, but he was not immediately free. Now Charles wanted to resuscitate the project, envisaging the panels as a memorial to his father, stressing his qualities as a wise ruler, peacemaker, and the architect of British unity. These, of course, were the themes of the court masques, and this is one reason why it seems likely that Inigo played a role in advising Rubens, unfamiliar as he was with the nuances of Stuart philosophy and iconography, on the specific subjects of the paintings.[23] The two men had much in common. Inigo was only four years older than the painter, and both had travelled in Italy during their formative years.

Rubens did not stay in London to complete the paintings. He returned to his Antwerp studio armed with the measurements of the empty panels and a detailed brief. By 1634 he had completed the work and two years later, after characteristic delays in obtaining payment from the King, the paintings had been shipped to London and installed on the ceiling of the Banqueting House, where they remain today in all their magnificence.

The central, oval panel illustrates James's apotheosis. He is seen being transported to heaven on the back of an eagle, in the company of figures representing justice and religious faith, while a winged Minerva, goddess of wisdom, waits to place a crown on his head – a clear allusion to the Stuarts' belief in the divine right of monarchs. The two large rectangular panels to its north and south also depict the King in person. In both he is portrayed as a latter-day Solomon, uniting England and Scotland to give birth to the new entity of

Great Britain, and affording protection to the symbols of peace and plenty while warding off warmongers who would disturb them. The six smaller, flanking panels illustrate the virtues that Charles attributed to his father: wisdom, genius, reason, heroism, kindness and magnanimity. These nine masterly panels are the only Rubens ceiling paintings to have survived anywhere.

Chapter Fifteen

A HOUSE FIT FOR A QUEEN

I N 1628 A SIGNIFICANT FIGURE entered Inigo's life. John Webb, then seventeen, joined him as his assistant and pupil, straight from Merchant Taylors' School. There may have been a family connection between the two. Both were born in Smithfield, although Webb's father hailed from Somerset. In a petition of 1660, in which Webb asked the newly restored Charles II to appoint him Surveyor-General, he described Jones as his 'uncle'. This is likely, though, to have been an imprecise reference to Webb's later marriage to Anne Jones, variously described as Inigo's niece or his cousin and suspected by some historians (probably mistakenly) of being his illegitimate daughter, on the grounds that she was the principal beneficiary of his will.[1] The most authoritative account of their relationship came from Webb's son James who, in a letter to an Oxford historian after his father's death, declared that his mother 'was not Mr Jones's daughter (as you suppose) but his near relation, her father and Mr Jones being cousin germans [first cousins]'.[2]

Since Inigo never married, John and Anne Webb, whatever their precise relationship to him, were the closest he had to a family, apart from his sisters. As time went on, Webb was to be given more and more responsibility in running the office and assisting his master with his designs for buildings and masque scenes. He was an excellent draughtsman, and many surviving drawings of Inigo's later work are in his hand. After some years he started to design his own buildings, very much in his mentor's idiom. In modern terms he could be likened to a junior partner in an architecture and design practice. After Inigo's death, Webb inherited his papers and drawings and was trustee of his estate. His short biographical introduction to the posthumously published book about Stonehenge is one of the few direct sources for several aspects of Inigo's life.

In the same 1660 petition, Webb said that Inigo took him on as an apprentice at the 'special command' of the King, with a view to training him up to succeed him as Surveyor to the Crown. This may well have been the case since Charles, only three years into his reign, was clearly wishing to make his mark as a builder of splendid palaces in the style of his European contemporaries. Inigo was almost the only English-born architect with any comprehensive grounding in classicism, and in 1628 he was in his mid-fifties. This was already a creditable lifespan for the period, and would have seemed especially old to the much younger Charles. Assuring succession is a constant royal preoccupation; so it would have seemed natural to the King to seek to arrange that his chief architect's attributes would not die with him.

As Webb began his apprenticeship, Inigo gave him a room in his house in Scotland Yard, adjoining the Surveyor's office. At this point, Inigo was still paying his £46 a year in rent for it, but in 1629 the King issued a warrant by which the Crown, recognising Inigo's 'good and faithful service done to our late dear father and to us', would henceforth pay his rent for him.[3] Although the sum was not great, the royal gesture was a tangible indication of how Inigo's stock at court was continuing to rise.

One of the first official assignments that came to the Surveyor's office after Webb began his apprenticeship was Inigo's second recorded design for a new theatre – like the first, converted from a former cockpit. In 1629 he was asked to transform the cockpit in Whitehall Palace, built for Henry VIII, into a small venue for plays, as distinct from masques. He did not alter the building's Tudor exterior but put a neo-Palladian theatre inside it, based primarily on Palladio's Teatro Olimpico at Vicenza, which he had visited sixteen years earlier.

The designs of other architects inspired some of the details. In his copy of Serlio's architectural work, he made a marginal note at a point where the author wrote about small cornices placed between pilasters to accommodate busts, 'as I made in the scene [*frons scenae*] of the Theatridium in Whitehall'.[4] The conversion of the Cockpit-in-Whitehall, as it was more generally called, took three years. A drawing of it by Webb, apparently made after Inigo's death, shows an octagonal auditorium, probably the original shape of the cockpit, fitted inside a square exterior. Minimal traces of it can still be found inside the Cabinet Office building in Whitehall.

In the first few years after Webb joined Inigo's office, much of their official work was concentrated on Somerset House, the main London residence of Henrietta Maria, forever seeking to upgrade and modernise the old Tudor palace in accordance with her exacting requirements. With the painter Matthew Goodrich, Inigo redesigned the Queen's Cabinet Room in the most sumptuous manner, with extensive panelling and a moulded ceiling, all in white and gilt, a colonnaded chimney-piece and a doorcase with a frieze and pediment, of which Inigo's drawing survives.[5]

Improvements were also made in the garden that led down from the house to the bank of the Thames. A fountain designed by Inigo and executed by Hubert Le Sueur was placed in a central position there in the 1630s. A female figure, with one hand clasped to her breast, stands on a plinth surrounded by sea monsters, dolphins, mermaids and cherubs. An early draft of the design, in Inigo's hand, is in the Duke of Devonshire's collection at Chatsworth and contains elements copied almost exactly from engravings of sixteenth-century fountains at Bologna and Augsburg. The fountain was moved to Hampton Court in 1656 on the orders of Oliver Cromwell and in 1713 placed in the centre of the round pond at nearby Bushy Park, on a tall base that was not part of the original. Known as the Diana Fountain, it remains there today and a comparison with Inigo's drawing leaves no doubt that he was its designer, even though his original nude female figure was clothed by the sculptor to protect her modesty.[6]

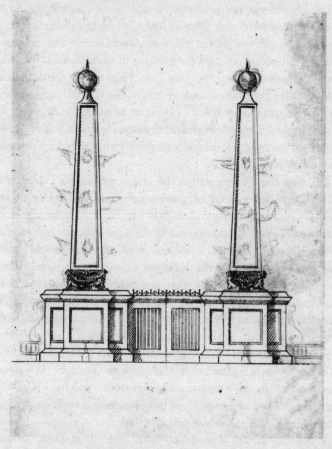

The water stairs at Somerset House

A drawing of the watergate and stairs that led from the garden of Somerset House to the river has been identified as possibly being by Webb.[7] The gate, incorporating carvings of river gods and ornamental vases, was framed in a pair of 'wings' that sloped down to the river wall. It was begun in 1628 and completed in 1632, by which time Inigo had resumed work on the Catholic chapel for Somerset House that he had abandoned when Charles failed to win the hand of the Infanta.

The chapel was not primarily for the Queen herself but for the eight Capuchin friars that Charles had allowed her to bring into her household to officiate at her religious observances. The beleagured Catholics of London regarded the granting of permission for the chapel as something of a triumph, perhaps even a signal that the old religion would one day be restored, and when the Queen laid the foundation stone they organised a colourful ceremony to mark the occasion. The site was swathed in tapestries and other costly materials; fragrant flowers were spread over the ground and a temporary altar rigged up, decorated with fine ornaments.[8]

The new chapel, larger than the one at St James's Palace, was a double cube stretching sixty feet on its longest side, well lit by eight large windows with Portland stone surrounds. The ceiling was flat where at St James's it was rounded. Again, and for the same political reason, it was unobtrusive, quite 'masculine and unaffected', on the outside.[9] Inside, though, Inigo complied with the client's desires and allowed himself more decorative licence. The altar was framed by an arch supported on two pillars. Behind it was an elaborate altar-piece, verging on the Baroque, made up of a series of seven oval frames containing angels sitting on clouds with, at the centre, a dove holding the holy sacrament, surrounded by cherubim and seraphim within rays of light. According to one of the Queen's Capuchins, Father Cyprian Gamache, it was 'most ingeniously contrived, with the aid of perspective and hidden lights, so to deceive the eye and to produce the illusion of a considerable space occupied by a great number of figures'.[10]

A delicate carved screen, on fluted and gilded Doric columns, marked the entrance to the Queen's closet. There were hints of French influence in all this elaborate decoration and it is probable that other designers, brought from the Queen's native land and no doubt sharing her faith, collaborated with Inigo on many of the interior details.[11] A Roman envoy in London reported that Inigo had been reluctant to work on this, his second Catholic chapel, because he was 'one of those Puritans, or rather people without religion'. Despite the urgings of the Queen, apparently coupled with some financial inducements, the chapel was not completed until the end of 1635.[12]

Its consecration that December was a solemn and lengthy affair. The Reverend George Garrard, Master of Charterhouse, described it in a letter to Thomas Wentworth, Earl of Strafford, then Lord Deputy of Ireland:

> The ceremonies lasted three days, massing, preaching and singing of litanies, and such a glorious scene built over their altar, the Glory of Heaven, Inigo Jones never presented a more curious piece in any of the masques at Whitehall; with this our English ignorant papists are mightily taken.[13]

At the end of the third day the crowds had to be cleared to allow the King to visit his wife's new chapel. Again according to Father Gamache, he spent a long time gazing at Inigo's handiwork, and finally said that 'he had never seen anything more beautiful or more ingeniously contrived'.

If Inigo really was a Puritan, he had clearly not on this occasion let his beliefs interfere with the requirements of the Queen. So much did the altar smack of popery that it was destroyed by Parliamentary soldiers during the Civil War. In the late 1630s Inigo carried out further improvements on Somerset House itself, including the provision of a classical frontage on the river side. It was all pulled down in 1775, with the chapel and the rest of the old Renaissance palace, to allow Sir William Chambers to erect his magnificent office building, now housing a set of museums.

Even if we accept the Roman envoy's account of Inigo's religious affiliation (supported a few years later by the Pope's representative, Gregorio Panzani),[14] it may not have been the sole reason for the delay in completing the chapel. An alternative explanation was that Inigo was working at the same time on a much more exciting project for the young Queen. The King had acceded to her request that the unfinished pleasure house at Greenwich, abandoned when Anne of Denmark died in 1619, should now be completed for Henrietta Maria. After consulting her, Inigo made some changes to his original design. The Great Hall at the heart of the house, where sculpture was displayed and where guests would assemble after they entered, was originally conceived as occupying only a single storey. Now he doubled its height, turning it into a perfect cube, divided horizontally by a balustraded gallery on all four sides.

Adding the second storey to both halves of the building, on either side of the road, meant that they could finally be joined by the unique 'bridge room'. It also allowed for the creation of another of the house's most unusual features for its time – the first-floor open loggia on the south side, overlooking the park. In 1615 Inigo had noted in the margin of his Palladio that a central loggia, 'a frontispiece in the midst', was one of the greatest ornaments a house could have. There are other references, too, to his enthusiasm for loggias, especially as they adorned the palazzos of Genoa. Although the English climate renders an open balcony rather less useful than in Italy, as well as more expensive to maintain, it was to become a feature of the English Palladian style.

On the resumption of the work, Inigo played less of a hands-on supervisory role than he had done during the initial phase. He delegated the day-to-day organisation of it to Henry Wicks, Master of Her Majesty's Works, who was paid a total of £7000, presumably including the cost of labour and materials, between 1632 and 1638. The date of 1635 appears on the north front, probably recording the year when the work was far enough advanced for the Queen to move in,[15] although additions to the interior decoration continued until the royal family were obliged to leave the London area on the eve of the Civil War in 1642. A distinctive aspect of the construction was the use of brick, uncommon in country houses in the early seventeenth century, despite all the official proclamations recommending and requiring it. Inigo had observed during his Italian travels that Palladio frequently used brick, often covered with stucco, for elements of his buildings. In the accounts for the Queen's House are payments for 750,000 bricks as well as 230 tons of stone.[16]

The renowned spiral 'tulip' staircase was installed in the Great Hall in the late 1630s, constructed by Nicholas Stone from Inigo's design.[17] It gets its present-day name from the motif on the wrought-iron balusters, possibly meant not as a tulip but a stylised fleur-de-lys, the emblem of the Bourbons, Henrietta Maria's family. Stone was also responsible for installing the grey and black marble floor.[18] In 1638 ten carved wooden pedestals for marble statues were placed in the hall, and on them were placed statues that came from other royal palaces, including some from the former collection of the Dukes of Mantua.[19] A bust of King Charles by Gianlorenzo Bernini, based on the well-known triple portrait by Van Dyck, was probably sited in a niche in the hall's south wall. (It was moved to Whitehall and destroyed when the palace burned down in 1698, but a copy based on a plaster cast of the original is at Windsor Castle.)

The ceiling of the Great Hall was painted white, with gold highlights, so as to set off the nine ceiling paintings by Orazio Gentileschi of Pisa, Charles's court painter since 1626. Their theme was the flourishing of peace and the arts under the English Crown. As at the Banqueting House, it is likely that, before the pictures were commissioned, Inigo designed the shapes of the ceiling panels where they were to be fitted. As Gentileschi was working on them he became ill – he died in 1639, aged 76 – and sent to Naples for his talented daughter Artemisia to help him finish them. One of the few professional women artists of her time, she had been at the centre of a scandal as a teenager when her father charged her tutor, Agostino Tassi, with raping her repeatedly.

In the early eighteenth century the Gentileschi ceiling paintings were removed from Greenwich by Sarah, Duchess of Marlborough, and are now at Marlborough House in London. Other elements of the original decorative scheme have also been dispersed over the years. What is thought to be one of Inigo's original fireplaces for the house is today installed at Charlton House nearby: a replica was made for one of the main bedrooms at Greenwich in the 1980s.[20]

While he was exercising his artistic judgment on these decorative details,

Inigo had to deal with all the frustrations involved in masterminding a major court construction project. It was particularly hard to secure the services of the best craftsmen. In February 1637 he made an official complaint that two of his best wood carvers, Thomas James and Richard Dirkin, had been press-ganged by the Admiralty – a recurring hazard of the time – to work on its ships and administrative buildings.[21] They were ultimately reassigned to him, but the advent of the Civil War meant that some of the decoration in the Queen's House was never completed as he had planned.

The centre of the ceiling in Henrietta Maria's bedchamber was meant to be adorned with the painting *Bacchus and Ariadne* by Guido Reni of Bologna, one of her favourite artists: his *Labours of Hercules* had been among the paintings acquired by Charles from Mantua. Reni's *Bacchus* was finished in 1640 but never despatched to London because Cardinal Barberini, who had commissioned it on behalf of the Queen, was worried about the artist's handling of the nude figures, which he characterised as 'lascivious'. He feared that it would scandalise England's Protestants and reinforce their reservations about Catholic morality. The picture was destroyed in France in 1650, apparently for the same reason, although an etching survives.[22]

The most ambitious decorative scheme for the Queen's House was a set of twenty-two paintings by Jacob Jordaens, a pupil of Rubens, that would have adorned the walls and ceilings of the withdrawing room on the first floor, illustrating the story of Cupid and Psyche. Inigo played a key role in the selection of the artist and in laying down the guidelines for the composition, commissioned in 1639. Both Rubens and Van Dyck were considered but Jordaens had less of a reputation, which meant that his agreed fee of £680 was about half what the other two would have demanded. Balthazar Gerbier, by now the King's agent in the Netherlands, was keen nonetheless to give at least part of the work to Rubens. He wrote that neither he nor Jordaens would 'seek to represent robustrious boisterous drunken-headed imaginary gods' but that Rubens was 'the gentlest in his representations, his landscapes more rare'.

Nonetheless, the commission stayed with Jordaens. Gerbier was instructed not to tell him the identity of the client, for fear that he would bump up his price if he knew it was the Queen.[23] Inigo, clearly worried by Gerbier's comments about Jordaens' lack of gentleness, wrote in March 1640 asking him to ensure that the artist represented 'the faces of women as beautiful as may be, the figures gracious and svelte'. The pragmatic Gerbier replied that he would do so, but he also urged Inigo to speed the payment to Jordaens, 'since painters' pencils move not without that music'.[24] Inigo, after nearly a quarter of a century in the employ of cash-strapped Stuart kings, would have needed no lessons from Brussels on the frustrations of trying to extract payment from the royal coffers.

A set of detailed instructions to the artist, almost certainly issued by Inigo, was transcribed and preserved by Webb. They pointed out that the figures on the ceiling should be drawn so that they could be seen from a distance of nineteen feet:

> The greatest piece in the middle of the ceiling to be of Cupid and Psyche in heaven, and Jove sitting presenting a cup of nectar unto her. About them as many of the gods as may be without confusion . . . For the other two square pieces in the ceiling he is to choose such parts of the story as will do best overhead and in shortening . . . The pieces on the sides about the room must be all of the same story of Cupid and Psyche, and the bigness of the nearest figures answerable to those on the ceiling.

The instructions went on to discuss the effect of the light from the windows and to demand that the paintings should be made of 'strong new cloth', and measured carefully so that they would fit into the allotted spaces. Each was to be sent to Greenwich as it was finished, rather than waiting for the whole set to be completed.

By 9 May Gerbier was able to tell Inigo that the first painting was about to be despatched, but he was still keen to persuade the King and Queen to let Rubens do some of the work, especially the ceiling. That effort ended abruptly on 23 May, when Gerbier wrote starkly to Inigo: 'There are none more to be expected of Sir Peter Rubens, who deceased three days past of a deflaction which fell on his heart after some days' indisposition of age and gout.' Ever practical, Gerbier added the advice that if the King or Thomas Howard wanted to buy any of the late painter's pictures from his studio, they should move quickly and send him bills of credit.

Only eight of Jordaens' twenty-two commissioned paintings were ever delivered to the Queen's House. On 5 December 1640 Gerbier wrote to Inigo complaining that the artist had been paid only £100 so far out of his promised £680. It is doubtful whether he ever received any more, for the looming Civil War would shortly put paid to the enterprise, as to much else.

The first two recorded court masques of Charles's reign, performed in January and February 1631, were to change the lives of their two principal creators. If any masques were staged during the preceding five years, they have left no trace. Inigo had been kept busy with building and refurbishment projects for the new King and Queen but, by contrast, his collaborator Ben Jonson had fared badly. With no certainty that regular commissions for masques would be resumed, he feared that the King, periodically urged by his advisers to make economies, could at any time discontinue the annual retainer of one hundred marks (£66) granted him by King James in 1616.

So in 1625, at the age of fifty-two, he returned to the commercial stage with *The Staple of News*, his first play since *The Devil Is an Ass* in 1616. Though not a tremendous success, it did not flop as disastrously as his next work, *The New Inn*, in 1629.[25] Following this second successive failure the playwright – now ill, grossly overweight and virtually bedridden following a stroke in 1628 – wrote an *Ode to Himself*, urging his alter ego to:

> Come leave the loathed stage,
> And the more loathsome age,
> Where pride and impudence in faction knit,
> Usurp the chair of wit:
> Indicting and arraigning every day,
> Something they call a play.

Denouncing your critics is a familiar theatrical convention. While indulging in it, Jonson felt obliged to shore up his position at court by penning a number of fawning verses in praise of Charles, as well as a petition asking for an increase of a third in his annual retainer to bring it up to £100. The King, who had already made the poet an *ex gratia* grant of £100 to help sustain him during his incapacity, agreed to the new annual sum, citing Jonson's 'good and acceptable service . . . and especially to encourage him to proceed in those services of his wit and pen'. For good measure, the King granted him forty-two gallons of Canary wine a year from the royal cellars. In the Stuart court, flattery would get you everywhere.[26]

Such practical evidence of royal favour was good news for the ailing poet, but better still was the resumption of the regular winter masques. This may have been done to satisfy the desires and influence of Henrietta Maria. As a child in France, she had enjoyed watching and taking part in court entertainments – an enthusiasm she shared with her mother, Marie de Medici.[27] Now twenty-one, the Queen had developed into a decisive, independent-minded woman, a fast learner in the skills of how best to exploit her status at court.

During the first years of their marriage, Charles had maintained distant and chilly relations with her, due in part to the manoeuvres of Buckingham. The King's most influential adviser feared that if she became too close to the King his own influence would diminish; he also suspected, with some justification, that the Pope and her French Catholic relatives would seek to use her as a means of persuading the English monarchy to revert to the true faith.[28] Since Buckingham's murder in 1628 the Queen had come to recognise the futility of any such single-handed attempt to alter the course of English Church history: the most she could achieve was to secure tolerance and some freedom of worship for herself and her fellow-Catholics. As for Charles, the violent death of his close friend and adviser spurred him into forging a mutually affectionate relationship with his Queen that would endure throughout his life and became the principal theme of court entertainments during his reign.

Masque costume for Charles I

The two 1631 masques set the pattern. The first, *Love's Triumph Through Callipolis*, was for the King. Callipolis was Plato's idealised city, the fount of beauty and virtue, where Charles and his fourteen fellow-masquers represented pure love. As Jonson declared in the Introduction, the masque had been devised 'for the honour of his court, and the dignity of that heroic love and regal respect born by him to his unmatchable lady and spouse, the Queen's Majesty'.

The second masque, *Chloridia*, was for the Queen, who equally personified unsullied love triumphing over evil and vicious influences. In the last four lines of the masque, Jonson, straining perhaps rather too hard to fulfil the brief, lauded her as

> Chloris, the queen of flowers,
> The sweetness of all showers,
> The ornament of bowers,
> The top of paramours!

The two masques represented the first manifestations in English court entertainments of the philosophy of platonic love, which had originated in France in the sixteenth century. Henrietta Maria was greatly taken with the notion of pure love unsullied by sexual desire. Seeing that she and Charles produced six children (the first died at birth), she cannot have carried all the elements of platonic love into her own marriage, but it did allow her to build an influential circle of male confidants, advisers and admirers without apparently compromising herself.

Contemporary comment suggested that platonic love was viewed at court with a measure of wry incomprehension. James Howell, a diplomat and a prolific correspondent of the time, wrote to his friend Philip Warwick in 1635:

> The Court affords little news at present, but that there is a love called Platonick Love, which much sways there of late; it is a love abstracted from all corporeal gross impressions and sensual appetite, but consists in contemplation and ideas of the mind, not in any carnal fruition. This love sets the wits of the town on work; and they say there will be a masque shortly of it, whereof Her Majesty and her maids of honour will be part.[29]

He was referring to William Davenant's masque *The Temple of Love*, performed at court that year, in which he wrote of platonic love:

> Certain young lords at first disliked the philosophy
> As most uncomfortable, sad and new,
> But soon inclined to a superior vote,
> And are grown as good platonic lovers
> As are to be found in an hermitage.

In the same year Davenant wrote a play called *The Platonic Lovers*, performed at the Blackfriars Theatre. It chronicled the attempt of the romantic hero to conduct his courtship on platonic lines – a bid that ended in betrayal and disaster. One of the characters explained the philosophy as:

> A new court epithet scarce understood;
> But all they woo, sir, is the spirit, face,
> And heart: therefore their conversation is
> More safe to fame.

And another fashionable playwright, Richard Brome, wrote a play called *The Lovesick Court*, on the same theme.

Perhaps because of the demands of having to come to grips with this new philosophy, made the more challenging by his debilitating illness, Jonson's texts for the 1631 masques were shorter than for most of the earlier ones. Inigo, though, carried on where he had left off, with characteristic scenes of clouds descending to reveal brightly lit figures inside, of high hills emerging from beneath the stage, of giant rocks split open by thunder and lightning, and of gaily clad dwarfs, elves and monsters in the antimasques. In *Chloridia* the antimasque ended with a storm, acted out by players representing the elements. One of his stage directions stipulated:

> Rain, presented by five persons all swollen and clouded over, their hair
> flagging, as if they were wet, and in their hands balls full of sweet water
> which, as they dance, sprinkle all the room.

This was, too, the first masque in which he employed a fly gallery above the proscenium, allowing for more complicated aerial scenes.[30]

Now that he was working for a French-born Queen, with her own views on appropriate stage designs, Inigo prepared himself with characteristic thoroughness. The records of Sir Robert Cotton, his old drinking companion and England's foremost book collector, show that in January 1631 the architect had five books out on loan. Two of them were illustrated accounts of the coronation ceremonies at pageants for the two queens of Louis XII of France, Anne of Brittany and Mary, sister to Henry VIII.[31] It must be assumed that he borrowed them before November 1629, when Cotton's library was closed on the orders of the Privy Council, who suspected that it contained subversive tracts. So Inigo would have had ample time to put any ideas gleaned from them into practice.

A revealing insight into his relationship with the Queen comes in a note that he wrote on his drawing of the dress he created for her to wear in *Chloridia*:

> The design I conceive to be fit for the invention and if it please her majesty to add or alter anything I desire to receive her command and the design again by this bearer. The colours are in her Majesty's choice but my opinion is that several fresh greens mixed with gold and silver will be most proper.[32]

Of most significance are four words that he struck out after 'her majesty's choice'. Instead of 'but my opinion is' he had started to write 'but I should humbly . . .' before thinking better of it. At this stage of Inigo's career and reputation he felt he no longer had to feign humility – as Ben Jonson was about to discover to his cost.

Chapter Sixteen

SUCH SWEET SORROW

THE IMMEDIATE CAUSE of the rift between Inigo and Jonson has been well chronicled. In essence it derived from an ancient theatrical tradition: the dispute over who gets top billing. It had become the convention for Jonson, familiar as he was with the world of publishing, to have the texts and stage directions for the masques printed and circulated soon after they were performed. The days had long passed when he would pay specific tribute in his introductions to Inigo's contribution to the enterprise. In the case of *Love's Triumph*, he thought it adequate to note on the title page: 'The Inventors: Ben Jonson, Inigo Jones.'

Inigo believed that his contribution to the masques was now more significant than Jonson's; so it followed that his name should have been listed first. He must have made his displeasure known to his collaborator, though it is unclear exactly how. Jonson responded with a final, characteristic act of defiance: when the time came to publish *Chloridia* he removed Inigo's name altogether.

It was a grave misjudgment. Inigo now had sufficient influence with both the King and Queen to damn Jonson with the seventeenth-century version of the Hollywood curse – you will never work in this business again. And he was ruthless enough to enforce the diktat, making no allowance at all for the playwright's record, reputation or failing health. Mercy was not among his qualities; even if it were, he knew Jonson well enough to be certain that any conciliatory gesture would surely be hurled back into his face by the irascible playwright. No; if the King could rule without Parliament, Inigo could make masques without Jonson. *Chloridia* was the last entertainment that the royal couple would invite the playwright to create for them.

Chloridia, 1631: The Dwarf Post from Hell

The row had not, of course, erupted from nowhere. Since the heady early years of their partnership the relationship between the two egotistical artists had been declining steadily. It was, after all, a dozen years since Jonson had told William Drummond that if he wanted a word to express the greatest villain in the world, he would call him an Inigo. Even earlier, as we have seen, Jonson had been unable to resist inserting oblique insults to his collaborator, and to the profession of architect, into many of his plays and poems.

Nor did Inigo now have any qualms about responding in public. Jonson's first play produced after the split was *The Magnetic Lady*. It was heavily criticised by Alexander Gill, an enemy of long standing, who advised the playwright to go back to bricklaying:

> Fall then to work in thy old age again,
> Take up thy trug and trowel, gentle Ben.
> Let plays alone.

He added that the only person in the audience to laugh was Inigo – and he did so mockingly, delighted that nobody found Jonson's jokes funny:

> And Inigo with laughter there grew fat,
> That there was nothing worth the laughing at.[1]

Yet though Jonson may have been down, he was not out. He was still nimble enough of mind to pen an instant riposte, pointing out that Gill had, not many years earlier, been convicted of insulting the King and Buckingham, and sentenced to the then fashionable punishment of having his ears cut off. He was pardoned only after the intervention of William Laud, an influential churchman and a friend of Gill's father. Describing his critic as a 'bawling fool', Jonson wrote:

> Shall the prosperity of a pardon still
> Secure thy railing rhymes, infamous Gill?

By having Jonson dropped from the masque-writing team Inigo had won the most important battle, but in the war of words he was always destined to be outgunned. The poet was, after all, a professional, and had many outlets in which to pursue the vendetta. In 1632 he wrote another play, *The Tale of a Tub*, featuring a character called Vitruvius Hoop, clearly supposed to represent Inigo in the most unflattering light. Before new plays could be performed they had to be submitted for approval to the King's Master of the Revels, Sir Henry Herbert. The references to Inigo in *The Tale of a Tub* were so obvious and so insulting that Herbert felt obliged to show the script to him before deciding whether to give his approval. Inigo objected strenuously, and took his complaint to the King, who told Herbert not to license the play unless the character of Hoop was removed. Herbert recorded that, for a fee of £2, he had agreed to license the play, with this proviso:

> Vitru. Hoop's part wholly struck out, and the motion of the tub, by command from my Lord Chamberlain, exception being taken against it by Inigo Jones, Surveyor of the Works, as a personal injury to him.[2]

Jonson reluctantly complied, but retained some of the most pointed barbs at Inigo, putting them into the mouth of another character, In-and-In Medlay.[3]

Medlay wanted to present a masque and spoke incessantly of his own qualities, refusing help offered by a poet and a painter. As the poet, Diogenes Scriben, said:

> He'll do it alone, sir, he will join with no man,
> Though he be a joiner[4], in design he calls it,
> He must be sole inventor. In-and-In
> Draws with no other in's project, he will tell you,
> It cannot else be feasible, or conduce:
> Those are his ruling words.

Those two words must have been among Inigo's favourites, since Jonson also put them into Medlay's mouth in discussing a possible venue for the proposed masque:

> If I might see the place, and had survey'd it,
> I could say more: for all invention, sir,
> Comes by degrees, and on the view of nature;
> A world of things concur to the design,
> Which makes it feasible, if art conduce.

The sally hit home. When Inigo watched the play at court in January 1634 he was furious, and urged the King to ban future performances. Charles needed little persuasion because, again according to Herbert's records, the whole play was 'not liked' by the court.

This setback did not deter Jonson from stoking the flames of the feud. Although barred from writing masques for the court, he maintained his official title of poet laureate and the pension that went with it. He still received occasional private commissions as well. The Earl of Newcastle asked him to compose a masque to be performed during a visit by the King and Queen to his seat at Bolsover, Derbyshire, in July 1634. Jonson was delighted. The request 'fell like the dew of heaven on my necessities', he told the Earl. It turned out that *Love's Welcome at Bolsover* was the last masque he would ever write. Its main theme, inevitably, was the undying love between the royal couple, but the defiant playwright could not resist inserting another satire on Inigo into the antimasque, in the person of Colonel Iniquo Vitruvius, a surveyor supervising a motley troupe of mechanics. When they performed a dance for him, Vitruvius responded:

> Well done, my musical, arithmetical, geometrical gamesters! Or rather my true mathematical boys! It is carried, in number, weight and measure, as if the airs were all harmony and the figures a well-timed proportion.

Harmony, proportion and mathematics – all among Inigo's preoccupations, and words that must, like 'feasible' and 'conduce', have characterised his vocabulary.

It would be unfair to Jonson to suggest that, at least from his viewpoint, the quarrel was purely about personalities. While his antipathy towards Inigo was certainly part of it, the poet also had genuine artistic reservations about the masques' growing emphasis on spectacle and the consequent devaluation of the spoken word. Jonson was essentially a man of the theatre, and the Elizabethan and Jacobean theatre placed little importance on scenery: it was the words, the inspired words of Shakespeare and his contemporaries, that counted. In *Timber, or Discoveries*, a collection of Jonson's thoughts and observations published after his death, he articulated his dislike of flashy spectacle and costume, chiding those who succumbed to their appeal:

> There is a great difference in the understanding of some princes, as in the quality of their ministers about them. Some would dress their masters in gold, pearl and all true jewels of majesty; others furnish them with feathers, bells and ribbons: and are therefore esteemed the fitter servants.

He went on to make the same point more pithily: 'Some love any strumpet, be she never so shop-like or meritorious, in good clothes.' In a more obvious allusion to Inigo, Jonson discussed the kind of people attracted to the royal service. The best were motivated by a simple desire to be of use, others simply wanted an easy life. The third sort set themselves up as authorities on 'craft and design (as the architects say) with a premeditated thought to their own, rather than their prince's, profit. Such let the prince take heed and not doubt to reckon in the list of his open enemies.'

The work that most directly reflected Jonson's contempt for Inigo, as well as their artistic differences, was his *Expostulation with Inigo Jones*, more than a hundred lines of undiluted bile written soon after *The Tale of a Tub*. Its first lines were:

> Master surveyor, you that first began
> With thirty pound in pipkins,[5] to the man
> You are; from them leapt forth an architect,
> Able to talk of Euclid, and correct
> Both him and Archimedes; ...
>   ... overbearing us
> With mistook names out of Vitruvius!
> Drawn Aristotle on us! And thence shown
> How much architectronics is your own!
> Whether the building of the stage or scene!
> Or making of the properties it mean?

Jonson went on to accuse Inigo of vanity and boundless ambition, and of having ideas above his station:

> What makes your wretchedness to bray so loud
> In town and court? Are you grown rich? And proud?
> Your trappings will not change you. Change your mind
> No velvet sheath you wear will alter kind.

And, in the most often quoted lines of the poem, he made an ironic reference to the fashion at court for spectacle rather than dialogue:

> . . . O shows! Shows! Mighty shows!
> The eloquence of masques! What need of prose
> Or verse, or sense t'express immortal you?
> You are the spectacles of state! 'Tis true
> Court hieroglyphics! And all arts afford
> In the mere perspective of an inch board! . . .
> Oh to make boards to speak! There is a task!
> Painting and carpentry are the soul of masque!
> Pack with your piddling poetry to the stage!
> This is the money-get, mechanic age!

Unrelenting, Jonson described how Inigo, not content just to design costumes and scenery, wanted to take over every aspect of the masques:

> The maker of the properties, in sum
> The scene, the engine! But he now is come
> To be the music-master, fabler too;
> He is, or would be, the main
> Dominus-Do-All in the work!

Although Jonson's achievements had earned him a degree of tolerance at court, to launch such a ferocious attack on a man so close to the King was a perilous strategy. Charles had shown his goodwill by his generosity at a time when the poet's fortunes were at a low ebb, but his patience was not inexhaustible. The diplomat James Howell, a good friend and neighbour, wrote warning Jonson of the dangers: 'I heard you censured lately at court, that you have lighted too foul upon Sir Inigo, and that you write with a porcupine's quill dipped in too much gall.' Jonson's reply has been lost, but it quickly provoked another letter from Howell, scolding him again for trying to destroy the reputation of the royal architect:

> For reputation, you know, is like a fair structure, long time a rearing but quickly ruined. If your spirit will not let you retract, yet you shall do well to repress any more copies of the satire on the royal architect; for, to deal plainly with you, you have lost some ground at court by it: and, as I hear from a good hand, the King, who has so great a judgment in poetry (as in all other things else) is not well pleased therewith.

Jonson took his friend's advice and destroyed all the copies he could, although one remained intact and was published after his death.

But this did not mean that he was yet done with the vendetta, for he wrote two other anti-Inigo verses. The first, *To Inigo, Marquis Would-Be*, suggested that his tormentor was seeking ennoblement, as had just been bestowed on the architect to the Spanish court.

> But cause thou hearst the mighty King of Spain
> Hath made his Inigo Marquis, wouldst thou fain
> Our Charles should make thee such? T'will not become
> All Kings to do the self-same deeds with some! . . .
> He may have skill and judgment to design
> Cities and temples! Thou a cave for wine
> Or Ale! He build a palace! Thou a shop
> With sliding windows and false lights atop!

The cave for wine or ale was presumably the drinking grotto in the basement of the Banqueting House. The shop with sliding windows and false lights may also have been the Banqueting House, or perhaps a reference to Inigo's ingenious stage devices.

The other poem, *To a Friend, an Epigram of Him*, may have been written after the exchange with Howell, for it appeared to announce that Jonson was, at least temporarily, suspending hostilities. Reacting to a suggestion that he was planning fresh verbal assaults on the Surveyor, he wrote dismissively:

> . . . Wretch, I quit thee of thy pain:
> Thou'rt too ambitious, and dost fear in vain!
> The Libyan lion hunts no butterflies,
> He makes the camel and dull ass his prize!

Inigo struck back with a verse, *To His False Friend Mr Ben Jonson*, found in a contemporary manuscript.[6] He railed against what he called 'satire, epigram or libel-play against the manners of the time', and replied in kind to Jonson's scorn for his professional pretensions:

> In reading of thyself, tickling the age,
> Stealing all equal glory from the stage,
> That I confess with like form thou has writ
> Of good and bad things, not with equal wit:
> The reason is, or may be quickly shown,
> The good's translation, but the ill's thine own.

It is tempting to envisage Inigo's memory being jogged here by something he had read in his copy of Plato's *Republic* where, on page 108, he had noted in the margin: 'What poesie is imitation . . . What poesie is not imitation.'[7] Yet for a man who himself borrowed extensively from foreign sources, in both his architecture and stage design, it was an impudent sally. In his fury, he was clearly not seeking to make a consistent or reasoned argument. The verse concluded with a lament that Jonson's talent was not matched by his nature:

> From henceforth this repute dwell with thee then,
> The best of poets but the worst of men.

If Inigo's own literary effort was laboured, he could call to his aid at least one old friend with a more obvious gift for poetry. The playwright George Chapman is today best known for his translation of the works of Homer, which so moved the poet John Keats nearly two centuries later. Chapman and Inigo probably became acquainted at the court of Prince Henry, to which they were both attached. They remained devoted friends for the rest of their lives. In 1614 they collaborated on *The Memorable Masque* for the Inns of Court, and two years later Chapman dedicated his *Divine Poem of Musaeus* to:

> the most generally ingenious, and our only learned architect, my exceeding good friend Inigo Jones esquire, Surveyor of His Majesty's works. Ancient poesie, and ancient architecture, requiring to their excellence alike creating and proportionable rapture, and alike being over-topped by the monstrous Babels of our modern barbarism ... yourself then being a chief of that few by whom both are apprehended.

Earlier in his career Chapman had worked with Jonson on the contentious *Eastward Ho!* and contributed verses in praise of Jonson's plays *Sejanus* and *Volpone*. They had remained friends at least until 1619, when Jonson told Drummond that Chapman and another playwright, John Fletcher, were 'loved of him'. But Chapman did not hesitate to rally to Inigo's support early in 1634 with an *Invective Against Ben Jonson*. Although Inigo is not mentioned in it, there is little doubt that it was provoked by Jonson's attacks on the architect. Chapman accused the playwright of some of the very vices he had mocked in Inigo, especially arrogance and vanity. Jonson, he wrote, thought of himself as:

> ... most great, most learned, witty most
> Of all the kingdom; nay of all the earth.[8]

Chapman died a few months after undertaking this final act of loyalty to his close friend. A grateful and sorrowful Inigo built a plain, Roman-style altar for his grave, with a Latin inscription, in the churchyard of St Giles-in-the-Fields, close to Covent Garden. The stone, after centuries of battering by the weather, has now been moved inside the church.

The usual perception of the quarrel between Jonson and Inigo casts the playwright as the earthy man of the people, the plebeian chronicler of the City's low life, pitted against the more refined and better educated architect, preoccupied with dry intellectual concerns. Paradoxically, that is almost the opposite of the truth. Jonson had the better education, with a good grounding in Latin and the classics from William Camden at Westminster School. Inigo, so far as is known, was largely self-taught. His architectural and design skills, to which he owed his influential position at court, were the fruit of hours of dedicated study of the buildings he encountered on his trips to Italy as a young man, and of the books he bought there. It is easy to see why that contrast in their backgrounds can only have fuelled Jonson's resentment of Inigo's pretensions.

Although it would be unfair to accept Jonson's characterisation of Inigo unreservedly, coloured as it was by so much raw spleen, there is every reason to suppose that the personality defects he identified in him were real enough. Jonson's satirical plays and verses were, after all, performed and circulated among people who would be familiar and in some cases intimate with the Surveyor-General – and satire, as its modern practitioners understand well enough, is effective only if based on a significant kernel of truth. There is, too, at least one other witness to support the view that Inigo was a vain and boastful man.

In January 1636 a consignment of pictures, a gift from Pope Urban VIII to Charles I and Henrietta Maria, arrived in London. It fell to Gregorio Panzani, the Pope's agent in London, to arrange delivery of them to the Queen at Somerset House. Hearing that they had arrived, the King and Inigo hurried from Whitehall to inspect them. Inigo was always impatient when it came to examining new works of art. That same year Lord Maltravers, Thomas Howard's son, had described in a letter how the Surveyor was 'mad to see' some pictures newly arrived from Naples.[9]

On the delivery of the batch from the Pope, Panzani reported:

> The very moment Jones saw the pictures he greatly approved of them, and in order to be able to study them better threw off his coat, put on his eye-glasses, took a candle and, together with the King, began to examine them very closely. They found them entirely satisfactory.

A few days later, in another despatch, Panzani gave a further description of this occasion. He said that Jones believed he had identified the sitter in one of the paintings, a portrait by Leonardo da Vinci, through the initials inscribed on her breast:

> As he is very conceited and boastful he often repeats this idea of his to demonstrate his great knowledge of painting. As the King had removed the names of the painters, which I had fixed to each picture, he also boasts of having attributed almost all the pictures correctly. He greatly exaggerates their beauty and says that these are pictures to be kept in a special room with gilded and jewelled frames, and in spite of his being a very fierce Puritan he said this publicly in the ante-chamber of the Queen.[10]

Panzani's description of Inigo's enthusiastic reaction to the paintings lends credence to Gerbier's account of how he swooned with passion before Buckingham's newly acquired Titian a dozen years earlier. More significantly, the papal agent's assessment of his character is entirely consistent with that of Jonson's creations, In-and-In Medlay and Colonel Iniquo Vetruvius – proud, vain, manipulative, brimful of self-importance and enamoured of the sound of their own voices. Jonson, by contrast, was stubborn, unsure of himself and lacking in the black arts that would have kept his position at court secure. He died on 6 August 1637, having never recovered fully from his stroke and without making his peace with his former collaborator, who was probably not to be counted among the hundreds of mourners who attended his funeral in Westminster Abbey. His estate amounted to £8 8s 10d.[11]

Inigo was to live another fifteen years, through a period of turbulence that Jonson, with roots both in the court and in the lives of common people, would have found it hard to cope with. No such divided loyalties afflicted Inigo, despite Panzani's probably inaccurate assertion of his Puritanism: his support for the Crown was instinctive. Although Jonson died a defeated man, in the final outcome both would earn a place of honour in the history of English art and literature. From twenty-five years of bitter rivalry, no outright victor would ultimately emerge.

* * *

Inigo was approaching sixty when the partnership broke up in 1631. Although his creative energy seemed unimpaired, there were indications that his bodily health was letting him down. In April 1633 the King issued a warrant exempting him from a range of taxes and other public obligations, such as jury service and knighthood, citing his long and faithful service to him and his father, as well as his declining physical condition. The reference to knighthood in the warrant has led to some confusion, prompting a belief that Inigo had been offered this honour but, for churlish or political reasons, had declined it and been forced to beg a royal pardon for his temerity.

In the seventeenth century, though, knighthood was an honour that had to be paid for. James I had made much use of a statute passed in 1227 by which all commoners with an income of more than £40 a year were obliged to attend a monarch's coronation to be knighted. Failing that, a fine was imposed on them, and once they had paid it they were entitled to the honour and benefits of knighthood. James raised considerable sums in this way, and was mocked for it by Jonson and other satirists. For Charles, ruling as he was without Parliament, it became an even more important source of revenue, and in the single year of 1630 he realised an impressive £173,537 in 'knighthood fines'.[12]

He did not, however, wish to dun loyal and important members of his court such as Inigo. So the 1633 warrant amounted effectively to an exemption from any taxation imposed by the King and Parliament, listed as 'subsidies, fifteenths, tenths, quotas, taxes, tallages' – a medieval tax forming part of the feudal system. Nor would he have to supply men, horses or arms to help the King wage war, as gentlemen were obliged to do on demand. The King gave these reasons for granting such favours to his Surveyor-General:

> He having constructed in architecture buildings and structures to our glory and honour, and also to the pleasure of those following, and in the knowledge that he will inspire others, who afterwards will devotedly serve in useful fashion, and that he educated workers constantly and without sleep day and night in our service, surpassing tirelessness and . . . our said servant now old, broken and by his labours frail

of body, now too tired to be permitted beyond further public work without detriment of his body.[13]

Since he was to live for a further nineteen years, and since there are no contemporary reports of his being seriously ill in the 1630s, to describe him as broken and frail may have been an exaggeration. There are, however, indications that he suffered from a chronic kidney complaint, aggravated by hypochondria and the fussiness often associated with ageing bachelors. As he approached his sixties he used the flyleaf of his prized edition of *I Quattro Libri* to make notes of recommended remedies for his ailments, and recipes for how to concoct them. They give a rare insight into a part of his private life.

He describes the chronic sickness that appears to have afflicted him since he was young as 'spleen and vomiting melancholy'. (The word melancholy was then used to describe a specific physical condition involving an excess of black bile, as well as in the modern sense of depression.) His remedy was to cook capers in vinegar, drain them and mix them with currants. Two spoonfuls of this insipid muesli should be eaten for breakfast:

> This cured me of the sharp vomitings which I had had thirty-six years, but it is the frequent use of them that does the effect . . . I sometimes use salad oil with them but it must be very good. I do sometimes eat them with meat for a salad if I cannot eat them in the morning.

The other disorders mentioned most frequently, from which it must be assumed he also suffered, were gout, wind and gallstones. Although he had no medical training, he turned his methodical mind to categorising ailments into 'four principal diseases whereunto almost all other diseases may be referred'. Gout was one of these. Inigo considered it to be the root cause of pains in the veins, teeth, abdomen and head. The other three basic conditions were leprosy, related to 'ulcers, itches, scabs, etc.'; dropsy, connected with fevers and indigestion; and falling sickness, the cause of excessive heartbeat, cramp, giddiness, apoplexy and shortness of breath.

He sometimes attributed the recipes to the people who passed them on to him. They included 'Mr Dimmock's man'; 'my Lord of Northumberland's corncutter'; a surgeon named Haydon; Lord Newcastle; and Dr Harvey, almost certainly William Harvey, physician to both King James and King Charles, famous for discovering the circulation of the blood. In December 1638, when Inigo had a stuffy nose, Lord Huntingdon told him to fill a pipe with tobacco, wrap a cloth round it and hold it under his nostrils. He tried it and it worked; but he went outdoors too soon afterwards and caught a cold. Another remedy for the same condition was to tickle his nose with a feather before meals, which 'purgeth the brain by the nose and mouth'. He added: 'I have used it for the pain in my neck and found ease.'

Lady Pembroke was mistress of Wilton House, where he had occasionally stayed and where he was to undertake his last significant architectural work. Her cure for kidney stones involved a mixture of wild and garden herbs: saxifrage, thyme, parsley, fennel seed and sliced horseradish roots. These should be gathered in May or June, when they would be at their best, shredded together and soaked overnight in a gallon of new milk. Mixed with an equal quantity of white wine, the medicine had to be taken regularly throughout the year, at the time of the new and full moons, and as a result 'you will find great ease, voiding many stones . . . without any pain at all'.

For 'dizziness in the head', another friend recommended crushing cloves and sage between two ovals of brown paper and wearing them on top of the head, presumably not in public. A headache might be cured by rubbing the head with aniseed, and there was a radical cure for stomach trouble, aimed at inducing vomiting:

> Eat and drink claret wine extraordinary much at dinner [mid-day] and at about five o'clock in the afternoon cast it [throw up] and it may bring away the humour. This I did on Thursday 8 September 1631 and it did the effect.

His cure for constipation was less dramatic but just as effective. He made a broth from a piece of chicken and neck of mutton, added fennel and parsley and discovered that 'it loosened my belly'. Generally speaking, though, he was opposed to eating too much meat, and reminded himself that 'the chiefest point of health consisteth in this, not to fill thyself with meat, nor to be slow in labours'.

Some of his hints were copied from a medical book whose title he abbreviated to 'Gen. Prac', which is probably not short for general practitioner. One of them advised that 'to strengthen the brain when you go to bed, swallow two or three pieces of frankincense'. Another bedtime tip was to take a piece of ginger before retiring, for it 'dries the brain and eases the stomach and protects against vapours that ascend to the head'. Various herb concoctions were recommended to improve the memory and combat melancholy. For the latter, music and sleep were suggested, as well as this uncompromising instruction: 'Copulation must be utterly eschewed, for that thereby the best blood of a man is wasted and natural strength enfeebled.'

It is unclear whether this was a general prohibition, designed to prevent the onset of melancholy at any time, or whether it was to apply only after the condition had already set in. Despite the modern theory that Inigo was part of a circle of Elizabethan homosexuals,[14] there is no contemporary evidence that he entered into intimate physical relationships, proper or improper, with people of either sex. If there were, Jonson would surely have brought it up in his insulting plays and verses, and it would also have been raised in references to him in the hostile Parliamentary press during the Civil War. It is therefore possible that he could have been a long-term practising celibate, however unusual that seems to have been then, as now. Cryptic annotations in his copy of Plutarch's *Moralia* do little to illuminate the question. He marked a passage discussing Epicurus's warnings against sex after meals, and wrote two tantalising words in the margin: 'nuptial delights'.[15]

The final, touching entry on the fly-leaf of the Palladio consists of three remedies for dimness of sight, the worst of all afflictions for a practitioner of the visual arts. It appears to be written in a different hand from the others. It could be that his failing eyes made writing more laborious or, more likely, that somebody else had to write it for him. One of the three recipes includes ivy, celandine and a spoonful or two of women's milk. There were, as well, one or two surprising non-medical tips, such as that you can measure an inch by laying three barleycorns from end to end – a slap-happy method for a man whose profession demanded precision.

From the vantage point of the sophisticated twenty-first century, it is easy to mock such homespun hints and forays into folk medicine, but the glimpse these notes give us of Inigo's home life in his declining years is essentially a sad one. Living as he did in a perilous age, when deadly plague was rife and the attentions of doctors were as likely to kill as to cure, we picture him alone in the fading light of his chaste rooms at Scotland Yard, afflicted periodically with the vomiting curse, solemnly brewing his potions from capers and mother's milk, swathing his head in brown paper and his pipe in a damp cloth, measuring inches with barleycorns, pondering mortality. As he had noted in the margin of his Vitruvius: 'Time ruins all things.'

Chapter Seventeen

ST PAUL'S: POLITICS AND PIETY

I NIGO HAD LITTLE TIME to savour his conclusive victory over Jonson, for 1631 was also the year when he was given two tremendous opportunities to extend his work as an architect. Both, though, would involve him in heated disputes that would sour the last two decades of his life and make enemies of people who would eventually be in a position to exact revenge.

In a politically charged era, nobody who worked for the court could escape controversy. Not even the nation's most talented architect and designer could expect his creative accomplishments to keep him above the fray. In his roles as Surveyor of the Works and magistrate, he was required to make decisions that could affect people's pockets and their living conditions. Inevitably, he was exposed to pressures from every quarter. It had become clear during his brief and unhappy career as an MP that politics was not his strong suit, at least not in the conventional sense of holding convictions and using rhetoric to persuade others of their rightness. He preferred the more subtle arts of forging tactical friendships, trading favours and exercising influence through persuasion. This was easier to do in Westminster and Whitehall, where connections at court counted for something, than in the independent-minded City of London, where if anything they were a liability.

A dispute that was to haunt Inigo for much of the rest of his life stemmed from the first of the two major projects that he began in 1631, an enterprise that he had every reason to look upon as the most important of his career. In January of that year the decision had finally been taken to go ahead with the plan to make major alterations to St Paul's Cathedral, badly in need of remedial work following nearly a century of neglect. Inigo was made supervising architect of the project, and can only have been delighted. At last he would be able to put his imagination and talents to work on the greatest and most prominent place of worship in the land.

It was twenty-five years since King James had first thought to initiate major repairs on the cathedral. Though he made several attempts during his reign to get the work under way, financial constraints limited him to essential maintenance. Now Charles, egged on by his ambitious Bishop of London, William Laud, was determined that a newly beautified cathedral would be part of his artistic legacy to a grateful nation, as well as symbolising the legitimacy of the Anglican Church and the monarch's role as its head. As he said in 1631 when he appointed a commission to organise the restoration, the cathedral was 'the goodliest monument and most eminent church of his whole dominions . . . the principal ornament of the City of London, the imperial seat of this his realm'.[1]

Inigo's work on it would come to be greatly admired, especially by John Webb, who as his lieutenant played an important role in the restoration. In 1665, just before it was lost to posterity in the Great Fire, Webb wrote that the restored cathedral represented 'a piece of architecture not to be paralleled in these last ages of the world'.[2] But for Inigo, such excellence came at a high political cost.

The first St Paul's, probably made of wood, was built at the beginning of the seventh century on top of Ludgate Hill, dominating the City and the river, on the site of a former Roman temple. After seventy years it burned down and was replaced by a stone building that lasted nearly 300 years until it was torn down by the Vikings in 962. The third cathedral survived little more than a century before it, too, was destroyed by fire in 1087. This was at the height of the Norman conquerors' initial burst of enthusiasm for constructing enormous monuments to themselves and their faith. They seized on the opportunity that presented itself at the heart of England's most important city. Work on a new building began with the ashes of the old one scarcely cool, but it took centuries to complete.

This fourth cathedral was conceived on a huge scale, 650 feet long and 325 feet wide, larger even than Sir Christopher Wren's present building.[3] Its spire rose higher than Wren's gigantic dome. The stone, from Caen in Normandy, was brought to the site by water. Work on embellishing the cathedral continued throughout the Middle Ages, and by the seventeenth century it contained examples of many different architectural styles. The oldest part, at the western end, was Norman, with characteristic round-headed windows, the doorway flanked by two bell towers. The choir, dating from the thirteenth and fourteenth centuries, was Gothic, with flying buttresses, pinnacles and a splendid vaulted interior. Within the precinct was a magnificent fourteenth-century chapter house, and over the years other buildings were added and the complex enclosed within walls.[4]

The cathedral, as the capital's most important centre of religious observance, prospered until the Reformation. That cathartic event not only changed the nature of worship, forcing churches to transfer their allegiance overnight from Rome to Whitehall, but also had a severe impact on their funding. The largest ecclesiastical buildings, needing constant maintenance, were the first to show symptoms of decline. At St Paul's, stones eroded by the acrid and pervasive London smoke were left unrepaired. In 1549 the high altar was demolished and replaced by a table, more in tune with the simpler trappings of the Protestant faith. The cathedral was no longer devoted exclusively to religious observance but became a social and business centre. Lawyers and moneylenders met their clients in the nave, traders set up stalls there and used the tops of tombs as counters, while the font became the recognised place for settling accounts. Many distinctly shady transactions took place there because people were safe from arrest. The actual church services had to be conducted in the choir.

A pamphlet published in 1607 described the chaotic scene:

> At one time, and in the same rank, yea, foot by foot and elbow, shall you see walking the knight, the gull [simpleton], the gallant, the upstart, the gentleman, the clown, the captain, the apple-squire [pimp], the lawyer, the usurer, the citizen, the bankrupt, the scholar, the beggar, the doctor, the idiot, the ruffian, the cheater, the Puritan, the cut-throat, the high-men, the low-men, the true man and the thief: of all trades and professions some, of all countries some. Thus while devotion kneels at her prayers doth profanation walk under her nose in contempt of religion.[5]

The phrase 'to dine with Duke Humphrey', meaning to go without dinner, originated in St Paul's at this time. One of the aisles was known as Duke Humphrey's Walk, because of the mistaken belief that it contained the tomb of the fifteenth-century Duke of Gloucester. Traditionally, people who could not afford to buy themselves a meal congregated there at dinner time, free from harassment by creditors.

All this had been going on for more than fifty years; certainly since before 1561, when a fire destroyed the wooden roof and spire and a pamphleteer saw it as God's judgment on the desecration of the cathedral. He gave a concise account of how the nave was used for various discreditable functions:

> The south alley for usury and popery, the north for simony [buying Church appointments] and the horse fair in the middle for all kinds of bargains, meetings, brawlings, murders, conspiracies, and the font for ordinary payments of money.

While funds were found after the fire to repair the roof (Queen Elizabeth donated £6000), the spire was never to be replaced.

In 1620, twelve years after failing in his first attempt to raise the wherewithal for the cathedral's improvement, King James appointed a royal commission to report on its state. Inigo was a member of it, as were two of his patrons, Thomas Howard and Lionel Cranfield, along with John Chamberlain, the prolific court correspondent. Some small and poorly executed repair work had already begun, as Inigo noted in a letter to Howard that year.[6] Yet the appointment of a commission was one thing; finding money to carry out its recommendations was quite another. Although stone was acquired from Portland it was not used on the cathedral and the Duke of Buckingham commandeered some of it to build the watergate at York House, his Strand palace.[7]

So matters stood at St Paul's until Laud pressed Charles into action in 1631. Another commission was formed, but it was still two years before the preparatory work would commence. The first thing to do was to remove buildings that were deemed to be too close to the cathedral walls to be safe or sightly. It was only to be expected that owners of several affected shops and houses would resist abandoning them, and some had to be removed by force.[8] This unpleasant task fell to Inigo, who had been appointed the surveyor, or chief architect and overseer, of the project, agreeing to serve without payment because he thought the cause so worthwhile. (His salary was well in arrears, in any case.)[9] Edward Carter, who worked for him in the Surveyor-General's office, acted as his deputy, and was paid 5s a day. The King gave the go-ahead for the reconstruction in February 1633, with one proviso: there had to be at least £10,000 in the coffers before work could begin.[10]

Inigo and his team began their preparations regardless, assuming that the money would ultimately be raised from local merchants and others interested either in improving the City's amenities or buying favour with the King. The agreement between Inigo and the two chief masons, Edmund Kinsman and Gilbert Arnold, was in fact signed a few days before the royal approval was made public. It included detailed descriptions of the work and materials required, and the prices to be charged for them: windows came in at £45 or £55, depending on their size, and pinnacles at £25 to £27 10s. The work was to be carried out 'strongly and neatly well and workmanlike' and completed by the last day of August 1634, or by Michaelmas at the latest. Arnold and Kinsman were obliged to find the necessary workmen – about sixty of them – and provide them with tools. They would be paid according to progress made.

The agreement was witnessed by John Webb, Nicholas Stone and Henry Wicks, Paymaster of the Works. One of its last clauses seems to have been included by Inigo in the light of his frustrating experiences with the craftsmen who absented themselves from the Banqueting House. Kinsman and Arnold had to promise to 'personally attend the work themselves and not undertake any other works until the said works be fully finished'.[11] The habits of builders have changed little over the centuries.

A memorandum addressed to the Church authorities, annotated by Webb, gives further details of how the work was organised. The 'surveyor's substitute', Edward Carter, was in day-to-day charge. Webb described his own contribution meticulously, stressing that Inigo's was the creative mind behind the alterations:

> Mr Webb copied all the designs from the Surveyor's invention, made all the traceries in great for the work and all the mouldings by the Surveyor's direction, so that what the Surveyor invented and Mr Webb made, the substitute saw put in work, and nothing else.[12]

The stress he laid on the limits of Carter's contribution suggests that he may have added that note after Inigo was deprived of his office by Parliament in 1643 and Carter appointed as his successor. Webb thought he had stronger claims to the position, and was probably seeking to belittle Carter's abilities.

Carter had to visit the site at least twice a day to be sure that everything was going ahead as planned. Other senior officers had to make more frequent checks to ensure that the men were applying themselves to their tasks, and to decide how much they should be paid. Inigo, although not on the site as often as he was when he had built the Banqueting House, personally signed the monthly accounts and took pains to ensure that the finished product would be as he wanted it. He had full-sized timber models made of the external decorative features and erected them in the appropriate positions so that he could judge their effect and make any changes that would improve the composition.[13] There is no evidence that he had done this for any of his other buildings – an indication of his determination to leave nothing to chance in a work which, now he had reached sixty, was likely to be one of his last, and among the two or three by which posterity would judge him.

In May 1633 the Commissioners reported that enough stone and other materials had been delivered to St Paul's for the work to begin, but that only £5413 13s 6d had been raised, little more than half what was supposed to be in hand before work could officially be started. They argued, though, that if the entire sum were to be devoted to paying for materials and labour, and not to compensating the owners of properties that had been pulled down in the vicinity of the cathedral, this would be enough for the work to get under way. If they had followed the strict letter of the King's stipulation, they would not have been able to begin until the following year at the earliest.[14]

The Privy Council told them to go ahead and the required sum was eventually raised after Laud, about to be promoted from Bishop of London to Archbishop of Canterbury, exercised his considerable powers of persuasion and patronage. In one of many dunning letters, he castigated city aldermen for giving only £10 each. Their parsimony, he argued, discouraged lesser citizens from giving more generously because it was not 'fit or convenient to give more than their superiors did'.[15] There were exceptions – Sir Paul Pindar, a wealthy merchant and former ambassador to Turkey, was a major donor – but for the most part the City fathers were reluctant to support a project sponsored by a monarch who was rapidly losing their favour. Charles himself had promised £500 a year, and paid at least the first two instalments.

Laud also persuaded the King to allow fines for moral offences, such as adultery and profanity, to be passed on to the rebuilding fund, giving short shrift to other claimants on the money. A wronged wife, Martha Helwys, wrote to him in February 1635 about her husband, Sir William Helwys, who had been fined £500 for 'several adulteries' and had apparently abandoned her. She had been awarded alimony but the errant knight had 'not paid her one penny' since June 1633. She now asked for the fine to be allotted to her, to relieve her distress, adding that the King had 'sundry times heretofore been graciously pleased to grant the benefit of such fines or forfeiture of bonds to poor distressed wives who, forced by their own misery, brought such suits'.

Laud was immovable. While he was glad to do all he could to help enforce the alimony order, God's work and the royal will had to take priority over individual cases of human hardship: 'For begging the fine I may not meddle because His Majesty hath been graciously pleased to allot all fines of that nature towards the repair of St Paul's.'[16]

In the summer of 1633 four foundation stones were laid in a formal ceremony – one by Inigo; one by Sir Francis Windebank, Charles's Secretary of State; one by Sir Henry Marten, a politician and judge; and the last by Archbishop Laud. Soon work began on repairing the choir, replacing damaged buttresses and tracery, before moving west to the transepts and nave. Here Inigo undertook more radical alterations, covering the Norman work with a skin of new stone, incorporating rustication and other classical details. As Samuel Pepys observed, when he inspected the ruins of the cathedral two years after the 1666 fire, Inigo had simply put a casing over the medieval nave, enclosing its ancient columns within the new walls.[17] The round-headed windows were retained but with Tuscan pilasters between them, topped by stone pineapples.[18]

Even when the initial £10,000 was raised, it would still go nowhere near to covering the cost of the most ambitious aspect of Inigo's design, the giant Corinthian portico that would enclose the west door and become one of his most notable creations. Its purpose was not simply to provide a grandiloquent entrance but also a venue for the secular and commercial activities – the gulls, the gallants, the apple-squires and the rest – that Laud was anxious to root out of the interior. The King was so enthusiastic that in 1634 he donated £10,000 from his own depleted coffers specifically to finance the portico, but he seems from that point to have stopped his annual £500 payments.

In designing it, Inigo might have been trying to recreate the lost portico of the Basilica of Maxentius on the edge of the Forum in Rome, as depicted on Roman coins.[19] Its eighteen columns, ten at the front and four at each side, were forty feet high, much larger than any that had been seen in England before. Above them was a balustrade incorporating plinths for statues but only two – of Charles I and James I, by Hubert Le Sueur – were ever put in place. The base of the portico, made of black marble from a quarry in Ireland, stood two and a quarter feet above ground level. Three doorways leading into the church were also cased in marble.

A formidable amount of work was involved in transporting, lifting and dressing the quantities and sizes of stone needed for the project. The biggest block weighed sixteen tons. They were shipped from the quarries to Paul's Wharf, then had to be dragged up the slope to the cathedral itself. Inigo designed a robust pulley system for lifting heavy pieces once they had arrived on site, basing it on illustrations in his Italian architectural books. Webb drew it in 1637, probably as a guide to the carpenters who had to make it. The detailed explanatory notes beneath the drawing are in Inigo's hand and show that, at sixty-four, he retained his fascination with the mechanical aspects of his profession.

The shipping of the stone, principally from Portland, was another headache. With the King's permission, the captains of ships that carried it to London were declared exempt from having their crews press-ganged to serve with the Royal Navy, an accepted seafaring hazard of the time. In April 1637 Inigo learned that the Admiralty had not kept to this agreement, because of a technical flaw in the official exemption certificates.[20] More seriously, as the political skies darkened, there were signs of mutiny from bodies that would normally have been expected to lend practical support to such a worthy royal project. The timber for the work came from the New Forest and it was expected that Justices of the Peace in Hampshire would provide the funds for its carriage to London. Despite the King's warrant, they refused – an act of defiance with ominous political overtones.[21]

The most serious and debilitating objections to the restoration of the cathedral came from the community in whose heart it stood. For centuries the rich merchants who administered the City of London had been careful to keep an arms-length relationship with the monarchy. They saw Westminster as a rival power base. Reasoning that they were largely responsible for creating the wealth that allowed the country and its rulers to prosper, they believed they deserved a large measure of autonomy in running their affairs. The feeling was intensified when it came to matters concerning the City's numerous churches. Protestants almost to a man, the City fathers suspected that the King, influenced by Henrietta Maria, was plotting to restore the Catholic faith. They were therefore reluctant to accept advice and instructions on redeveloping their places of worship from Inigo: however great his architectural expertise he was, in their eyes, acting on royal instructions, to further the King's secret and sinister objectives.

Before the work began, the Commission for Pious Uses, established that year to expedite the repair and renewal of churches, asked Inigo to look into whether St Gregory's Church, sited perilously close to the west end of the cathedral, could threaten the proposed alterations. Inigo visited the church in May 1631 and met some of its leading parishioners. From the tone of his report, issued the following month, it appeared to have been a useful and cordial meeting. The parishioners explained that an arch in the old church had been in danger of collapse and they were about to repair it, and to replace some rotten timbers.

Inigo approved of these works and was clearly impressed by the parishioners' commitment to keeping their church in a safe condition. In his report, he stated that he did not think the church's proximity to the cathedral in itself constituted a danger; nor would it block any significant light from its larger neighbour. Aesthetically, the church and the adjoining Lollards' Tower did not, in his view, spoil the aspect of the cathedral, and he could find no more convenient site for a new St Gregory's in the vicinity. There was just one minor worry, spelled out in his report's final and most significant paragraph. It seemed innocuous enough:

Lastly, I finding a vault now digging for burials (as the parishioners say) close to the foundation of St Paul's, have forbidden them the proceeding therein, and ordered them to fill in the earth again and make their vault (if they will have it) on the other side, which they are willing to do.[22]

Those last six words turned out to be premature. In his naivety, Inigo assumed that because those parishioners he spoke to were willing to accept his recommendation for relocating the vault, it would automatically be put into effect.

Soon it became apparent that other, more stubborn members of the congregation were unwilling to accept his verdict without seeking a second opinion. They brought in their own experts, who advised them that, contrary to what Inigo had asserted, the vault they had begun to dig would in no way undermine the cathedral. On the other hand, if they accepted the Surveyor's recommendation and started digging on the opposite side of the church, in the direction of the churchyard, the stability of St Gregory's itself might be threatened. In July, the parishioners petitioned the Privy Council to be allowed to go ahead with the original vault, but their plea was rejected.

The following February Inigo went back to St Gregory's for another inspection. He found that the parishioners had followed his instruction and filled up their original vault, and had dug another one. They had not, however, taken his advice about where to position it. It was not on the side of the church closest to the churchyard, but to the south of the cathedral near the tower. In digging it, they had lain bare part of the cathedral's foundations. Inigo, now angry about this challenge to his authority, reported:

Although I cannot say there is any present danger to the church[23] or tower by digging the said vault, yet in my opinion I hold it not fit that the foundation of so great and noble a work should be underwrought upon any occasion whatsoever, seeing the parishioners might have digged their vault towards their churchyard, and not have come near to the walls of the said church or the tower.

By now this had become an issue of principle for both sides. Positions had been taken and neither was willing to give way. The parishioners flatly refused to fill in the second vault, and soon the repairs to the cathedral got under way. By 1639, when they were well advanced, Inigo had become convinced that St Gregory's and its vault had become a real hindrance to the completion of the work. He had part of the church demolished without the parishioners' consent and ordered them to pull down still more of it. The furious congregation would have taken the matter to Parliament were it not still in suspension. In the event, they felt they had no immediate alternative but to comply with the instruction of Inigo and the Privy Council.

In his single-minded determination to leave a permanent mark on the City landscape by restoring the cathedral to its former glory, Inigo may have failed to grasp how rapidly the political climate was changing. In 1640 Charles was forced to recall Parliament, after eleven years of personal rule, to finance his ill-advised campaign against the Scots. This was a signal for the anti-monarchist forces – and that included most citizens of London – to flex their muscles. Craftsmen working for Inigo on the cathedral raised formal protests through their guilds about inadequate payment for the work, and the verdict usually went in their favour.[24] And as soon as Parliament was recalled, the tenacious parishioners of St Gregory's presented a complaint to the House of Commons about Inigo's high-handed behaviour. The Commons sent it up to the Lords, who summoned the Surveyor to appear before them.

Echoing Jonson's characterisation of Inigo as a 'Dominus Do-All', the parishioners asserted that he wanted to be 'sole monarch' of the restoration work on the cathedral. Having had some of St Gregory's demolished without consulting them, he then 'threatened that if the parishioners did not take down the rest of it, then the galleries should be sawed down, and with screws the materials of the said church should be thrown down into the street'. The stubborn congregation said they were warned that they would be 'laid by the heels' [put into the stocks] if they refused to comply. Intimidated, they had given in, but now sought redress. Their church, they maintained, was unusable and they calculated that it would take £3000 to restore it.

Inigo was now clearly worried that Members of Parliament, in vengeful mood after their long absence from Westminster, would seek to impose a heavy fine on him, or even a term of imprisonment. He managed to postpone any final resolution of the case by claiming the right to hire lawyers. The Lords agreed to an adjournment but, hearing a rumour that he planned to leave the country, issued an order preventing him. Eventually they referred the case to the Commons, who declined to take an immediate decision, but in 1643, with the Civil War under way, they gave the parishioners some of the stone originally earmarked for the cathedral, so that their church could be rebuilt. The issue had become a cause célèbre, and Inigo's high-handedness a symbol of the intolerable oppression of ordinary people by the King and his placemen. Two years later, when Inigo was captured by Oliver Cromwell's troops at the siege of Basing House, one Parliamentary pamphleteer had thought it sufficient to describe him merely as 'the famous surveyor and great enemy to St Gregory'.[25]

In the meantime Inigo had become involved in a second bitter dispute over rebuilding a City church, this one with the parishioners and churchwardens of St Michael le Querne, on an island site at the western end of Cheapside. As with St Gregory's, it was the church's location that attracted the interest of the central government in its restoration plans. For centuries Cheapside had been London's principal thoroughfare, at the heart of the City's commercial and social life. Its chief glory had been Goldsmiths' Row, on the south side of the street towards the west. Its uniform four-storey houses, built in 1491, had shops on the ground floor, every one occupied by a goldsmith.

In the early years of the seventeenth century, though, the goldsmiths began to move west, outside the City limits, following the example of their well-heeled customers. Their shops were taken over by practitioners of other trades. In 1622 Chamberlain lamented:

> It is a strange sight and not known in this age till within these two or three years, to see booksellers, stocking men, haberdashers, pointmakers [lacemakers] and other mean trades crept into the Goldsmiths' Row, that was wont to be the beauty and glory of Cheapside.[26]

The Goldsmiths' Company sought to lure the goldsmiths back into their traditional home, and won the backing first of King James and then of Charles; but the campaign had only limited success, and eventually became another cause of contention between the City and the Crown.

It was the King's interest in upgrading Cheapside that in 1637 brought the plans for St Michael le Querne to the attention of the Privy Council. Its parishioners wanted to restore and enlarge the dilapidated church, at that time capable of accommodating barely half its parishioners. One obstacle to the plan was a tumbledown shop at its east end, owned by one Edward Brooke, who was proving reluctant to vacate it. The Council ordered work on the church to be halted to allow time for Inigo and four other Buildings Commissioners to inspect the site and persuade Mr Brooke to vacate the shop. They were also to look at the possibility of resiting the water conduit just east of the shop, and to examine some more shops at the west end of the church, likewise in a poor and unsightly state.[27]

Mr Brooke evidently had friends among the churchwardens, who proved reluctant to carry out the Council's recommendation. They visited Inigo several times to discuss ways of enlarging the church without demolishing the shop: their account book shows that they paid one shilling each on eight occasions for the river journey from the City to the Surveyor's office at Scotland Yard. Inigo drew a plan showing the church enlarged at the east end, after the shop's demolition, but the churchwardens said that the proposed eastern extension would be too narrow to be of much use. They produced their own alternative plan and made a model of it which they took to Oatlands to show the King, and to Bishop Laud at his palace in Croydon.[28]

Inigo insisted that his scheme, involving the demolition of Mr Brooke's shop, should prevail, and was supported by the King. The churchwardens dug in their heels, accusing the Surveyor of holding up the essential works. Inigo defended himself in a petulant report to the King, pointing the finger of blame at Mr Binyon, a silk merchant and the most unyielding of the churchwardens. When Inigo asked for his plans back so that building could begin, it was Binyon who told him they had been mislaid. Then when the Surveyor asked to borrow the parishioners' own model, so that he could assess the cost of their scheme, they refused to send it to him.

Citing the 'false and impertinent objections' made to his scheme, Inigo wrote that Mr Binyon was 'resolved, as is given out, that either the church shall be built after their way or not at all'. He asked Charles to give orders that the silk merchant 'desist from his malicious vexation', to allow Inigo to get on with the other important works that he was undertaking for the King and Queen.[29] Mr Brooke's house was not finally demolished until 1640, when the church was duly enlarged. It burned down in the Great Fire of 1666 and was not replaced.

The West Front of St Paul's before the Great Fire

Work on rebuilding St Paul's Cathedral was still in progress when the outbreak of the Civil War brought it to a premature halt in August

1642. Nothing significant had been done to the interior, and plans to renew the tower and replace the former spire were never realised. During the war the statues of the two kings were torn from the parapet above Inigo's portico and the cathedral was damaged by Parliamentary troops, who used it variously as a barracks and a stable. In the years of Oliver Cromwell's rule, shops were built within the portico, with lofts above them for storage and accommodation.

After the Restoration of Charles II in 1660, Christopher Wren was making plans for further work on the Cathedral when the Great Fire of 1666 intervened, destroying much of what Inigo had created. There was some surprising technical criticism of his work from Dr William Sancroft, a future Archbishop of Canterbury and one of the churchmen placed in charge of the rebuilding. Examining the cathedral ruins, he noted that the weight of the stone in the upper walls was being borne by the groins of the vaulting and not by the pillars, and that the lack of keystones to tie the new cladding to the medieval work meant that the walls had already begun to bulge out.[30] Assuming he was right, such structural failings are surprising in the work of a man who, to judge from the notes in his text books, approached his craft in such a meticulous fashion.

The fire left Inigo's great portico relatively unscathed but Wren, after some consideration, decided not to incorporate it into his new cathedral, and it was demolished in 1687.[31] In 1996, parts of it were discovered in the basement. To judge from contemporary drawings, the survival of what Inigo regarded as one of his major works would scarcely have burnished his reputation. Most modern critics share the view of the architectural historian John Summerson that it amounted to 'a gallant attempt to make a classical silk purse out of a Gothic sow's ear'.[32] The application of a Roman portico to what remained an essentially medieval building inevitably involved compromises and, even if completed, Inigo's work could never have achieved the sublime integrity of Wren's masterpiece.

Chapter Eighteen

COVENT GARDEN:
SHAKING THE MONEY TREE

THE SECOND OF THE PROJECTS that Inigo began in 1631 took him into the broader field of creative town planning. On his visits to Italy and France he had not only been studying the individual buildings of Palladio and his compatriots, and the earlier Roman ruins, but had witnessed ground-breaking advances in laying out whole areas of cities. He had seen and admired the Place Royale (now the Place des Vosges) in Paris and the main squares, or piazzas, of Turin and of Livorno, where a church occupied one of the four sides. All three were elegant examples of rows of uniform, arcaded dwellings surrounding a spacious and airy central square, to make a natural focus for meeting, strolling and transacting business: a latter-day variant of the Roman forum. Where Palladio wrote of piazzas in his *Quattro Libri*, Inigo had noted in the margin: 'Piazzas necessary for divers purposes. Piazzas giveth ornament. In sea towns near the port. In land in the middle.'[1] How splendid if he could introduce the same liberating concept to Londoners, most of whose houses, even some of the grandest ones, were wedged awkwardly into narrow, twisting, foul and overcrowded streets, their pattern little changed for centuries.

By the end of the 1620s the two principal populated areas of London had spread west from the City and east from Westminster, until they were all but conjoined. Lincoln's Inn Fields had already partly succumbed to the developers.[2] The proclamation on building restrictions that the King had issued in 1625 had failed to limit the sprawl, although it may have helped pay some of his debts as developers stumped up substantial sums to be granted exemption from the regulations, or paid fines for breaching them. In 1630 the proclamation was reinforced and transgressors threatened with higher fines. The timing of this second initiative, just a year after Charles suspended Parliament, was almost certainly linked to his need to increase his revenues from non-Parliamentary sources.[3]

After Lincoln's Inn Fields, the largest area of open land between the City and Westminster was Covent Garden, just north of the Strand between St Martin's Lane and Drury Lane. Once the site of a large Saxon settlement called Lundenwic, since the early Middle Ages it had belonged to Westminster Abbey, being used as an orchard and vegetable garden for its convent: hence the name. In 1540, when the monasteries and convents were dissolved, Henry VIII gave the ground to John Russell, the first Earl of Bedford, whose family mansion was on the Strand. Edward Russell, the third Earl, put a wall round the former garden in the early seventeenth century and began to build some houses on Long Acre, along its northern edge, until the Buildings Commission made him desist and pull some of the houses down.

In 1627 the third Earl died and was succeeded by his entrepreneurial cousin, Francis Russell, who saw the huge scope for developing Covent Garden as London's first planned residential square. The idea may have stemmed from an approach made to him by William Laud, the influential Bishop of London, early in 1629. Laud asked Russell whether he could have a church built in Covent Garden because St Martin's-in-the-Fields, at the western end of the Strand, was becoming overcrowded. Under the terms of the 1625 building proclamation the King had to give his formal permission for this new building, and the application would be passed through Inigo, as Surveyor-General. This is probably why, when permission to build the new church came through, it was conditional on Inigo being commissioned to design it.[4]

The following year the Privy Council ordered Russell to make improvements to Long Acre, whose unmade carriageway and half-finished, abandoned houses had offended the King when he drove along it on his way to Theobalds Road, the route to his Theobalds estate. Russell took the opportunity of seeking a licence to resume the building work begun there by the previous Earl, and in return promised to pave the street. He also applied to make a further breach of the 1625 and 1630 proclamations by building an up-market residential complex in the heart of Covent Garden, of which Laud's new church would form part.

Charles had little hesitation in giving his approval. Although technically any building on new foundations flouted the regulations that he had recently reiterated, the true purpose of the proclamations was not to call a complete halt to construction in the capital but to exert a measure of control on the types of building that went up, and specifically to deter the erection of low-grade, unhygienic housing. The scheme proposed by the Earl was for a development centred on a small number of high-quality town houses that, if properly executed, would feed the King's ambition, encouraged by Inigo, to bring to London some of the elegance and Renaissance splendour of such admired cities as Venice, Florence, Rome and Genoa.

Because of his difficulties in persuading Parliament to vote him funds, Charles could not afford to underwrite such projects himself: that was why most of his schemes to embellish his capital never progressed beyond the drawing board. For instance, he wanted to improve London Bridge by erecting a rail to separate pedestrians from wheeled traffic, but he could not raise the necessary £5000.[5] Much more would have been needed to finance his ambitious scheme for a new Whitehall Palace that would be the envy of Europe.

The attraction of Russell's proposal was that the Earl would be paying for it, and moreover could be charged £2000 for permission to breach the rules. The King gave his assent in January 1631, in a warrant stipulating that the scheme as a whole should amount to a 'distinguished ornament' for London[6] and the new houses be 'fit for the habitations of gentlemen and men of ability', some of whom helped Russell fund the scheme by buying leases in advance. The formal licence issued the following month further insisted that all the houses must be built of brick and stone, and be for single-family occupation.[7]

By April the building work had begun, under the direct supervision of Isaac de Caux, the nephew of Solomon de Caux, who had been part of Prince Henry's household twenty years earlier. There is little doubt, though, that Inigo's was the dominant vision. He had already been designated as the architect of the church, and almost certainly was involved in drawing up the regulatory guidelines. According to one contractor's record, his role even extended to personally enforcing strict standards about the quality of the bricks.[8]

Covent Garden, by Wenceslaus Hollar

Here at last was his chance to introduce the concept of the piazza to London; although with the new St Paul's Church occupying most of the west side of the square, and the outer wall of the Bedford House garden to the south, the arcaded rows of houses – eighteen in all – would fill only the north and east sides. Each house had a front door recessed within the arcade, while the front room on the first floor extended outwards, flush with the columns. A block of the houses on the north side remain today, rebuilt in the nineteenth century in something like their original form.

An incidental result of the development was the introduction of a device that would become integral to English towns. Tenants of long, unbroken rows of houses needed convenient places to stable their horses, so a parallel alley had to be created behind them, called a mews, the name deriving from the royal stables at Charing Cross. Hart (now Floral) Street, was London's first mews, running behind the terrace of colonnaded houses on the north side of the Piazza, and continuing west to serve the same purpose for the houses in King Street. Maiden Lane was the mews for Henrietta Street, a block south. Later in the decade, mews were provided for the houses designed by Inigo and others on Lincoln's Inn Fields and Great Queen Street.[9]

The new church was flanked by two arched and pedimented gates leading to the churchyard, with two detached three-bay houses, uniform in design, filling the Piazza's north-west and south-west corners. Today the portico provides a sympathetic backdrop for the street entertainers who use that part of the Piazza as their stage. Scarcely higher than the neighbouring buildings, the church has never dominated its immediate surroundings, reflecting the secular spirit that ruled at the time of its construction.

St Paul's was the first church built in London since the Reformation, and was unlike anything seen in England before. The story most often told about Inigo's approach to it could well be true, in essence if not necessarily in detail. The Earl of Bedford, a strict Protestant, was anxious that the new church should eschew any of the elaborate decoration that characterised Catholic places of worship, especially in mainland Europe. The restraints that Inigo had worked under when designing the exterior of his two chapels for the Queen had, in the case of St Paul's, to be be applied to the interior also. Nor did the Earl want to spend any more money on the church than was absolutely necessary. He therefore instructed Inigo that 'I would not have it much better than a barn,' to which the architect is reputed to have replied: 'Then you shall have the handsomest barn in England.'[10]

The plain, pitched roof, projecting beyond all four walls, is its most barn-like feature. For the columns and pilasters supporting the pediment on the east side, facing the Piazza, he chose the least decorated of the classical orders, the Tuscan, adding no statues or other adornments. The portico, supported by rectangular pillars at the ends and circular ones in the middle, adhered strictly to the proportions laid down by Vitruvius.[11] It was designed to resemble the main entrance of a Roman temple, but in the event the effect was purely cosmetic, because the church has always been entered from the west, through the churchyard. Inigo's original plan was to have the altar at the west end, to allow entry from the Piazza, the logical place. Although this would have gone against tradition, he must have felt that Protestant worshippers would not object to this deviation from the strict Catholic line. His view was not shared by Bishop Laud, a High Anglican and a traditionalist, who insisted that the altar should be at the east end.

The total cost of construction came in at under £5000,[12] but achieving that price meant cutting a few corners, and defects soon appeared. St Paul's Church has been patched and modified many times over the centuries but the exterior remains much as Inigo designed it, despite having to be reconstructed, in stone instead of the original stucco, following a fire in 1795. One important change, affecting its overall impact, is that originally the whole building stood on a low plinth, a foot or two from the ground, but the gradual raising of the street level has meant that the floor of the portico is now flush with the external pavement. And the sides of the portico, originally closed in, are now open arches.

Some local residents were disconcerted by the plainness of the decoration and the modesty of the building as a whole. They felt it lacked the overall commanding presence they expected in a place of worship. This was just one of several objections to the scheme – many politically based – that dogged it from the outset. In a time of turmoil, with the citizens of the capital prominent among those growing increasingly resentful of the King's autocratic style of rule, his every act came under close and critical scrutiny. A petition to him from future parishioners of the new church in 1638 complained that 'wanting a steeple and bells it cannot properly be called a church'. The eighty-seven petitioners (from a total of 359 parishioners) said they would have to spend some £4000 of their own money to provide those and other essential amenities – although in the end they found they could after all worship adequately without them.[13]

Like the church, the Piazza itself has had to endure much over the years, including more than a century as the heart of London's main wholesale fruit and vegetable market. It is hard today to envisage the initial impact on Londoners of its unfamiliar sense of space and uniform frontages. The King took a keen interest in the project, appreciating the style and glamour that it added to his capital, and he personally suggested some changes to Inigo's original plans. He and his ministers were less enthusiastic, though, about Russell's construction of several hundred lower-cost houses in the surrounding streets, which were being occupied by people 'of mean and loose condition'. Apart from anything else, they added to the sewage problems that had already been exercising Inigo, with the night soil again encroaching on Whitehall Palace and giving further offence to the royal nostrils.

In 1634 the Earl was hauled before the Star Chamber and dunned a further £2000 for these transgressions, in spite of asserting that he believed he was complying with the conditions of his licence. Inigo, meanwhile, was asked to take another look at the drains.[14] He ordered that the 'great gutter', carrying soil from Covent Garden to the Strand, should be blocked up; in 1635 a new sewer was built in St Martin's Lane that would carry the stinking waste into the Thames without coming within sniffing distance of the palace.[15]

Inigo must by now have been London's greatest expert on drains: in 1635 he was asked to advise on a major sewer project in Moor Ditch, north of the City. The problem was that a drain above the ditch, taking waste into the Thames, regularly became blocked and overflowed into the ditch itself, 'which is very foul and dangerous to infection'. His suggested remedy was to build a large new sewer big enough for a man with a wheelbarrow to enter and clear it out, and then to fill in the ditch.[16] He may not have found all this as demeaning and unpleasant as it seems, for the notes he made in his copy of Palladio show that he was as much fascinated by the technical aspects of construction and design as he was by the aesthetics.

His fine houses around the Piazza succeeded for a while in attracting the wealthy residents they were designed for. More and more people of their class were now travelling through the Continent, as Inigo had done twenty years earlier. They greatly admired the stylish town houses that they saw in French and Italian cities, symbols of the potential pleasures of urban living – and thus undermining the official attempts to persuade them to remain in their country seats. Among early tenants of the Piazza were the Earls of Peterborough and Stirling and Thomas Wentworth, later Earl of Strafford and one of the King's most powerful advisers.[17]

Before the end of the century, though, the aristocrats began to move west, to the splendid new streets and squares being laid out in Soho and Bloomsbury, then in Mayfair and St James's. Covent Garden was now left to raffish actors, writers and artists (Sir Peter Lely and Sir Godfrey Kneller had studios there) and later to shady clubs, coffee houses and brothels. Yet the influence of Inigo's innovatory town planning lived on; for the elegant eighteenth-century squares in the West End were based to a significant extent – mews and all – on his Covent Garden model. London today would not look the same without him.

The development of prime building land has been among the most profitable of human activities through the ages and, in consequence, chronically prone to corrupt practices. There were strong hints of shady deals surrounding the construction of the new houses on the Piazza and, especially, those in the adjoining strets – the meaner houses that had caused so much trouble with the drains. One developer's name crops up frequently. William Newton was a Bedfordshire landowner who decided, shortly before the Covent Garden development, to seek his fortune in property speculation. The records show that he regularly received permission to build rows of houses that were clearly in breach of the King's regulations, and it can be assumed that he contributed generously to the royal coffers in return for these favours.

In 1629 he acquired Cup Field, one of the Lincoln's Inn Fields that was supposed to be protected by the commission on which Inigo sat.[18] In 1638 Newton bought the adjoining Purse Field from Lady Cornwallis and sought permission to build thirty-two houses there, pointing out that the development would greatly increase the Crown's revenue from the land. The Society of Lincoln's Inn protested that the proposed buildings would generate 'offensive and unhealthful savours', as well as interrupting the students' studies.[19] The complaint was overridden and permission granted for the houses, including at least one attributed to Inigo himself. It is Lindsey House, the only original building still standing in Lincoln's Inn Fields, built in about 1640 but taking its name from a later owner. Though it has been somewhat altered over the years the essential features of the frontage remain largely intact. It is a pleasing composition. The rusticated ground floor is surmounted by six tall Ionic pilasters made of brick, covered with stucco to mimic stone, and there is a balustraded parapet at the top.

By August 1641 most of Purse Field was covered with houses and Newton wanted to build on the other two fields. His plan was thwarted not by Inigo and the Commissioners but by the newly recalled House of Commons, whose members, flexing their muscles for their ultimate act of defiance, looked askance at any schemes that seemed to have the approval of the court.[20] William Prynne, a virulent Puritan propagandist who denounced Catholic influence in high places, wrote a pamphlet called *Hidden Works of Darkness Brought to Public Light*. In it he accused Newton of being a front man, developing the properties on behalf of wealthy Catholics, especially those in the circle of Henrietta Maria.[21] Newton was certainly well acquainted with the Queen, and many of his applications for royal consent for his development plans were passed through her. In October 1638, his petition for a licence to build fourteen houses on Pickett's Field was first addressed to the Queen, and began: 'The King, at the instance of your Majesty, has granted petitioner licence to build sundry messuages upon part of the fields near Lincoln's Inn.'[22] A year later permission for the fourteen new houses came through.[23] Newton's close connection with Henrietta Maria is confirmed by his presence in the Queen's party when she fled to the Netherlands in 1642, at the start of the Civil War.[24] He died the following year.

While Inigo himself did not invest in any of the new houses, at least two of his close associates did: Edward Carter, his Deputy Surveyor, and Isaac de Caux.[25] In terms of today's politics the personal relationships between those who authorised the development and those who profited from it would be termed cronyism and sleaze. That it was predominantly a court project is confirmed by the names of the principal streets leading into the Piazza: King, Henrietta, James and Charles (now gone). Great Queen Street, off Lincoln's Inn Fields, was another development in which both Newton and Inigo were involved.

More measured criticism than Prynne's, though no less potent for being less savagely expressed, came from the playwright Richard Brome in his comedy *The Weeding of Covent Garden*, subtitled 'The Middlesex Justice of Peace.' With Inigo recently appointed JP for Westminster and Middlesex, the subtitle signalled unambiguously that he was the target of the satire. In the play the architect, Rooksbill, and the JP, Cockbrain, were separate characters, symbolising both aspects of Inigo's role in the development. In the first scene, heavy with irony, Cockbrain complimented Rooksbill on the quality of his work:

> Here's architecture expressed indeed. It is a most sightly situation, and fit for gentry and nobility . . . A hearty blessing on their brains, honours and wealths that are projectors, furtherers and performers of such great works . . . I like your row of houses most incomparably. Your money never shone from your counting-boards as in those structures.

Brome wanted to leave no doubt that in his view the principal motive for the project was financial. Rooksbill, like Cockbrain, was concerned with the money side, pointing out that he had spent £1000 on walls and windows, and was now worried that the houses would not be taken up by 'worthy persons'. Cockbrain was reassuring and continued to flatter, in a speech mocking long-winded architectural jargon:

> It will all come again with large increase . . . The Surveyor (whate'r he was) has manifested himself the master of his great art. How he has wedded strength to beauty; state to uniformity; commodiousness with perspicuity.

David Howarth is probably right to interpret Brome's play primarily as an attack on property speculation and greed, with the inference that Inigo and the Crown were deeply implicated in it.[26] He points out, too, that Brome was a friend, protégé and former servant of Ben Jonson, who had written a poem in his praise. So his satire on Inigo was not simply motivated by the politics of urban development, but represented a further sally in the feud between the two great men: it had become the talk of the town, and everyone felt they had a right to take sides.

Inigo was continuing to work for private clients. His 1638 drawing of a town house for Lord Maltravers, Thomas Howard's son, is at Worcester College, Oxford. A plain building in Lothbury, in the City of London, it was apparently planned primarily as an office. It has two floors of flat-topped windows, five on the first floor and four at ground level, to make room for the modest central doorway. Three dormer windows adorn the hipped roof.[27]

Two surviving buildings in the London area have been attributed speculatively to Inigo. One is Ashburnham House, built in 1640 and today part of Westminster School, retaining among its original interior features a fine balustraded staircase. The other is a plain brick garden house, with Tuscan pilasters, in the grounds of the early Jacobean Charlton House, the former home of Sir Adam Newton, tutor to Prince Henry when Inigo was employed as his Surveyor. The garden house (now used as a public lavatory) dates from about 1630, the year Sir Adam died and left Charlton House to his son Henry, who made some improvements to it. One of the fireplaces in the main house is similar to two drawings by Inigo in the collection of the Royal Institute of British Architects, and may have been moved to Charlton from the Queen's House at Greenwich.[28]

While demand for housing in London continued to increase, the early seventeenth century was not a prolific period for the construction of English country houses. In the tense and uncertain political climate, monied landowners were too preoccupied with examining their loyalties and safeguarding their futures. To build splendid country piles would have demanded a degree of long-term confidence that they found hard to muster. Of the few great houses that date from this time, any showing signs of being influenced by European classicism have over the years been attributed to Inigo, with varying degrees of conviction but without hard evidence. As James Lees-Milne observed:

> There is scarcely a county in England or Wales – or Scotland – in which some Jacobean house with, say, a window, gable or porch displaying a more or less regular use of the classical orders, has not been classified by over-zealous topographers as an Inigo Jones building.[29]

While the architects of royal buildings can be identified with certainty, because records of payments for work on them can be found in the state archives, the relevant papers of the private families who commissioned the houses have often disappeared. Three mansions in Northamptonshire, though, have been linked to Inigo with some plausibility: Stoke Park, Kirby Hall and Castle Ashby. All include elements that clearly owe something to his influence, but their exact attribution remains conjectural. John Webb and Nicholas Stone may have been involved in some of them, with or without Inigo's collaboration.

Stoke Park, the earliest of the three, is the most tantalising. What remains of it today are two charming pavilions, part of a house built in 1630 for Sir Francis Crane, who had founded the Mortlake tapestry works at the behest of James I and used some of the money he made to give financial support to the hard-pressed Charles. In return, the King granted him 400 acres of land near the village of Stoke Bruerne, south of Northampton, where he began to build what is thought to be the first genuinely Palladian country house in England, with the main part connected by a curved colonnade to two flanking cubic pavilions. When Crane died in 1636 only the colonnade and pavilions – one serving as the library, the other as the chapel – had been put up. The central part was built to a different design by a successor in the 1660s, but the pavilions remained as they were.

John Bridges, the eighteenth-century historian of Northampton-shire, says that Crane acquired the original design of his house from Italy and 'received the assistance of Inigo Jones' in executing it. The two men would have become acquainted when tapestries from Crane's Mortlake factory were commissioned for the Banqueting House, and by the 1630s they were both prominent members of Charles's court. Certainly no other architect of the period is known to have possessed the sophisticated understanding of the Palladian style and method evident in the two pavilions, slightly altered over the years but still beautifully balanced and 'proportionable according to the rules'.

The most significant of the contested attributions is the splendid Wilton House, near Salisbury – then, as now, inhabited by the Earls of Pembroke. The family had always been close to the monarchy. The first Earl, whose Welsh father was an ally of Henry VII, was the brother-in-law of Catherine Parr, Henry VIII's last wife. When the monasteries were dissolved, Henry granted Wilton Abbey to the Earl, who built there one of the largest and most splendid Tudor houses in the region. Both King James and King Charles liked to stay in it. James included it on the itinerary for his first progress through his kingdom in 1603, when Shakespeare is said to have played the part of Adam in a command performance at Wilton of *As You Like It*. Inigo had been a guest there at least once.

When the fourth Earl, Philip Herbert, succeeded to the title in 1630, he thought it was time for the old house to be brought up-to-date in accordance with modern architectural principles. King Charles encouraged him in this. According to the antiquarian John Aubrey:

His majesty intended to have it all designed by his own architect, Mr Inigo Jones, who being at that time, about 1633, engaged in

His Majesty's buildings at Greenwich, could not attend to it; but he recommended it to an ingenious architect, M. Solomon de Caux, a Gascon, who performed it very well; but not without the advice and approbation of Mr Jones.[30]

Aubrey had the wrong de Caux. Solomon, the former architect to Prince Henry, had died in 1626, and he was not a Gascon but a Norman. The architect involved at Wilton was his nephew Isaac, who had worked with Inigo at Covent Garden.

At Wilton, the garden was laid out first. Despite Aubrey's assertion, historians now believe that Inigo provided more than 'advice and approbation' and was largely if not wholly responsible for its design, as well as that of the south front of the house. Some of the backdrops to the masques of the 1630s include gardens derived from French engravings, broadly similar to the spacious, formal design at Wilton, complete with its celebrated grotto.[31] De Caux was certainly employed to supervise the work and produced a set of engravings of the garden. There is also evidence that Nicholas Stone, Inigo's friend and colleague, played a part.[32]

A painting by Leonard Knyff gives an idea of the splendour of the garden at the end of the seventeenth century. An account of how it looked in 1635, just after its completion, comes in a 'Description of a Journey made into the Western Counties' by an anonymous army officer.[33] He wrote of the 'double ranks of pleasant green walks, one above another, and set all along with pots for flowers of the best kind'. He described the 'four white square fountains, with four white alabaster statues', along with statues of Flora and Bacchus 'both most artificially [expertly] cut'. After crossing a wooden bridge over a stream, the visitor came to four pools, with fountains spouting from rocks in their centre – all amounting to a 'delightful garden journey'.

In 1636, to complete the composition, work began on the house itself. The original plan was for the south frontage to stretch almost the whole width of the garden, some 330 feet. A drawing of the garden with the projected house in the background was discovered by Howard Colvin at Worcester College, Oxford, in 1954. It shows a three-storey building with a hipped roof and a central colonnaded portico crowned by a pediment, the portico aligned with the central avenue of the garden.

In the event the building was modified and foreshortened, probably for reasons of cost. The central portico was lost and distinctive 'pavilions' were added at each end, one storey higher than the central block, apparently derived from designs by Palladio and Scamozzi. They counteracted the long, flat look of the original design.[34] Given that the work was broadly contemporary with Inigo's completion of the Queen's House at Greenwich it is significant that in both cases a considerable amount of the new construction was of brick, which had still not come into general use in country houses.[35]

The south front of Wilton House

A fire at Wilton in 1647 destroyed much of this new south wing. The following year, despite the prevailing political uncertainty, the Earl determined to have it rebuilt. Although he had once been a friend of the King he had supported the victorious Parliamentary cause in the Civil War, so his estate was not subject to punitive fines. This time Isaac de Caux does not seem to have been involved in the venture.

Webb was the principal architect, with Inigo, so far as he could manage at the age of seventy-five, acting as consultant. Both were Royalists, but Pembroke did not let political considerations interfere with his desire to employ the best talent available. Nor would Inigo, at that late stage of his career, be inclined to turn down commissions out of loyalty to a defeated monarch.

From this reconstruction date the glorious interiors of Wilton's south wing, including the 'cube' and 'double cube' rooms, among the most perfect surviving examples of seventeenth-century interior design, conforming strictly to the classical proportions laid down by Vitruvius and Palladio. In the former, all three principal dimensions are thirty feet, and the latter is sixty feet long. The core design of both rooms, with their coved ceilings, is simple enough, yet their decoration is the height of sumptuous sophistication, strongly influenced by the French manner that Inigo had been developing in his work for Henrietta Maria, especially in the chapels at Somerset House and St James's Palace. The chimneypieces are recognisably based on designs of the French architectural writer Jean Barbet.[36] The pine-panelled walls are richly decorated with carved and gilded wood, the ceilings and coving with paintings illustrating classical or symbolic themes. Surviving drawings confirm that Inigo collaborated with Webb in designing at least some of the doors and ceilings for these and other major rooms in the house, although part of the detail of the decoration has been modified over the years.

The double cube room contains a collection of portraits of the King, Henrietta Maria and their children, as well as of the third and fourth Earls of Pembroke, painted by Van Dyck or his pupils. It is fitting that Inigo's last attributed work, however limited his actual contribution may have been, should contain these flattering images of his principal patrons.

Chapter Nineteen

PICTURES WITH LIGHT AND MOTION

AFTER THE BREAK WITH JONSON, the procedure for composing court masques became more clear-cut. Inigo, in close consul-
tation with the King and Queen, would devise the plot, then engage
somebody to write the words. There were plenty of aspiring poets and
jobbing playwrights to choose from, happy enough to accept a subser-
vient role in the creative process in return for gaining royal attention.
The first two masques produced under the new arrangement, in January
and February 1632, had scripts written by Aurelian Townshend, a poet
who already boasted connections at court. He had once been a steward
to Robert Cecil, Earl of Salisbury, and was one of Jonson's closest friends
in the early years of the century. In 1608 he had toured Europe with
Edward Herbert, whose brother Henry, as Master of the Revels, was
now in charge of court entertainments.

The first of Townshend's masques, *Albion's Triumph*, was dedicated
to the King and performed on Twelfth Night. The companion piece
for the Queen, *Tempe Restored*, was presented on Shrove Tuesday. In
Albion's Triumph the poet, under Inigo's close scrutiny, produced a more
overtly topical and political text than had been Jonson's custom. He

glorified the King's right and ability to rule wisely without Parliament, as he had already been doing for more than two years. In celebrating Charles's declaration of independence from the restraints imposed by less worthy men, it has been suggested that Inigo also had in mind his own release from the difficulties of working with Jonson.[1] With hindsight we can judge that while both breaches may have been expedient in the short term, ultimately they involved forfeiting something integral to the two projects.

Whatever the masque's subtext so far as Inigo's own position was concerned, it is hard to imagine that Charles would have authorised any very different theme at that particular stage of his reign. Townshend dutifully celebrated the benefits the King had already brought to his kingdom – peace, prosperity and a reduction in street crime:

> Arms are laid by: early and late
> The traveller goes safe to bed;
> Men eat and drink in massie [heavy] plate
> And are with dainties daily fed.
> Why should this isle above the rest
> Be made, great God, the Halcyon's nest?

(The halcyon is a mythical species of kingfisher said to have built its nest on the sea, which remained miraculously calm during its breeding season – the halcyon days.)

Townshend's celebration of the King's peaceable nature seems devastatingly ironic in view of the calamity that would overtake the nation ten years later:

> That which the murdering cannon cannot force,
> Nor plumed squadrons of steel-glittering horse,
> Love can . . .

Charles danced the part of the benign king Albanactus, meaning Scots-born.[2] Inigo's design for a stage palace for this exemplary monarch was influenced by the King's recent acquisition of the Mantuan paintings and sculptures. There were borrowings from Mantegna's *Triumph of*

Caesar series and three of the most important sculptures of the collection were represented on the proscenium, on either side of the royal arms, emphasising the King's exquisite taste. The first scene depicted a Roman atrium, with columns on each side and statues of gold on round pedestals between them. In some ways it resembled the sculpture gallery that Inigo had designed for Thomas Howard to house the pieces they had bought in Italy, although it was also strongly influenced, like much of his work, by Italian stage designers.[3]

The proscenium arch was decorated with figures labelled as representing theory and practice, 'showing that by these two, all works of architecture and engineering have their perfection'. This was based on the design of the title page of Scamozzi's book, which Inigo had bought in Italy.[4] Here he was following his own rather than the King's agenda, promoting his view of architecture as a craft that covers many disciplines. His message was that to leave the design of a building to masons and carpenters, as had been the custom in earlier times, meant that it lacked the academic underpinning that only a well-read architect could provide. At the same time the architect always had to take account of the technical aspects of turning his design into a workable building. So theory and practice were both integral to the process.

The Queen's 1632 masque, *Tempe Restored*, was yet another paean to platonic love. Tempe, the idyllic haunt of the Muses, was for a time inhabited by Circe and her court of 'intemperate beasts', as they were described by Inigo in his explanation of the allegory. They were driven out by a combination of Divine Beauty and Heroic Virtue, personified by the Queen and King. Inigo appears to have written the explanation of the allegory and the description of his scenic effects himself. The King, he wrote, 'transcends as far common men as they are above beasts', while the Queen's beauty 'may draw us to the contemplation of the beauty of the soul, unto which it hath analogy'.

Released from Jonson's restraints, he was unstinting with praise for his own achievement, especially at the point where Divine Beauty descended from the sky in layers of clouds that vanished to reveal more clouds, then bright stars:

And above all, in a chariot of goldsmith's work richly adorned with precious gems, sat Divine Beauty, over whose head appeared a brightness full of small stars that environed the top of the chariot, striking a light round about it . . . The sight altogether was, for the difficulty of the engining [engineering] and the number of the persons, the greatest that hath been seen here in our time. For the apparitions of such as came down in the air, and the choruses standing beneath, arrived to the number of fifty persons, all richly attired, showing the magnificence of the court of England.

As he wrote in his initial description of the scene, almost certainly recalling his artistic differences with his former collaborator: 'These shows are nothing else but pictures with light and motion.'

Tempe Restored has a special place in the history of the English stage as the first known occasion when actresses played speaking and singing roles in anything but a strictly private performance.[5] The first step towards breaking this taboo had been taken by Henrietta Maria in 1626, but her speaking part in the French-language *Artenice* was seen only by the King and a very restricted circle of intimates who could be relied upon not to take offence.[6] Inigo would have seen actresses at work in Italy, where they appeared from about the middle of the sixteenth century, and probably in France, where they were in evidence some fifty years later.[7] As the main begetter and producer of *Tempe Restored*, he must be given much of the credit for this far-reaching innovation, although Henrietta Maria would have had to approve and might have been instrumental in choosing the actress who played Circe, a Frenchwoman named in the text as Madame Coniack. There was also a Mrs Shepherd, representing Harmony.

Now that a precedent had been set with *Tempe Restored*, the Queen was anxious to resume her own acting, which appears to have been dormant since *Artenice*. Towards the end of 1632 Inigo was instructed to design a theatre in the courtyard of Somerset House, where he had already begun work on the delayed chapel for the Queen. The theatre was to be 'purposely made' with the timber work 'properly done', as the venue for a pastoral by Walter Montagu, the Francophile courtier who had acted as proxy for Charles at his marriage ceremony and later became a Catholic. The plan for this theatre, perhaps in Inigo's hand, survives in the Lansdowne manuscript collection in the British Library. It has an apron stage jutting into a rectangular block of seats, with a deep area at the back for wings and shutters that would allow several changes of scene.[8] A drawing in the Chatsworth collection probably represents one of the backdrops. It shows a geometrically formal garden that seems to be derived from an etching by Jacques Callot of a garden at Nancy. (The garden designed by Inigo or Isaac de Caux at Wilton House may have been inspired by the same etching.)[9]

Although not a great writer, Montagu was certainly a prolix one: *The Shepherd's Paradise*, performed on 9 January 1633, lasted seven hours and was four months in rehearsal.[10] The Queen played a central role, this time speaking in English. As was almost inevitable, the marathon work's principal theme was a celebration of platonic love. Inigo devised eight scene changes, but even so the patience of the audience was sorely tested. Inigo managed to recycle some of his designs a year later for another pastoral at Somerset House, *The Faithful Shepherdess*, an old work by the popular Jacobean playwrights Francis Beaumont and John Fletcher.[11]

The easing of the restrictions on women appearing on stage, with overt royal sanction, was bitterly opposed by Puritans, who saw it as proof positive of the immorality that pervaded court life. The most insistent critic was William Prynne, the pamphleteer who attacked the Queen's role in the Covent Garden development.[12] His notorious denunciation of the Jacobean stage, *Histriomastix*, was published a few months after the production of *Tempe Restored*. In it, he characterised the lavish spectacle of the masques as a surreptitious revival of Catholic ritual, the dancing as a 'Devil's mass'. He was incensed, too, that performances were sometimes staged on Sundays, when public playhouses were closed at the insistence of the Church.[13]

Prynne's book contained an especially vicious attack on women who took part in masques, even in non-speaking roles. It was the reference in the index to 'Women actors, notorious whores' that prompted Laud to persuade the King to take action against Prynne. The words were interpreted, and probably intended, as a treasonable insult to the thespian Queen. After a trial in the Star Chamber, in which fifty allegedly treasonable passages in the book were cited, Prynne was sentenced in 1634 to life imprisonment in the Tower of London, a £500 fine and to have both his ears removed in the pillory.

In the Tower he continued to write inflammatory Puritan pamphlets and was hauled back to the Star Chamber, where he was sentenced to the removal of those parts of his ears that remained intact after the first mutilation. Contrast that grisly image of brutality with the 'softnesses of courts', as celebrated by Jonson and his successors. Here was one traveller in Charles's peaceable kingdom who did not go safe or comfortably to bed: Prynne could have detected no evidence of divinity, beauty or love – platonic or any other sort – in the treatment meted out to him by his sovereign.

His sole offence, after all, had been to hold and express deep convictions and to remain true to them. As Inigo must have calculated early in his career, England under the Stuarts was one of those recurring periods of history when to hold convictions is a deadly dangerous self-indulgence, when beliefs are the very stuff of murderous dispute. Only when Charles was forced to recall Parliament was Prynne's sentence declared illegal. Disfigured but unrepentant, he was released in 1641.

Prynne had been a member of Lincoln's Inn since 1621. Although he was summarily expelled following his first trial in 1634, his disgrace had still placed the four Inns of Court under a cloud in the eyes of the King and his supporters, who felt that some form of restitution was called for. They persuaded the leading lawyers of the Inns that, if they wanted to return to royal favour, they must mount a masque in the Banqueting House 'as an expression of their love and duty to their majesties'. This would demonstrate in the most direct way that they did not share their former colleague's prejudices against the splendours of stage performance. It would also mean that the King and Queen could enjoy the pleasures of a masque without its being a charge on the royal exchequer.

James Shirley was asked to write *The Triumph of Peace* and Inigo to provide his usual effects, scenes and costumes. The performance, in February 1634, was preceded by a spectacular evening parade, also designed by Inigo, involving the masquers and members of the four Inns. It started at Ely House in Holborn, close to Gray's Inn, progressing along Chancery Lane and the Strand, thence to Whitehall. It was a sensational occasion, the talk of the town for weeks, and more than one detailed account has survived. At the head of the parade the King's Marshal and his assistants, bearing torches, cleared the way for one hundred lawyers – twenty-five from each Inn – riding on horseback, brilliant in gold and silver lace:

> The richness of their apparel and furniture glittering by the light of a multitude of torches attending on them, with the motion and stirring of their mettled horses, and the many and various gay liveries of their servants; but especially the personal beauty and gallantry of the handsome young gentlemen, made the most glorious and most splendid show that ever was beheld in England.

Then came the musicians and the actors playing in the antimasque, some of them boys disguised as birds. Several other antimasque characters represented comical tradesmen seeking to purchase monopolies. One, for example, carried 'a bunch of carrots upon his head and a capon upon his fist, describing a projector [entrepreneur] who begged a patent of monopoly as the first inventor of the art to feed capons fat with carrots'.[14]

The meaning could scarcely be clearer. This was a direct sally at the King's policy of granting monopolies to replace revenue that would normally come from Parliament. The lawyers were then, as now, a powerful group in themselves, less dependent than many on royal patronage. Because they had ultimate control of the masque's content, it was not as fawning as those written directly for the King and Queen. Its theme, appropriate in the circumstances but daring nonetheless, was the need for any monarch to operate within the rule of law.[15]

After the antimasquers came the principal masquers, seated in replicas of Roman triumphal chariots, each drawn by four horses and accompanied by scores of torchbearers. The men wore doublets, hose and caps, 'as thick with silver spangles as could be placed', while the horses were covered with crimson and silver cloths, sporting red and white feathers on their heads and rear ends.

The torches and flaming huge flambeaux born by the sides of each chariot made it seem lightsome as of noonday, but more glittering, and gave a full and clear light to all the streets and windows as they passed.

When the parade came by the King and Queen, watching from a Whitehall Palace window, were so impressed that they asked for it to turn round and do the last stretch again. Then the masque began, its scenery described as 'most curious and costly': the bill for the whole evening set back the Inns of Court some £21,000. Among the most admired scenes was the forum or piazza of peace, one of several of Inigo's designs that appear to have been copied from the work of the Italian designer Giulio Parigi in a comedy produced in Florence in 1608.[16] Inigo is known to have had drawings of stage settings sent over from the Continent at this period, and had no compunction about reproducing them almost exactly.

Another of the artistic successes in *The Triumph of Peace* was the music, composed by Bulstrode Whitelocke, a young lawyer who, as Master of the Revels of the Middle Temple, was on the committee that had organised the event. His score was so popular that whenever in future he appeared in the audience at a public theatre, the musicians would interrupt their performance and begin to play it – probably the first signature tune in the history of British entertainment.[17]

At the end of the masque the participants kissed the hands of the King and Queen and were treated to a splendid banquet. The festivities continued until nearly morning, but still the Queen had not had her fill of Inigo's and Shirley's creation. Despite its ambiguous political theme, which she may not wholly have understood, she declared that she would like to see it again. The Lord Mayor of London was persuaded to invite the royal couple to the City a week later for a repeat performance of both the parade and the masque, mounted this time at the Merchant Taylors' Hall.[18]

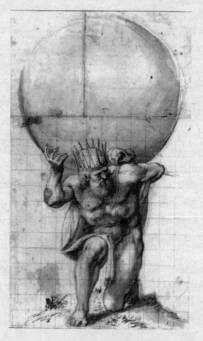

Atlas holds up the world, from *Coelum Britannicum*, 1634

The court masque for 1634 was presented only a few days later, on Shrove Tuesday, 18 February. *Coelum Britannicum*, or the British Heaven, written by the poet Thomas Carew, has been described as 'the most complete celebration of the court of Charles and Henrietta Maria'.[19] The couple's moral purity was cited as a model for English society, their court likened to Jove's heaven. The King took a leading role but, unlike his wife the previous year, a silent one, confining himself to dancing to the music composed by Henry Lawes, the house musician at the Chapel Royal. Both the King and Inigo received at least one good review, from Inigo's old friend Thomas Howard, in a letter to Thomas Wentworth in Ireland. After first describing the Inns of Court masque,

Howard wrote: 'But his majesty on Shrove Tuesday last far surpassed it, not only in dancing but in the scene, where in Mr Surveyor did his masterpiece.'[20]

Inigo shared his friend's high opinion of his achievement. In his initial 'Description of the Scene', after enumerating the uplifting inscriptions, the branches, foliage and lilies (the flower of France), he wrote: 'All this ornament was heightened with gold, and for the invention and various composition was the newest and most gracious that hath been done in this place.'

For the mechanical effects, he went through his by now familiar repertoire of stage devices: clouds drifting, rising and falling; the moon breaking and waning; mountains emerging from beneath the stage; rocks cracking open to reveal caves. The most sensational moment, again according to Inigo's own testimony, came when three actors representing the kingdoms of England, Ireland and Scotland were seated on a rock. A cloud descended and drifted up again to the heavens:

> At that instant the rock with the three kingdoms on it sinks, and it is hidden in the earth. This strange spectacle gave great cause of admiration, but especially how so huge a machine, and of that great height, should come from under the stage, which was but six foot high.

When he described his inventions as pictures of light and motion, Inigo ought to have added 'illusion'.

Carew's lengthy text was notable for several passages in the anti-masque that boldly described the sins of courtiers and citizens during the reigns of Charles and James. These were put into the mouth of Momus, the son of night and god of ridicule. One speech echoed James's complaint that it was the wives of gentlemen who persuaded them to abandon duties in the countryside and hasten to the fleshpots of the capital:

> Edicts are made for the restoring of decayed housekeeping, prohibiting the repair of families to the metropolis; but this did endanger an Amazonian mutiny, till the females put on a more masculine resolution

of soliciting businesses in their own persons, and leaving their husbands at home for stallions of hospitality.

There was, too, a pointed reference to the prevalence of homosexuality in King James's late court:

Ganymede [Jupiter's cup-bearer and lover] is forbidden the bed-chamber, and must only minister in public. The gods must keep no pages nor grooms of their chamber under the age of twenty-five, and those provided of a competent stock of beard.

But the proceedings could not end without the compulsory deification of the royal couple:

> And as their own pure souls entwined,
> So are their subjects' hearts combined . . .
> And their fair fame, like incense hurled
> On altars, hath perfumed the world.
> Wisdom, truth, pure adoration,
> Concord, rule, clear reputation,
> Crown this king, this queen, this nation.

Unless there were special events to celebrate, court masques were customarily staged shortly after Christmas, in the first two months of the year. In 1634, though, Inigo found himself having to work on one for the Queen in November. It was written by Thomas Heywood, a prolific and popular playwright and actor, born in the same year as Inigo. Most of Heywood's work was for the commercial theatre (he claimed to have had a hand in 220 plays), and *Love's Mistress* is his only known masque. It had its first performance, without scenery, at the Phoenix in Drury Lane – the theatre that Inigo had designed for Christopher Beeston more than a decade earlier. The Queen saw it there and commanded that it be brought to Somerset House, where the King could also enjoy it as part of the celebrations for his thirty-fourth birthday.

Inigo was asked to design the settings for this second performance at short notice, and the scant details of them that survive suggest that he may have borrowed some devices from *Coelum Britannicum*. In any case, Heywood was impressed, or at least he was determined not to make Jonson's mistake of taking his collaborator for granted:

> For rare decorments which now apparelled it, when it came the second time to the royal view . . . I cannot pretermit [neglect] to give a due character to that admirable artist, Mr Inigo Jones, master Surveyor of the King's Works etc., who to every act, nay almost to every scene, by his excellent inventions gave such an extraordinary lustre; upon every occasion changing the stage to the admiration of all the spectators: that, as I must ingeniously confess, it was above my apprehension to conceive, so to their sacred Majesties and the rest of the auditory; it gave so general a content, that I presume that they never parted from any object, presented in that kind, better pleased, or more plenally satisfied.[21]

For Inigo, the trouble with being the recipient of such consistent adulation, ever more extravagantly expressed, was that you came to expect it, and to resent anything that smacked of faint praise – or even, perish the thought, a hint of criticism. That is what lay behind his next major personal feud, with no less a dignitary than Thomas Wentworth (later Earl of Strafford). Originally a harsh critic of the King, Wentworth, an opinionated Yorkshire landowner, was now one of his most powerful advisers, serving in an important role as Lord Deputy of Ireland, ever the kingdom's most troublesome province.

Wentworth unwittingly fired the first volley against Inigo in December 1634. Keen to exert his authority in Dublin soon after his arrival, he decided to tackle the city's physical condition, asking for money to repair his castle and to be sent a copy of the restrictive building regulations that Inigo had drawn up, but only spasmodically enforced, for London. The requests were passed through the Secretary of State, Sir John Coke, and both were complied with. In acknowledging the grant of funds for the castle, Wentworth wrote:

> I will be as good a husband of it as possibly I can, and trust to prove as thrifty a surveyor as the best; nay, without offence to Mr Jones,

or pride in myself be it spoken, I take myself to be a very pretty architect too.[22]

This could scarcely have been a deliberate attempt to rile Inigo, for Wentworth cannot have known that his note would be shown to the Surveyor-General. But it was, and Inigo was predictably stung by the Lord Deputy's nerve in daring to compare his amateur dabbling with the work of the country's greatest architect. Thomas Howard, a friend of both men, tried to head off the incipient bad feeling but managed only to make things worse. He wrote to Wentworth in January saying that Inigo 'hopes your Lordship will one day acknowledge him to be the better architect'. Wentworth, meanwhile, had drawn up a set of building restrictions apparently based on Inigo's for London, although he claimed he had never received them. Howard wrote to him again in March:

> For the Proclamation of Buildings Inigo told me long ago he had sent it unto your Lordship and so saith still, which he avows he did out of his duty and to propagate the arts but not to beg suffrage [approval] for his ability in his own profession, which he understands so well, as though he be not worthy to look upon your Lordship's abilities in all things else, yet in this particular he would be sorry your Lordship's skill should presume to enter the lists with his.[23]

This drew from Wentworth an ironic response that soured the relationship still further. He assured Howard that he desired peace with 'the great and good genius of architecture Mr Inigo Jones', and acknowledged himself to be 'one of the lesser intelligences in the high and noble art'. But he went on:

> Thus I shall be willing to borrow from and acknowledge his authority. But if he look big and disdainfully upon us, I shall not forbear to tell him, I have built a better stable for the King here in Ireland than ever he did in England. That a worm if trodden on will turn again.

On his return from Ireland in 1639 Wentworth became the King's principal adviser, masterminding two of the miscalculations that prepared the ground for civil war: the recall of Parliament and the invasion of Scotland. He was created Earl of Strafford in 1640, but the same year he was impeached by the House of Commons and sent to the Tower of London, to be tried in Westminster Hall in March 1641. It fell to Inigo to draw up plans to rig up the hall for his antagonist's trial, just as he had done twenty-five years earlier for the trial of the Earl and Countess of Somerset in the Overbury affair. It is hard to believe that even so powerful a hater would have tackled the assignment with any satisfaction or relish. When Strafford was found guilty, Charles was persuaded, against his will, to sign the death warrant of his ally and supporter, who was executed in May. The worm would turn no more.

Whatever Inigo's personal feelings about designing the stage for the show trial, it led him into yet another dispute, this time with the carpenters who carried out the work. Hollar's engraving of the trial shows that a substantial amount of construction was involved, and it had to be done with remarkable speed. Inigo had designed about a dozen rows of steeply banked wooden seats on each side of a central well, with a raised dais for the King's throne, a covered gallery for members of his family and a stout wooden stall for the prisoner. The master carpenter, Arthur Cundall, agreed to provide all this for £100, including all the timber. Working day and night, he and his men completed the hall's transformation within five days.

When the trial was over, the carpenters returned to dismantle and remove the timber, which they believed still belonged to them. In a statement to the court when the issue was taken to law, they maintained that their fee covered only their labour costs, and that the wood and other materials were together worth 'the sum of £204 and upward'. They were prevented from taking it away by the Earl of Lindsey, Lord Great Chamberlain, and two men acting for him, one named as Peter Cannon, 'confederating themselves with the said Inigo Jones, Thomas Baldwin [Comptroller of the Works, who had died in 1641] and Henry Wicks [Paymaster of the Works]'. Maybe someone had an inkling that the materials might be needed for other show trials to come.

Answering the complaint, Inigo and Wicks denied 'to their best remembrance that the said agreement was set down in writing' and declared that they had not told the carpenters specifically that they could take possession of the timber. Their aim had been to 'make a good and profitable a bargain and agreement for His Majesty'. They denied, too, being in league with Peter Cannon and said they had not taken any of the disputed materials for themselves.[24]

The case dragged on even while Inigo absented himself from London in the first years of the Civil War. When he returned it became a cause of such concern to him and his co-defendant Wicks that in 1646 they petitioned the House of Lords to protect them from Cundall's demands, which if successful were 'likely to become a precedent to others who have money owing them from His Majesty in the said office, to the petitioners' utter ruin'. By then Inigo had been forced to pay a hefty fine to punish him for his Royalist allegiance[25] and was clearly feeling insecure, both financially and psychologically. The Lords accepted his and Wicks's petition and on 27 June issued a recommendation to the Committee of Revenue that 'some course may be taken for the payment of such monies that are due' from the public purse.[26]

It would be misleading to infer from all this that Inigo's social talents were now limited to quarrelling and making enemies. Although he appears to have long retired from the companionable drinking clubs at the Mermaid and the Mitre, he still had many friends at court. Some, no doubt, genuinely admired his qualities and others felt it politic to remain on good terms with a man who exerted so much influence. Among the most eminent of those in the former category was Sir Anthony Van Dyck, the prolific and brilliant Flemish portrait painter, follower of Rubens, who came to Whitehall from Italy in 1632, at the age of thirty-three. He had been invited by the King to be his court painter in place of the less well regarded Daniel Mytens, and was soon knighted. His recruitment was a signal of Charles's determination to turn the royal palace into a haven of the finest in Continental culture. Van Dyck's many portraits of the royal family fulfilled the same image-building function as the court masques, idealising them as models of elegance, dignity, wisdom and courage.

The young artist had first visited London thirteen years earlier, as the guest of Thomas Howard. Inigo would presumably have met him then, and as Surveyor he became officially involved in the painter's second stay when, in August 1633, he was asked to help find him a house.[27] Van Dyck usually spent the summer at the royal palace at Eltham, Kent, and had been lodging the previous winter in a house in Blackfriars owned by Edward Norgate, a court organ restorer. Now he sought a more permanent London base.

There is good evidence that Inigo and Van Dyck admired each other's work. John Webb, in his short biography of his mentor, quotes the Dutchman's commendation of Inigo's drawing skills, unequalled by the great masters for his 'boldness, softness, sweetness and sureness of his touches'. Both were much taken with the design of a fragment of an ancient frieze excavated at Pergamon in Turkey, depicting two female heads: Inigo used it in one of his set designs for *Albion's Triumph*, and Van Dyck as a background to more than one of his works.[28]

A portrait of Inigo by Van Dyck is today at the Hermitage Museum in St Petersburg. Originally owned by John Webb, it was acquired by Sir Robert Walpole for his renowned art collection at Houghton Hall in Norfolk and in 1779 was sold, along with other highlights of the collection, to Catherine the Great. The same artist's drawing of Inigo (later to form the basis of a posthumous portrait by William Hogarth) is in the Duke of Devonshire's collection at Chatsworth. In both pictures he is gazing pensively out to his left, but they differ somewhat in mood and character.

The Hermitage painting is austere by comparison with Van Dyck's flattering and vivacious portrayals of exquisitely dressed aristocrats. It concentrates on Inigo's head, enclosed in an oval. His long, dark hair curls untidily beneath a black skull-cap, making a contrast with his neatly trimmed white beard and moustache. He is wearing a plain collar over a black topcoat. His expression suggests a formidable intellect weighed down by the burdens of his position: he does not look as though he would be the life and soul of any party. In the drawing, we see more of him – his whole upper body instead of just his torso. Dressed in the same fashion, he is leaning a little backwards, his right arm resting on what seems to be a plinth draped in a curtain. In his hand he loosely holds a plan of one of his buildings, half concealing his portly stomach. The face again suggests gravity and intelligence but the brow is more furrowed than in the painting, the eyes a little steelier.

At about the same time, or perhaps a year or two later, Inigo drew one of several self-portrait sketches, also now at Chatsworth. Here he was even harder on himself than his Dutch friend had been, revealing a man altogether less serene, the eyes more troubled, the lips pursed. Seen together, along with the later portrait by William Dobson reproduced on the front cover of this book, the pictures suggest a contrast between the confident public figure and his less self-assured private persona. It is not hard to read into them the vanity and the obsession with his own importance revealed in his clashes with Jonson and Wentworth and in the comments of some of his contemporaries.

In March 1636 Inigo and Van Dyck were guests at a dinner of the Painter-Stainers Company at its headquarters in Little Trinity Lane, close to the river. One of the oldest of the city livery companies, the Painter-Stainers sought to regulate all aspects of the decorative trades, embracing artistic 'picture makers' as well as workaday house and furniture painters. Inigo was a freeman of the company and it is likely that the invitation to Van Dyck came through him. The record shows that the painter's 'wife' was also present:[29] this must have been his mistress Mary Ruthven, whom he married two years later at the insistence of the King. Another guest was Christopher Wren senior, Dean of Windsor, whose son would eventually inherit Inigo's role as Surveyor-General and his reputation as the nation's leading architect.

The dinner may have been intended as a gesture of peace after a dispute among the Painter-Stainers in which Inigo had become involved. Like all the City guilds, one of the company's recurring concerns was to protect the livelihood of its members from competition from outsiders or 'strangers' – practitioners who were not members, either because they had not served appropriate apprenticeships, or could not afford to buy their way in, or had been rejected for other reasons. They often worked for lower rates than members, and were able to employ cheap, untrained assistants.

In 1627 the guild drew up a list of foreign artists who were practising in London without authorisation. Several of them, including Daniel Mytens and Orazio Gentileschi, were working for the King, and one, Abraham Van der Doort, became keeper of the royal collections.[30] Van Dyck himself was not a freeman of the Painter-Stainers, but there is no record of any attempt being made to bar him from working. Technically he did not come under their jurisdiction because Blackfriars, where he lived and worked, was a 'liberty', an area where the writ of the livery companies did not run.[31] This could have been why Inigo found a house for him there.

Because so many court artists were not among its members, the guild had been inhibited from demanding sanctions against strangers. Criticising the King's employees was a risky business. Some members were more robust, though, and in 1635 a dozen of them, led by one Thomas Johnson, decided to take the law into their own hands. Using a statute passed in the middle of the sixteenth century, they hauled some of the strangers before the Middlesex Sessions at Hicks Hall in Clerkenwell, where one of them, a Mr Crosse, was committed to the counter, the municipal prison.

This was probably Michael Cross, a Spanish-born painter (originally Miguel de la Cruz) who had been copying some Italian and Spanish pictures for Charles and was on the royal payroll. On his behalf a complaint was made to the King against the disgruntled guild members who had prosecuted him. After taking Inigo's advice, Charles wrote to the company urging 'the toleration of strangers', and Cross was released. When the matter came before the court of the Painter-Stainers in January 1636, they asked Henry Isaacson, a senior officer of the company, to write to Inigo explaining their position. It was probably as a result of this letter that Inigo – 'very lovingly', according to the company's minute book – accepted the invitation to dinner two months later.

His role as a regulator had expanded, then, to embrace the worlds of art and of the livery companies, who were also beginning to call on his services as an architect. He and Webb worked on the headquarters of at least one of the important guilds, the Barber-Surgeons, and he

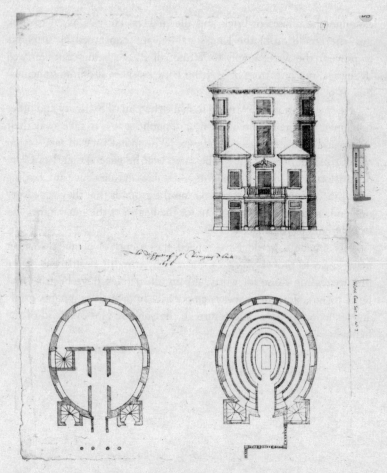

Lecture theatre for the Barber-Surgeons Company

seems to have been instrumental in persuading the Goldsmiths to hire his friend Nicholas Stone to design their hall.

Jonson's characterisation of Inigo as Dominus Do-All became ever more apt as the decade wore on and he undertook a growing number of civic responsibilities, as well as being called on to make rulings on contentious matters of town planning and public health. In 1638 he was appointed to a commission to regulate porters and another to examine the abuses of brick and tile makers. He was asked to look into the condition of the King's stables, and continued his attempts to prevent the water supply to Whitehall Palace being contaminated by sewage, not only from St Martin's Lane but now also from some new houses in Piccadilly.[32]

He spent part of 1639 trying to make the Earl of Salisbury and other noblemen pay their share of the cost of public sewers to take away their waste, and in his role as a Middlesex JP he found time to take action to control the price of lime. The same year he gave the Earl of Clare permission to pull down tenements and stables in Reindeer Yard, leading from Lincoln's Inn to Westminster, on the grounds that they were 'very unseemly and noisome, dangerous for the health of the inhabitants and troublesome to passengers'.[33]

His schedule would have sapped the energy of a much younger man, and was probably one of the reasons why his health was giving him increasing cause for worry. All in all, it must have been a great relief to be able to turn away temporarily from such mundane, grimy and malodorous tasks, and return to the sublime fantasy world of the masques.

Chapter Twenty

THE LAST MASQUES

WILLIAM DAVENANT'S *The Temple of Love*, his paean to the platonic tendency, was performed on Shrove Tuesday, 1635. It was the first royal commission for Davenant, an up-and-coming playwright and impresario in his late twenties who asserted that he was Shakespeare's illegitimate son. (The questionable claim was based on the fact that his father and mother ran an inn at Oxford where the playwright would stay on his journeys between London and Stratford.) A libertine in his youth, Davenant was disfigured by the loss of his nose as a consequence of contracting syphilis.[1] His talents, along with his devotion to the Royalist cause, were no less appreciated at court for that. The Queen was so delighted with *The Temple of Love* that in 1638, shortly after Ben Jonson's death, she used her influence to have Davenant inherit his position of poet laureate.

The masque had an oriental theme, with camels and elephants depicted on the proscenium. Two of Inigo's detailed drawings for costumes for the Brachmani – Brahmins, or Indian priests – have notes in his hand written on the back, demonstrating the fertility of his imagination. One was to have 'an old face with great spectacles on his nose, a beard red and white grizzled, long hanging locks, a wand

315

in his hand of green'. And the other 'a robe of russet girt low with a great belly like a swollen man, long moustachioes, the sleeves short . . . buskines [calf-length sandals] to show a great swollen leg, on his head a cap coming forth before like a peak and from it great leaves hanging down with great ears, a great head'.[2]

The published text included Inigo's by now familiar compliments to himself, this time at the very end:

Thus this masque, which for the newness of the invention, variety of scenes, apparitions and richness of habits was generally approved to be one of the most magnificent that hath been done in England.

It was also, although he may not have known it at the time, the last masque to be performed in his Banqueting House. In October 1635 Rubens's magnificent ceiling paintings were finally delivered, to be installed over the winter. In December, when the Queen wanted to stage another French pastoral, *Florimène*, the Banqueting House was out of commission because of the ceiling work, and Inigo had to rig up a stage in the Tudor great hall of the palace itself – a stage sophisticated enough to accommodate six scene changes. However the installation of the Rubens canvases had a knock-on effect that does not seem to have been anticipated until they were actually in place.

Inigo's ambitious lighting schemes were the problem. The candles, oil lamps and flaming torches he used to create his glittering images took the audience's breath away in more than one sense. They produced smoke, and the more spectacular the effect the more pollution they generated. Nobody minded too much about damage to the spectators' lungs, but the threat of depositing soot and grime on the precious new paintings was an entirely different matter. The King would pay (after the customary delay) £3000 to the Dutch artist for his work: he did not want such expensive masterpieces damaged or dimmed by the smoke and heat. This meant that Inigo's great Banqueting House could no longer be used for one of the principal purposes for which it had been designed. This was a blow for the Queen especially, and for a while she improvised by using other locations within the royal palaces for the stage performances she so loved.

On 29 August 1636 the royal couple went on a state visit to Oxford and Inigo was summoned to design the scenery for the two plays that were to be presented to them there, William Strode's *The Floating Island* and William Cartwright's *The Royal Slave*. Unlike his previous visit to Oxford some thirty years earlier, his efforts this time were universally well received. One commentator described the scenery and effects in the first play in detail and with relish:

> It was acted on a goodly stage, reaching from the upper end of the hall almost to the hearth place, and had on it three or four openings on each side thereof, and partitions between them, much resembling the desks or studies in a library, out of which the actors issued forth. The said partitions they could draw in and out at their pleasure on a sudden, and thrust out new in their places according to the nature of the scene, whereon were represented churches, dwelling houses, etc., which for its variety bred very great admiration.

He was describing the sidewings and shutters that Inigo had introduced to London masque-goers some years earlier. Other marvels that impressed the Oxford enthusiast included:

> the perfect resemblance of the billows of the sea rolling, and an artificial island, with churches and houses waving up and down and floating, as also rocks, trees and hills. Many other fine pieces of work and landscapes did also appear at sundry openings thereof, and a chair also seen to come gliding on the stage without any visible help. All these representations being the first (as I have been informed) that were used on the English stage.[3]

The Royal Slave had an oriental setting, similar to that which Inigo had designed for *The Temple of Love*. The plot involved a slave, captured as a prisoner of war, being allowed to rule as a king for three days, in place of the weak king who held him captive. The fictional queen was so impressed by the slave's nobility that a bond of affection – platonic, of course – grew up between them. When the real king became uneasy at this development, she explained the theory of platonic love and he was mollified. Again, Inigo's contribution was greatly admired, containing:

> as much variety of scenes and motions as the great wit of Inigo Jones
> (well skilled in setting out a court masque to the best advantage) could
> extend unto. It was very well penned and acted and the strangeness of
> the Persian habits gave great content.[4]

Henrietta Maria was much taken both with the play and its setting and asked the Chancellor of the University, who had commissioned the scenery and costumes from Inigo, whether they could be transported to Hampton Court, so that the play could be performed again for her enjoyment. He agreed, on condition that the used costumes were not eventually donated to the common players, a charitable practice of the time.[5]

Staging entertainments at Hampton Court was all very well, but this and the other rural palaces were far from the centre of court life and fashionable society. To present plays and masques there was the equivalent of putting on a present-day show in a fringe theatre rather than in London's West End. So in 1637 the Queen persuaded the King to find the money to erect, alongside the Banqueting House, a wooden masquing house of the same dimensions, its tiled roof supported by twelve massive timber posts.[6] Galleries afforded extra seating for spectators and Inigo took advantage of the opportunity to construct the most elaborate and flexible stage yet seen in London, fitted out so that scenery could slide in from the wings more easily and rapidly, without the need to bring in special equipment for each production.[7] It meant that he could finally abandon his old 'triangle machines', the *periaktoi*, in favour of flat scenery, allowing more changes. The building went up in two months and the last three masques of the reign – indeed of any English reign – were presented in it, all of them written by Davenant.

After a gap of three years the prospect of the 1638 masques, to be performed on Twelfth Night and Shrove Tuesday, had been engrossing the court for weeks, according to despatches sent home by Benedetto di Cize, the agent for Savoy. On 6 December 1637 he reported that preparations were well under way for the first of them, the King's masque *Britannia Triumphans*, adding laconically, 'otherwise there is nothing going on at present in this court except for plays twice a week'.

A month later he reported that the Queen was in serious training for her own masque, *Luminalia*: 'She spends every evening practising for it, with the result that both of them [the masques] will come off very well.'[8]

Britannia Triumphans was the most overtly topical of all the masques of Charles's reign. It was presented at the height of the dispute over ship money, which the King was using to shore up his finances while ruling without Parliament. Traditionally the tax, supposedly earmarked for the maintenance of the national battle fleet, had been levied only on coastal ports and only at times of imminent national danger. From 1634 Charles began to collect it annually from all areas, including inland towns, even though the country was not at war. In 1636 John Hampden, a former and future Member of Parliament, took a public stand against the tax and refused to pay, declaring that the King had no authority to levy it. The court found against Hampden, albeit narrowly, but he gained widespread sympathy and the case added to the King's unpopularity.

The masque sought to justify Charles's demands by glorifying the Navy. In the text Inigo's proscenium was described as being decorated on one side with a woman holding the rudder of a ship, signifying naval victory, and on the other with a man carrying a sceptre and a book, representing 'right government'. The message could hardly have been clearer: good government required command of the waves. The frieze depicted 'a sea triumph of naked children, riding on sea horses and fishes, and young tritons with writhen trumpets and other maritime fancies'. The plot was outlined in the introduction:

Britanocles, the glory of the western world, hath by his wisdom, valour and piety not only vindicated his own but far distant seas, infested with pirates, and reduced the land, by his example, to a real knowledge of all good acts and sciences.

The King, naturally enough, danced the part of Britanocles. Before his appearance came the antimasque, whose first scene was played in a setting that represented the City of London and the Thames. Inigo liked to promote his own architecture in his stage designs when he could. Just as in *Time Vindicated* in 1623 he had included the Banqueting House on the backcloth, so now he depicted his acclaimed west portico for St Paul's Cathedral. After a wordy debate between actors representing Action and Imposture, Merlin appeared, announcing that he had summoned 'the great seducers of this isle' to appear before him, at which 'the whole scene was transformed into a horrid hell, the further part terminating in a flaming precipice'.

To characterise the evil seducers, Inigo devised a menagerie of unprecedentedly grotesque and fantastic figures. They included a crier of mousetraps, the master of two baboons and an ape, a ballad singer, a harlequin, a mountebank and an old, lame charwoman. Inigo's drawings for their costumes included others not mentioned in the text, such as a tooth drawer and corn cutter. Accompanying them were 'four old-fashioned parasitical courtiers', a political comment on the perceived change in the nature of the court since Charles had come to the throne. A more direct and prescient reference to the state of the nation was the inclusion amongst these degenerate figures of 'rebellious leaders in war' – John Cade, Robert Kett and Jack Straw, who had in earlier centuries taken up arms against the Crown. In incorporating these characters, and designing their costumes, Inigo and Davenant must have had in mind the increasingly militant and unruly mood of the King's opponents. Their description left their opinion of them in no doubt – 'The apparel of these in part showed their base professions, mixed with some soldier-like accoutrements' – and Inigo's drawings of them underlined the point.

The scene changed again to a forest, where a 'mock romanza' was played out by a dwarf, a giant, a knight and a damsel. When it was over,

the earth opened and there rose up a richly adorned palace, seeming all of goldsmiths' work, with porticoes vaulted on pilasters running far in ... When this palace was arrived to the height, the whole scene was changed into a peristilium [cloister] of two orders, Doric and Ionic, with their several ornaments seeming of white marble, the bases and capitals of gold.

(Inigo copied this design from one by Giulio Parigi, as he had the principal setting of *The Triumph of Peace* six years earlier.)[9]

So the stage was set, in its classical splendour, for the arrival of Britanocles, the glory of the western world, heralded by Fame. The palace sank beneath the stage and the masquers appeared, accompanied by more songs in praise of the King. In the final scene of a spectacular seascape, crowded with ships from Charles's fleet, Inigo made full use of the advanced technology installed in his new masquing house:

Some ships were discerned sailing afar off several ways, and in the end a great fleet was discovered which, passing by with a side wind, tacked about, and with a prosperous gale entered into the haven, this continuing to entertain the sight whilst the dancing lasted.

The ship money, then, had been well spent.

Having paraded his talent for inventing spectacle on Twelfth Night, Inigo concentrated on beguiling lighting effects on Shrove Tuesday for the Queen's masque, calling it *Luminalia: the Queen's Festival of Light*. The opening scene was a moonlit rustic view, generally thought to be based on a work by Adam Elsheimer, a German landscape painter who died in 1610 and was greatly admired by Rubens.[10] A river ran through a tree-fringed meadow, with the shadows of the trees and the light of the moon reflected in the water.[11] Because the masque was written for the Queen, the plot glorified beauty and culture rather than strong government. The Muses, driven from Greece by the Thracians and from Italy by the Goths and Vandals, had been forced to wander in an inhospitable world until finding refuge in peaceful Britain, through the grace of its King and Queen. Britain had thereby assumed the mantle of ancient Greece as the fountainhead of the arts.

The idea was expressed in an aerial ballet where again Inigo made full use of the technical resources of the new masquing house. And in the final scene, where Henrietta Maria descended from the skies, there was more innovative lighting: 'Behind all was a bright sky, and in the midst, above the Queen majesty's seat, was a glory with rays, expressing her to be the queen of brightness.'[12]

The brightness would soon fade, however, and would not be restored until the King was dead and the Queen much chastened. For all their magnificence, the masques were transitory, insubstantial pageants, leaving scarcely a rack behind. The Doric and Ionic pillars in *Britannia Triumphans*, topped and tailed in gold, were constructed of flimsy wood and canvas and in a few weeks would have been consigned to some scenery store, never to be admired again. If Charles wanted to bequeath to the nation more lasting evidence of his affinity with the Muses, he would have to turn to the other aspect of Inigo's genius. It was time to fulfil the dream of transforming London into one of the great classical cities of Europe, centred on a Renaissance palace in Whitehall whose size and splendour would serve as an enduring memorial both to Inigo's artistry and to Charles's golden, enlightened reign.

Several designs for spectacular London buildings, mostly drawn by Webb to Inigo's instructions, date from the late 1630s. One of the most appealing was for Temple Bar, the symbolic link between Whitehall and the City. It was a stately, classical, three-sectioned arch, resembling the Arch of Constantine in Rome, topped with an equestrian statue of the King on a massive plinth. If built, it would have made a fittingly grandiose approach to the new portico at St Paul's Cathedral, a few hundred yards to the east. By contrast Sir Christopher Wren's more modest Temple Bar, constructed some forty years later, reflected a restored monarchy with fewer pretensions.

A second unfulfilled scheme of Inigo's, along the same east-west route, was for a new Strand frontage for Somerset House, by then the main London residence of Henrietta Maria. The unbroken terrace of thirty-five bays would have dominated the eastern end of the street. The cost would have been substantial and it proved too much even for a King so anxious to please his Queen. He did, however, buy her

Inigo's unfulfilled design for Temple Bar

a country house in Wimbledon in 1639, and Inigo undertook some building work there at a cost of £558 10s 11d.

Many features of the abortive Somerset House design recur on a much grander scale in the series of plans for the immense new Whitehall Palace conceived in the late 1630s – although the surviving designs, drawn by Webb but probably prepared under Inigo's guidance, appear to date from more than one period. Inigo devised at least two schemes, one for a brand new palace in St James's Park and another that would involve demolishing most of the old palace and building afresh on its site.

The drawings for the second scheme portray an immense complex of six or seven courtyards covering a site 725 feet square, facing the river on one side and St James's Park on the other, straddling present-day Whitehall. There were two sets of royal apartments – on the river side for habitation in summer, on the park side for winter. In what appears to be the most considered of the designs, the Banqueting House would have been incorporated into the palace, balanced by an identical structure that would have served as a chapel. One of the courtyards was shown as being circular and arcaded, possibly to accommodate some kind of performance area. A picture painted by Thomas Sandby in the eighteenth century, based on some of the drawings, shows how the new palace would have dominated Westminster had it been built. Nothing on its scale has ever been constructed in London. John Harris has called it 'the greatest might-have-been in English architecture', although the chance of its ever becoming a reality must always have been remote.[13]

The King's idea was to finance his proposed new palace, at least in its initial stages, through revenue that he had raised from the City of London in settlement of a long and rancorous dispute involving Ireland. As part of the vain bid to introduce the Anglican Church into the troublesome province, the town of Derry had been occupied by English troops and its Catholic rebels suppressed. In 1610 James essentially passed over responsibility for the town and its nearby plantations to the City of London, changing its name to Londonderry.

One stipulation was that the livery companies should send over English or Scottish Protestant tenants for the individual farms. In the event they did not send anything like enough of them, so tenancies were granted to native Irish Catholics, destroying the main point of the exercise. In 1635 the Crown took legal action against the livery companies in the Star Chamber, accusing them of falling down on their responsibilities. As a result, the companies were fined a colossal £70,000, but in 1637 a settlement was reached whereby only £12,000 was demanded.[14]

The fact that the King, already desperately short of funds, was initially prepared to devote this money to the new Whitehall Palace is a measure of the project's importance to him. But very soon it became apparent to his advisers that any available money had to be used to finance the disastrous military campaign, urged on him by Laud and Strafford, to enforce use of his new Anglican prayer book in Scotland. The Scottish Covenanters were rigid Presbyterians and thought that Laud's prayer book smacked too much of popery. After initial successes, Charles's soldiers suffered several setbacks and eventually had to concede defeat.

The outbreak of full-scale civil war in 1642 would force the plans for the new palace to be shelved again. Yet even after the King was captured by Parliament he clung desperately to the dream. According to Webb, the captive monarch raised the subject with him when he went to see him at Hampton Court and at Carisbrooke Castle on the Isle of Wight, in the years immediately before his execution.[15] The proposed palace had become a symbol of Charles's faith in divine providence, of his conviction that he would ultimately defeat his Parliamentary opponents and return to govern even more gloriously than before. Neither dream would be fulfilled.

Without any such major project to occupy him, Inigo had to exercise his architectural talents on a more modest scale. One commission, undertaken at the King's behest, was for an impressively large screen for Winchester Cathedral. The severely classical work was more in the nature of a triumphal arch than a traditional church screen. On top of the central opening was a pediment with reclining figures draped on its sloping sides. Two columns, decorated in the Corinthian order, flanked the archway, with another at each end of the screen. In the wings, between two pairs of pilasters, were niches for bronze statues by Hubert Le Sueur of Kings James and Charles.[16]

Its style was gratingly incongruous in the context of the Gothic interior, just as the portico Inigo had placed on the west end of St Paul's was never truly of a piece with the rest of the cathedral. No doubt he would have preferred to design complete Palladian buildings from scratch, but if nobody had the money to construct them he had to make do with these stylistic compromises. The Winchester screen was dismantled in 1820. The statues remain in the cathedral, near the west door, but the central arch, columns and pediment, minus the reclining figures, were removed in 1912 and now form part of the Cambridge Archaeological Museum – where, it must be said, they look equally out of place.

Webb continued to refine the plans for a new Whitehall Palace after Inigo's death and after the Restoration, but nothing was to come of them. James II, during his brief reign, had Christopher Wren put up a new range just south of the Banqueting House, but William and Mary, who succeeded him, preferred to live in Kensington and Hampton Court, away from the city smoke. Whitehall had effectively been abandoned as a royal residence before the fire in 1698 that destroyed most of it, leaving the Banqueting House as the only remnant of Charles's scheme to create there, on a scale befitting its theme, a permanent symbol of the Stuarts' glorious rule – a monument to Britannia triumphant, to the triumph of peace, to the golden age restored.

To judge from Inigo's drawings of its scenery and costumes, the last masque of Charles I's reign, *Salmacida Spolia*, has claims to be his most splendid. By virtue of its timing, it was also the most poignant. It was mounted at the beginning of 1640, the year that set Charles's reign irretrievably on its course to disaster. Probably with an eye to economy, it was decided that there should not be separate masques for Charles and his Queen this year: a single one would honour the two of them. Both took part in it, even though Henrietta Maria was carrying her eighth child (the total includes three who did not survive beyond infancy). Her son Henry, the future Duke of Gloucester, was born the following July.

The suburbs of a great city, from *Salmacida Spolia*, 1640

Artistically, *Salmacida Spolia* was one of Inigo's greatest successes. Some of his diagrams of the complex stage mechanisms have survived, as well as drawings of the costumes and scenery, so it is possible to discern to some extent how he achieved his spectacular effects.[17] The plans show that the stage was slightly raked – seven feet from the ground at the front and eight feet at the back. The backdrop rose forty-seven feet from the stage. The King and Queen, seated, were to arrive on the scene from the skies and their thrones were drawn by pulleys along a groove some twenty feet above the level of the stage. Wheels that controlled these and other pulleys were located both below the stage and below the floor of the auditorium. Clouds descended from the roof by means of one of the seven side shutters. Seats for the masquers were at the rear of the stage and could be lowered beneath it when not in use.

Another diagram shows a plan of the auditorium, with the names of the dignitaries to whom boxes had been allocated.

Inigo added informative notes to some of the plans, revealing his techniques and his willingness still to experiment at the age of sixty-six. On the back of a drawing of a large cloud he wrote:

> The great cloud which comes forth and opens and discovers the Queen seated in a bright cloud. To try if this great cloud may come down between the grooves and then be drawn open and whether the shutters and this great cloud may not be drawn away both together.

But in Whitehall in 1640, the audience's minds were on other matters than innovative stage effects. According to a letter from Sir Henry Vane, Secretary of State, the King began practising his dancing steps for the masque only a day before he announced his fateful decision to recall Parliament the following April, for its first sitting in eleven years, to raise funds for the Scottish war.[18] The King recognised that to persuade Members to cooperate he would have to appear conciliatory and this, again according to Vane, was to be the principal message of *Salmacida Spolia*. It was significant that at least four of the ten male masquers who took part were prominent supporters of the Parliamentary cause – Lord Herbert, Lord Fielding, Lord Russell and his younger brother.

The very title underlined the masque's message. It was based on an adage quoted in Inigo's introduction: 'Salmacian spoils, achieved without bloodshed or sweat, rather than a Cadmian victory when destruction falls on the victors themselves.'[19]

The allusion is to two ancient legends. In the first, a group of barbarians ravaging Halicarnassus was subdued and civilised by tasting the sweet water of Salmacis. In the other the Cadmians (Thebans), having been defeated by the Peloponnesians, escaped to their home city. The victorious enemy pursued them there but was repulsed, with heavy losses on both sides. Inigo drove home the moral: 'His Majesty, out of his mercy and clemency . . . seeks by all means to reduce tempestuous and turbulent natures into a sweet calm of civil concord.'

The King danced the part of Philogenes, a dedicated, benign but misunderstood monarch having to ride out a severe tempest – a chance for Inigo to give rein to all the tricks of dramatic staging that he had learned over more than thirty years. His drawings of the 'horrid scene' of the tempest are brimful of ferocity and turbulence. As he described it: 'No glimpse of the sun was seen, as if darkness, confusion and deformity had possessed the world and driven light to heaven.'

This was soon transformed into a scene of calm and prosperity. A chariot broke out of the clouds, bearing figures representing Concord and the Good Genius of Great Britain. They sang the praises of 'the great and wise Philogenes':

> O who but he could thus endure
> To live and govern in a sullen age,
> When it is harder far to cure
> The people's folly than resist their rage?

There followed a further complicated antimasque. Among the listed actors in it was the celebrated dwarf Jeffery Hudson, then nineteen years old but reputedly only eighteen inches high, although he later grew to about three feet. As a boy he was adopted by the Duke of Buckingham, who once served him in a pie to King Charles; later Hudson joined Henrietta Maria's household. During his colourful life he was twice captured by pirates, but lived until the age of sixty-three. Inigo portrayed him in one of his surviving masque drawings, captioned 'The damsel, the dwarf and Lanier [the musician]'. Davenant wrote a poem about Hudson and nearly 200 years later Sir Walter Scott included him as a character in *Peveril of the Peak*.[20]

With the scene now changed to a rocky landscape, Concord and the Good Genius reappeared to sing the praises first of Marie de Medici, Henrietta Maria's mother, who attended the performance, then the King, who had made his appearance seated in a golden throne surrounded by palm trees and heroic statues. It was a pointed justification of Charles's eleven years of personal rule, even though it was known by then that the imminent recall of Parliament would bring them to a close:

> Since strength of virtues gained you Honour's throne,
> Accept our wonder and enjoy your praise!
> He's fit to govern there and rule alone
> Whom inward helps, not outward force doth raise.

Then the Queen came down from the heavens in 'a transparent brightness of thin exhalations, such as the gods are feigned to descend in'. Both were accompanied by their masquers, and the dancing began.

Peace, order and love had been restored. The setting changed to a townscape of 'magnificent buildings', an idealised version of London, with crowds of men and women, coaches and horses crossing a Roman-style bridge over the Thames.[21] The masque concluded with of one of Inigo's most spectacular cloud effects. The first cloud accommodated eight people, representing the spheres. Two more clouds joined them, each containing a group of musicians, playing, as 'a heaven opened full of deities'.

In this final tableau, rejoicing that the royal couple were 'loved even by those who should your justice fear', the company sang out:

> All that are harsh, all that are rude,
> Are by your harmony subdued;
> Yet so into obedience wrought
> As if not forced to it, but taught.

In the febrile political atmosphere of 1640, with many courtiers and gentry undergoing earnest self-examination to decide where their sympathies truly lay, it would have been surprising if the masque's message of tolerance and harmony had been accepted by all spectators in the spirit in which it was offered. Where Charles and Henrietta Maria – and presumably Inigo and Davenant – regarded the masque as an affirmation of truth, a growing band of sceptics could see it only as a denial of reality. Some deliberately absented themselves from it, including one Robert Read, who wrote to his cousin, Sir Francis Windebank, saying that while he had chosen to stay away he had heard that 'the disorder was never so great at any [masque]'.[22] He was probably not referring to scenes of debauched excess such as characterised the events in James I's day, but to discontent among members of the audience who disapproved of the skewed political message.

The King and Queen, though, were so delighted with Inigo's and Davenant's creation that they insisted on dancing it again, on Shrove Tuesday. It was their final attempt to persuade their opponents – the harsh and the rude – that the idealised image of the couple presented in Van Dyck's portraits was a true account of their boldness, wisdom and sense of justice. When it was over, Inigo's brilliant lights were snuffed out for almost the last time. (He and Webb designed a performance of a five-act play called *The Queen of Aragon* for Henrietta Maria in March.) The musicians gathered up their instruments, which would not be needed again during Charles's reign.

Can the King really have deluded himself that Davenant's verses would inculcate obedience into the upstarts? When they did not, he had no choice, according to his rigid view of his regal duty, but to go for the Cadmian, not the Salmacian option – and it proved as disastrous for him as it had for the Peloponnesians. Parliament, recalled the following April, refused to grant him the funds he sought for the unpopular Scottish campaign unless he would accept limits on his freedom of action. After three weeks he testily sent its members home; but he was rapidly losing control of events. After a second defeat by the Scots he was forced to recall Parliament again in November.

By this time the Parliamentarians were flexing their muscles, no longer willing to be creatures of the King's whim, summoned whenever he felt short of money and summarily dismissed when he discovered he had nothing to gain from them. They first insisted that he agree to call a Parliament at least every three years and not to dissolve it without the approval of members. Then they made him consent to Strafford's trial for treason and his execution in May 1641.

Tension increased towards the end of the year. In November the Commons voted in favour of a 'Grand Remonstrance' that set out all their grievances and would have obliged the King to accept their choice of ministers. There were, too, an increasing number of street disturbances in London as citizens became divided between supporters of the Crown and Parliament. On 29 December Inigo and two other magistrates were called upon to examine three men who had been involved in a fracas outside Whitehall Palace. Men carrying clubs and swords paraded, shouting: 'No bishops, no Papist lords', at which seven or eight courtiers climbed over the palace railings, drew their swords and struck out at the demonstrators.[23]

In January 1642, Charles, citing his divine right to rule, went to the House of Commons in an attempt to arrest the five main leaders of the dissident group; but they made themselves scarce before he arrived. His action only increased popular resentment against him and next morning he fled from London, initially to Hampton Court, while Henrietta Maria went abroad to try to gain military and financial support in Europe for the royal cause. There was to be no more dancing, no more harmony. The wooden masquing house, only ever meant to be temporary, proved more so than had been envisaged. Parliamentary supporters, seeing it as a symbol of the court's decadence, nicknamed it 'The Queen's Dancing Barn'; in 1645 they tore it down, plank by plank.

Chapter Twenty-One

TIME RUINS ALL THINGS

T HE ROYAL COUPLE would never return to their London palaces. In April 1642 Charles travelled north and in August he raised his standard at Nottingham, signifying the start of the Civil War. From then on, with a progressively dwindling group of courtiers, he would flit from one royal stronghold to the next, several times narrowly avoiding capture, until he established his temporary capital in Oxford.

Inigo stayed in London for a few months after the King's departure, still operating as Surveyor-General. The nature of some of his duties sprang from the troubled times. In May – while in the throes of his own legal problems concerning the St Gregory's parishioners – he was instructed by the House of Lords to prepare another hall for a show trial, this time of Sir Robert Berkeley, a judge of the King's Bench who had played a significant role in levying the despised ship money.[1] After half a lifetime designing stage scenery, Inigo was now creating theatrical settings for real-life dramas. He can scarcely have avoided reflecting that, before the run ended, he would be lucky to escape being cast as the villian and forced to play a starring role.

There can never have been any doubt in his mind about which side to take in the looming conflict. He had become inextricably identified with the extravagance of the court through his masques, and with its reputation for tyranny through his duties as Surveyor. It was unthinkable that he could now desert his monarch and patron. In July he proved his loyalty by responding to a request from the hard-pressed King for a loan of £500.

When Charles made the request he was with the royal army in Beverley, preparing to lay siege to Hull, and Inigo gave the money to John Webb to carry north. Recalling the adventure in a petition to the restored Charles II in 1660, Webb described how he sewed the cash into the lining of his waistcoat before crossing territory held by Parliamentary forces. On his way back to London, having delivered the money safely, his mission was somehow discovered: maybe he was carrying with him the King's receipt, which has been preserved in the State Papers.[2] Webb was imprisoned for a month before being allowed to return to London. That did not, however, deter him from fulfilling his duty, as he saw it, to the King. In the same petition – admittedly self-serving – he claimed to have supplied Charles with details of all the fortifications placed around London by the Parliamentary forces, 'their proportions, the number of guns mounted on them, how many soldiers would man them, how they might be attempted and carried and all particulars relating thereto'.[3]

There is no other evidence that Webb performed this loyal, even heroic service to the King. If he did, the fruits of his espionage were untested, for Charles was never in a position to mount an assault on London. By the end of 1642 Inigo had left the capital, as much for his personal safety as to escape the fines that Parliament was now exacting almost routinely on those overt Royalists wealthy enough to pay. The eighteenth-century antiquarian George Vertue records that, before Inigo left town, he and Nicholas Stone buried their savings and valuables near the Surveyor's office in Scotland Yard – safe, as they thought, from the long arm of the Parliamentarians. But they were spotted by at least four bystanders. Parliament had recently issued an edict stating that anybody aware of such secret stashes, and who informed the authorities of their location, would receive half the amount discovered. Inigo and Stone therefore moved the money rapidly to a new burial place south of the river, on Lambeth Marsh.[4]

Inigo was away from London for most of the first three years of the Civil War, but he maintained his official residence at Scotland Yard throughout the 1640s, according to records of the poor rates and other imposts on property owners and tenants.[5] He left Webb in charge of the Surveyor's office until 1643 when, in Webb's own words, he was 'thrust out, as being entrusted for His Majesty', and replaced by Edward Carter, a senior member of Inigo's staff who had played an important role in coordinating the works at both Covent Garden and St Paul's Cathedral, but who was now prepared to declare his support for the Parliamentary cause. Webb remained in Inigo's house alongside the Surveyor's office, despite having been removed from his post.

Inigo's whereabouts between 1642 and his capture at Basing House in October 1645[6] cannot be traced with certainty. The belief that he spent some time with the King in the north of England, passed down through generations of biographers, seems to be based on a misreading of the circumstances of the £500 loan received by Charles at Beverley. The fact that the money was delivered by Webb argues against Inigo's presence. When the exiled court was established at Christ Church, Oxford – where Henrietta Maria rejoined her husband in July 1643 – Inigo's enemies assumed that he was there, too. In October of that year, one of the Parliamentary news sheets reported:

> The Queen will not have so many masques at Christmas and Shrovetide this year as she was wont to have other years heretofore; because Inigo Jones cannot conveniently make such heavens and paradises at Oxford as he did at Whitehall; and because the poets are dead, beggar'd or run away, who were wont in their masques to make gods and goddesses of them, and shamefully to flatter them with attributes neither fitting to be ascribed or accepted of; and some are of opinion, that this is one of the innumerable vanities which have made them and us become so miserable at this day.[7]

Another piece of evidence seems to support his being at Oxford. At about this time William Dobson painted the last known portrait of the architect. Hanging today at Chiswick House (and reproduced on the cover of this book), it depicts him as a deeply troubled old man, disillusioned by the turmoil of the times. Dobson, born in 1611, succeeded Van Dyck as court painter at the start of the Civil War and stayed at Oxford with the exiled royal family, painting portraits of many courtiers, until his death in 1646. His depiction of Inigo appears to date from that period.

Yet Webb, in another 1660 petition, claimed that the story about Inigo being in Oxford with the royal household was a false one. He believed it had been spread by Carter in his successful bid to discredit Webb, Inigo's protégé, and take over as Surveyor-General.[8] Inigo himself, in a self-justifying deposition in 1646 to the Committee of Compounding – assessing how much he should be fined for his 'delinquency' – declared unambiguously that he 'never was in the King's quarters nor any part of them since the beginning of this unhappy war, nor ever gave intelligence thither or received any intelligence from thence'.[9] He added that he had been living 'in the country' since leaving London, and it is possible that he had spent much of that period at Basing House. If the news sheets were accurate in asserting that he had been there advising on its defences, he must have arrived some time before those defences were built in the months leading up to the first siege of the house in 1644.

The fall of Basing House in October 1645 marked a watershed not just for Inigo personally but for the progress of the war in the south-west; it had been the King's principal remaining stronghold after his crushing defeat at Naseby that June by the New Model Army of Sir Thomas Fairfax and Oliver Cromwell. A series of further military setbacks made it clear to nearly everyone except Charles himself that Parliament was in the ascendancy and the Royalist cause lost. For formerly loyal Crown servants such as Inigo, self-preservation was now the priority. They had no option but to come to terms as best they could with the new state of affairs. Those who had not been involved directly with the King in the conduct of the war, or in framing the policies that led to it, could expect to be allowed to live peacefully after they had paid a fine large enough both to bring home to them the extent of their misjudgement and to replenish the Parliamentary war chest.

Delinquency, which literally means failure to fulfil responsibilities, was a word used by Parliament to describe virtually any act of support for the Royalist cause. The Committee for Compounding was established in 1643 to raise money to pay the Parliamentary army – initially its Scottish component – by exacting forced loans or levies from anyone thought able to afford them. After a while, the focus shifted to imposing fines on delinquents. The first targets were large landowners, made to pay twice the annual rental value of their estates, based on the higher rents that applied before the Civil War began. If they did not, the estates would be taken from them.[10]

The Committee began to examine Inigo's affairs while he was still absent from London. After his capture, he was summoned to appear before it at Goldsmiths' Hall on 7 March 1646. The report of the proceedings described him as 'a very aged, infirm man, scarce able to walk abroad'. From the contrasting handwriting on his deposition before the Committee, he appears to have dictated it to a clerk and then signed it. In it, he gave a detailed account of his financial position. He was owed substantial amounts of money: £2000 by the King and Queen for work he had done for them in his capacity of Surveyor-General, and other debts amounting to £168. Property to the value of £40 had been confiscated in his absence and the bailiffs who came to look for it had damaged his house to the extent of another £40. He declared his assets as being chiefly 'goods and instruments mathematical and other things of that nature belonging to my profession' worth £500, and 'certain models [probably architectural drawings] and other like commodities which I only used and keep for my pleasure but of no profit, yet cost me £200 and upwards'.

The most intriguing paragraph came close to the end:

> I left some ready money and plate in trust with a friend when I left this city and went into the country, to the value of £2000 or thereabouts, which is very questionable whether I shall ever get it again or no.[11]

This could be a veiled reference to the money he and Stone had buried in 1642. It is unclear whether Stone was able to retrieve his share before his death in London in 1647, but the fact that Inigo died relatively rich, despite being fined by Parliament, suggests that he at least may eventually have recovered his buried fortune.

Inigo accepted that he was totally at the Committee's mercy. He undertook to pay whatever sum it decided would discharge his obligations and allow him to enjoy the rest of his property without fear of further harassment from the authorities. To mitigate his delinquency, he pointed out that he was not among those who had actually taken up arms against Parliament; but that was not enough to excuse him from the two acts of penitence that were integral to the sanctions at the Committee's disposal. First he had to take the 'negative oath', or Oath of Abjuration, dissociating himself from the King and his misdeeds. Then he had to swear allegiance to the National Covenant, pledging support for a Presbyterian United Kingdom. He did this in front of a minister of the Church, three days after the Goldsmiths' Hall hearing. For a proud man, who had set such store by the strength of his beliefs, it was all an abject humiliation; but that of course was the whole point. A subversive ballad of the time suggests that the opponents of Parliament, though they had no option but to take the oaths, defiantly refused to accept their implications:

> Since Goldsmiths' Committee
> Affords us no pity,
> Our sorrows in wine we will steep 'em.
> They force us to take
> Two oaths, but we'll make
> A third, that we ne'er meant to keep 'em.[12]

A few days after Inigo had taken the Covenant oath, the Committee delivered its ruling. His wealth was assessed at just under £5000, chiefly made up of the money he was owed by the King and Queen and the £2000 'in trust with a friend'. His immediate fine came to ten per cent of that sum, plus £60 for arrears of rent. That brought the total to £557

13s 6d.[13] In order to avoid any future demands for levies he volunteered to make that up to £1000 – in essence an insurance payment. On 2 June the Houses of Lords and Commons jointly confirmed the settlement, authorising his pardon for having 'adhered unto the forces raised against Parliament' and ordering the restitution of his goods, chattels and estates. A rider was added that if it was discovered that Inigo owned property that had not been disclosed to the Committee, he would be subject to a further fine.[14]

By this time the first and principal stage of the Civil War was over. In April 1646 the King, disguised as a servant, had been forced to flee a besieged Oxford. He joined up at Newark with the Scottish Covenanters, to whom he effectively surrendered. From then on he was a prisoner, although still enjoying the comforts appropriate to his position. Efforts were made to negotiate a settlement by which he would keep his throne, with a severe reduction of his powers; but he stood firm by his God-given royal prerogatives. At the same time, divisions were widening between the leaders of Parliament and the increasingly powerful, radical and Puritan Army. In August 1647 the Army marched on London to assert its authority and demand its back pay.

The dissension among his opponents encouraged Charles to engineer a resumption of hostilities. While a prisoner at Carisbrooke Castle, on the Isle of Wight, he came to an agreement with the Scottish Presbyterians, who in 1648 took up arms on his behalf: the so-called Second Civil War. In August of the same year the Scots were defeated at Preston and the Royalist garrison at Colchester surrendered, marking the end of the short but bloody renewal of the conflict.

The idea of executing the King, formerly unthinkable, grew out of the Army's anger with him for his role in reigniting the war. With Parliament purged of its moderate elements, the remaining Members voted to establish a special court to try Charles for treason. The trial began on 20 January 1649 in Westminster Hall, which had been fitted out according to much the same plan as Inigo had devised for Strafford's trial in 1641. Charles consistently refused to recognise the court's authority, on the ground that no earthly power could claim supremacy over a king. On 27 January he was sentenced to death as a tyrant, traitor, murderer and enemy of the people. Three days later, on a cold Tuesday afternoon, he walked out of a first-floor window of Inigo's Banqueting House onto a platform where, still expressing defiance, he was beheaded with a single blow from the executioner's axe.

Inigo was probably too infirm, even if he had the inclination, to join the thousands who gathered to witness that barbaric act committed in front of perhaps his most gracious building. Yet even if he was not among the throng he could certainly, from his house only a few hundred yards away, watch them assemble and hear the collective gasp of horror as the King's head tumbled onto the wooden planks of the scaffold. He had designed the Banqueting House to flatter and delight the Stuart kings and their queens, to convey to the outside world the extent of their refinement, divinity and majesty. It can only have been a deliberately ironic act to use his classical façade as the backdrop to regicide. His scenery, as always, was immaculate; but on this occasion he had no control over the script.

Charles I executed outside the Banqueting House, January 1649

The death of the King ushered in the eleven years of the Common-wealth, under Oliver Cromwell. Inigo, after settling his affairs with the new regime, continued to live at the Scotland Yard house next to the office of the Surveyor-General, despite the fact that he no longer enjoyed any official status. Webb and his family also lived there and probably looked after the increasingly frail old man. He had not given up his work entirely. As described in Chapter Seventeen, he was involved in the reconstruction of Wilton House after the 1647 fire. And a few years later he may well have provided designs for Sir George Pratt's new house, Coleshill in Berkshire, described by James Lees-Milne as 'the perfection of English seventeenth-century classicism'.

Amongst Inigo's drawings at Chatsworth are three labelled as being for Coleshill, and although they are in Webb's hand they have more in common with Inigo's style than his. A young joiner on the estate remembered some years later that Inigo had visited several times while the house was being built, in the company of Roger Pratt, Sir George's cousin, who has long been credited as Coleshill's principal architect.[15] Pratt was only thirty in 1650, and had just come back from Italy, as enthused by its Palladian buildings as Inigo had been thirty-six years earlier. He would later design other country houses and play an important role in rebuilding London after the Great Fire of 1666. However, the maturity and quality of Coleshill's exterior design, and of some of the principal ceilings, make it more plausible to attribute the larger role to Inigo, even though the house was not completed until 1660, some years after his death. It was destroyed in a fire in 1952.[16]

On 22 July 1650, Inigo made his will. This was a task that in those days normally waited until death appeared imminent; but to the last he proved a tough survivor and was to live for two more years. According to a nineteenth-century biographer the final months of his life were filled with disappointment and a sense of under-achievement:

> Tradition says that the sorrowing old man was sometimes to be seen wandering in the vicinity of Whitehall and St Paul's Cathedral, looking at those splendid but incomplete works.[17]

Inigo died on 21 June 1652 at Somerset House, a few days before his seventy-ninth birthday. The place of death presents a slight mystery.

Since Henrietta Maria had fled London at the start of the Civil War, Somerset House had been used as lodgings for Members of Parliament and senior army officers.[18] Given that one of the first acts of the new inhabitants was to trash the chapel that Inigo built for the Queen, it is unlikely, in the prevailing political climate, that he would have been offered a home there. In any case, the rating records show that he kept his Scotland Yard house almost to his death: the last appearance of his name on the register for the address was in 1651, and only the following year was it replaced by Webb's.[19] And his will describes him as living in the parish of St Martin-in-the-Fields, which included Scotland Yard. Somerset House was in the parish of St Mary-le-Strand.

The most likely explanation is that, when he became terminally ill, he went to stay with Richard Gammon, a former employee in the Surveyor's department who had married Elizabeth Jones, a relative of Inigo's. Gammon joined Inigo's staff in 1634 and was made clerk of the works at Somerset House. As such he was allotted an apartment there and the rating records show that he was allowed to keep it after the Parliamentarians moved in – indeed he stayed there until 1679.[20] His importance to Inigo in the last years of his life is clear. His was the first name mentioned in the will and he and John Webb, the executor, were made responsible for ensuring that the legacies were properly administered.

Despite the architect's fall from official favour and the fines he was forced to pay to Parliament, the bequests in the will amounted to slightly more than £4000. Webb's wife Anne, Inigo's cousin, was allotted half, with another £1000 to be divided among her five children. After those two major sums, the largest bequest was the £500 left to Gammon, along with half of Inigo's clothing. Gammon and Webb were also to share equally in the bulk of the proceeds of any payment made in eventual settlement of money owed him by the late King and Henrietta Maria. Henry Wicks, the Paymaster of the Works, would be given the first £50 of any such settlement, as an incentive to him to speed up payment. There is in fact no record of its ever being paid. In 1668 Webb was still petitioning the King to try to get it back.[21]

Inigo made several bequests of £100: to the widowed Mary Wagstaffe, 'my kinswoman', plus another £100 to be divided among her five children; to John Damford, a carpenter; and to Stephen Page, 'for his faithful service'. Two donations of £10 went to the poor of St Martin's parish, where he lived, and the poor of St Benet's parish, where he would be buried.

The tomb Inigo designed for himself, sketched by John Aubrey

As well as earmarking £100 for his funeral expenses, he left another £100 for a white marble monument to be built to his own design and erected on his tomb in the chancel of St Benet's, next to where his mother and father were buried. John Aubrey sketched the monument. The rectangular base bore reliefs portraying the two buildings that Inigo regarded as his finest: the St Paul's Cathedral portico and the Banqueting House. On top, his bust was placed between two tall obelisks.[22] At the very least the tomb would give future generations an inkling of how great a man he was, even if circumstances had conspired against his leaving many great works to posterity.

Perhaps his most perceptive obituary was written by the nineteenth-century architectural historian Alan Cunningham, in *The Lives of the Most Eminent British Painters, Sculptors and Architects*:

> Quiet-tempered and generous, Inigo was vain of his credit at court and of his importance in the world, and proud above all things of being considered an unrivalled architect. He could not well be blamed for saying that the art of design was but imperfectly known in England till he appeared – still less for speaking with sarcastic contempt of those who, calling themselves gentlemen, scorned him as a mechanic.

His visits to Italy had engendered a sense of revelation, of liberation from the crabbed confines of the old order. Returning, he embarked on a mission to construct in England buildings that could inspire equal passions. In his copy of Vasari's *Lives of the Architects* he had translated the epigram: 'Rich princes should leave behind them a fame of building richly' – but the times were against the princes and against him. Not even his memorial to himself was destined to survive. St Benet's Church was destroyed in the Great Fire of 1666, and when Sir Christopher Wren rebuilt it he found no place to commemorate his proud predecessor.

Ben Jonson's paean to the Stuart court and to the art of masque, quoted in an earlier chapter,[23] presented a rose-tinted picture of a haven of grace, love, pleasure, softness, laughter and sport. It was from *The Fortunate Isles and their Union*, the last masque of King James's reign. From the time of his son Charles's accession, the fortunes of the Fortunate Isles had progressively declined, to end in bloodletting and regicide. For Inigo the pleasure, the laughter and the sport had vanished long before his death in Somerset House. But then he was by no means the only man in Stuart England whose ambitions and dreams had been scotched by the turbulence of the times; by other men's stubborn folly.

Chapter Twenty-Two

REVIVAL

A SIDE FROM BEING OUSTED as Acting Surveyor-General in 1643, and his short time in captivity after his mission to the King at Beverley, John Webb suffered no other direct sanctions on account of his Royalist sympathies and his association with Inigo. But he can have had no realistic expectation of appointment to an official position while the King's opponents retained power. He appears to have continued to live in Scotland Yard but, drawing no salary, relied on irregular architectural commissions to sustain himself and his family. The unstable times meant that, during and immediately after the Civil War, noblemen were reluctant to commit themselves to building costly new mansions; but as people grew accustomed to life in Cromwell's Commonwealth, something approaching normality returned. Noblemen willing to acquiesce in the new order were allowed to retain the bulk of their wealth, and began to feel secure enough to spend it. In the 1650s Webb designed buildings for the gentry at Cobham Hall, Belvoir, Gunnersbury, Lamport Hall and Amesbury, all in the meticulous classic idiom that he had absorbed from his mentor.[1]

In 1653, the year after Inigo died, Webb bought an estate in Butleigh, Somerset, for £8420, part of which must have been Anne's inheritance. There is, too, evidence to suggest that he was boosting his income by selling off some of his former master's property. In 1660 one Henry Carter (probably unrelated to Edward Carter, Inigo's successor as Surveyor-General) petitioned the newly restored Charles II, claiming that six years earlier he had bought 'from John Webb, executor to Inigo Jones, a naked Venus, a foot long, for £20'. This had now been identified as having belonged to Charles I, and was being reclaimed by the Crown in its attempt to reassemble the late King's collections. The petitioner wanted Webb to be ordered to return his money.[2]

Whatever the outcome of that case, the Restoration initially brought Webb hope. He assumed, understandably enough, that he would soon be appointed to the position of Surveyor-General for which Inigo had been preparing him throughout his adult life. Edward Carter had been succeeded in 1653 by John Embree, a former master plumber at court with a taste for fine art. (When the King's paintings were being disposed of after his execution, Embree acquired a group of pictures, including a Titian and two Tintorettos, in lieu of back pay of £174.) Embree had become too closely associated with the Commonwealth period to be acceptable for a position under the restored monarchy and was dismissed as soon as Charles II assumed power in 1660.

Webb immediately petitioned the House of Lords, seeking appointment to the post he regarded as being his by right – asserting that, in training him for it, Inigo had been acting on the specific instruction of Charles I.[3] If professional qualifications had been the only criterion, Webb was the obvious successor; but senior positions at court have never been awarded solely on merit. During his years of exile in Europe, Charles II had gathered round him a group of loyal servants committed to him and to his restoration. One of them was John Denham, a rakish poet who had been with the exiled Henrietta Maria in France, then in Holland with her eldest son.

Hearing that his coveted post was likely to be awarded to Denham – a man with no experience in architecture, or even plumbing – Webb sent off another plaintive petition, this time to the new King himself. He maintained that after being displaced by Carter he had 'patiently acquiesced in confidence of your majesty's glorious return'. Moreover he had recently been preparing the royal houses for that happy event, all in the space of a fortnight and at a cost of £8140 5s 2d, of which he had so far been reimbursed only £500. He therefore requested that he be appointed to the position

whereunto your royal father designed him [Webb] and to that end only ordered his education . . . Otherwise after his many sufferings and imprisonments during the late wars for his loyalty to the Crown your petitioner . . . instead of reaping the fruits of his fidelity and long studies may together with his whole family be ruined at last for ever without your Majesty's royal favour.[4]

The petition was accompanied by 'a brief on Mr Webb's case' giving more details of his qualifications and of his loyalty to the Crown during the Civil War, and ending with a none too subtle denigration of the man who sought to usurp his office:

Mr Denham may possibly, as most gentry in England at this day, have some knowledge in the theory of architecture but nothing of the practice, so he must of necessity have another at his Majesty's charge to do his business, whereas Mr Webb himself designs, orders and directs . . . without any other man's assistance. His Majesty may please to grant some other place more proper for Mr Denham's ability and confirm unto Mr Webb the Surveyor's place.

His Majesty was pleased to do no such thing, and was moved only to the extent that he granted Webb the reversion of the office: he would be first in line when Denham quit or died. Despite Denham's objections that Webb was the older man – forty-nine against his forty-five – and that he had hoped to make money from selling the reversion himself, the King's promise to Webb was confirmed. He was also made one of Denham's deputies and awarded several royal commissions. They included a theatre at Whitehall, some fortifications at Woolwich and the design of the new King's House at Greenwich – his most important surviving building, later incorporated into the Royal Naval Hospital.

He also enlarged the Queen's House by building extra rooms above the road, concealing Inigo's original H plan.[5]

Denham, made a knight in 1661, married a woman of eighteen in 1665 but a year later she had a scandalous affair with the Duke of York, later James II. It became the talk of the town and Denham went temporarily insane, claiming to be the Holy Ghost. His young wife died early the following year and he was widely suspected of having poisoned her.[6] But through all this turmoil he clung to office until his death in 1669 heralded yet another disappointment for Webb. This time his nemesis was a young astronomer with star quality, who had already caught Charles's eye.

Christopher Wren came from a family with impeccable Royalist credentials. His father had been Dean of Windsor and his uncle Matthew was imprisoned in the Tower of London throughout the Commonwealth period because of his refusal to renounce Laud's High Church practices. When Inigo died, Wren was twenty. He had just graduated from Oxford and was about to begin five years of scientific research at All Souls, concentrating on astronomy. In 1657 he was appointed Professor of Astronomy at Gresham College in London, where a few years later he would be one of the founder members of the Royal Society.

In 1661 the King had made him an offer that it had proved surprisingly easy to refuse. As part of his marriage settlement to Catherine of Braganza, the Portuguese princess, Charles had been granted control of the North African port of Tangier. He asked Wren to spend a year or two out there, designing the defences of its harbour. As a lure, he was offered the reversion of the office of Surveyor-General, despite its already having been promised to Webb – an indication of how unreliable such undertakings could be.

Wren turned down the Tangier post and instead became Professor of Astronomy at Oxford. In 1662 he designed a chapel for Pembroke College, Cambridge, followed by his first major building, Oxford's Sheldonian Theatre. Based on the Theatre of Marcellus in Rome, it included many of the classical elements that Inigo had introduced to England, its south front divided into seven bays by columns and pilasters, with a raised central pediment. The semi-circular north front was less formulaic, an early signal that Wren would not be content to adhere strictly to the precedents that Inigo had set. His visit to France in 1665 – the only time he ventured outside Britain – further widened his architectural horizons and enhanced his appreciation of the Renaissance style. The domed churches in Paris, notably Jacques Lemercier's Sorbonne and Val de Grace, were fresh in his mind when he was asked to draw plans for completing the restoration of St Paul's Cathedral that Inigo had left unfinished.

In 1666 Wren was appointed acting surveyor during Denham's temporary insanity. The ink was scarcely dry on his drawing of the dome that he proposed for the cathedral when the Great Fire, consuming virtually the whole City of London, changed the nature of the project from restoration to building afresh. His initial proposal was to create a whole new stately city, with wide boulevards lined with resplendent buildings and monuments. This was rejected because of its cost, and property owners began to rebuild piecemeal, sticking to the old street pattern. For the authorities, the priority was to reconstruct the churches, for no community could function without its places of worship.

Clearly the Surveyor-General would have a key role to play in rebuilding the City; but in 1669, before much progress had been made, Denham died. Despite the promise to Webb, and to nobody's real surprise, the post was offered to Wren. Webb may well have been familiar with Shakespeare's *Henry VIII*; and if he was, he will have brooded on the line: 'O how wretched is that poor man that hangs on princes' favours.' In his despair, he sent another petition to the King, pointing out that 'though he [Webb] acted under Sir John Denham, a person of honour, he conceives it much beneath him to do the like under one [Wren] who in whatever respects is his inferior by far'.

So he proposed a compromise by which the office would be shared between the two contenders:

May your Majesty please if not to confirm your petitioner's grant, as in the honour of a king you appear to be obliged, then to join him in patent with Mr Wren and he shall be ready to instruct him in the course of the office of your works, whereof he professeth to be wholly ignorant.[7]

Again, the King did not agree. Even without Webb's help, Wren proved to be a fast learner. So London's churches and cathedral came to be rebuilt in his version of the Baroque style rather than in Webb's interpretation of Inigo's purer Palladianism.

In 1670 Parliament levied a tax on coal to provide the funds needed to construct the new cathedral and fifty-one of the eighty-seven churches that had been destroyed. Work on the churches had already begun, but it was not until 1675 that the first stone was laid for the cathedral, and it would take thirty-six years to complete. Such had been Inigo's impact on the architectural thought of the seventeenth century that the idea of rebuilding the churches in their former Gothic form was not seriously considered, except by a few diehard traditionalists. Yet Wren, while he had certainly absorbed the mathematical principles of Vitruvius and Inigo's version of classicism, was not a man to adhere unthinkingly to a formula. In his 'Tracts on Architecture', published by his son after his death, he criticised 'modern authors' (presumably including Serlio and Palladio) as being 'too strict and pedantic' in their interpretation of the rules of classical architecture, which were, after all, no more than the fashions of the time when they were propounded.[8] His designs incorporated elements of the Baroque churches that he had observed on his visit to France, and many other details that derived directly from his own vivid imagination.

It would in any case have required considerable ingenuity to deploy a strictly classical style on the restricted sites of London's old Gothic churches. Rules of scale, balance and proportion had to be reinterpreted for buildings that could not spread themselves in the manner of grand palaces and mansions on spacious great estates, and his solutions to such problems gave rise to some of the most startling and innovative aspects of his work. Yet in other contexts he was certainly capable of adhering to the classical rules, as he showed in his sober and distinctly Jonesian design of the library at Trinity College in Cambridge. All these influences came together most effectively in St Paul's Cathedral, where he achieved his most sublime blend of the classical with the Baroque.

While Wren was in no sense a disciple of Inigo, he clearly recognised the important position that his predecessor occupied in the history of English architecture. He gave serious consideration to incorporating the west front portico, relatively undamaged in the fire, in his design for St Paul's, and when he came to build the Royal Hospital at Chelsea he wanted to transpose one of Inigo's surviving towers from the cathedral, but the ecclesiastical authorities would not give their approval.[9] The sheer quantity, energy and originality of Wren's work justifies his reputation as Britain's most gifted architect; but Inigo's influence on future ages was, surprisingly perhaps, to prove the longer lasting. Although Wren's disciples, Nicholas Hawksmoor and James Gibbs, along with Sir John Vanbrugh, persevered with the Baroque style well into the eighteenth century, a reaction was setting in against them even before Wren's death in 1723, as a group of enthusiasts emerged who sought a return to uncompromising Palladian purity.

Inigo's most important tangible legacy to Webb was his collection of books, drawings, engravings and plans. They included the drawings by Palladio and Scamozzi that he had bought in Italy; his library of architectural and philosophical works, heavily annotated in his hand; and an enormous archive of his own architectural drawings and designs for the costumes and scenery of the masques. Webb used some of them as the basis of his own designs, but he realised that their greatest value lay in the record they provided of Inigo's life, work and influences. When he died in 1672 he left the entire collection to his second son William, instructing in his will 'that he shall keep them entire together without selling or embezzling any of them'.

William began to defy that instruction almost immediately, and by 1675 some of the books had already come on to the market.[10] A few years later the bulk of the collection had been split in two. Most of the books and some drawings were acquired in the early eighteenth century by Dr George Clarke, a Member of Parliament, Lord of the

Admiralty and amateur architect, who in 1736 bequeathed them to Worcester College, Oxford, where they remain. Many more drawings were sold by William Webb to John Oliver, the City Surveyor. From him they passed to the architect William Talman, who designed part of the Duke of Devonshire's house at Chatsworth, Derbyshire, and worked for Wren in the Surveyor's office. He bequeathed them to his son John, a minor artist, who in turn sold them to Richard Boyle, the third Earl of Burlington, a liberal patron of the arts and one of those most responsible for the revival of interest in Inigo in the eighteenth century. That collection is now divided between the Royal Institute of British Architects and the Duke of Devonshire, who keeps his part of it, including Inigo's copy of Vitruvius's *I Dieci Libri*, at Chatsworth.[11]

Burlington's principal ally in fashioning the Palladian/Jonesian revival was Colen Campbell, a Scottish lawyer who had also become passionate about Palladian architecture. In 1715 Campbell published the first volume of *Vitruvius Britannicus*, a set of plans of one hundred buildings in the classical style, some from life and some from his imagination. Inigo's most important creations are included, as well as some attributed to him that are now known to have been designed by others.

In the introduction Campbell argued that British architects had generally been underrated, and were in truth just as capable of inspired work as their more admired Continental counterparts. In saying that, he was not seeking to downgrade Palladio, 'who has exceeded all that were gone before him' in his 'great manner and exquisite taste'; but he decried the Baroque and Mannerist tendencies in other Italian architects, and he made it clear from the very beginning that the 'British Vitruvius' of his title was Inigo:

> It is then with the renowned Palladio we enter the lists, to whom we oppose the famous Inigo Jones: let the Banqueting House, those excellent pieces at Greenwich, with many other things of this great master, be carefully examined and I doubt not but an impartial judge will find in them all the regularity of the former, with an addition of beauty and majesty in which our architect is esteemed to have outdone all that went before.

The Banqueting House, 'this incomparable piece', inspired his most lyrical praise:

> Here our excellent architect has introduced strength with politeness, ornament with simplicity, beauty with majesty; it is, without dispute, the first room in the world.

In the year his first volume was published, Campbell began work on Wanstead House in Essex, England's first strictly classical building of the eighteenth century. And that same year saw the appearance of an English translation of Palladio's *I Quattro Libri*, with illustrations by Giacomo Leoni. Shortly before those two seminal books were published in England, the young Burlington had begun to rebuild Burlington House in Piccadilly (now the Royal Academy), initially employing Gibbs. Reading them on his return from a trip to Italy, he was overwhelmed by an intense obsession such as only a twenty-one-year-old can muster. He immediately changed his plans for Burlington House, appointing Campbell as the chief architect. (Campbell went on to design about a dozen Palladian houses, notably Mereworth in Kent, based on Palladio's Villa La Rotonda at Vicenza.)

Burlington went back to Italy in 1719 to study the Palladian style in greater detail. He also managed to buy a batch of about sixty of Palladio's original drawings and soon married these with the substantial portion of Inigo's collection that he had bought from John Talman. Thus armed, he felt able to design buildings for himself. In Rome he met an English painter named William Kent, who shared many of his enthusiasms, including a passion for Inigo's architectural ideas. The two men returned to England together and remained inseparable until Kent's death in 1748. The artist's first assignment for the Earl was to produce murals and ceiling paintings for Burlington House, including a sentimental tribute to their common idol. *The Apotheosis of Inigo Jones*, above the main staircase of the house, portrays the muse of architecture flanked by a portrait of Inigo and a plan of the house, indicating that its design was inspired by the master's example and philosophy.

In 1725 Burlington designed his best-known building, Chiswick

House – another spin-off from La Rotonda, but a less exact copy than Mereworth. Again, in case there should have been any doubt about his sources of architectural inspiration, he placed statues of Inigo and Palladio on either side of the main entrance, and brought Jones's gateway from Beaufort House in Chelsea to place in the garden.

Chiswick house, designed by Lord Burlington

The new building was not, however, universally admired. To those used to the traditional comforts of the English country house it seemed cold, soulless and inconveniently laid out. Lord Hervey, a friend of Burlington's, described it as 'too little to live in, and too large to hang on one's watch'. It never had a kitchen: food had to be cooked in the older family home alongside, linked to the new house by a covered gallery. Such practicalities were low on the list of Burlington's priorities. His principal aim was to create a building imbued with the spirit of ancient Rome and the vision of Palladio and Inigo.

In 1727 Burlington financed Kent's publication of *The Designs of Inigo Jones*, in which, like Campbell, Kent attributed to Inigo a good many drawings now known to be by Webb. His admiration of his subject was just as uncritical and passionate as Campbell's:

If the reputation of this great man does not rise in proportion to his merits in his own country, 'tis certain in Italy (which was his school) and other parts of Europe, he was in great esteem; in which places, as well as in England, his own works are his monument and best panegyric; which, together with those of Palladio, remain equal proofs of the superiority of those two great masters to all others.

Burlington, being both an accomplished architect and an influential aristocrat, was in a position to ensure that his aesthetic preferences were reflected in appointments to posts that had a bearing on the direction of British taste. His friend Richard Arundell was made Surveyor-General in 1726, and Kent became his master carpenter, eventually rising to deputy surveyor. In 1734 Burlington collaborated with Kent on one of the most distinguished houses of the period, Holkham Hall in Norfolk. Another protégé, Henry Flitcroft, who would later design Woburn Abbey, was made clerk of the works for Westminster and succeeded Kent as deputy surveyor.

By this time the pattern of British architecture for the remainder of the century had been set. The fashionable view was well expressed by James Forrester in a 1734 essay in verse, *The Polite Philosopher*:

> That true politeness we can only call,
> Which looks like Jones's fabric at Whitehall;
> Where just proportion we with pleasure see,
> Though built by rule, yet from all stiffness free.

Later eighteenth-century architects such as Robert Adam and John Nash were simply embellishing the Jonesian principles that had become embedded in British taste through the efforts of Burlington, Kent and Campbell. The cool, elegant Georgian buildings that grace many of our cities, as well as the classical country houses of the period, would not have been possible without Inigo's Palladian inspiration.

Inigo's reputation is today eclipsed in the popular mind by the achievements of the more prolific and imaginative Christopher Wren. Yet if historical accident dictated that Inigo's output was meagre by comparison, with little of it remaining for our enjoyment, we can still stroll through the Georgian terraces of London, Edinburgh, Dublin and Bath in the knowledge that we are looking at the legacy of a proud, vain, quarrelsome hypochondriac with the clarity of vision and tenacity of purpose that allowed him, in the most difficult possible political environment, to exercise his genius in revolutionising British architecture and design.

VISITORS' GUIDE

Many works once speculatively attributed to Inigo are now thought to have been designed by others. This is an alphabetical list of buildings and monuments – discussed in detail in the body of the book – where his connection is certain or has been plausibly established. I have included some practical information for visitors.

All Saints' Church, Conington, Cambridgeshire

Two wall monuments erected for Sir Robert Cotton around 1615 have recently been attributed to Inigo, and the case is quite strong. He was a friend of Cotton's and the monuments are designed in a stern classical style that was unusual in England so early in the century. In care of the Churches Conservation Trust. Off Junction 15 of the A1(M) near Peterborough. (Do not confuse it with the village of the same name between Huntingdon and Cambridge.) For access to the key, ring the Trust on 020 7936 2285.

Ashburnham House, London

The attribution to Inigo, made by Isaac Ware in the eighteenth century, has never been established, although there is a bust of him on the staircase. The original Jacobean house, now part of Westminster School, has been greatly altered over the years. Underground: Westminster.

Banqueting House, London

Inigo's best and most celebrated building stands halfway along Whitehall, only a few hundred yards from his home in Scotland Yard. Completed in 1622, its elegant, superbly balanced frontage was revolutionary for its time. Although the classical style had been popular in parts of Europe for more than a century, English architecture was still rooted in the exuberant Tudor tradition. The splendid new Whitehall Palace, of which the Stuart monarchs dreamed, was never to be, but in succeeding centuries the Banqueting House exerted a dominant influence on the architects of neighbouring buildings, providing a historical context for the imposing government offices that surround it today. The interior has been restored to something like its original form, with a canopied throne of state at the southern end. Mirrors directed at the ceiling allow detailed examination of Rubens's magnificent paintings honouring James I. Underground: Westminster or Embankment. Open Monday to Saturday, 10 a.m.–5 p.m.

Basing House, near Basingstoke, Hampshire

Only the foundations remain of this once splendid mansion where Inigo was captured by Cromwell's rampaging Roundheads in 1645. But you can still see the outline of the star-shaped defensive ramparts that he designed in a vain attempt to keep the enemy at bay. Near Basingstoke, Hampshire. Open April to September, Wednesday to Friday, 2 p.m.–6 p.m.

Bushy Park, Hampton, Middlesex

A drawing at Chatsworth suggests that Inigo designed the so-called Diana Fountain in the centre of the round pond in this royal park, although the present tall base was not part of the original composition. It was sculpted by Hubert Le Sueur in the 1630s and placed in the garden of Somerset House. Oliver Cromwell had it taken to Hampton Court in 1656 and in 1713 it was moved the few hundred yards to its present site. A ten-minute walk from Hampton Court rail station, the park is open during daylight hours.

Cambridge University Museum of Archaeology and Anthropology

The central arch of the massive screen that Inigo designed for Winchester Cathedral was rather incongruously built into the museum in 1912. Downing Street, Cambridge. Open Tuesday to Saturday, 2 p.m.–4.30 p.m.

Charlton House, London

This fine early Jacobean House, built for Sir Adam Newton, tutor to the ill-fated Prince Henry, is worth visiting in its own right, whether or not you accept the traditional attribution to Inigo of a garden house in the grounds, now used as a public lavatory. One of the fireplaces in the main house is believed to be based on his design, possibly moved there from the Queen's House at Greenwich. A ten-minute walk from Charlton rail station. To arrange a visit, phone 020 8856 3951.

Chiswick House, London

A gateway that Inigo designed for Beaufort House in Chelsea was moved into the garden here in the eighteenth century by Lord Burlington, the leading proponent of the Palladian revival. There is also a bust of Inigo and the original of the William Dobson portrait on the cover of this book. A fifteen-minute walk from Chiswick rail station. Open daily, 8.30 a.m. to dusk. (House open April to September, 10 a.m.–6 p.m., October 10 a.m–5 p.m.)

Covent Garden, London

Nothing remains of the original buildings designed by Inigo, but St Paul's Church and a short row of colonnaded buildings on the north side of the Piazza have been reconstructed as he envisaged them. The temple-fronted church, with its dour, plain Tuscan columns, is one of London's most distinctive landmarks. Underground: Covent Garden.

Hatfield House, Hatfield, Hertfordshire

Inigo is thought to have had some input into the design of the south front and the clock tower of this splendid Jacobean mansion. Certainly he was close to its owner Robert Cecil when the work was going on: he is recorded as visiting the house in October 1609 and of being paid £10 for unspecified architectural work in February 1610. If he was involved, it would amount to one of his earliest essays in architecture. Hatfield is twenty-one miles north of London and the rail station is opposite the house entrance. Open daily, Easter to the end of September: house 12 noon–4 p.m., park 11 a.m.–5.30 p.m.

Lindsey House, London

Inigo's only surviving townhouse is at 59–60 Lincoln's Inn Fields. The interior is not open to the public but the frontage, set back from the street, its five bays divided by tall pilasters, gives a good idea of the original grandeur of this mid-seventeenth-century housing development, constructed not long after Covent Garden. Underground: Holborn.

Queen's Chapel, London

Built for Queen Henrietta Maria as a Catholic place of worship, the plain exterior masks an exquisite interior with a vaulted and compartmented roof and a splendid east window. It stands on Marlborough Road, between St James's Palace and Marlborough House, on a site that was once within the palace grounds. Underground: Green Park. Open only for Sunday services from Easter until mid-July, and a pre-Christmas carol service. Ring 020 7930 4832 for details.

Queen's House, Greenwich, London

Although it was not completed until the 1630s, Inigo appears to have made few changes from his original design, which he began for Anne of Denmark in 1616. So this appealing, unassertive house, that once straddled a main road, ranks as his oldest surviving building. The interior has been altered over the years but the impressive cube entrance hall, with its 'tulip' staircase, is still there. The house also contains a copy of the Dobson portrait of Inigo hanging at Chiswick House (q.v.). Rail stations: Greenwich, Maze Hill. Open daily 10 a.m.–5 p.m. (10 a.m.–6 p.m. in summer).

St Chad's Church, Norton-in-Hales, Shropshire

The monument to Sir Rowland Cotton and his wife Francis is one of Inigo's earliest known works, attributable to him through a drawing in the collection of the Royal Institute of British Architects. That original design was for a tomb for Francis Cotton, who died in 1606, but it was later adapted by someone else to accommodate Sir Rowland as well. Three miles north-east of Market Drayton. Usually open in daylight hours.

St Giles-in-the-Fields, London

Inigo's weather-beaten monument to his friend, the poet George Chapman, in the form of a Roman tombstone, now stands near the north-east corner of the church in St Giles High Street. Underground: Tottenham Court Road. Open daily.

St Paul's Church, London

See Covent Garden.

Stoke Park Pavilions, near Towcester, Northamptonshire

These two charming pavilions, featuring giant pilasters and linked by a colonnade, are all that remain of a Palladian house begun in 1630 for Sir Francis Crane, founder of the Mortlake tapestry works. It has long been accepted – but never proved conclusively – that Inigo was the architect. If he was, this is one of the few surviving examples of his work on country houses. Seven miles south of Northampton off the A508. Open for thirty-one afternoons in the summer, on an irregular schedule. For details, ring 01604 862172.

Wilton House, near Salisbury, Wiltshire

The south front of this magnificent house, and the famous cube and double cube rooms, represent Inigo's last known works, and they rank among his finest. He was in his seventies when, after a disastrous fire in 1647, he and John Webb began to reconstruct the south wing for the Earl of Pembroke, whose descendants still live here. Few traces remain of the original garden, which may also have been designed by Inigo. Three miles west of Salisbury, Wiltshire, off the A36. Open April to October, daily 10.30 a.m.–5.30 p.m.

SOURCE NOTES

Books and articles are listed separately in the bibliography. Where the name of the author appears in capital letters it is a reference to an article, otherwise to a book.

Abbreviations used in notes:

APC   Acts of the Privy Council
BL   British Library
CSP   Calendar of State Papers
DNB   Dictionary of National Biography
HMC   Historic Manuscripts Commission
JHL   Journal of the House of Lords
PRO   Public Record Office
SP   State Papers

Chapter One: Terror at Basing House

1 Godwin, p. 244
2 Tindall, p. 80
3 *Mercurius Britannicus*, 20 October 1645
4 This book, together with the bulk of Inigo's library, is now at Worcester College, Oxford
5 Godwin, p. 211
6 Godwin, p. 236
7 *Moderate Intelligencer*, 15 October 1645
8 *A Diary or an Exact Journal Faithfully Communicating the Most Remarkable Proceedings of both Houses of Parliament*, 15 October 1645
9 *A Perfect Diurnall of Some Passages in Parliament*, 15 October 1645
10 Godwin, p. 244
11 Godwin, p. 248
12 See pp. 336–9, 15 October 1645
13 *Mercurius Britannicus*, 20 October 1645
14 PRO C82/2096 fo. 28, translated from Latin by Dr Nicholas Barrett
15 Inigo's copy of Vitruvius's *I Dieci Libri dell' Architectura* is at Chatsworth

Chapter Two: Foundations

1 Harris, Orgel and Strong, p. 16
2 Cunningham, A., p. 71
3 Lee and Onions, p. 211
4 Harris, p. 12 (For a fuller discussion of Inigo's sexual inclinations, see p. 261
5 Strachan, p. 15
6 BL, Add. ms. 39853, fo. 77v
7 Gotch, p. 43
8 'The Honesties of This Age' (1614)
9 Bates, p. 288
10 Lee and Onions, pp. 218–9, and Bates, p. 241
11 Bates, p. 363
12 Harris, p. 11
13 Lees-Milne, p. 84
14 Gotch, p. 26
15 Strong (3), p. 110, quoting the *Diary of Sivert Grabbe*, Copenhagen Royal Library mss. Uldallske sams. 499, f.147
16 Peacock, p. 7.

Chapter Three: Inigo's London

1. Schofield, p. 140
2. Brett-James, p. 40
3. Slack, p. 58
4. Leapman, p. 14 (quoted with Andrew Saint's permission)
5. See pp. 241–3
6. Banham, p. 106
7. Bradley and Pevsner, p. 60
8. Cooper, p. 17
9. Cooper, p. 29
10. Summerson (1), p. 33
11. Summerson (2), p. 15
12. Cooper, p. 19
13. Cook, pp. 40 and 49
14. Summerson (1), p. 25
15. Summerson (1), p. 22
16. Bradley and Pevsner, p. 60
17. SMUTS (1), p. 117
18. Pevsner and Cherry, p. 53

Chapter Four: Palladio the Peerless

1. WITTKOWER (2), pt. I
2. *Dieci Libri* (trans. Daniele Barbaro, Venice, 1567), p. 100
3. WITTKOWER (2), pt. II
4. Palladio, Book 1, p. 5
5. Muraro and Marton, p. 44
6. WITTKOWER (2), pt. II
7. WITTKOWER (2), pt. I
8. WITTKOWER (2), pt. I
9. Palladio, Book 1, pp. 52–5
10. Palladio, Book 2, p. 4
11. Palladio, Book 2, p. 45
12. See pp. 259–62
13. Palladio, Book 3, p. 31
14. Palladio, Book 1, p. 48
15. Johnson (2), p. 40 *et seq.*
15. Johnson (2), *passim*

Chapter Five: The Odd Couple

1 Lindley, p. 216
2 Peyton, p. 338
3 Riggs, p. 113
4 Riggs, p. 70
5 Riggs, p. 105
6 Weldon, pp. 2–5
7 Riggs, p. 112
8 Willson, p. 194
9 Hutchinson, p. 42
10 *Secret History of the Court of James 1*, vol. 2, p. 346
11 Simpson and Bell, p. 1
12 Peacock, p. 2
13 Harris, Orgel and Strong, p. 83
14 Peacock, p. 2
15 GORDON (2)
16 Harris, Orgel and Strong, p. 35, quoted with permission
17 Wilson, p. 31
18 ORRELL (4)
19 Peyton, p. 369
20 See pp. 178–80
21 Gurr, pp. 203–8
22 Brown, p. 197
23 Arber, p. 539

Chapter Six: The Looks, the Laughter and the Sports

1 ORRELL (5)
2 Howarth (2), p. 25
3 Simpson and Bell, p. 10
4 Orgel and Strong, p. 39
5 Herford and Simpson, vol. X, p. 450
6 Lindley, p. 216
7 Simpson and Bell, p. 10
8 Wilson, p. 31
9 Herford and Simpson, vol. X, pp. 448–9, quoting *Winwood Memorials* ii, p. 44
   and SP14, vol. xii, no. 6
10 Simpson and Bell, p. 90
11 Simpson and Bell, p. 63
12 Simpson and Bell, p. 65
13 Orrell, p. 33

14 Strong (3), p. 150
15 Orrell, p. 109
16 Orrell, p. 4
17 Orgel and Strong, p. 46
18 Simpson and Bell, p. 104
19 Orgel and Strong, p. 43
20 Simpson and Bell, p. 38
21 Simpson and Bell, p. 20
22 Orgel and Strong, p. 7
23 Orrell, p. 31
24 Nichols, vol. I, p. 238
25 Orrell, p. 31
26 Orgel and Strong, pp. 824–6
27 Chute, pp. 150–5
28 Chute, pp. 155–7
29 GORDON (1)

Chapter Seven: First Steps in Architecture

1 Gotch, p. 32
2 See p. 23
3 Nichols, vol. II, pp. 53–69
4 Skovgaard, p. 126
5 Nichols, vol. II, p. 69
6 See pp. 259–262
7 Weldon, p. 361
8 Lindley, p. 221
9 Lindley, pp. 28–9, and Campbell, Lily, p. 169
10 Weldon, p. 361
11 GORDON (2)
12 ORRELL (5)
13 Gotch, p. 45
14 Simpson and Bell, p. 7
15 Simpson and Bell, p. 13
16 Mathew, A.H., p. 93
17 Donaldson, p. 602
18 STONE (2), p. 106
19 McClure, vol. 1
20 Mathew, A.H., pp. 94–5
21 Orgel and Strong, p. 31
22 Riggs, p. 157

23 STONE (2), p. 116
24 STONE (2), p. 121
25 Donaldson, p. 602
26 Colvin (3), vol. III, p. 148, and NEWMAN (2), p. 360
27 See pp. 183–4
28 Thurley (1), p. 17
29 Summerson (2), p. 19
30 Harris, Orgel and Strong, p. 83
31 Simpson and Bell, p. 12
32 PRO Rolls of the Treasurer E 351/543 p. 214
33 SP 78 (France) 55/122
34 BL Harleian ms. 288, folio 282
35 HIGGOTT (1) and NEWMAN (3)
36 CHANEY (2), p. 633 and Smuts (2), p. 99
37 STONE (1), p. 118
38 WORSLEY (1), pp. 230–7

Chapter Eight: A Prince Among Men

1 Strachan, p. 12
2 Danish National Archives, England 1602–25, parcel II, Microfilm S1727
3 Cunningham, P. (1), pp. x–xiii
4 Skovgaard, p. 128
5 Strong (3), p. 184 *et seq.*
6 Strong (3), pp. 26–9
7 Smuts (1), p. 29
8 Strong (3), p. 26
9 PRO E403/2730
10 Strong (3), pp. 140–5
11 HMC 15th rep., appdx. 2, Hodgkin mss., p. 276
12 *Annals* p. 992, quoted in Smuts (1), p. 31
13 Gotch, pp. 52–3
14 Simpson and Bell, p. 43
15 Strong (3), p. 155
16 Strong (3), p. 170
17 See p. 81
18 Simpson and Bell, p. 4
19 Peacock, p. 188
20 Brown, p. 197
21 Cunningham, P. (1), p. ix
22 Strong (3), pp. 108–10

23 Colvin (3), vol. III, p. 125
24 Riggs, p. 192
25 BL Harleian ms. 6018, ff. 179–80
26 Wright, pp. 49–57
27 See Chapter Seven
28 Strachan, p. 146
29 Nichols, vol. 2, p. 400, quoted in DNB
30 Prestwich, p. 101
31 Osborn, pp. 288–91
32 Jardine, pp. 468–9
33 Piatigorsky, p. 63; Findel, p. 117
34 Knoop and Jones, pp. 33–4
35 Strong (3), p. 174
36 Hopwood, vol. 2, p. 559
37 Quoted in Strong (3), p. 221
38 Cunningham, P. (1), pp. xv–xvi
39 Osborne, p. 268

Chapter Nine: Pilgrim's Progress

 1 Smuts (1), p. 94
 2 Orgel and Strong, p. 23
 3 See p. 79
 4 Lindley, p. 237
 5 Strong (3), p. 180
 6 Cunningham, P. (2), p. 16
 7 Gotch, p. 69
 8 Clarendon, 'History of the Rebellion and Civil Wars in England', quoted in Howarth (2)
 9 Harleian ms. 6272, fol. 170, quoted in Smuts (1), p. 104
10 Howarth (2), p. 30
11 Hervey, p. 176
12 Details of journey from Hervey, unless otherwise attributed
13 HARRIS (1), pp. 147–52
14 Thomas Coke to Earl of Shrewsbury, 23 November 1612, Arundel archive. Autograph letters 1585–1617, no. 186
15 Stoye, p. 74
16 Hervey, p. 75
17 Harris, p. 12
18 Griffiths, pp. 20 and 78

Chapter Ten: In the Steps of the Masters

1 All Inigo Jones's comments are from his margin notes in Palladio's *I Quattro Libri*, except where otherwise noted. See Allsopp, *passim*

2 Shrewsbury to Coke, 13 January 1614, HMC, 23, Cowper 1, p. 80, quoted in Howarth (2)

3 Johnson (2), p. xxix

4 Stoye, p. 77

5 Howarth (2), pp. 51 and 230–1

6 Bates, p. 376

7 Howarth (2), p. 46

8 HOWARTH, p. 691

9 Simpson and Bell, p. 25

10 Howarth (1), p. 31

11 Howarth (2), pp. 47–8 and 230

12 Coke mss. quoted in Howarth (2)

13 Chaney, pp. 188–9

14 Gotch, p. 75

15 Gotch, p. 32

16 PRO CSP Venetian, 1613–15, p. 155, item 320, quoted in Howarth (2)

17 Gotch, p. 76

18 BL Add. ms. 15970

19 Howarth (2), p. 51

20 Chaney, p. 208

Chapter Eleven: On Their Majesties' Service

1 McElwee, p. 48; Parry, E., pp. 77–8

2 Jones and Stallybrass, pp. 71–87; BELLANY, p. 206

3 *Narrative History*, p. 12

4 McElwee, p. 148

5 McElwee, p. 200

6 Danish National Archives, England A1, microfilm S1727, no. 74e

7 PRO SP14/83, fo. 21

8 Jones and Stallybrass, p. 72

9 Bellany, p. 78

10 ORRELL (1), pp. 304–5

11 Arundel Archive: autograph letters 1585–1617, no. 196

12 Howarth (2), pp. 60–1

13 Howarth (2), p. 106

14 Harris, Orgel and Strong, p. 100

15 Riggs, p. 216

16 *Narrative History* (Abstract of His Majesty's Revenue)
17 Cunningham, P. (2), p. 47
18 Colvin (3), vol. III, p. 106
19 Webb, p. 119, quoted in Colvin (3), vol. III, p. 129
20 Colvin (3), vol. III, pp. 130–1
21 Colvin (3), vol. III, p. 138
22 See also p. 204
23 Bold (1), p. 44
24 Bold (1), p. 36
25 Colvin (3), vol. III, p. 138
26 Harris, Orgel and Strong, p. 95
27 Lees-Milne, plate 59
28 See pp. 183–5
29 Orrell, pp. 39–62
30 Leith-Ross, p. 94
31 Lees-Milne, p. 72

Chapter Twelve: The Banqueting House – Harmony Amid Disorder

1 DNB; Gotch, p. 45
2 See pp. 71–2
3 Orgel and Strong, pp. 283–4, and Lindley, p. 248
4 Orgel and Strong, p. 285
5 Riggs, p. 253
6 Gotch, pp. 96–7
7 Hadfield, pp. 69–71
8 McClure, p. 169
9 Lubbock, p. 29
10 McIlwain, p. 343
11 Brett-James, p. 79
12 Smuts (1), p. 133
13 Smuts (1), p. 134
14 Brett-James, p. 90
15 Brett-James, pp. 152–4
16 *Moderate Intelligencer*, 13 April 1645
17 Brett-James, p. 98
18 Orrell, p. 79
19 Palme, p. 2
20 DNB
21 DNB and Lees-Milne, p. 73
22 Palme, pp. 26–7

23 NEWMAN (3), p. 66

24 CSP, 19 April 1619

25 Palme, p. 44

26 Colvin (2), p. 209

27 BAGFORD, BL Harleian ms. 5900

28 Summerson (1), p. 77

29 NEWMAN (3), p. 24

30 Allsopp, p. 55

31 Palme, p. 204

32 Thurley (1), pp. 84–5

33 Johnson (2), p. 24

34 Palme, p. 227

35 Colvin (3), vol. IV, pp. 331–3

36 Palme, p. 78

37 PRO Jour. 29 1612–14, fo. 243–243V; Summerson (1), p. 78 and Lees-Milne, p. 75

38 Colvin (3), vol. IV, p. 329

39 CSP, 16 August 1620

40 Arundel archive: autograph letters 1617–32, no. 245

41 Colvin (3), vol. III, p. 132

42 HMC, 4th report, p. 310

43 Palme, p. 268

44 Palme, p. 41

45 See p. 49

46 Colvin (3), vol. IV, p. 333, and Palme, p. 66

Chapter Thirteen: The Weakness of Princes

1 Cunningham, A., p. 107

2 Lubbock, p. 162

3 Mowl and Earnshaw, p. 87

4 See p. 126

5 *Parliamentary History*, vol. 1, p. 1190

6 NEWMAN (1), p. 696

7 *Parliamentary History*, vol. 1, p. 1339

8 APC 1619–1621, p. 330

9 Arundel archive: autograph letters 1617–32, no. 245

10 Summerson (2), pp. 49–53; Harris, p. 13; HARRIS (2), p. 37

11 CSP Domestic, James I, vol. CXIII, p. 134

12 Harris, Orgel and Strong, pp. 186–7

13 Lees-Milne, p. 72

14 Chaney, p. 217
15 BETCHERMAN, p. 252
16 See also p. 257
17 Gotch, p. 134
18 Colvin (3), vol. IV, p. 340
19 Palme, p. 21
20 CSP Venetian, 1621–3, p. 216
21 Riggs p. 273
22 Peacock, p. 138
23 Cokeley was a well-known professional jester
24 See p. 57
25 Orgel and Strong, p. 348
26 Townshend, p. 42
27 Colvin (3), vol. IV, p. 248
28 Harris, p. 14
29 Baldwin, p. 133 and GAPPER, p. 83
30 A herbinger is someone sent ahead to seek lodgings for dignitaries or soldiers
31 McClure, p. 501
32 Hibbert, pp. 51–62

Chapter Fourteen: Honour Thy Father

1 Herford and Simpson, vol. X, pp. 658–60
2 Harris, Orgel and Strong, p. 136
3 PEACOCK, pp. 2–3
4 Lees-Milne, p. 83
5 Smuts (2), p. 94
6 Lees-Milne, p. 82
7 Audit Office 2425/58, October 1627–September 1628
8 Brett-James, p. 105
9 Colvin (3), vol. III, p. 142
10 St Martin-in-the-Fields vestry minutes 1623–52, F2002, Westminster Archives
11 SP Domestic, Charles I, p. 371
12 CSP Domestic, Charles I, 1 October 1634
13 APC 1630–1, p. 347
14 Harris, Orgel and Strong, pp. 160–1
15 Riggs, p. 295
16 Hervey, p. 242
17 Hervey, p. 264
18 MacGregor, p. 210 (Francis Haskell)

19 Van der Doort, *passim*
20 Gotch, pp. 160–1
21 Wilson, p. 111 *et seq.*
22 Hervey, p. 283
23 Sharpe and Lake, p. 238 (J. Newman)

Chapter Fifteen: A House Fit for a Queen

 1 Lees-Milne, p. 160
 2 PRITCHARD, p. 140
 3 Cunningham, P. (2), pp. 47–8
 4 Peacock, p. 276
 5 Colvin (3), vol. IV, p. 262
 6 FISHER and NEWMAN, p. 533
 7 Colvin (3), vol. III, p. 137
 8 Veevers, p. 136
 9 Summerson (2), p. 68
10 Harting, pp. 8–9
11 Harris, Orgel and Strong, p. 153
12 Lees-Milne, pp. 86–9
13 Gotch, p. 242
14 See p. 18
15 Bold (1), p. 53
16 HEWARD, p. 99 and see p. 133
17 Lees-Milne, p. 71
18 Bold (1), p. 70
19 Bold (1), p. 65
20 Bold (1), p. 63
21 CSP, 6 February 1637
22 Bold (1), p. 73, and MacGregor, pp. 221–2
23 MacGregor, p. 225
24 Sainsbury, pp. 211–30
25 Riggs, pp. 295–308
26 Chute, pp. 322–3
27 Wilson, p. 169
28 Veevers, pp. 75–6
29 Veevers, p. 134
30 Veevers, p. 112
31 BL Harleian ms. 6018, ff. 179–80
32 Simpson and Bell, p. 59

Chapter Sixteen: Such Sweet Sorrow

1 Herford and Simpson, vol. X, p. 692
2 Adams, p. 19
3 Chute, pp. 330–1
4 The pun supports the belief that carpentry was Inigo's original trade
5 A pipkin is an earthenware pot. The allusion is obscure
6 Gotch, p. 234
7 Johnson (2), p. 77
8 Herford and Simpson, vol. X, p. 697
9 Hervey, p. 335
10 Johnson (2), p. xxxi
11 Chute, p. 346
12 Howarth (1), p. 46
13 PRO C82/2096 fo. 28, translated from Latin by Dr Nick Barratt
14 See p. 16
15 Johnson (2), pp. xliii and 65

Chapter Seventeen: St Paul's – Politics and Piety

1 Sharpe and Lake, pp. 250–1 (Newman)
2 Bold (2), p. 168
3 HART, p. 414
4 Weinreb and Hibbert, p. 778
5 Dugdale, p. 106
6 Lees-Milne, pp. 90–1
7 Gotch, p. 170
8 HART, p. 416
9 CSP Domestic, Charles I, 3 November 1635
10 CSP Domestic, Charles I, 4 February 1633
11 BL Add ms. 75846
12 INIGO JONES AND ST PAUL'S, p. 42
13 NEWMAN (3) p. 71
14 CSP Domestic, Charles I, 22 May 1633
15 SP 16/259, no. 22
16 SP 16/283, no. 72
17 Pepys's Diary for 16 September 1668
18 HART, p. 424
19 Sharpe and Lake, pp. 249–50 (Newman)
20 CSP Domestic, Charles I, 11 April 1637
21 CSP Domestic, Charles I, 20 July 1639
22 Gotch, pp. 155–61

23 The word 'church' in this extract refers to the cathedral, a word that was not in general use at this period
24 Guildhall ms. 25574, St Paul's mss.
25 Colvin (3), vol. III, pp. 154–5; *Moderate Intelligencer*, 15 October 1645
26 Griffiths and Jenner, p. 177
27 PC 2/47, pp. 426–8
28 COLVIN, pp. 36–9
29 SP Domestic 16/370, 1637
30 HART, p. 424
31 Colvin (3), vol. III, p. 152
32 Summerson (1), p. 82

Chapter Eighteen: Covent Garden – Shaking the Money Tree

1 ALLSOPP, vol. 3, p. 31
2 See pp. 185–6
3 *Survey of London*, vol. 36, p. 26
4 DUGGAN, p. 143
5 CSP Domestic 1635, p. 385
6 Webber, p. 11
7 *Survey of London*, vol. 36, p. 26
8 DUGGAN, p. 148
9 WORSLEY (2), p. 89
10 Weinreb and Hibbert, p. 776
11 Lees-Milne, pp. 85–6
12 SUMMERSON, p.177
13 Webber, p. 16
14 DUGGAN, p.158
15 *Survey of London*, vol. 36, p. 32
16 CSP Domestic 1635, p. 302
17 Richardson, p. 13
18 See pp.183–6
19 *Survey of London*, vol. 3, p. 9
20 Brett-James, p. 155
21 *Survey of London*, vol. 36, p. 28
22 CSP Domestic, 1638–9, pp. 56–7
23 CSP Domestic, 1639, pp. 482–3
24 Taylor, p. 259
25 *Survey of London*, vol. 36, p. 28
26 Howarth (1), p. 289
27 Colvin (2), p. 162

28 Cherry and Pevsner, p. 251; Harris, Orgel and Strong, p. 151; Bold (1), p. 63
29 Lees-Milne, p. 105
30 Bold (2), p. 57
31 Mowl (2), pp. 1–10
32 Colvin (2), pp. 136–57
33 *Camden Miscellany*, vol. XVI, 1936
34 Colvin (2), pp. 136–57
35 HEWARD, p. 99
36 Bold (2), p. 65
37 Bold (2), pp. 58–60

Chapter Nineteen: Pictures with Light and Motion

1 Peacock, p. 326
2 Smuts (2), pp. 78–9 (Martin Butler)
3 Peacock p. 303; Simpson and Bell p. 62
4 Bold (2), p. 14
5 Lindley, pp. 260–1
6 See pp. 222–3
7 Brown, pp. 120–1 and p. 225
8 ORRELL (6), pp. 13–19
9 Mowl and Earnshaw, pp. 32–3
10 Orrell, p. 114
11 Simpson and Bell, p. 20
12 See p. 287
13 Butler, p. 97
14 Orgel and Strong, pp. 539–42
15 Orgel and Strong, p. 64
16 WELSFORD, pp. 399–401
17 Butler, p. 92
18 Orgel and Strong, pp. 538–45
19 Lindley, p. 263
20 Howarth (1), p. 204
21 Orgel and Strong, p. 826
22 Howarth (1), p. 201
23 Howarth (1), p. 207
24 PRO: C5/598/199 and C8/91/99
25 See pp. 336–9
26 HMC, 6th report, p. 123
27 CSP Domestic, Charles I, vol. 23 (addenda) p. 457

28 Howarth (2), p. 82
29 Englefield, p. 105
30 Guildhall ms. 5667/1
31 Ashton, p. 164
32 CSP Domestic, 15 June 1638, 18 September 1638, 30 September 1638
33 CSP Domestic, 3 May 1639, 25–27 May 1639, 15 November 1639

Chapter Twenty: The Last Masques

 1 Banham, p. 281
 2 Simpson and Bell, p. 90
 3 Wood, quoted by Southern, pp. 37–8
 4 Wood, quoted by Orgel and Strong, p. 829
 5 Butler, p. 44, Veevers, p. 71 and Campbell, Lily B. p. 190
 6 Orrell, p. 155
 7 Orrell, p. 149
 8 ORRELL (4), pp. 76 *et seq.*
 9 WELSFORD, pp. 399–401
10 Simpson and Bell, p. 117
11 Peacock, p. 202
12 Peacock, p. 327
13 Harris, Orgel and Strong, p. 146
14 Ashton, pp. 158–60
15 Bold (2), pp. 108–125
16 Colvin (3), vol. III, p. 153
17 BL, Lansdowne ms. 1171
18 Healy and Sawday, p. 65 (Martin Butler)
19 Lindley, pp. 201 and 270
20 Cunningham, P. (2), p. xii
21 Peacock, p. 108
22 SP Domestic, 23 January 1640, quoted in Gotch, p. 212
23 CSP Domestic, 1641 p. 215

Chapter Twenty-One: Time Ruins All Things

1 JHL, v., 1642–3, p. 52
2 CSP Domestic, 28 July 1642
3 SP 29/5 74.I, quoted in Bold (2), pp. 181–2
4 Vertue, vol. 1, p. 91
5 Westminster Archives, St Martin's Parish Records, rolls 1545–7
6 See Chapter One

7 *Mercurius Rusticus*, 26 October 1643, quoted in Raymond, p. 101
8 HMC, 7th report, p. 92
9 SP 23/177, fo. 780
10 Green, vol. 1, pp. iii–xiii
11 SP 23/177, fo. 782
12 Hardacre, p. 22
13 SP 23/177, fo. 777
14 JHL, vol. 6, p. 350
15 Lees-Milne, pp. 211–6
16 Mowl and Earnshaw, pp. 48–59
17 Cunningham, A., p. 138
18 Weinreb and Hibbert, p. 819
19 Westminster Archives, St Martin's Parish Records, roll 1820
20 Westminster Archives, St Mary-le-Strand Parish Records, roll 1900
21 PRO Prob 1/39 (and Prob 11/224, fo. 227); SP Domestic, 1668, p. 297
22 Harris, Orgel and Strong, p. 209
23 See p. 77

Chapter Twenty-Two: Revival

1 Bold (2), pp. 52–102
2 CSP Domestic, 1660, p. 379
3 HMC, 7th report, p. 92
4 SP 29/5 74
5 Bold (1), p. 77
6 DNB
7 SP 29/251 120, quoted in Bold (2), p. 182.
8 Tinniswood, p. 247
9 Tinniswood, p. 267
10 Bold (2), p. 9
11 Lees-Milne, p. 164

BIBLIOGRAPHY

Books

(published in London except where stated)

Adams, Joseph Quincy (ed.), *The Dramatic Records of Sir Henry Herbert, Master of the Revels, 1623–1673*, Yale University Press, New Haven, 1917

Allsopp, Bruce (ed.), *Inigo Jones on Palladio*, Oriel Press, 1970

Amos, Andrew, *Great Oyer of Poisoning: The Trial of the Earl of Somerset*, Richard Bentley, 1846

Arber, Edward (ed.), *A Harmony of the Essays, etc., of Francis Bacon*, Southgate, 1871

Ashton, Robert, *The City and the Court, 1603–1643*, Cambridge University Press, Cambridge, 1979

Baldwin, David, *The Chapel Royal, Ancient and Modern*, Duckworth, 1990

Banham, Martin (ed.), *The Cambridge Guide to the Theatre*, Cambridge University Press, Cambridge, 1995

Barker, Felix and Jackson, Peter, *London: 2000 Years of a City and its People*, Cassell, 1974

Bibliography

Bates, E.S., *Touring in 1600*, Constable, 1911

Bellany, Alastair, *The Politics of Court Scandal in Early Modern England: News Culture and the Overbury Affair, 1603–1660*, Cambridge University Press, Cambridge, 2002

Bold, John, (1) *Greenwich: An Architectural History of the Royal Hospital for Seamen and the Queen's House*, Yale University Press, New Haven, 2000

Bold, John, (2) *John Webb: Architectural Theory and Practice in the Seventeenth Century*, Clarendon Press, Oxford, 1989

Bone, Quentin, *Henrietta Maria: Queen of the Cavaliers*, Peter Owen, 1973

Bradley, Simon and Pevsner, Nikolaus, *The Buildings of England: London 1: The City of London*, Penguin, 1997

Brazell, J.H., *London Weather*, Her Majesty's Stationery Office, 1968

Brett-James, N.G., *The Growth of Stuart London*, George Allen & Unwin, 1935

Brome, Richard, *Dramatic Works*, John Pearson, 1873

Brown, John Russell (ed.), *The Oxford Illustrated History of Theatre*, Oxford University Press, Oxford, 1995

Butler, Martin, *Theatre and Crisis 1632–42*, Cambridge University Press, Cambridge, 1984

Campbell, Colen, *Vitruvius Britannicus*, 1721

Campbell, Lily B., *Scenes and Machines on the English Stage During the Renaissance: a Classical Revival*, Cambridge University Press, Cambridge, 1923

Carlton, Charles, *Charles I, the Personal Monarch*, Routledge & Kegan Paul, 1983

Chaney, Edward, *The Evolution of the Grand Tour*, Frank Cass, 1998

Cherry, Bridget, and Pevsner, Nikolaus, *The Buildings of England: London 2: South*, Penguin, 1983

Chute, Marchette, *Ben Jonson of Westminster*, Souvenir Press, 1978

Colvin, Howard M., (1) *A Biographical Dictionary of British Architects*, Yale University Press, New Haven, 1995

Colvin, Howard M., (2) *Essays in English Architectural History*, Yale University Press, New Haven, 1999

Colvin, Howard M. (ed.), (3) *History of the King's Works* (vols. III and IV), Her Majesty's Stationery Office, 1975

Cook, Olive, *The English Country House*, Thames and Hudson, 1974

Cooper, Nicholas, *Houses of the Gentry, 1480–1680*, Yale University Press, New Haven, 1999

Cunningham, Alan, *The Lives of the Most Eminent British Painters, Sculptors and Architects* (vol. IV), John Murray, 1831

Cunningham, Peter, (1) *Extracts from the Accounts of the Revels at Court in the Reigns of Queen Elizabeth and King James I*, Shakespeare Society, 1842

Cunningham, Peter, (2) *Inigo Jones: A Life of the Architect*, Shakespeare Society, 1848

Dallington, Robert, *A Method for Travel*, 1605

Donaldson, Ian (ed.), *Ben Johnson: A Critical Edition of the Major Works*, Oxford University Press, Oxford, 1985

Dugdale, William, *The History of St Paul's Cathedral in London*, 1818 (originally published 1658)

Englefield, W.A.D., *The History of the Painter-Stainers Company of London*, Chapman and Dodd, 1923

Findel. T.G., *History of Freemasonry*, Asher & Co, 1866

Fleming, John; Honour, Hugh and Pevsner, Nikolaus, *The Penguin Dictionary of Architecture* (revised edition), Penguin, 1991

Godwin, G.N., *Civil War in Hampshire and the Story of Basing House*, Elliot Stock, 1882

Gotch, J. Alfred, *Inigo Jones*, Methuen, 1928

Green, May Anne Everett (ed.), *Calendar of the Proceedings of the Committee for Compounding, etc., 1643–1660*, Her Majesty's Stationery Office, 1889

Griffiths, Antony, *The Print in Stuart Britain, 1603–1689*, British Museum Press, 1998

Griffiths, Paul and Jenner, Mark S.R. (eds.), *Londinopolis: Essays in the Cultural and Social History of Early Modern London*, Manchester University Press, Manchester, 2000

Gunther, M.A. (ed.), *The Architecture of Sir Roger Pratt*, Oxford University Press, Oxford, 1928

Gurr, Andrew, *The Shakespearean Stage, 1574–1642*, Cambridge University Press, Cambridge, 1992

Hadfield, Miles, *A History of British Gardening*, Penguin, 1985

Hardacre, P.H., *The Royalists During the Puritan Revolution*, Martinus Nijhoff, The Hague, 1956

Harris, John, *The Palladians*, Trefoil Books/Royal Institute of British Architects, 1981

Harris, John; Orgel, Stephen and Strong, Roy, *The King's Arcadia: Inigo Jones and the Stuart Court*, Arts Council of Great Britain, 1973

Harting, Joanna H., *Catholic London Missions*, Sands and Co., 1903

Healy, Thomas and Sawday, Jonathan (eds.), *Literature and the English Civil War*, Cambridge University Press, Cambridge, 1990

Herford, C.H. and Simpson, P. & E., *Ben Jonson, the Works* (11 vols.), Oxford University Press, Oxford, 1925

Hervey, Mary, *The Life, Correspondence and Collections of Thomas Howard, Earl of Arundel*, Cambridge University Press, Cambridge, 1921

Hewlings, Richard, *Chiswick House and Gardens*, English Heritage, 1989

Hibbert, Christopher, *Charles I*, Penguin, 2001

Hopwood, Charles Henry, *Middle Temple Records*, 1904–5

Hosking, G.L., *The Life and Times of Edward Alleyn*, Jonathan Cape, 1952

Howard, Clare, *English Travellers of the Renaissance*, John Lane, the Bodley Head, 1914

Howarth, David, (1) *Images of Rule: Art and Politics in the English Renaissance, 1485–1649*, Macmillan, 1997

Howarth, David, (2) *Lord Arundel and his Circle*, Yale University Press, New Haven, 1985

Howell, James, *Instructions for Foreign Travel (1642)*, English Reprints, 1869

Hutchinson, Lucy, *Memoirs of the Life of Colonel Hutchinson*, Phoenix Press, 2000 (originally published 1806)

Jardine, Lisa, *On a Grander Scale: The Outstanding Career of Sir Christopher Wren*, HarperCollins, 2002

Johnson, A.W., (1) *Ben Jonson: Poetry and Architecture*, Clarendon Press, Oxford, 1994

Johnson, A.W., (2) *Three Volumes Annotated by Inigo Jones*, Abo Akademi University Press, Finland, 1997

Jones, Ann Rosalind, and Stallybrass, Peter, *Renaissance Clothing and the Materials of Memory*, Cambridge University Press, Cambridge, 2000

Kent, William, *The Designs of Inigo Jones*, Gregg Press, Farnborough, 1967 (originally published 1727)

Knoop, Douglas, and Jones, G.P., *A Handlist of Masonic Documents*, Manchester University Press, Manchester, 1942

Leapman, Michael (ed.), *The Book of London*, Weidenfeld and Nicolson, 1989

Lees, S. and Onions, C.T. (eds.), *Shakespeare's England*, Clarendon Press, Oxford, 1916

Lees-Milne, James, *The Age of Inigo Jones*, Batsford, 1953

Leith-Ross, Prudence, *The John Tradescants: Gardeners to the Rose and Lily Queen*, Peter Owen, 1984

Lindley, David (ed.), *Court Masques: Jacobean and Caroline Entertainments 1605–1640*, Oxford University Press, Oxford, 1995

Lubbock, Jules, *The Tyranny of Taste: the Politics of Architecture and Design in Britain, 1550–1960*, Yale University Press, New Haven, 1995

McClure, N.E. (ed.), *The Letters of John Chamberlain*, Philadelphia, 1939

McElwee, William, *The Murder of Sir Thomas Overbury*, Faber and Faber, 1952

MacGregor, Arthur (ed.), *The Late King's Goods*, Alistair McAlpine/ Oxford University Press, Oxford, 1989

McIlwain, C.H. (ed.), *Political Works of James I*, Harvard University Press, Cambridge, Mass., 1918

Magum, Ruth (ed.), *The Letters of Peter Paul Rubens*, Harvard University Press, Cambridge, Mass., 1955

Mathew, Arnold Harris, and Calthrop, Annette, *The Life of Sir Tobie Matthew, Bacon's Alter Ego*, Elkin Mathews, 1907

Mathew, D., *The Jacobean Age*, Longmans, Green and Co., 1938

Moryson, Fynes, *An Itinerary*, James Maclehose and Sons, Glasgow, 1908

Mowl, Timothy, (1) *Elizabethan and Jacobean Style*, Phaidon, 1993

Mowl, Timothy, (2) *Gentlemen and Players: Gardeners of the English Landscape*, Sutton Publishing, Gloucestershire, 2000

Mowl, Timothy and Earnshaw, Brian, *Architecture Without Kings: The Rise of Puritan Classicism Under Cromwell*, Manchester University Press, Manchester, 1995

Muraro, Michelangelo and Marton, Paolo, *Venetian Villas*, Könemann, Cologne, 1999

A Narrative History of King James for the first Fourteen Years, 1651

Nichols, J., *The Progresses of King James I*, 1828

Orgel, Stephen and Strong, Roy, *Inigo Jones: The Theatre of the Stuart Court*, Sotheby Parke Bernet and UCLA Press, Los Angeles, 1973

Orrell, John, *The Theatres of Inigo Jones and John Webb*, Cambridge University Press, Cambridge, 1985

Osborn, L.B., *The Life, Letters and Writings of John Hoskyns*, Yale University Press, New Haven, 1937

Osborne, Francis, *Traditional Memoirs in the Reign of King James I*, John Ballantyne, Edinburgh, 1811

Palladio, Andrea, *I Quattro Libri dell' Architettura*, Rome, 1570

Palme, Per, *Triumph of Peace: A Study of the Whitehall Banqueting House*, Almqvest & Wiksell, Stockholm, 1956

Panzani, Gregorio, *Memoirs*, Birmingham, 1793

A Parliamentary History of England, 1762

Parry, Edward, *The Overbury Mystery*, J. Fisher Unwin, 1925

Parry, Graham, (1) *The Golden Age Restor'd: The Culture of the Stuart Court, 1603–42*, Manchester University Press, Manchester, 1981

Parry, Graham, (2) *The Seventeenth Century: The Intellectual and Cultural Context of English Literature 1603–1700*, Longmans, 1989

Peacham, Henry, *The Compleat Gentleman*, Clarendon Press, Oxford, 1906 (originally published 1634)

Peacock, John, *The Stage Designs of Inigo Jones: The European Context*, Cambridge University Press, Cambridge, 1995

Pevsner, Nikolaus and Cherry, Bridget, *The Buildings of England: London 1: The Cities of London and Westminster*, Penguin, 1972

Peyton, Edward, *The Divine Catastrophe of the Kingly Family of the House of Stuarts*, James Ballantyne, Edinburgh, 1811 (originally published 1652)

Piatigorsky, Alexander, *Who's Afraid of Freemasons? The Phenomenon of Freemasonry*, The Harvill Press, 1997

Prestwich, Michael, *Cranfield: Politics and Profits Under the Early Stuarts*, Oxford University Press, Oxford, 1966

Raymond, Joad (ed.), *Making the News: an Anthology of the Newsbooks of Revolutionary England*, The Windrush Press, Gloucestershire, 1993

Richardson, John, *Covent Garden Past*, Historical Publications Ltd., 1995

Riggs, David, *Ben Jonson: A Life*, Harvard University Press, Cambridge, Mass., 1989

Sainsbury, W. Noel (ed.), *Original Unpublished Papers Illustrative of the Life of Sir Peter Paul Rubens as an Artist and a Diplomatist*, Bradbury and Evans, 1859

Schofield, John, *The Building of London from the Conquest to the Great Fire* (3rd edition), Sutton Publishing, Gloucestershire, 1999

Sharpe, Kevin and Lake, Peter (eds.), *Culture and Politics in Early Stuart England*, Macmillan, 1994

Simpson, Percy and Bell, C.F., *Designs by Inigo Jones for Masques and Plays at Court*, Walpole and Malone Societies at Oxford University Press, Oxford, 1924

Skovgaard, Joakim A., *A King's Architecture: Christian IV and his Buildings*, Hugh Evelyn, 1973

Slack, Paul, *The Impact of Plague in Tudor and Stuart England*, Routledge and Kegan Paul, 1985

Smuts, R. Malcolm, (1) *Court Culture and the Origins of a Royalist Tradition in Early Stuart England*, University of Pennsylvania Press, Philadelphia, PA, 1987

Smuts, R. Malcolm (ed.), (2) *The Stuart Court and Europe: Essays in Politics and Political Culture*, Cambridge University Press, Cambridge, 1996

Southern, Richard, *Changeable Scenery: Its Origin and Development in the English Theatre*, Faber and Faber, 1952

Spiers, Walter Lewis, *The Note Book and Account Book of Nicholas Stone*, The Walpole Society at Oxford University Press, Oxford, 1919

Starkey, David (ed.), *The English Court from the Wars of the Roses to the Civil War*, Longman, 1987

Stow, John, *The Survey of London*, Everyman, 1987 (originally published 1598, revised 1603)

Stoye, John, *English Travellers Abroad, 1604–1667*, Yale University Press, New Haven, 1989

Strachan, Michael, *The Life and Adventures of Thomas Coryate*, Oxford University Press, Oxford, 1962

Strong, Roy, (1) *Art and Power: Renaissance Festivals 1450–1650*, University of California Press, Berkeley, 1984

Strong, Roy, (2) *Britannia Triumphans: Inigo Jones, Rubens and Whitehall Palace*, Thames and Hudson, 1980

Strong, Roy, (3) *Henry, Prince of Wales, and England's Lost Renaissance*, Thames and Hudson, 1986

Summerson, John, (1) *Architecture in Britain, 1530–1830*, Penguin, 1953

Summerson, John, (2) *Inigo Jones* (revised edition), Yale University Press, New Haven, 2000 (originally published 1966)

Survey of London, London County Council and Greater London Council, 1900 onwards

Taylor, I.A., *The Life of Queen Henrietta Maria*, Hutchinson, 1905

Thurley, Simon, (1) *The Lost Palace of Whitehall*, Royal Institute of British Architects, 1998

Thurley, Simon, (2) *Whitehall Palace*, Yale University Press, New Haven, 1999

Tindall, Gillian, *The Man Who Drew London: Wenceslaus Hollar in Reality and Imagination*, Chatto & Windus, 2002

Tinniswood, Adrian, *His Invention So Fertile: a Life of Christopher Wren*, Jonathan Cape, 2001

Townshend, Dorothea, *Life and Letters of Mr Endymion Porter*, T. Fisher Unwin, 1897

Van der Doort, Abraham, *Catalogue of the Collections of Charles I*, Walpole Society, 1960

Veevers, Erica, *Images of Love and Religion: Queen Henrietta Maria and Court Entertainments*, Cambridge University Press, Cambridge, 1989

Vertue, George, *Note Books, Vols. 1–4*, The Walpole Society at Oxford University Press, Oxford, 1930–6

Webb, John, *A Vindication of Stone-Heng Restored*, (originally published 1655)

Webber, Ronald, *Covent Garden: Mud-salad Market*, J.M. Dent and Sons Ltd, 1969

Weinreb, Ben and Hibbert, Christopher (eds.), *The London Encyclopaedia*, Macmillan, 1983

Weldon, Sir Anthony, *The Court and Character of King James*, John Ballantyne, Edinburgh, 1811 (originally published 1651)

Willson, D. Harris, *James VI and I*, Jonathan Cape, 1956

Wilson, Michael I., *Nicholas Lanier, Master of the King's Musick*, Scolar Press, Aldershot, 1994

Wittkower, Rudolf, *Palladio and English Palladianism*, Thames and Hudson, 1974

Wood, Anthony à, *The History and Antiquities of the University of Oxford*, 1817

Wright, C.J. (ed.), *Sir Robert Cotton as Collector: Essays on an Early Stuart Courtier and his Legacy*, British Library Publications, 1997

Articles and pamphlets

Bagford, John, 'Notes for a History of Printing (early 18th century)', British Library Harleian ms. 5900 (short biography of Inigo on folios 57–9)

Bellany, Alastair, 'Mistress Turner's Deadly Sins: Sartorial Transgressions, Court Scandal, and Politics in Early Stuart England', *Huntington Library Quarterly* (vol. 58) 1996, pp. 179–210

Betcherman, Lita-Rose, 'The York House Collection and its Keeper', *Apollo* (vol. 92), 1970, pp. 250–4

Burns, Howard, 'Palladio and the Foundations of a New Architecture in the North', *Palladio in Northern Europe* (papers from a symposium), Skira, Milan, 1999

Chaney, Edward, (1) 'A New Model Jones', *Spectator*, 13 January 1996, pp. 34–6

Chaney, Edward, (2) 'Review of "Inigo Jones Vitruvius Britannicus"', *Burlington Magazine* (vol. 130), August 1988

Colvin, Howard M, 'Inigo Jones and the Church of St Michael le Querne', *London Journal* (vol. 12), 1986, pp. 36–9

Duggan, Dianne, 'London the Ring, Covent Garden the Jewel of that Ring', *Architectural History* (vol. 43), 2000

Fisher, Geoffrey, and Newman, John, 'A Fountain Design by Inigo Jones', *Burlington Magazine* (vol. 127, no. 989), August 1985, pp. 531–3

Gapper, Claire, 'The impact of Inigo Jones on London Decorative Plasterwork', *Architectural History* (vol. 44), 2001, pp. 82–7

Gordon, D.J., (1) 'Hymenaei: Ben Jonson's Masque of Union', *Journal of the Warburg and Courtauld Institutes* (vol. 8), 1945

Gordon, D.J., (2) 'The Imagery of Ben Jonson's "The Masque of Blackness" and "The Masque of Beauty"', *Journal of the Warburg and Courtauld Institutes* (vol. 6), 1943

Gordon, D.J., (3) 'Poet and Architect: The Intellectual Setting of the Quarrel between Ben Jonson and Inigo Jones', *Journal of the Warburg and Courtauld Institutes* (vol. 12), 1949

Harris, John (1), 'Inigo Jones and the Mystery of Heidelberg Castle', *Apollo*, 137, March 1993, pp. 147–52

Harris, John (2), 'Inigo Jones and the Prince's Lodging at Newmarket', *Architectural History* (vol. 2), 1959, pp. 26–40

Hart, Vaughan, 'Inigo Jones's Site Organisation at St Paul's Cathedral', *Journal of the Society of Architectural Historians* (vol. 53:4), December 1994, pp. 414–27

Heward, John, 'The Restoration of the South Front of Wilton House: the Development of the House Reconsidered', *Architectural History* (vol. 35), 1992, pp. 78–117

Higgott, Gordon, (1) 'Inigo Jones in Provence', *Architectural History* (vol. 26), 1983

Higgott, Gordon, (2) '"Varying with Reason": Inigo Jones's Theory of Design', *Architectural History* (vol. 35), 1992

Howarth, David, 'Lord Arundel as an Entrepreneur of the Arts', *Burlington Magazine* (vol. 122), 1980, pp. 690–2

'Inigo Jones and St Paul's Cathedral', *London Topographical Record*, (vol. 18), 1942, pp. 41–3

Keith, W. Grant, 'Some Hitherto Unknown Drawings by Inigo Jones', *Burlington Magazine* (vol. 22), 1913, pp. 218–26

Lethaby, W.R., 'Inigo Jones and the Theatre', *Architectural Review* (vol. 31), 1912

Mowl, Timothy and Earnshaw, Brian, 'Inigo Jones Restored', *Country Life*, 30 January 1992, pp. 46–9

Newman, John, (1) 'A Draft Will of the Earl of Arundel', *Burlington Magazine* (vol. 122), 1980, pp. 692–6

Newman, John, (2) 'An Early Drawing by Inigo Jones and a Monument in Shropshire', *Burlington Magazine* (vol. 115), 1973, pp. 360–7

Newman, John, (3) 'Inigo Jones's Architectural Education before 1614', *Architectural History* (vol. 35), 1992

Newman, John, (4) 'Nicholas Stone's Goldsmith's Hall: Design and Practice in the 1630s', *Architectural History* (vol. 14), 1971, pp. 30–9

Orrell, John, (1) 'The Agent of Savoy at the Somerset Masque', *Review of English Studies (New Series)* (vol. 28), 1977, pp. 301–5

Orrell, John, (2) 'Inigo Jones and Amerigo Salvetti: a Note on the Later Masque Designs', *Theatre Notebook* (vol. 30), 1976, pp. 109–114

Orrell, John, (3) 'Inigo Jones at the Cockpit', *Shakespeare Survey* (vol. 30), 1977, pp. 157–68

Orrell John, (4) 'The London Court Stage in the Savoy Correspondence', *Theatre Research International* (vol. 4), 1979, pp. 79–94

Orrell, John, (5) 'The London Stage in the Florentine Correspondence, 1604–18', *Theatre Research International* (vol. 3), 1997–8, pp. 157–76

Orrell, John, (6) 'The Paved Court Theatre at Somerset House', *British Library Journal* (vol. 3), 1977, pp. 13–19

Peacock, John, 'Inigo Jones's Catafalque for James I', *Architectural History* (vol. 25), 1982, pp. 1–5

Pritchard, Allan, 'A Source for the Lives of Inigo Jones and John Webb', *Architectural History* (vol. 21), 1978, pp. 138–40

'A Relation of a Short Survey of the Western Counties Made by a Lieutenant of the Military Company in Norwich in 1635', *Camden Miscellany* (vol. 16), 1936

Shapiro, L.A., 'The Mermaid Club', *Modern Language Review* (vol. 45), 1950, pp. 6–17

Smuts, R. Malcolm, (1) 'The Court and Its Neighborhood: Royal Policy and Urban Growth in the Early Stuart West End', *Journal of British Studies* (vol. 30), 1991, pp. 117–149

Smuts, R. Malcolm, (2) 'The Puritan Followers of Henrietta Maria in the 1630s,' *English Historical Review* (vol. 93), 1978, pp. 26–45

Stone, Lawrence, (1) 'The Building of Hatfield House', *Archaeological Journal* (vol. 112), 1955

Stone, Lawrence, (2) 'Inigo Jones and the New Exchange', *Archaeological Journal* (vol. 114), 1957

Strong, Roy, 'Inigo Jones and the Revival of Chivalry', *Apollo* (vol. 86), 1967, pp. 102–7

Summerson, John, 'Inigo Jones (Lecture on a Master Mind)', *Proceedings of the British Academy* (vol. 50), 1965, pp. 169–92

Welsford, Enid, 'Italian Influence on the English Court Masque', *Modern Language Review* (vol. 18), 1923

Whinney, Margaret, (1) 'Inigo Jones: a Revaluation', *RIBA Journal* (vol. 59), 1952, pp. 286–9

Whinney, Margaret, (2) 'John Webb's Drawings for Whitehall Palace', *Walpole Society*, (vol. 31), 1942–3, pp. 45–107

Wittkower, Rudolf, (1) 'Inigo Jones, Architect and Man of Letters', *RIBA Journal* (vol. 60), 1953, pp. 83–90

Wittkower, Rudolf, (2) 'Principles of Palladio's Architecture', *Journal of the Warburg and Courtauld Institutes* (vol. 7, part I, and vol. 8, part II), 1944 and 1945

Worsley, Giles, (1) 'Inigo Jones and the Hatfield Riding House', *Architectural History* (vol. 45), 2002, pp. 230–37

Worsley, Giles, (2) 'Inigo Jones and the Origin of the London Mews', *Architectural History* (vol. 44), 2001, pp. 89–95

ACKNOWLEDGEMENTS AND PICTURE CREDITS

Easily the most enjoyable part of writing this book was the research trip to northern Italy, where my wife Olga and I followed, as far as possible, the route that Inigo took through the region's historic towns and cities nearly 400 years ago. It would have been much less rewarding had it not been for the unstinting efforts of our good friends Ugo and Cristina Tesler and their son Marco. As well as offering bountiful hospitality in Milan and driving us to the top of the St Gothard Pass, they activated a range of knowledgeable contacts in other cities. These included Anna Regge and Vilma Fasoli in Turin, Marta Montolivo Saccomanno and Marina Firpo in Genoa and Andrea Nante, who took two days off from running his superb diocesan museum in Padua to guide us around the Palladian villas and palazzos in the vicinity of his city and Vicenza. Chapters Nine and Ten could not have been written without their generosity, enthusiasm and expertise.

All modern work on the seventeenth-century court masques leans heavily on the illuminating scholarship of Stephen Orgel and Roy Strong, who have been kind enough to give me permission to quote passages from their work. Andrew Saint has allowed me to reproduce his vivid description of Elizabethan London in Chapter 3. At the very beginning of the project John Bold, the ranking expert on the Queen's House in Greenwich, generously gave me a conducted tour of the building and shared his unrivalled knowledge. The distinguished art historian Oliver Millar kindly put me right on some details concerning Van Dyck and his sojourn in London.

I am grateful to the London Library for the depth of its resources and the unfailing patience and professionalism of the staff. That applies also to the British Library, where I spent many intriguing and productive hours in the Manuscripts Department, and to the library of the Royal Institute of British Architects. Individual librarians who went out of their way to help were Joanna Parker at Worcester College, Oxford, where the bulk of Inigo Jones's surviving library resides; and Sara Rodger at Arundel Castle, which holds an archive of Thomas Howard's correspondence. Thanks, too, to Tyge Krogh at the Danish National Archives for sending over microfilm of letters to and from Anne of Denmark and her son Prince Henry; and to Nick Barratt for translating from Latin the document that excused Inigo Jones from accepting a knighthood and paying various royal imposts.

The idea for this biography was brought to me by Lindsay Symons and Heather Holden-Brown at Headline. Lindsay moved on as I was about to deliver the manuscript, at which point Celia Kent seamlessly assumed her editorial role. I owe a great deal to their support, as I do to Olga for her insights and the formidable research skills that she deployed at the Public Record Office and a number of local authority archives.

PICTURE CREDITS

Colour section

Categna Trust 7 above
Country Life Picture Library 8 below
Crown Copyright: Historic Royal Palaces 4 below, 5
Devonshire Collection, Chatsworth. Reproduced by permission of the

INDEX

Note: Buildings and streets are listed under their cities, towns or villages; any places now within Greater London (e.g. Greenwich) are listed under London.

Page references in bold type are to illustrations within the text. Page references in italic type are to illustrations in the plate section.

Index